WARATAH

HA-LE THAI

COMPLIMENT FOR WARATAH

An enthralling tale of motherhood, war, betrayal, and love.
Sam Cawthorn ~ ~ *International Best Selling author and CEO/Founder of Speakers Institute.*

The Waratah, is an exceptional piece of writing. Ha-Le's words take the reader on an extraordinary tale of personal tragedy, heartbreak and perseverance. The Waratah is an incredible read oozing with openness and vulnerability. It's pages are filled with adventure, curiosity, and strong links to Vietnamese culture. It's a fantastic read!
Kirsty Salisbury ~ *Speaker - Podcaster - Coach & Author - Auckland- New Zealand.*

A Poignant and Powerful Tale of Love, Pain, and Growth.
Ha-Le's story is incredibly moving and powerful.
The story weaves the past and present together so beautifully.
Jenifer Higgins~ *Author, Teacher- USA*

I admired Ha-Le's courage to share her life struggles and
the many obstacles she overcame in her life.
Her love of life is undeniably contagious.
Muna Nedimovich~ *Project Manager – Finance- Vancouver, BC Canada*

Captivating. A story of adversity told with wisdom and humility. I found I couldn't put it down- there were so many inspiring moments!
Lisa Harvey~ *High school teacher- Sydney –Australia*

Amazing life journey with full of courage and inspiration!
Vyle Nguyen~ *Senior International Auditing Manager- USA*

From the moment I picked up Ha-Le's memoir, I could not put it down. There were moments the completely took my breath away. Piece by piece, the past and present all came together. Ha-Le is the true representation of strength, resilience, courage, and love.
Sharon Muscet~ *Expert Authority, Speaker and Author – Adelaide- Australia.*

Ha- Le's life journey touched my heart. She had shown that nothing is impossible for a human being!
Thu Tran~ *Manager of Public Bank Vietnam*

Take nothing away from the love a mother has for her child and commend her efforts more if she's bold enough to tell the tale even amidst all the trials, travails and difficulties. It's a long one from Ha Le, but it's definitely worth picking up to read this masterpiece memoir.
Prince Olayode Oluwatobi M.~ *Nigeria*

A book with a rollercoaster of emotions and very relatable to my culture. After chapter one, I didn't want to put it down!"
Kiki Wong ~ *Director at The Silent Company-Voice over talent, Professional backing vocalist- Hong-Kong*

An incredible story of hardship, survival, cultural differences and of love, forgiveness and TRIUMPHANT JOY.... the power of FAITH and HOPE! Riveting! Couldn't put the book down!
Trudie Morris~ *Senior Pastor, Church planter, Lecturer & international conference speaker- Melbourne –Australia*

This is not just the story of a lady who has suffered tremendously, it is a story of 3 generations of strong and courageous women, their Culture and Traditions, generational patterns and prejudice, and finally it is a story of transformation.
Linda Thackray~ *Psychosomatic Therapist of Finding Magic Within Registered Teacher of Psychosomatic Therapy College*

Printed in the United States of America
First Printing, 2018

Cataloguing-in-Publication details are available from
the National Library of Australia www.trove.nla.gov.au

Hardback: 978-0-6484486-5-5
Paperback: 978-0-6484486-9-3
Ebook: 978-0-6484486-6-2

Edited by: Cate Hogan, Jen Higgins, and Rainy Warf
Proofreading and line edited by: Dr Minh Duc Thai
Cover design: Nonon Tech & Ha-Le Thai
Interior design: Nonon Tech and Design
All photographs: Gia Khanh Phan –Pixabay - Lama Jabr

Published by: Waratah Publisher
Address: 67 ROWE DR Potts Hill, NSW 2143

Visit: www.halethai.com.au

DEDICATION

To Hong-An and Minh

ACKNOWLEDGEMENT

I want to thank my beloved daughter, Hong-An, who taught me the games of life through trials, pains, hurt, and depression until I became triumphant. She was the one who indirectly inspired me to write this memoir.

I am also so humbled and grateful to my parents who brought me to this life and whose unconditional love gave me the wings to soar in the universe freely, as well as to dare dream big dreams that really scared me. They have also made it possible for me to have a great journey that I can now share to the world.

Thank you, Minh, for being my longest friend in my life journey after leaving Vietnam. He played a big part in helping me to become a fearless warrior. He was also one of the first persons that encouraged me to put the pen down for my memoir.

I say thank you to my four beloved brothers, Hiep, Hien, Hung and Hai who shaped me better to be a warrior at a very young age.

Thank you, my son in law, Travis who came to my life as one of the biggest gifts that God gave to me, and my life has never been the same again.

I couldn't say thanks enough to Irene Graham who taught and coached me about memoir writing. Through her training, I developed a great understanding of how to write a good memoir and that blessed me with the courage to write my life story and to bring it to the world now!

My sincere gratitude for the constant support of Cate Hogan, who was my coach, my supporter and my great editor. Without her love and care to check on me in last three years, this book would not have come for its second edition.

To Michael Collins who worked very hard with me for a year to pull, push and put this story together. I very much appreciated his care, passion, and integrity. I thank him so much for his tolerance with my accent throughout the time when I worked with him to relate my journey and to bring this book to life.

My special thanks go to Jenifer Higgins and Rainy Warf for being the other editors. I very much appreciated their thoughtfulness and sensitivity in editing my book with all their hearts.

I am greatly indebted to Minh, my husband, who did a final check on the manuscript with great passion. I can say the book is in its best shape for readers now!

I'd like to express my deepest gratitude to Leb Raingam (Nonon Tech & Design) who spent so much time and a considerably huge amount of effort in book cover, formatting, internally designing and materialising this book from a raw word document. Leb didn't mind going back to the manuscript countless times to insert, remove and adjust for the book to come out in such a beautiful form as it looks now.

I am humbled and grateful to Dr Joe Subino, Dr Bruce Lipton, Bob Proctor, Wayne Dyer, Brian Tracey, Sam Cawthorn, Dr Bradley Nelson, Sharon Pearson, Joe Pane, John Assaraf, Herman Muller, Marie Muller, Dr Tad James, Dr Adriana James, Arthur Bablis, Linda Thackray, and Sean Jason who have been my teachers, my masters, my coaches and have taught me so many things directly and indirectly and these have helped me to transform my life in different states and to bring out the best shape for this memoir.

Special thanks to Sam Cawthorn, Linda Thackray, Conor Healy, Lisa Harvey, Kirsty Salisbury, Sharon Muscet, Trudie Van Zyl Morris, Kylie Hancox, Vyle Nguyen, Muna Nedimovich Melissa A Wiringi, and Leanne Shelton who were patient enough to read my book and provide their reviews of it.

Lastly, I thank all who have believed me and been very fond of my journey. Those who have encouraged me to share my life story to the world. More specifically, I am grateful to Mellisa Wiringi, Thu Tran, Vyle Nguyen, Lisa Harvey, Jackie King, Judy Truong, and Lai Le.

Ha-Le Thai

TABLE OF CONTENTS

PROLOGUE

The first time my writing was read aloud was when I was a child, in Year Three. This was when I first realised that writing was a connection to other people, a way to evoke emotions, to move them and put into their heads the things already in my head. The story was about a cat. It was a simple story, but I'd worked so hard on it, using all of my descriptive abilities to evoke the image of a cat in the minds of my classmates. My cheeks were flushed and hot as my teacher read from my paper, but despite my reddened face, I was happy. I was even more so when my teacher finished and all the rest of the children clapped their hands for me. My heart was bursting with pride at what I'd done. My imagination was set on fire, and from that moment on, all my little mind wanted to do was write.

Despite so many things that have happened in my life, a burning desire to write never left me. It was always smouldering in my heart, keeping itself alive on the glowing embers of my passion, my wish to speak to the hearts of others. The written word is a powerful tool. It connects us, across time and across culture.

When I was younger, I often wanted to write about my world, the sadness and worry that engulfed me, the small joys and triumphs in the life of young Ha-Le, but the struggles of making it from day to day didn't leave me much time to pursue this craft. I said to myself, 'I will write my story when I grow up. I'll write all about it for the world to read.' I saved up everything that I wanted to write about, storing in my little heart all of the things that I wanted so desperately to say. I carried these memories in my body for so many years, for so many decades.

It seemed there was always something in my way, and writing down the events of my life had to be delayed time and time again. Even after making it to Australia, I had a daughter to raise and a business to get off the ground. When my daughter was older and my business was flourishing, this was when my health problems began. I was far too sick, both physically and mentally, to sit down and pen the words clamouring about in my soul.

The first cancer was Thyroid cancer. Before my diagnosis, I had been in the midst of preparing to start my memoir, and many people in my life encouraged me. 'You must write your story, Ha-Le!' they said, and I wanted to. But then, the cancer came. It took over my body, zapping me of all my passion and enthusiasm. Every day was a struggle. The cancer left me weak and listless. I didn't have the energy to sift through the pain of the past. I put my dreams aside, yet again.

I survived this cancer, feeling so blessed and grateful to God. I was rejuvenated and ready to take on the world, and I started to think that now, finally, I could pen my tale.

But shockingly, another cancer hit me. This time it was Ovarian cancer. After all that I'd lived through, I couldn't believe the universe still had challenges for me to overcome. But I did overcome it, because that is what life is. Life is a series of new challenges, ongoing, one after another. Writing my memoir, finding the time and the energy, turned out to be one of these challenges. But I am now so pleased to say that I have overcome them like the other struggles life put ahead of me.

When I was speaking with a coach, Nick Harding from Speaker Institute, about my life story and the finding for the right title of my memoir, he told me that I should use a flower to represent my journey.

'Your life should be symbolised with a lotus since you are Vietnamese,' he said. 'The lotus is a beautiful flower. It manifests its beauty even when it is growing in mud.'

I liked his idea, but I didn't feel the lotus was the best symbol for me. I knew of a better flower, a far more resilient and stronger flower, because if I knew anything about myself, I knew this: I was strong, and like the flower I'd chosen. I had proven time and again that I could bloom even under the most strenuous circumstances. I showed Nick a picture of a waratah.

People may wonder why I chose WARATAH as the title of my book. I found my great passion for waratah flower when I visited the Blue Mountains for the first time. This was in 1991, after we'd been living in Australia for a few months. The vibrant red colour caught my eyes and drew me closer. It was like a gorgeous drop of blood seeping vividly into the surrounding landscape. I did not yet know the flower's name, but I loved the way it looked. I felt captured by its beauty.

Life never goes in the way that we wish! I could not believe that third cancer hit me and this time, it was Non- Hodgkin Lymphoma!

For finding more ways to rescue myself, I went to a psychosomatic training. It was part of my effort to heal myself through knowledge and self-growth. One morning, my Master, Linda Thackray held a card reading. I was given a card that read, 'Waratah- Become the true you. Show the world who you really are and what you were born to do. It's time to focus on your true passions and purposes to become Your Authentic Self. Share your gift and talents with the world and blessings will come your way.'

From that moment, I knew the name of my favourite bush flower- WARATAH after twenty five-years seeing it. And it has become my attribute, the token of my fiery emotions. Waratah represented my fighting and survival characters and everything I'd gone through.

The more that I researched about waratah, the more that I found myself in awe of it. The waratah is nearly impossible to kill. Not even bushfires can destroy the waratah. When a bushfire occurs, the flower may burn up, but then from the ashes of destruction, a new waratah bud will bloom, growing from the same seeds. The bud is new, but the plant is the same. Flames cannot extinguish this large red flower. No matter what engulfs the waratah, it will continue to grow, change and never die.

Waratah is like a phoenix. Each destruction is a rebirth. Through the waratah, we can see how loss can be gainful. We can see how entropy becomes creation. I love the waratah, and I hope to always have the spirit of the waratah flowing through me.

I kept trying to find the perfect name for my memoir, the perfect title that captured the essence of my story. I wanted a title that told others I was a survivor. I kept on choosing different names related to survival, but I was never happy with any of them.

One day, in the middle of my meditation, I pictured myself as a warrior, standing tall and looking back through all the battles I'd fought through. I had been thinking of the title, 'A Vietnamese Warrior', but the name didn't give my heart a punch. I played with the title in my mind, picking it apart one word at a time. I landed on the last word.

'Warrior! Warrior! Warrior!'

I chanted and chanted this. That is the punch that I'd been waiting for struck me in the heart.

I cried out with excitement, 'WARATAH!'

I gave birth to my memoir's name after keeping the waratah in my heart for such a long time.

This memoir has been a journey in and of itself, and I humbly thank you for taking the time to read my words. I have carefully chosen them in the hopes of bringing others into the past, giving others a glimpse into the realities that I have lived. My life has been rife with pain and joy, suffering and bliss, anger and love, and through it all, I've learned so much. I hope to share all that I have experienced with you.

Be Waratah. Be an unconquerable spirit. Take the ashes of loss and use them as fertile ground for new blooms. Resiliency is possible. There is a waratah within every one of us.

CHAPTER ONE

WHAT MISTAKES ARE MADE OF

My daughter and my escape from Vietnam share the same anniversary. The overwhelming nausea I felt when the sun finally ended that first rough night in the overcrowded fishing boat turned out to be morning sickness. Had I known just how dangerous and torturous the journey would be, I would never have set foot in the boat. But in the larger arc of our lives, there is no room for regrets. I took a risk to follow my dreams, and it has paid off – indeed, it paid off hugely. The past brings you to the present, and the present is all that we can control. I needed to find a way to shape the present for my daughter's future.

I shifted uncomfortably in my deck chair and tried to appreciate the moment: the afternoon sun on my face and the light breeze carrying distant sounds of coconut palms. A neighbouring resort was playing music a little too loudly, but the rhythm combined pleasantly with the persistent pulse of the ocean – the same ocean that encircled my childhood town, fifty kilometres north. The same ocean the three of us escaped into. The same ocean that I had since flown back over so many times.

I watched my daughter wading deeper into the waves, her Australian fiancé beckoning her further in. He looked strong and handsome from a distance. Many things are not what they appear from a distance. I clenched my fists and felt my stomach twist. I felt a furious sort of wistfulness, a longing for everything that might have been. They were happy, for now, and I wished that I could support that. But all I could see was the pain that he was leading her towards. Life with him would be a burden for Hong-An. I wanted to stop them, but I felt helpless.

I continued to watch them playfully frolicking in the surf, their eyes alight with love. He reached out, taking my daughter's hand. He spun her around as if they were ballroom dancing in the waves and I saw her face then, laughing and lit with joy. I only looked away when he leaned in to kiss her, just as when I was an eight-year-old watching 'Wild! Wild! West!' on our first television. The present moment is all there is, I told myself. It is all you can control. I couldn't control the past.

Travis had already asked Hong-An to marry him, and he had done it without first asking for her parents' permission. After many years in Australia, I was very used to Australian customs and social norms. I knew that there were many differences between the Australian way of life and the Vietnamese way, yet still, I found myself reeling from the shock of Travis's proposal. My husband, Minh, and I found his way of asking for Hong-An's hand to be so thoughtless. But, despite this, here we were, the four of us in Vietnam, introducing Travis to our homeland and the rest of our family.

The actual proposal had taken place one month earlier back in Australia. It had all started with Travis shocking us with an announcement from the back-seat of our car as the four of us drove to church. It was a Sunday afternoon, and we were making the drive from Birrong to Chester Hill. I was wholly unprepared for the conversation that was about to take place.

'I'll be proposing to Hong-An soon.'

I felt my stomach drop. He might as well have pulled the pin on a grenade and thrown it onto the dashboard. Minh's hands gripped the steering wheel; I froze, not believing what I'd just heard. He would be? He was informing us.

Look at us, I felt like saying. Look at your girlfriend's lovely face. We are Vietnamese. Your girlfriend's first language is Vietnamese. There is a way to ask for her hand in marriage in my culture. You do not just tell us. You get down on your knees in humility, in a proper place! You ask.

This was not the kind of conversation to be having in a car, but this violation of our traditional values was not our biggest concern, and Hong-An knew that. Minh and I were already worried for other reasons about Travis. But twenty-one years in Australia had also taught me that sometimes it was better to hold my tongue. I turned around and smiled at them, taking a moment to notice Travis had his usual expression of gloom and fatigue, which only cemented my dismay that he intended to be my son in law soon.

'Congratulations.' I said, only for my daughter's benefit, and to save Travis from the embarrassment of the silence that followed his words.

I felt two-faced and dishonest, but I didn't know how else to respond at that moment. I was put on the spot. My mouth felt like it was full of sand. I turned back, and in the awkward silence, I sensed them both looking at Minh for his response. He remained silent and white-knuckled. Hong-An leaned forward so she could see him in the rear-view mirror, but he did not return her look.

Travis probably had no idea that on that peaceful afternoon, our worlds were crashing down around us. He had no idea that although it seemed like we were just driving along quiet suburban Sydney streets on the way to Church, the Earth had opened up and we were falling into unimaginable depths. But Hong-An must have known. She should have known. We parked and made our way to the church, just as we always did, but this time I felt like I was walking with strangers.

That night when we arrived back home, I told Minh to try and talk some sense into his daughter. He sighed and slowly turned the page of his book. His forehead was creased with worry lines. We didn't want to hurt anyone, but we both knew that we couldn't stay silent.

But now here on the beach, this all seemed like a distant memory. We were happy and strong together. This fateful car ride had taken place weeks ago back in Sydney, and now, here we were in Hoi An Vietnam. But despite the smiles and palm trees blowing happily in the breeze, I once again, found myself rallying my husband to talk to our daughter.

'You have to be the one to talk to her,' I said as I got up from the deck chair. 'When you talk, she knows that it is serious.' Minh nodded in agreement.

I walked down to the shoreline, dipped my feet into the water, and looked out at the ocean; at the lonely islands, the wispy clouds, and the fishing boats returning. The ocean is indiscriminate to borders, politics, and family issues. Sometimes gentle, sometimes violent, occasionally blue as the sky, and sometimes black as death. I bent down to pick up an empty plastic bottle which had washed ashore, nudging against my ankle. I traced the sun-faded letters on the label, remembering how I had done the same over fifty years ago when my younger brother proudly brought home a Fanta bottle. I had never seen anything like it before.

I allowed myself to put on a smile, despite my mood. Some things don't change at all. Unable to throw it back into the sea, I hesitated just as Hong-An and Travis appeared, dripping wet, hand in hand.

'You should swim, Mẹ,' Hong-An said in English. 'Mẹ' is what she called me, even when speaking English. This was the sweetest word that Vietnamese sons and daughters called their mothers.

We had spent our whole lives talking to each other in Vietnamese. It was one of the things I was most proud of. Hong-An was fluent despite never having lived in the country, but for the sake of her fiancé, she now always spoke in English with me. It was not the language that had connected us for the twenty-three years of her life.

'Yeah,' Travis added. 'The water is awesome.'

I looked at them. The playful vigour I had just witnessed had disappeared, revealing just how tired and drawn-out they both were. They clung onto each other as if it was necessary just to hold themselves up. I knew it was the burden of living a life like Travis' – a life that would soon become Hong-An's forever. I didn't want to see my daughter with that tired and heavy look always on her face, a look that came from him, a look that was the result of bearing his burden of a heavy soul. Minh and I had worked so hard to give her a better life. We had done the suffering so that she wouldn't have to.

'I'm OK here,' I said. I had hoped to sound polite, but my words came out sounding twisted and bitter. By the tone of my voice and expression on my face, Hong-An could see right through me. We could never hide from each other.

'Just try to enjoy yourself,' she said. 'Please.'

How could I?

We had visited Vietnam many times before, just the three of us.

'The Three Musketeers,' she had said, coining our favourite family phrase. This time, there was four of us, and our beautiful family balance had been completely broken.

'I'm thrilled we came here.' Travis said, doing his best to smooth over the now-obvious tension between us. There was an earnestness in his face, but he really had no idea who we were and what we needed; or what my daughter really needed. He did not understand that loving her with all his heart was not enough for my daughter's life.

'I'm glad you are glad,' I said calmly, not wanting to hurt Travis intentionally. I turned and walked back to the deck chair where the waiter had just delivered a cocktail in my brief absence.

Later, I watched Minh talking with Hong-An. They both sat under a coconut tree. Minh looked sad. My daughter sat calmly next to him on the wooden bench, playing with her engagement ring.

That ring, oh that ring, just seeing it now on the beach, brought back all the memories of the first day I saw it. It was in Sydney, the day after Travis's shocking announcement in the car on the way to church. I had rung my daughter from work. I had already stayed at the office for more than two hours just to think.

Hong-An was very confident, smart, sensible, and trusted her parents. How could I make her see reasoning? She had always been respectful towards her mother all her life. There was still time to question her about her true feelings, I assured myself. I had high hopes that Hong-An would make the right choice for her future.

There were so many times in the past that she fought with me, throwing tantrums over my suggestions, but in the end, with a beautiful smile and hug, she always conceded with: 'You are right, Mẹ!' I comforted myself with these thoughts. There was still time. Travis had only just announced his intentions the day before.

It was a busy Monday as usual at my preschool.

Children laughed and sang my favourite songs to greet their brand-new day, but I was not as happy as usual when hearing them. My thoughts were only on Hong-An.

Why didn't I let Hong-An know that we would talk today about Travis's announcement before I went to preschool? It was Monday, and Travis would come back to Maroubra as usual. I wished he hadn't stayed with us last night. If he had gone home, that would have given Minh and I a chance to talk.

I went into my office and shut the door. I had to call Hong-An and talk this through. I was on edge as I waited for her to pick up the phone.

She did not answer. I could feel that something was wrong and rushed home. All that I kept thinking was, don't tell me that Travis has proposed already! Please, that can't be the case!

My entire body shook with the thought.

When I got home, I found the house empty. Usually, she would leave a note, but there was no evidence that she had been around except for a few dirty breakfast dishes in the sink. It was like she had disappeared. My heart hammered rapidly against my ribs. I tried calling her phone again and was beyond thankful when, this time, she picked up right away.

'Sweetheart,' I said. 'Where are you now? Mẹ is home, and I want to have lunch with you.'

'Guess what, Mẹ? I got engaged!'

Her voice was pitched high with excitement, the way she would cry out to Minh and me when, as a little girl, she got a sticker or an award at school. 'Travis proposed to me this morning at our house. We are now at Sydney Harbour having lunch.'

Each word stung like a thousand bullets in my soul. I was not quick enough to give her my advice. They had known each other for only eight months!

'Mẹ... are you there?'

'Congratulations,' I said, with my tongue twisted and with a hollowness in my soul. I was a liar again. 'It's so... soon.'

I put down the phone a little too quickly and steadied myself against the kitchen bench. My head was exploding the way it did when I was watching the Vietnam War on our first TV. I was afraid that my entire body was about to collapse. The shock was far too much.

I'd been sure that there was still time to discuss this with Hong-An. At dinner, I had taken the time to ask Travis when he would be proposing to Hong-An. I wanted to get a sense of how serious he was and to find out if I had time to talk to my daughter about it.

'Where and when are you planning to propose to my beloved and precious daughter? Sapa? Halong Bay? Or Hoi An?'

Travis looked at me, smiled and answered, 'I don't know yet!'

I was flooded with relief. I had imagined that his usual lack of assuredness and apathy would give me time to talk things over with my daughter. But now, not even twelve hours later, he had already proposed. He had given me hope and then snatched it away.

I ended the call with Hong-An feeling a dead weight in my heart. I felt lost, utterly unsure of what to do next. Almost immediately, I wanted to ring her back and tell her my true feelings, but I held back. I was still unable to shake my concern.

I texted her instead, two hours later.

Actually, I'm disappointed. It's too quick. You accepted the ring without talking with us and considering your parents' feelings.

I intended to write more, but my hands were shaking. Travis had skipped too many steps. He had completely burned the process of proposing.

I sent my text message off to Hong-An and then burst into tears, feeling trampled upon. She was supposed to feel on top of the world today. This should be a happy time, filled with smiles, high-fives, and jumping around in joy and congratulations. This was what Minh and I dreamed of seeing one day, but everything had gone all wrong.

Every choice that I'd made in life had been for Hong-An. Everything I did was for Hong-An's survival and happiness. I couldn't accept the fact that all of my sacrifices for my daughter would be for Travis' benefit. This dreary lump of a man could not make her happy. My daughter was not born to bear his struggles. Her stamina was not very high, and she became grumpy very quickly when something bothered her. She needed someone high spirited, not Travis, with his sleepy eyes and weary smile.

I knew that Minh would react to the news of Travis's sudden proposal in the same panicked and desperate way that I had. This was going to crush him. I texted Minh at 10 a.m. He had a work meeting all day, so I had almost seven fun-filled hours to anticipate his anger before he called back at 4:40 p.m.

'No! It cannot be!' he growled. 'How rude. He cannot be Hong-An's husband. He cannot look after her!' Minh exploded out his words as if he'd learned them by heart.

'We can't do anything now – Hong-An has a ring!' I responded, my voice shaking.

'She will listen to us. She knows we have always been right in the past! She will listen to us and reconsider her decision!' Minh reassured me.

It was true! Hong-An had been a perfect daughter, and she trusted our intuition. We had a great bond for twenty-three years.

When Minh came home, he was tired, furious and took his phone out to call Hong-An straight away.

'No, please don't,' I pleaded, 'Don't call her when you are angry. You will only hurt her.'

I knew Minh well when his temper was fired up. Despite everything, I still wanted my daughter to feel happy and blessed, but my feelings were conflicted.

'You didn't consider your parents in this,' Minh snapped when she picked up. 'You accepted his proposal without asking us. Come home at once, and don't bring Travis with you.'

I shook my head in disbelief. He had said the words I wanted to say, but I felt so guilty.

When Minh ended the phone call, his face was red with anger. He turned to me with an accusatory tone, 'It's all your fault! You arranged a Vietnam trip and made Travis and Hong-An think we fully support their relationship because you invited him!'

'That has nothing to do with anything,' I argued. 'The trip is so that Travis can understand where we come from and understand Hong-An, and us, as Vietnamese.'

But even as I denied Minh's allegations, I worried that maybe he had a point. Was this trip one of the reasons why Hong-An accepted the ring? Was this why she hadn't thought to talk to us first? My kindness had killed me!

We waited in the lounge room like jury members for her to return, one in a rage and the other caught in a dilemma. When she finally came through the screen door, we were surprised to see Travis following her.

Minh leapt to his feet.

'Travis,' he said firmly, 'we have some vital family matters to discuss. Please respect our family time and go home.'

'No,' he said. 'I will not leave. I'm here to protect my fiancé.'

'Protect her? She is our daughter. We have done nothing but protect her for her whole life, and we intend to keep protecting her. That is why I am asking you to go.'

Travis snorted and shook his head as if he were disgusted with me. I felt myself drawing up in defence. I didn't think Travis was right for Hong-An, but I'd always thought he was a nice and respectful boy. Now, I couldn't believe the way he was acting, and the next words that came out of his mouth shocked me, and what followed only solidified my feelings that there was something just not right about him.

'No. I am here for Hong-An.'

Travis had never shown such an attitude, and I wanted to pull my hair out with frustration.

'Tell Travis to go, Hong-An, and we can have our family meeting.' I said.

'It is up to Travis. I cannot ask him to go,' she responded.

I could tell Hong-An needed an ally. She knew she was in trouble.

I spoke to Hong-An in Vietnamese. 'This is very important, darling. It is a matter of respect. We honestly can't believe that you would do this to us.'

I grabbed her hand and held the ring up toward her face. 'Hong-An, this is a costly ring. Look at the size of the diamond. He must have been planning this for a long time, and he did not even think to ask us?'

Hong-An pulled her hand away and let it fall by her side. 'It's a two-dollar ring, Mẹ,' She said flatly, responding in Vietnamese. 'It's fake.'

I did not think it was possible to be even more shocked than I already was. Her future husband proposed to her with a two-dollar ring?

'Now you know the value of his love.' I said.

'It is just a symbol, and the ring's value doesn't decide our happiness, Mẹ.' Hong-An reasoned.

'English, please,' Travis demanded. 'What are you saying? What are they saying, Hong-An?'

'He is now intervening in our family meeting and even dares to command us! How rude!' Minh shouted in Vietnamese.

Hong-An was silent and then translated: 'They got a shock with your proposal. They needed to know first, and you acted so quickly.'

Travis almost laughed. 'But you are living in Australia. You have to accept that things are not like that here.'

Minh banged on the table, 'You need to go home and tell your parents to come and talk to us, visit us, and ask us for our permission.' Minh's voice became loud and high-pitched with anger. His eyes went wide. 'We are Vietnamese,' he said. 'You are Australian. We are totally different, and you need to respect our culture when proposing to our daughter. Tell your parents to come and talk to us!'

Minh's face was purple with rage. He may have been discussing culture, but I knew he wanted to bring up the real reason for our concern, Travis' chronic health issues and character, but he kept these words to himself. We had accepted a lot already. More than most Vietnamese parents would. He did not consider Travis an equal in this conversation and was not used to being challenged so openly.

Travis was lucky that both Minh and I had been exposed to a lot of Aussie friends, and we did not keep the Vietnamese tradition very high; otherwise, the rooftop would explode with the imminent problem.

'Ba, please calm down,' Hong-An said through thin shaking lips. Knowing her father was very hurt and I was in despair, her voice was quiet and weak.

Responding to Hong-An's tone, Travis changed tack. 'Christ died for us. He gave his love so that we could love one another.'

'Yes, I know,' Minh interrupted, 'but could we talk as parents?'

'This is a matter for us too!' Travis snapped back, then suddenly burst into tears. I was shocked, and my heart melted when I saw Travis with wet eyes.

'Calm down, Minh. Calm down, Travis. Let's sit down at the table and talk about this,' I said, probably less calmly than I had hoped. 'We have a problem. We can find a solution together.'

Travis then turned to me and said the words that would continue to haunt me for many years, 'Ha-Le, you are a sick woman with a dysfunctional family. Let your daughter do what she wants.'

An electric shock ran through me from head to toe. It was my good intention to make peace but Travis' words shot me down. He said that I was sick. What could I have done to make Hong-An tell him that I was ill?

'What do you mean, I am sick?'

'You asked Hong-An to do this and that, eat this and that and do exercise, blah blah ....'

Oh! My love gestures and advice to my daughter had annoyed her, and she'd told Travis everything. Maybe that was why he viewed me as a sick woman? Was it sick to devote myself to her? Was it sick to want her to live her best life? Was this how Travis viewed our relationship? Or was this something that Hong-An had said to him?

Either way, I felt so hurt by Travis's words. My respect for him diminished at that moment. All I could feel was this was not right. It was not me who was sick. It was him. There was nobody in my life who insulted nor treated me that way, and he certainly wasn't going to either. I wouldn't allow it. At that moment, I wanted him gone. I wanted him out of my house, and I never wanted to see him again.

'You don't know who I am yet, Travis!' my lips were trembling with the enormous hurt in my heart.

Minh got up and left the room, banging the door on the way out.

We stood in a horrible, wounded silence for a few moments as his words sunk in further. What was sick about caring about my daughter's well-being? Sure, I had been ill. I had survived cancer twice already, but that is not what he meant. He meant 'sick-in-the-head' - a phrase Hong-An had taught me once. A sick woman with a dysfunctional family? It was the worst insult imaginable, and every wound I had ever endured was instantly exposed.

My Hong-An was born in the most difficult of situations. All her life, I had done everything, given everything, sacrificed everything, to give her the best life possible, and to afford her every opportunity to live a better life. Yet, all I wanted for her was the life I never had, the mother I never had, and now she was walking out of the door, and it was all being thrown back in my face.

CHAPTER TWO

VISIONS OF THE PAST

From as early as I can remember, I spent much of my time longing for my mother's presence. She would leave early in the morning when the sun hadn't yet risen and returned late at night, usually when I was already asleep.

'Where does Ma go every day, Chi Thoi?' I asked my babysitter once.

'She goes to work, stupid,' she said, 'How do you think you get your food? She makes money for us, and I do everything else.'

She stopped scrubbing the clothes and stared into the bucket, perhaps at her reflection. She was only fifteen, but through my three-year-old eyes, she was a responsible adult, the person that did everything for me, all the things that a mother would usually do, but without any care or love. I looked at her soft, pale face and her long, dry, curly, red-coloured hair. She always kept it tied back in a low ponytail. I remember watching it swing back and forth as she worked. It seemed like she was always busy with something. I used to wonder if that was the reason why she was so mean. She always wanted me to go away and leave her alone. I used to watch her scrub the floors or do the laundry and thought that if Chi Thoi had some time to stop and play, then maybe she would smile and laugh sometimes.

I loved Chi Thoi's hair colour. No one else I knew had a hair colour like her.

'I was in the rice fields at a very young age grazing the buffalo, so my hair got burnt and dry.' She told me on one of the rare occasions that she was in a good mood.

I dreamt of having a hair colour like hers. Red and dry hair. I told her this.

'Don't be silly! People dream of having shiny and silky hair like yours,' Chi Thoi said, turning her scary eyes on me.

I never whined to my mother about wanting red and dry hair since then.

I had been told she was a relative from my father's side, but that didn't mean anything to me. At that point in my life, my father was a stranger to me. I didn't feel a connection to him or a connection to Chi Thoi. It was only my mother that I felt any sort of connection to, and she was hardly around. When she was, I would cling to her, but she was much too tired to deal with the aggressive affection of a love-starved toddler. Chi Thoi's presence only reminded me of my mother's absence. She went on about her difficult tasks; cooking, cleaning, looking after my two brothers and me.

'Where does Ma go to?' I pressed Chi Thoi.

Chi Thoi looked up from the bucket and narrowed her eyes as if I had somehow offended her. 'Across the river.'

Across the river? I was sceptical. It sounded magical. Impossible.

The next day I went off by myself and walked to the riverbank. I looked across to the other side and tried to imagine my mother selling barbecued pork at the market. The thought made me very hungry.

Below me, the water looked cool and refreshing, and I jumped down onto the sand and dipped a toe in. I heard the delighted laughs of a group of children splashing and playing in the river further upstream. And unable to control my curiosity, I tiptoed into the water up to my ankles, then my knees.

I could only make out motorbikes on the other side, smoke rising from over houses of wood and corrugated iron. My belly rumbled, and I took another step. The sand under my feet was now mud. Suddenly, it seemed that the water was running very fast around me, and I realised I was sinking up to my waist. The cool, calm river was now a mighty, turbulent force around me, attacking my limbs with surprising force.

'Come back. Come back!' Said a voice in the distance. Was that my mother's? It seemed so far away.

I felt myself being lifted high by a pair of rough hands. I was carried back to shore and placed back onto the land.

'Silly girl,' the voice belonged to an old woman. She had waded out into the river and whisked me out of danger. 'Where did you think you were going?'

'Ma. To see Ma.'

The incident weighed heavily on me, though it did not deter me from continuing to go to the river. I dared not dip a toe into the water again, but I would play on the bank and watch the ferry go back and forth for hours every afternoon. I imagined surprising my mother as she walked home.

She would greet me warmly, pick me up, and twirl me around. I imagined her carrying me home, on her hip, as the other mothers did with their children. I imagined the pride I would feel when the neighbours saw us walking by. 'There goes Ha-Le and her mother.' But my mother would never arrive, and my hunger or boredom drew me back home without fail.

I never let anyone know that I went to the water; not even Hiep, my older brother, and Hien, my younger brother. If Chi Thoi knew, I would have had my face smacked.

I knew that the river was endless and that I would never reach my mother, who was somewhere on the other side of the bank. The river was an impossible barrier, keeping my mother away from me. This thinking made me feel hopeless and miserable.

Even at that young age, I felt a deep longing from the very depths of my soul. I longed for the mother-daughter connection that should be so strong and constant. I longed for that ethereal and eternal love that should flow between us. And of course, my mother did love me a lot, and I loved her, but the love never seemed to flow between us. Instead, it came in drips and drops. And I was always, always, thirsty for more.

❤ ❤ ❤ ❤

But now, I was both a mother and a daughter, and while the love never did begin to flow like a mighty river between my own mother and me, I wanted it to in my relationship with Hong-An. I'd always been close to her. She had always trusted me to guide her to do what was right. She knew that I would never leave her to flounder and drown. I would always help her stay afloat. I would hold tight to her in any storm. The wildest waves and strongest current would never cause her to lose her balance, not with me beside her.

I was proud of the relationship that Hong-An and I had built. We were not just mother and daughter; we were friends in a way that only mother and daughter can grow to be. But now, there was a boulder in front of us, one that threatened to divide the current of our river.

I had brought her into the world, and it was my responsibility to stick by her and guide her. I wouldn't stand by and watch her make a mistake that would drown her in sorrow. I had to help her see that Travis was not the right man for her!

I understood struggle first hand. Minh and I had had challenges in our marriage, same as anyone, but he was a good father, and it brought me great joy to see how he sacrificed and cared for our Hong-An. My own father had not been around very much when I was a child, and at times, he'd felt like a stranger to me. I would look at him and feel as though I should feel some sort of connection to him. I felt the burden of our shared blood and felt that we ought to know each other better than we did. This caused me a great deal of regret and sadness. But, on the other hand, I felt proud of knowing the father of my own child was present and involved in his daughter's life.

But maybe both of us were too involved.

I had always struggled to build a good life for my little girl. I had fought like a warrior, and I was proud of all that I'd done. But, Hong-An was so young, and she hadn't lived through any hard times.

Travis and his chronic illness would bring Hong-An many periods of sorrow, this I knew. They each lacked the strength to care for the other. She was still learning life skills, and although fiercely independent, she was nonetheless only twenty-three years old. Minh and I still did everything for Hong-An. Minh would even wash and sort her clothes for her.

'Hong-An is a smart girl; she will learn quickly enough when it is time for her to care for her own family,' I would say to Minh when he complained about Hong-An's household skills, but I wasn't sure that I believed it myself.

I had to admit it to myself that I liked spoiling Hong-An. I wanted to let her dance and laugh her way through life.

'Let me make her happy,' I would say, and Minh would always let me. But now with this fiancé, I didn't know how she was going to cope. She never had to cross big rivers or yearn for the love of a mother that wasn't there. We had not lived the same life, her and I. I hadn't prepared her for this suffering she would face.

♥ ♥ ♥ ♥

Minh and I had managed with effort and love to recover from that awful fight with Travis and Hong-An. We were trying to accept that this marriage would happen whether we liked it or not. We had done our best to heal the wounds inflicted on that terrible day when Hong-An had stormed out of our family home. We wanted to be happy and settled before leaving Australia for our holiday in Vietnam. But once in Vietnam, we couldn't just sit by any longer during the whole trip together. The true colour of Travis's well-being and the differences between our two cultures scared us. It was then on that beach that we realised that there was no way we could accept this marriage.

Minh spent a long time talking with Hong-An. I paced back and forth in the resort room, waiting for his retort and praying that Hong-An would be receptive to all that he said. I usually did the talking, and I was hoping that with Minh taking the lead, Hong-An would know that we were serious.

I jumped to my feet as Minh came back into the room.

'How did it go? What did you tell her?' I asked. He looked worn out, almost resigned.

'I told her the story of the man and the horse.'

Minh had a PhD in Linguistics. He was extremely intelligent and loved to use metaphors to explain complicated ideas. I remembered the story but wanted to hear the whole conversation.

'What story?' I continued.

Minh sat down on the bed and slowly took off his shoes. 'A man and a horse can be great partners on a long journey. If the horse is healthy, the man can ride it, and they both reach the destination easily and quickly. But if the horse is crippled, the man has to carry the horse the whole way.'

'It's a good metaphor,' I responded, a part of me almost feeling proud of Minh. 'So, what did she say?'

Minh placed his shoes neatly beside the bed. 'She said they were both humans, not horses.'

Hong-An was smart, like her father.

'But I told her she was missing the point,' Minh continued and narrated exactly what he'd told her. 'If you marry Travis', he said, 'your mother and I fear that you will suffer a lot. We raised you; we know who you are and what skills you have. I am your father. I have lived two times your life. I believe I can share with you some knowledge and wisdom. The wisdom I have gained from being with your mother.'

As he finished speaking, he looked at me and raised his eyebrows for an acknowledgement, but I continued.

'And so, what did she say?'

She said, 'Ba, I don't need wisdom. It's simple. I love him, and he loves me.'

Minh frowned, visibly fighting the contradiction in his mind. Finally, he shook his head and said defeatedly, 'I couldn't argue with that, you know? You can't argue with love.'

'I am glad you summoned the courage to talk to Hong-An,' I said as I patted him on the back, tears streaming from my eyes. I felt drained. I knew we both broke our daughter's heart. I did not want to discuss love with my husband right now. The conversation might result in someone getting hurt, so I decided to focus all my attention on my daughter at the moment.

'How can Hong-An know about love after only eight months? For her whole life, she has looked to us for advice and guidance. She had trusted us and wanted our support as she learned and grew,' I said.

It was true. Our whole community looked at our little trio as an example of a perfect family. People would say things like: 'Hong-An is such a good girl.' 'So smart.' 'So lively and positive.' 'I wish my daughter was like her.' 'You are so blessed.'

This was what I had always wanted. I remembered the daydreams I'd had as a child, dreams of a mother I didn't have. I dreamed of my mother scooping me up on her walk home from the river, and me clinging to her as she bounced me on her hip. I'd imagined the smiling faces of our neighbours, looking at us as the example of perfect mother-daughter love. This was just a dream. I hadn't had any of this in my childhood. I was lucky, I may not have had this with my own mother, but I'd been blessed with this kind of relationship with Hong-An.

But now, I did not feel blessed. The horrible truth was that Travis was a crippled horse. I had sensed it much earlier on. Before Minh and I had ever met Travis, Hong-An had mentioned a new friend, and it hadn't taken me long to figure out that this new friend was more romantic than platonic.

When she borrowed my car a couple of times during the week, I noticed that the passenger seat was pushed very far back.

He's tall, I had thought. He must be Australian. I was excited for her and desperately curious to know more about him, but she would not answer any of my questions, even when I kept joking and chanting, as usual: 'I can feel the love in the air,' I'd say, and Hong-An would just roll her eyes.

I looked at her recent pictures on Facebook: dinners with her girlfriends, selfies on the ferry, and university events. Then one struck me as odd; a group photo where only one person was not Asian. He looked like Aragorn among the Hobbits. I went to his profile. He had strong features with light sweet brown eyes and a big honest smile. A rush of emotion flooded through me, but as I clicked through the photos, a note of concern rose up as well. Underneath his striking, handsome features, he looked worn out and somehow deflated, as if he was perpetually just out of bed. Something was wrong with this young man. He did not look healthy.

'Show Mẹ your boyfriend's picture,' I asked her. But Hong-An refused to answer. She insisted, 'He doesn't look as good in pictures as he does in person. So you should wait to meet him. I will bring him home soon, Mẹ.'

I felt so happy when Hong-An talked to me about her new relationship. I was sure that sooner or later, she would tell me everything about him. My heart danced with the rhythm of love for my daughter, and I tried to push aside my worries. Maybe Hong-An was right. Perhaps the young man just didn't photograph well. Maybe I was too protective. I wanted Hong-An to be happy and in love, so I pushed my misgivings aside, convincing myself that I imagined things.

She finally brought him home for lunch on the very day the three of us were flying to Europe for a holiday.

Minh objected to the idea straight away. My husband wanted everything planned perfectly and needed a lot of time for this important event. While I was spontaneous, and I could transform nothing into something in a short time.

'It's OK for Hong-An to bring her boyfriend home to see us. We've arranged everything, and we will take a taxi to the airport after lunch.'

'Lunch? How about coffee?' Minh asked, getting a little easier with the idea as he started to accept his beloved daughter's wish.

'I can cook - leave everything to me,' I offered. I wanted to spoil my daughter as usual and impress her boyfriend.

'Nothing left in the fridge!' Minh declared, alarming me.

The only meal I could pull together was quail curry - an unusual dish, especially for such a momentous occasion.

I collected all the leftover vegetables and the last pack of quail in the fridge. My heart was beating very fast, and I felt excited with the thoughts running through in my mind.

'It's him, the one in the picture that I showed you,' I whispered to Minh when I saw Travis through the window.

Hugs and kisses were exchanged, and I was pleased to see Travis from the first moment. He had the most beautiful and honest eyes that I had ever seen, with a broad open smile. As it turned out, he looked much better than the photos I had seen.

'He's so hot, Hong-An! Good job,' I whispered to her. Her chin was up, there was a lot of love in the air.

My hands shook as I brought the dish to the table.

'He is from the Gold Coast but now lives in Sydney,' Hong-An had briefed us before his arrival after repeated demands for information. 'I met him at a Christian conference. He is my age and works for a solar engineering company. He was the school captain and very successful academically. He surfs, plays soccer, rugby, cricket, and came second at running in all of Brisbane. He travelled the country a lot and met John Howard and many well-known men and women in the world.'

'He sounds perfect. Like Chris Hemsworth. Is your boyfriend Chris Hemsworth?' I joked. 'I am thrilled that you have brought a very charming and healthy boy to this family. You have listened to your mummy well.'

It was an impressive list of facts, uncannily fitting my wish for her to be with a healthy, strong, supportive man. 'No unhealthy man is welcome in this home, OK! We need a hero to look after all of us!' I knew sickness could strain a marriage, and it was something I didn't want my daughter to have to go through. When I'd first snooped on Facebook and had seen Travis's pictures, I'd been struck with the worry that he might be unwell, but meeting him in person, these fears vanished, and I was so glad to be able to release them.

We had a great lunch, and to my delight, Travis loved my quail curry. He was full of praise for my daughter, and we taught him how to say, 'Thank you,' or 'Cam on' in Vietnamese. The next hour, we left for Europe - the Three Musketeers, with high hopes for our daughter's new relationship.

❤ ❤ ❤ ❤

When we returned to Australia from our holiday, the undercurrent I had sensed in the photos began to show. Travis invited us around to his apartment with the promising offer of cooking us a pasta dish.

'He cooks too,' I said to Hong-An in the hallway, winking playfully. But the confident man who had come to our house for lunch was now dishevelled and awkward as he prepared the meal for us. It seemed like he could not focus on anything, and his features were sunken.

'It's just the flu,' he said when I asked him if he was feeling OK. I made an excuse of needing to get something from Chinatown, which was just around the corner and motioned for Minh to join me.

'They need a bit of space,' I said when we were out the door. 'He looks so ill. How about we take him back to ours and look after him until he is better? He needs a bit of care and attention as his family is far away.'

Minh looked sceptical. He rejected the suggestion but eventually relented, knowing the benefits of my care and attention very well.

'I want to do this for Hong-An,' I told him. 'She is delighted when her boyfriend is around.' However, I felt sorry to cause Minh trouble, as he looked tired and wanted to have his privacy.

When we returned, he had not really made any progress in the kitchen, and Hong-An now looked almost as worn out as he did.

I took control. 'You have the flu. Let's go back to our house, where you can get some rest and good Vietnamese hospitality.' For just a moment, I thought I had offended him, but then he breathed a long sigh and smiled his big, honest smile.

'That would be amazing.'

Hong-An jumped up and down excitedly and held his hand.

'Let's leave the pasta here, shall we?' she said, and we all laughed.

♥ ♥ ♥ ♥

It was brave and open of me to invite an Aussie into our home. I didn't know him that well. Two meetings weren't enough to form a solid opinion. I mostly followed my natural inclinations, but it was also a strong, silent message that we welcomed their relationship. Travis coming to stay at our house was the first step to allow him into our lives with trust and assurance. I felt buoyed by my courage, despite hardly knowing him.

I felt so happy hearing my daughter giggling and laughing with Travis in the rumpus room while I was dancing in the kitchen. There was indeed a lot of love in the air.

Travis stayed with us and went back to the city for work the next day. Hong-An seemed to want him there forever. I extended my invitation without consulting with Minh. 'Our two bedrooms at the back are empty with a lot of space. You are welcome to stay with us anytime.'

Travis's eyes sparkled. 'Really? Thank you,' he said, seemingly unable to believe what he'd heard from his Vietnamese girlfriend's mother.

I made apologies to Minh later, but I was pretty sure that he also wanted to see his daughter happy.

I rearranged the house to make sure he had a place to sleep and assured him that he was welcome any time. Hong-An jumped up and down with her beautiful smiles. She acted like a little girl with a special treat, like when I bought her a purple dress or announced that we would have a picnic on the beach. I watched Hong-An, and my heart sang with joy.

'You love your daughter so much and cooked a lot for her boyfriend despite your tiredness after a long day at the preschool,' Minh said. But I didn't mind.

I was willing to do whatever I could. I would trade anything for the happiness of my daughter. However, I did sometimes wonder about my intentions. Was I doing all of this out of unconditional love for Hong-An? Or was I trying to make up for my own mother's lack of attention, by doing for Hong-An what I'd always wanted done for me? When I really thought about it, I knew that the answer was both. I did love Hong-An unconditionally, but I also knew that my own childhood very much guided my actions. The past informs the present, but the present is all that we ever have control over. I couldn't go back in time and give my young self any comfort or make my mother pay more attention to me, but I could be a better mother to my own daughter.

❤ ❤ ❤ ❤

Over the next few weeks, Travis came over often and became more and more comfortable in our family home. Hong-An jumped up and down with joy when I arranged surprise visits for her with Travis after he finished work in the city.

I began to educate him on Vietnamese cuisine, serving him as many unique dishes as I could. I also bought and served him mangos - his favourite fruit. He loved it, but behind the appreciation in his eyes, there was a kind of profound lethargy. His enthusiasm was muted as if he was constantly swimming against the current of a darker force inside himself. It wasn't long before I found out exactly what that dark force was.

He opened up to us one day as we sat together over morning coffee. He said that he had something to tell us, and we sat nervously waiting, unsure of what to expect. Finally, Hong-An placed her hand over his on the table and motioned for him to begin.

'When I was in Year 12, I went to England for the gap year, and I developed a severe depression,' he began.

The words seeped into our consciousness slowly, like drops of dye on cloth.

Travis's voice was shaking with the gravity of his words. 'After seeing a couple of psychologists, I was one of the first people to try a new medication that had just arrived in Australia. And it worked. Well, it made me more stable, at least for my university years. But honestly, it's still hard. I feel like I only have 50% of the energy I used to have, and it affects everything. Working is extremely tiring,' he fidgeted in his chair and cleared his throat. 'So, yeah, I just wanted to tell you because maybe it will explain why I can seem sick and tired sometimes, and I want to be honest about my situation with you both. I'm OK, really, but yeah, it's hard...' he trailed off, leaving us to our own thoughts.

I felt for him deeply, but to be honest, my thoughts were mostly for my daughter. No wonder she looked so drained recently. She was not built to handle the burdens of others. I had spoiled her as much as I could her whole life. I had shielded her from all of the pain and suffering that threatened her from every direction. Hong-An had looked nervous when Travis spoke. She clearly understood what Minh would think of his words.

'I'm sorry, Travis!' I said. 'That is such an awful burden on you, especially when you were so young'. His shoulders were completely sunken, and he actually looked like a seventeen-year-old boy now, weak and vulnerable across the table. 'Will you go off the medication eventually? I mean, do the doctors have a plan?' I asked.

Hong-An shot me a warning look, which Travis acknowledged with a squeeze of her hand.

'Um. No. There is no plan. It's just something I have to take,' he replied. 'I don't know. It's just part of my life, I guess. But Hong-An is great, and she really understands me. She says you will too, and I'm glad to have told you so that you can understand,' he offered a version of his smile, but it was unconvincing. The strong, healthy hero Hong-An had promised was now as exposed as a jellyfish in the sun.

It was a monumental moment. Just these few words left us with deep a concern that hung darkly around the table. His honesty both brought us together and further tore us apart. This simple revelation became a mountain we couldn't climb. It was now impossible for me to differentiate his illness from his personality.

After Travis had told us about his depression and all of the challenges he faced, Minh and I had tried to remain calm, but we were worried for our daughter. We felt sympathy for Travis, and we cared about him too, but our own daughter was always our priority. Once we knew about Travis's mental illness, many strange behaviours, such as his perpetual tiredness and seeming so sluggish and distracted, finally made sense.

I started to observe Travis more and more, paying attention to his behaviours. He left a bottle of pills on the table once. I saw the name, and I checked to find out what the side effects were. All of the blood in my body went cold when I read that long list. The side effects were nausea, increased appetite, weight gain, loss of sexual desire and other sexual problems. Not to mention fatigue, drowsiness, insomnia, and blurred vision, the list went on and on.

I cried out to Minh, 'All of those side effects! That can't be good for Travis, poor thing!'

So it was no wonder that Travis left the table at 10 am, announcing that he would take a nap. This was not normal for a young man. Only a very old or unwell person should need a nap so shortly after waking up.

One night during dinner, Travis made an announcement which gave me even greater cause to worry about what kind of partner he would be for Hong-An.

'I've lost my job,' he announced. There was a blank expression on his face.

Hong-An rushed to defend him. 'His boss was so mean to him.'

'No one could hire him for long-term, with his health issues always acting up like that,' Minh said later, as both of us were about to go to bed.

Travis stayed with us more while he was out of a job. I remained kind and welcoming.

And then I found that I had missed something. Something had changed in our house, and it wasn't fair to us. We spoke more English in our house than Vietnamese, the language of love of our trio for years since Hong-An was born.

At first, we were OK and tried to please Travis and helped him to get along with us, but now, Hong-An seemed to please Travis and not speak Vietnamese with us at mealtime.

'Hong-An needs to respect our family traditions and teach Travis to respect values. We are Vietnamese, and we have our roots,' Minh complained to me. I totally agreed with him, but I mostly kept quiet. I didn't want to add to Minh's worry by sharing my fears.

We tried to give Travis some credit. We kept on trying to find ways to connect with him and accept him into our family. We wanted to be reassured. He was honest and polite, but that wasn't enough. I wanted more for Hong-An. I wanted more for our family.

I kept trying to move past my negative thinking; I tried to reassure to both Minh and myself. 'Let them spend time together,' I said. 'Then the truth will be revealed.'

CHAPTER THREE

~

WHEN THE PAST MET THE FUTURE

'We could stay in a good hotel, but grandma's house is big, and we'll stay there to make her happy,' Hong-An and Travis accepted my suggestion. After all, the purpose of the trip was to get closer to family and show Travis our culture.

'We want to introduce you to both sides of Hong-An formally,' I explained.

We were formally introducing Travis to both sides of Hong-An.

'Looking at Travis, Hong-An said, 'Don't worry. It's just a formality. They are not that full-on about tradition.'

'Looking at Travis, Hong-An said, 'Don't worry. It's just a formality. They are not that full-on about tradition.'

It's not just a formality, I thought, and Hong-An knew it. I was disappointed with the way she was acting. I felt like I was losing her. While we had always been so close, she seemed so far away now; it was like we were standing on opposite banks of a vast and raging river. I had to figure out how to get across to her. I wanted my Hong-An back.

We had initially planned this trip before Travis proposed to Hong-An; it was meant as a kind gesture and a way to introduce him to our culture. I could never have imagined what had transpired before the trip. I was so disappointed in Hong-An for going against our wishes and accepting Travis's proposal; I was disappointed with how quickly everything had happened. I was disappointed with Travis for skipping steps and going about his proposal in such an inappropriate way, and for all the attitude that he had shown to us. That deep resentment boiling inside of me had not disappeared. I had only pushed it down and glossed over it. For everyone's sake, I was trying desperately to keep these feelings bottled up inside and not let them slip out. I wanted to have a happy family again, this much I was sure of.

We had planned this trip, and we were certainly going to make it happen, even if now it felt like the trip itself was supporting their marriage plans. But I was a good mother, so I would go through the motions of days at the beach and introducing Travis to my family, even if my troubled thoughts lingered. Despite the outward kindness, I planned to find a way to save Hong-An from this future. Maybe Hong-An would come to her senses. I held on tightly to this deep hope.

When we arrived in Hoi-An, my youngest brother, Hai, his wife, and their six-month-old baby flew from Saigon to Da Nang then to Hoi-An to unite with us and welcome Travis. Of her four uncles, he was the uncle that Hong-An was closest to.

Two days later, Hai borrowed the car from Hung and came to Hoi An to take us to Da-Nang.

My brother was chatting constantly to Travis and complimenting him. I felt so sad and frustrated with my brother's excitement toward his future Aussie nephew-in-law. Only two days earlier when his family came to visit us at the beach, I had talked to my brother about my apprehension. I had cried as I told him how I feared for Hong-An's happiness and future. He had said that he agreed with me and that Hong-An wasn't strong enough to support someone with lifelong mental health issues. Now, he was so friendly and warm towards Travis. I didn't want him to give Travis more hope.

Hai showed Travis The Marble Mountain with a cheerful face as we passed by. 'This is Ha-Le's and my favourite childhood place,' he said beaming.

'We are a very modern Vietnamese family. You are a lucky guy, Travis,' Hai added, reassuring Travis that he was in good hands.

♥ ♥ ♥ ♥

My family gathered at my mother's house to welcome us and meet the family's newest member - an Australian. I winced and had to hold myself back from saying something when I saw the outfit that Travis had chosen to wear. He was wearing shorts, a t-shirt, and flip-flops. This wasn't very comfortable to Minh and me, as our family was gathering to meet Travis for the first time and celebrate my mother's 72nd birthday. What he was wearing might have been fashionable in Australia, but here in Vietnam, that was the kind of clothing that cycle drivers would wear. It wasn't at all appropriate for this formal occasion, and I was disappointed in Hong-An for not correcting him. I knew that my family would welcome and adore Travis right away. That's just the way they are. But, Travis had nothing to impress them with, apart from having a handsome Australian face. Hong-An looks like a movie star in front of her loved ones in Vietnam, and they were looking to meet another movie star to match her.

With Hong-An translating, the guest of honour was introduced to an overwhelming welcoming party. My four brothers, their partners, as well as a handful of nieces and nephews all bowed and shook hands politely. I was so proud of my extended family in Vietnam for how they comported themselves in front of Travis.

My mother, the matriarch, was the only one seated, her back straight with elegant poise, her hair pinned neatly back, a string of pearls around her neck. She looked very dignified, formidable even. I had missed her. It was hard for me, with her always being so far away, and seeing her again every time was like a true feeling of peace.

My mother got up from the table, gently gesturing for me to join her. I was happy to have this extra time with her. We sat side by side on the sofa. It was a warm tropical evening which felt like a comfortable memory from my childhood. I needed a bit of comfort. I needed someone to sit with my feelings, to hold them for me as I let them out just a bit. I started and stopped and started again.

'Everything has collapsed now Ma, and I am so worried about Hong-An's future. She is a smart and mature girl but not yet ready for a new family and an unwell husband. There is too much for her to cope with.'

I intended to add more words but held back. I did not want to burden my mother too much and add to her sadness. She had had enough already for a lifetime.

She listened intently to my words. Her eyes were dry but had the full depth of many lifetimes of struggle and wisdom reflected in them.

She looked at me, her gaze piercing my heart with love.

'All mothers love their children,' she started, 'But you, I would say, you love your daughter so much that you have laid down your life for her.'

My mother's words brought me to tears. Her acknowledgement illuminated our unspoken burden that she knew she never gave me the love I needed. I was so moved by her concern for me that I suddenly didn't care about impressing her. She could see exactly how I was feeling, and her support warmed me.

Only a mother could be so patient with her child. My mum let me go on and on. Once I started talking, it was like I couldn't stop. My mother nodded sympathetically and let me get it all off my chest. I wondered how a woman who had lived such a hard life could still be so caring. I could feel our relationship mend tiny broken cracks in this quiet moment together, even if the river was still wide between us. We had never been close, but that wasn't my fault or hers. She had done the very best that she could, given the suffering in her own life.

I knew the story of my mother. I knew what she had endured. I had heard all the stories. The stories of how mum was born to be a servant for her whole family, how she was born to be abused and neglected. I had heard about the time her father had tied her to a pole and beat her. I knew how she had to sell her body to feed herself and her sister. I knew how a soldier had raped her at gunpoint. She had suffered so much more than most humans could imagine enduring. How could I ever blame her for her own inabilities as a mother?

At twenty-one, she fell in love with an army priest.

One day, coming home from a picnic, my mother tripped and badly hurt her head. The priest carried her to a nearby village, where they found some bandages and a place to sleep for the night. Her prettiness, her vulnerability, and the relative privacy of an unfamiliar room were too much temptation for the priest to resist, and soon enough, she discovered that she was pregnant.

When she met up with him to tell him the good news, he was very clear. 'That child is not mine,' He had said and disappeared. He broke my mother's heart, and she made a vow that a priest would never be near her child, and she would never have a man in her life again.

As an owner of a coffee shop, she got a lot of officers, even an army captain admiring her, but she refused them. Some good men with good positions in the community asked if they could be the child's father, but she ignored them all, keeping to her vow. Then, one day, my father came to her coffee shop.

My father had just come out of Thua Phu- Hue prison after six years in there. Orphaned at a young age, he grew up with his cousins and relatives in a rural area controlled by the Viet Cong. The Viet Cong educated him, and when he was around sixteen years old, he was selected to become part of a secret mission. They covertly sent him with a group to the North to be trained as infiltrators of the South Vietnamese Government; however, on the way to the North, he was caught and put into prison in Hue, where the Southern Government tortured him. Immediately after his release, he wandered into my mother's coffee shop. She saw him, alone at the table, his good looks still shining through his naturally kind face.

'He looked like a man with high morals,' Ma would often recall with love in her eyes. 'He would be much respected and standing out because of his handsome features and strong build; he was my hero.'

She was confident, capable, beautiful and strong to my father, and they were drawn together like pieces of a puzzle. She felt he was a man that she could trust.

When my mother told my father she was pregnant, he didn't seem to mind. The vulnerability of her situation possibly made him feel empowered to step into a role of responsibility. After being in prison with a lot of mental and physical torture, he said that he just wanted to settle down and live a quiet family life. They planned to tell the neighbourhood that it was his child she had, and they had a small party instead of a big wedding, just to let everyone know they were a couple. My father was still labelled a political prisoner, so finding a job was very difficult. And so, my elder brother was born into this new, complicated relationship, and I followed two years later.

I felt the weight of generations of suffering, sitting there in the dark with my mother. It would have been almost unimaginable for her to consider having an Australian as a grandson-in-law, but she seemed to be dealing with the engagement much better than me.

Hung, the number four sibling among us, passed by with his skin reddened by beer. 'I like Travis so much! He is a nice boy!' Then he added something that made me even more disappointed with Travis. 'He called you Ha-Le! Why not calling you Mẹ yet?' He raised his eyebrows as he waited for an answer. 'You have to explain to Travis about our culture,' he said. 'We are Vietnamese, and we have our values for the family's relationship. It is weird and rude when he called Minh and you by name.'

Hung was so sharp and direct as usual. I knew it was weird and rude for Travis to keep calling me by my first name. Being called Mẹ was a wish of all Vietnamese mothers-in-law. The title was meant to bring us closer together and cement the new familial connection. Travis and I had no connection, and it didn't look like this was going to change anytime soon. He knew that I longed for him to call me Mẹ in the Vietnamese language, but he didn't value what I valued at all. He acted like he had no regard for my feelings. I had expressed my wish to Hong-An and him many times after he proposed to my daughter.

'Aussie kids have a lot of freedom, and they just do what they want to do!' I explained, trying to cover my pain.

'Tell Hong-An to teach him about our culture.'

Hung was right. I couldn't get Travis to change. Hong-An was the only one who could do that.

'Shoo! Go away, so your sister can rest,' Mum raised her hand to pretend to smack him. He slid to the other side and kissed our mother's hand before he walked away with his beer.

I could remember Hung's life had created in me so many horrible memories at the earliest time of our lives. I watched him move to where Travis and Hong-An sat, my heart full of love for him. I still had echoes in my mind of his frightened cries. They reached out from the past, clinging to my heart. We had been through so much together.

CHAPTER FOUR

~

RECOLLECTIONS AND A REALISATION

I was only a child when the war started. Night after night, American planes would fly over Da Nang, rattling our little wooden house and forcing my elder brother and I to hide under the table. We would cry and hug each other until the piercing noise stopped. I remember thinking, then, that monsters had arrived in the sky.

'They are just practising,' my mother would say, but we didn't really know what that meant. To us, huge monsters were practising in the sky to show off their power. The big people never knew that they scared two little souls to death. Even my elder brother, who was supposed to protect me from harm, was just as scared as me. His hands held me so tightly that I knew he was experiencing extreme fear.

'You are my big brother! You have to be strong for me!' I yelled at him over the deafening noises of the monsters. He cried louder and dreaded the noise even more. At this point, I was not sure if it was my angry face or the noise of the aeroplane he feared, but I was certain of one thing, my older brother was the first person I rescued from fear at the tender age of three.

Then the war arrived on our doorstep in the form of a strange, uniformed man I had never seen before. Instinctively cautious, I crept into the background, but my mother ran to him and embraced him lovingly.

I could not remember there ever being a grown man in our house. My elder brother was the biggest man, but he was not big to me after the aeroplane incident. I held his eyes with an uncertain curiosity and his smile deepened. Kneeling down, he put his canvas bag on the floor and extended his arms towards me.

'Come to Ba!'

I did not run to him. His eyes were kind, however, a bit too overwhelmingly so. Instead, I ran behind the chair and observed him from a distance for the rest of the evening. He was tall and lean but unmistakably strong, with full lips and what I would later call a Western nose. I watched him pretend to play cards with my elder brother, Hiep and my younger brother, Hien, slapping his thigh in mock disappointment as they continued to beat him in a game that apparently had no rules. When dinner was ready, I ate quietly and shyly, stealing looks at my father across the mat.

I had seriously mixed feelings about his arrival. I'd heard my mother talk about my father before, but I'd never known what to expect. Now that he was here, I was confused, but I was also filled with pride. I thought to myself, He is my dad. I have a daddy like all of the other children do! I was sorting through a mixture of emotions, including excitement, fear, and reluctance. I wasn't sure that I wanted to see my house grow bigger. He was an unfamiliar sight in a home that had always been familiar to me. I didn't recognise our family with him suddenly present.

'Ha-Le has grown,' my father said to my mother fondly.

My mother raised her eyebrows. 'So has her appetite.'

Hien laughed with a mouth full of rice. 'Mostly for sweets and to hold food in her mouth for ages,' he said. 'Chi Thoi would always squeeze her face because of that,' he added innocently with a smile.

I put my spoon down, embarrassed. It was true. I had developed a craving for anything sweet: sweet bean soup, lollies, coconut jelly. The moments when I could savour a sweet snack were the best moments of my life. It was also true that mealtimes were the times that I faced Chi Thoi's power over me. I was so scared when Hien mentioned my suffering that I wanted to fly over and punch his back. My mum had always said, 'You have to listen to Chi Thoi, but if she hits you, let mum know!' I never told her as I knew that worse could happen.

Chi Thoi, overheard the conversation about the sweets and sensed that she was somehow to blame. She walked into the room, holding her head down, avoiding my parents' eyes. No one said anything.

My father rescued me from my awkwardness, 'A little princess deserves only the best sweets.'

I kept my face down but could not help a warm smile spreading across my cheeks—a princess. I had never been called a princess before.

'She is very smart, seems to know everything - quite abnormal for her age,' Mum added. More credits for me.

After dinner, I lay down in our shared bed and drifted off to sleep to the muttering sounds of my mother and father talking. My dreams were interrupted later by the sharp sound of a bottle hitting the floor and the heavy steps of my father, the stranger, walking across the room. It took me a few seconds to remember who he was. I kept my eyes shut and listened to his breathing until I, too, drifted back to sleep, but this time, my dreams were confusing and scattered.

In the morning, my father was in the kitchen tinkering with a small American-made radio. From the corner, I heard words I couldn't understand. Strange, I thought. There are a lot of people in that box, and they keep talking. His face was very stern as he kept turning the radio dial as if trying to find something inside that he had lost. They had music too. How could they do that? I wanted to see them one day, in the box. When he saw me, he brightened up and turned it off quickly.

'The princess has woken up,' he announced to the whole house.

I fidgeted silently, still shyly.

'I thought we could go and see Ma today at the market. Just you and me. What do you think?'

My eyes went wide with excitement, and I automatically glanced towards Chi Thoi, who was preparing breakfast with a pot. She kept looking at her work, apparently unmoved.

My father followed my eyes and then addressed me again, more quietly, 'just you and me.'

He winked, and my heart melted. At that moment of delight, I just wanted my father to tell Chi Thoi to stop hitting me. I knew he could do that, but I couldn't open my little mouth. What if Chi Thoi hit me more when no one was home? So, I kept quiet.

♥ ♥ ♥ ♥

Across the river!

My father was asking me to go across the river with him, and I couldn't believe it. This stranger had come and suddenly answered my prayers. I became hyperactive with joy, or relief, or happiness, I'm not sure. The same emotions came again when we stood on the deck of the ferry later that morning. Even though he was not working, he had dressed in his army uniform. He looked so handsome, and I could tell that many people were looking at him. He leaned out over the water, with one foot on the edge of the boat fearlessly. I looked up at him proudly from his side, this striking man in a smart uniform, as he laughed and joked with the other passengers. A few times, the boat rocked a little too much for my liking. I held onto my father's pants to steady myself, but also, I thought innocently, to save him if he fell in the water. The two of us were protecting each other as we crossed that previously un-crossable expanse of water that had separated me from my mother.

My mother was surprised and happy to see us. She gave each of us a bowl of pork and rice with pickles, and we sat together on little chairs that were close to the ground. For the first time, I was out in public with my parents. Hundreds of people walked past, a few of them saying hello to my mother and raising their eyebrows towards my handsome father. We must have looked like a happy little family, and I felt buoyed with confidence. My father reached into one of his many pockets and brought out a couple of shiny coins. 'The princess must now have her sweets.' He said, holding the coins out towards me. When I took them, he grabbed my hand and pulled me towards him in a hug, sniffing my cheeks and squashing me into his broad chest. Almost suffocating, I was forced to press my own nose against his uniform and absorb his unique smell. It had a peppery aroma, mixed with the ghost of laundry detergent and almonds. It was sweet, like dark, herbaceous honey and strong and soothing, like the first rain of the monsoon. I began to love my father at that moment, and I longed for that scent in his absence.

'OK, enough of that,' my mother said, waving her hand to dismiss me. 'Go and buy your sweets before the customers start avoiding us.'

I ran around the market to find the best sweets I could. I bought some squares of coconut jelly, some sweet sticky bananas wrapped in little leaf parcels, and a small bag of toffees to share with my brothers. It was heaven to go across the river with my father and see my mother at the market.

But heaven did not last long.

A few nights later, my parents began fighting, and I cupped my hands over my ears to try and muffle the shouting, just as I did when the American planes flew over our house. I heard only a few words. Money. Kids. Food. I couldn't piece these clues together into a complete puzzle. I just knew that I was scared and that I didn't want them to be angry at each other anymore. Someone smashed a plate, and I closed my eyes shut and hummed a song to myself to drown out the noise.

The monsters were back, but not in the sky. They were now in my house.

❤ ❤ ❤ ❤

But this was the past. Just a memory, I was no longer this little girl hiding from monsters. I was a mother myself. The past was over. It was only a ghost now. It couldn't be changed or brought back to life. I knew that I couldn't let the past control the present. But I was also so afraid. There had been far too much fighting in my family lately. My heart felt like it was aching and bleeding on the floor. Worry coursed through my body. I was worried about so many things. I was not just worried about the present with all the anger that hung in the air, but also worried for the future, Hong-An was choosing for herself. I was aware of how my feeling of past loss affected my present emotions. I wanted to feel safe in my relationships like the people I loved were not going anywhere. I didn't want to have a house full of monsters like I did as a little girl, I didn't want her to either. Love was a strong but tense emotion for me. It brought me both joy and fear.

Being in this big house in Vietnam, the country of my childhood had brought back so many memories. After my brothers, sisters in law, nephews and nieces had all gone home, I left the party, and then I left my mother sleeping in the back room. The night had made me very sentimental, and I wanted to take a taxi to the river for a walk. I asked Hong-An to join me. Maybe we could have some mother and daughter time. We hadn't had a moment alone since we had arrived. I wanted us to talk the way we used to. We had not managed to enjoy such a moment for the whole holiday. Every step of the way, she clung to Travis, and so I was not surprised when she refused. 'I can't leave him here with all the relatives. And, anyway, we want to get some rest'.

Hong-An reminded me of what had happened just last week. We arrived finally in Sapa in the morning after finishing a three-day trip at Ha Long Bay. We were still the Fantastic Four even as Minh and I stuck together like two old monkeys while Travis and Hong-An ventured out on their own.

'We go on a holiday as a family, not a double date,' Minh half-joked and half-showed his disappointment at not having the family time we used to have with Hong-An. I was disappointed too, but I tried to keep the energy high for the four of us.

I was so proud that the four of us reached Sapa together. Three of us were there with my brother Hai in 2008, and I really loved the place and wanted to take Travis to the best part of Viet Nam. Despite the rough trip from Ha Noi, I enjoyed the night in a train cabin. It was so small, and with such a low ceiling, Travis hit his head on everything, making us laugh – real, happy laughs as a family. I enjoyed every moment of us in the cabin with meals and snacks that we bought from

Ha Noi. We hugged and cheerfully kissed each other goodnight. It was the real family time that I had desired. We had been working hard to accept that Travis and Hong-An would be married, and during this time, it seemed that our hard work was starting to pay off. We were all finally getting along.

But our happiness didn't last. Travis fell ill that evening. He was vomiting and in great gastrointestinal distress. He was so pale and out of breath. My heart twisted for him. He looked so miserable. With Travis's sickness, all the plans for the Sapa adventure were cancelled for the Fantastic Four. Minh, Hong-An, and I tried our best to look after Travis. It was scary that there was no medical assistance up the high mountains. Minh gave Travis some medication that he bought, but it didn't seem to work. Travis struggled for a night and a day before he got better.

We were about to celebrate Travis being out of the woods when Hong-An came down with the same condition.

'You got it from Travis because you cared for him for the first day,' Minh said.

In one day, Hong-An only had her skin and bones left! Waiting for the bus to get us back Lang Son and then Ha Noi to rescue Hong-An, I felt like I was in hell. Seeing my daughter become skinnier and skinnier shook me. Like the time we were in Hei Ling Chau camp, and five-month-old Hong-An had a mystery fever at night with the door of the room locked.

I had to admit watching them care for each other as they were sick that I was jealous of Travis. My baby leaned on him and held his hand while I just watched the two of them at a distance. It was like I had been replaced; it had all happened so quickly. I was astounded at myself for having these thoughts. I worried that I was losing something big in my heart. But how could I not feel this way watching Travis sit there like a lump on the couch as I tried to do the things that I knew Hong-An needed. I was jealous of Travis; it all seemed so unfair. I was jealous of the affection that Hong-An showed him. As hard as I tried, I couldn't accept the two of them together. I wasn't ready to do it. Not yet.

I wondered if I ever would be.

CHAPTER FIVE

HOW WE ALL FELL APART

I sat on the bank of Bach Dang River, feeling as though I were a fifty-year-old child. I longed for Hong-An. As I relived my memories, I got stuck with a strong sense of Deja-vu. Here I was, once again sitting on the bank of this same river, longing for the company of someone I loved. Only instead of it being my mother, it was now my daughter. This trip was not turning out to be what I had expected at all. I had wanted so much to show Hong-An and Travis that I was an open-minded Australian-Vietnamese woman who was willing and able to welcome him into the family. For a long time, I had considered it my responsibility to adapt my culture to the Australian customs and expectations. We became well-known in the Vietnamese community in Sydney as a family that had created an excellent benchmark for living with two cultures. Hong-An had been a shining example of a girl who embraced modern Australian life while still respecting her cultural roots. Except for his love for Vietnamese food, which was hardly unique, Travis did not have any interest in our culture. He had not even bothered to learn any more than 'cam on' which means 'Thank you' in Vietnamese.

A few days after we had arrived here, I had asked him what he thought of his fiancé's homeland.

'It's great,' he replied. 'It's kind of like China.'

It was like saying Australia was kind of like America.

During our short holiday, my disappointment in the new Aussie member of our family only grew. I felt disrespected by his disinterest. I'd thought this trip would open his eyes to our culture, and it was only right that he makes an effort to learn about who we were. He wanted to marry our daughter after all. He was taking our only daughter, not just her time but her spirit. It was like you could watch him take her zest for life away the longer they were together.

Coming to Vietnam only brought the issues we'd been dealing with into a clearer focus. It was even more evident to Minh and I that our daughter was heading down the wrong path. She was less and less like herself and more disconnected from the extended family. She also changed her style of fashion to a very casual style to match Travis'. I wondered what power Travis had to make my daughter change so much about herself. I felt like something was not right. I needed to rescue her from this situation. It was my duty as her mother.

As evening fell, I looked out across the Bach Dang River. There was nothing worse than the separation of a child from their parents. Heartache rose like a tide inside me. The time for being careful and polite was over.

I had compartmentalized my disapproval of the marriage into a thousand manageable pieces. Now, it had coalesced into a ball of fire. I went home but couldn't sleep. I tossed and turned all night, dreading what I knew in my heart needed to happen. We had a final battle to face. This tension was going to come to a head whether I liked it or not. We couldn't live forever in anxiety.

The next morning, I woke up decided. I knew what needed to happen.

I cornered Minh, 'You were too soft on her when you spoke to her in the resort. This is her future, her happiness. We cannot beat around the bush. We have to tell Hong-An straight out what we think about her future. We should speak up rather than watch. She might blame us later if we don't give her advice on what we know will happen to her.'

Minh sighed, and I took a shaky breath before continuing on. I started to vent about everything that had happened while we had been on holiday, all of the unhealthy changes we had seen in Travis. It was evident to both of us that Travis was struggling with his depression. Not only that, but Hong-An was starting to show her stress. My worst fears were realized. I'd been right: Hong-An couldn't take the burden of Travis's illness.

Minh stared at me as my voice started to rise. I didn't want to fight with Minh. A fleeting memory intruded on my thoughts. A memory of my own parents fighting as I cowered under the covers as a child. I didn't want to repeat this in my own marriage. I didn't want to hurt our relationship with unkind words. I told myself that I shouldn't blame him for what was happening. None of this was really his fault, but I couldn't stop. It was like all of my pent-up and repressed emotions over the past few weeks were finally exploding. I couldn't contain them anymore.

'Marriage is hard enough,' I said. 'Why didn't you tell Hong-An how shocked you were when Travis got up and started drinking those beers in the middle of the night? Even after he went on Facebook last month to announce his success in weaning off the alcohol permanently.'

I trailed off, feeling stuck and unable to go on. My heart was heavy, and my eyes filled with tears.

My husband took off his glasses and cleaned them. His hands shook slightly as he put them back on his face. His instincts were apparently fighting with his analytical brain.

Finally, he nodded. 'You are right. Let's talk to Hong-An before we fly back to Australia.'

♥ ♥ ♥ ♥

It was about 10 a.m. when I walked to the room where Hong-An was rearranging her luggage, Minh, following a few paces behind me. Travis was not there. It was perfect, as we only wanted to talk to our daughter. I took a breath and opened my mouth.

'Can we talk, my darling?'

I tried to be polite and gentle to her as usual.

'What do you want to talk about Mẹ?' Hong-An countered in an icy voice.

I sensed that she knew exactly what I wanted to talk about.

'Ba talked to you three days ago about your relationship.'

'I don't want to hear anything about my relationship,' Hong-An stated stubbornly. I knew now the price of over-spoiling her: she didn't care a bit about what I had to say.

I talked very fast, my voice quivering with emotion.

'He is sick! I expect you to have a healthy husband to look after you; you know this. You should know how difficult it was for us when your father was sick. Being unwell is hard on a family! It will wear on your marriage!'

'There's nothing wrong with Travis, I love him, and I will be his wife.'

It felt like I was talking to three-year-old Hong-An. She was still very naive. Both of them were.

Minh's voice rang out, 'How will you manage when Travis is like a drug-affected koala? Your mother and I have been observing, and Travis does not show any signs that he will be the head of the family. You must be able to see what we see too. What's wrong with you this time? Will you be able to deal with this condition for your entire life?'

'We can handle it. We love each other,' Hong-An retorted.

'There are a thousand things you need to manage a family,' Minh said. 'Love for each other is not enough.'

'You are demanding so much, Mẹ,' Hong-An said, 'I love him and will marry him. He has just been tired since we have been in Vietnam. Everything has been hard for him to cope with here,' she persisted.

'A healthy boy would cope well in many different situations!' I countered.

'People are different! You can't make Travis be someone else!'

'I've studied him,' Minh stated, 'and I can clearly see the state of his health. I'm worried for your future if you marry him.'

'There have been a lot of changes, that's all, Ba,' Hong-An said with a flat voice.

I had weeks of frustration built up inside me, only further fuelled by countless sleepless nights, disappointments, and worries. Hong-An's words at this moment set me on fire. I couldn't hold back any longer. Without any thought to what I was saying, I threw out a bomb.

'Enough is enough, Hong-An! Travis is not the right partner for you, and I think you know that. He is sick, and you cannot carry that with you your entire life. I know you well and we are aware of your capability. You know what you need to do. If you marry him, you will have to change your entire life for him.'

My daughter remained on the bed, staring at me in disbelief. My words were like grenades, igniting the immense tension that we had carried throughout the holiday.

I continued the barrage. 'I can see that you have more lust than love for him. Listen to your wise mother. Lust never has a good outcome. Stop it now before it is too late. Honestly, if the rush to get married is about lust, then you'll pay a big price.'

Hong-An's eyes grew wider with every explosive sentence. At the last few words, she burst into tears and stood up.

My heart sank. I had meant what I'd said, but I couldn't stand to see my daughter in pain, especially when it was because of something I'd said. I had only ever meant to warn her, not to hurt her.

'You are unbelievable, Mẹ. Un-be-lievable. I can't believe those words just came out of your mouth,' she yelled, her voice choked with tears.

I had been so confident that my message would come through and was shocked at her reaction. Even without her shoes on, she was two inches taller than me, and so I straightened my back to hold her gaze, ensuring that she didn't lose the seriousness of my words. But in my heart, I felt devastated.

'Mẹ is right about everything,' Minh said tensely. 'I am of the same opinion. We love you, and it took all our courage to talk to you. You cannot stay with.'

His words were interrupted by the arrival of my mother who burst into the room, quickly followed by Travis.

'What's wrong?' my mother asked in Vietnamese.

'What's wrong, darling?' Travis repeated in English.

He held my daughter in his arms as people do in movies when they protect someone from the enemy and looked at me with resentment. 'I knew you would do something like this to my fiancé, Ha-Le.'

I narrowed my eyes. *You are the enemy here, not us,* I wanted to say. *What button do I press to erase him permanently from our lives?*

My mother grabbed my arm and led me into the dining room. There was no longer any tenderness in her touch.

Despite my mother's age, her grip was firm, and I winced at the pressure on my arm.

'Let's eat together as a family,' she said, picking up a large plate of fresh spring rolls. She had arranged a goodbye feast, and it seemed like the whole neighbourhood was involved. There were people everywhere. I couldn't find a place to scream. I longed for solitude, to be left alone to recover from the horrible scene in the bedroom. I ran to my mother's family altar, relishing that I had found this quiet corner to hide away.

I saw the picture of my father, his younger face smiling handsomely from the gold frame. I missed him desperately at that moment. I lit a stick of incense and placed it in the container of sand next to him, not to idolize him but to show my respect. My tears were already falling. I closed my eyes and remembered his smell when he would hug me tightly as a child. I just wanted him to pick me up again and protect me from the mess I had created, to take me wherever he was now. But he just stared out at me from the gold frame, smiling, as distant in death as he had been in his later years. I heard my daughter sobbing from the other room with Travis and the muted chaos of my brothers' families and the people downstairs. It felt like a family funeral.

I looked at my father's picture, and I sobbed. Seeing my father's kind smile brought back old guilt and hurt that suddenly caught up with me. Ten years ago, when he passed away, I couldn't say my final goodbye to him. I was in Japan for a holiday and planned to be in Vietnam just a few days later. I believed that my father was holding on just so my family could come home to have time with him.

That year, I'd promised myself that I would not go anywhere with my friends or with my family in Da Nang. I would just spend time with my father, telling him how much I loved him. But sadly he had a stroke and was gone in a day before I had the chance. I could now only place my hands on his picture in guilt and pain. His sudden departure taught me a lesson. I have to do whatever I thought was right for my loved ones, act as quickly as possible, and say something that needed to come out; I needed to be present with life. This was part of what had propelled me to talk to Hong-An.

After a few minutes, my mother came in and joined me in lighting an incense stick. We sat before my father's shrine in silence. I reached over and held my mother's hand. Her hand was an old woman's hand now. I could feel her pain join with mine as we sat there together in the corner. My ears tuned to the sounds of the house and the legacy of the disaster I'd created. I thought about my relationship with my daughter and felt sorrowful for the distance growing between us. I thought of my father, who was no longer with us. I thought of the love that my mother and father had once shared. I was the person that connected them both, the living and the dead.

I closed my eyes, letting my tears fall where they might. I cried by my mother's side, a raging river of tears.

CHAPTER SIX

~

SCARS THAT LAST

As a child of only three and a half years old, it was impossible for me to comprehend all of the politics and horrific nuances of war. I didn't understand that war was something considered traumatic and out of the ordinary, because for me, the war had been a nearly constant reality in my life.

I came to understand war better, just as I began to understand the world, and the two were inseparable for a long time. Apart from the planes in the sky, there was no other evidence of the war in Da Nang. But the more I came into the orbit of my father and his life, the closer I got to the effects of war until it eventually became a harsh, brutal reality.

After my father's sudden departure, that night that I'd lain awake listening to the scary sounds of him fighting with my mother, he would still come to visit us sometimes. He would show up in Da Nang ever so often. I was always ready to forgive him and give him all of my love as if nothing had happened. I learned that although he wore a soldier's uniform, he was actually an army nurse. He was stationed far away in Tam Ky, where there were army barracks and a hospital. Hiep, my older brother, told me he didn't fight the bad guys but helped the good guys when they were hurt and bleeding.

When I felt strong, I imagined my father as a confident, smart doctor, applying bandages and writing secret, important things on papers in a beautiful, white hospital room. When I was scared and feeling helpless, all I could imagine was blood. I had seen blood before, and it scared me senseless. Part of our house was rented to a man who would get drunk and cut himself late at night with a broken bottle; I saw him through the crack in the wall once. His face was covered in blood, and he was crying into his hands. I could easily imagine my father hurt and bleeding. I would imagine his beautiful uniform, stained with dark, red blood; the thought made me very afraid.

He would only visit for very short periods of time. My heart broke whenever it was time for him to leave again. He had become my hero.

Each morning, when he was home, I saw him take a small bottle of pink pills from the windowsill and swallow one. They looked almost like the lollies sold at the market. Once, I asked him for one, and he told me sternly that they were for adults only. Lollies for heroes, I thought. I longed to taste them, so one day, when no one was around, I used a chair to reach up to the windowsill and took down the plastic container. I pulled one of the pink lollies out and gingerly licked it. It was sweet. I sucked it a little, but it became so bitter that I spat it out onto the windowsill. It now looked like a large piece of unhulled rice. I looked around, but no one had seen me. Carefully, I pulled out another and licked the sweetness artfully, placing it on the windowsill next to the other. They all looked shiny, coated with my spit. Then I had another, and another, creating a neat line of pills.

'They look pretty!' I cried out with delight.

When my father found them there, laid out in a neat little line, he looked straight at me. His eyes were narrow and very serious, making me feel very scared because I could tell that I was in big trouble.

'Princess, you are very lucky. These pills are very dangerous. If you had eaten them, you would have died.'

Rather than smacking me, my father just looked at me with deep concern and laid his hand on my head. 'Ba needs to take these pills so he doesn't get sick when he is in the jungle.'

'What do you do in the jungle, Ba?' I asked.

He was silent for a while and then picked me up. 'Let's go and get some real lollies,' he said, and I buried my face in his shoulder.

The pills were to prevent malaria, and my father was in the jungle attending to soldiers who had been wounded in Viet Cong attacks. It would be a long time before I understood who the Viet Cong were. At the time, they were just the bad men who hurt the soldiers that my father would heal. They were also the reason that my father had to leave us, and so a flame of hatred began to burn quietly inside of me. The Viet Cong were the reason that my Ba could not be with me.

♥ ♥ ♥ ♥

One afternoon, during my nap time, Hien came to wake me up.

'Sister, sister. Ma went to see Ba.'

At only two years old, he was already very bright and had worked out that when my mother walked in the bus stop direction, it meant that she was on her way to see my father in Tam Ky.

'Let's go,' he said. 'Sister, let's go too.'

We rushed out the door before Chi Thoi could stop us and ran down the dirt road towards the direction where, apparently, my mother had just left.

After what seemed like an hour, we both knew that we were totally lost. I held my little brother's hand tightly and looked around. There was nothing around me that I recognised, I kept looking around in reckless abandon, hoping to find something or someone that I knew.

'Come on, Hien,' I told him, 'we can't stay in the street.'

I pulled him back over to the concrete. He was still sobbing as we sat down, watching a long line of army trucks and jeeps drive past. The noise of the vehicles rumbling down the road, combined with the sounds of Hien's crying, was all too much for me. I started to cry too, matching Hein in volume and rhythm. I was sick with fear, we had gone out searching for our parents, and now we might never find our way home again.

Thankfully, people around realised that we were lost, and assisted us to the police station and we eventually made it home.

On a good day, I already felt abandoned.

But today I was so ashamed of myself and felt truly and utterly alone.

What made my shame worse was the reaction I received from Chi Thoi later after my mother had left for work. 'Come here, Ha-Le!' Chi Thoi snapped at me from the other side of the room.

A change in expression that I had not seen before had come over her face. It was as if a mask had been taken off to reveal a genuinely bitter and mean person. She pursed her lips tightly together, her nostrils flaring. She scared me, but I knew I had to accept some punishment for leaving the house without asking and, of course, causing so much trouble getting lost, but there was something wild and terrible in Chi Thoi's eyes. There was a monster inside of her, and it was revealing itself now that my mother had left.

'Come here, Ha-Le!' she repeated, and I crossed over to her and bowed my head.

She slapped me firmly on the face; then, using my cheeks as a grip, took my weight in her hands and brought me closer to her face. I closed my eyes and squirmed in pain.

'When your mother is gone, you do what I say. Look at me, Ha-Le. I am the boss. You are just a little girl who knows nothing. Look at me, Ha-Le.'

I opened my eyes and saw that she meant it. It was a deep and dark threat, and I nodded as best as I could in her grasp before falling to the floor.

My action had broken something in Chi Thoi, or maybe it had exposed something that was there all along. From that point, she was nice to me when my mother was home, but as soon as she left, the monster overtook her. It did not take much to earn a slap on the hand, a pounding on the back, a tug on the hair, or an attack of insults.

Inspired by her nastiness, I began to hate her. She often left us alone for long parts of the day, but I didn't want her to slap me or yell, so I didn't tell my mother. I learned how to survive.

'Ha Le, you need to listen to Chi Thoi. Ma has to go to work for your clothes and food,' my mother told me whenever Chi Thoi complained about my naughtiness.

As time went on, I learned to blend with Chi Thoi to be beaten less by her. I started learning how to survive with her. At mealtime, I gobbled my rice, I did what I was told and I tried to ingratiate myself to her friends.

After I took up these survival strategies, Anh Hiep and Hien became Chi Thoi's victims. I felt so hurt in my heart when I heard their screaming and crying. I wondered why Chi Thoi was so angry and mean to me all the time. She seemed to have a monster inside of her.

My own childhood had been disturbed, but I'd devoted my life to children as an adult. I loved and cared for my daughter and for the children at my preschool. My job brought me so much joy. This was a small way I could care for and heal the wounds from this time.

In my daily life as a preschool teacher, I vowed to protect and care for all of the children who attended my preschool. From my own experience, I knew that many children might be afraid to speak up for fear of upsetting their abusers more. I carefully watched all of the kids at the preschool for signs of abuse. I knew first-hand that abuse leaves scars that can last a lifetime. Scars that never fully heal. I wanted to do everything I could as an adult to prevent what I was unable to stop as a child. Even if I couldn't fully admit it to myself, I knew deep down that my attempts to protect Hong-An from life's hardships were also the attempts to heal these wounds. As an adult, I could be the protector that no one had been for me as a child.

💜 💜 💜 💜

One night when I was a child, my mother only came home briefly to get changed before heading straight out again. This ritual had been happening more and more often. Sometimes I would watch her go and try desperately to stay awake until she returned but to no avail. This time, it was too much to bear. I slipped out the door and followed her for a few metres, but she sensed my presence and led me back to the house.

'Stop her from following me, Chi Thoi,' she said.

'Of course, Aunty.'

My mother patted me on the head, and I smelled a strong aroma of perfume. Her face looked beautiful with her makeup done so perfectly. I thought she was going out to have some fun and I wanted to join her. I watched her walk away again.

The sense of unfairness and abandonment grew in me like a rising tide. I missed her so much during the day. I followed her again, despite Chi Thoi telling me for the third time to go to sleep. At some point, I couldn't bear it any longer, and I let out a scream for her. I had no words to express the complexity of my feelings, but I let out scream after scream. I screamed with hatred for my babysitter. I screamed because I hated how Chi Thoi hit us. I screamed because she hurt my brothers and I couldn't stop her. Most of all, I screamed for my mother, who was almost always gone from the house. I wanted her to stop leaving all the time. I wanted her home with me, kissing and cuddling and playing with me. I screamed with the pure love of a daughter for her mother. My cries tore at my throat and left me burning with rage.

I screamed and ran after my mother. 'Let me go with you!'

'Go home with Chi Thoi. Ma will come back later,' she said to me.

My mother walked faster, and then two strange men appeared so suddenly that in my shocked state, they looked like monsters. They held me by my arms, shook me and yelled at me to stop screaming. I squirmed against them and tried to bite their hands, but they were too strong. After a brief exchange of hushed words with Chi Thoi, they carried me outside to the well, turned me upside down and dangled me head-first into the dark abyss.

'Stop screaming, or we will drop you in,' one of the men shouted above my shrieks of terror.

My screams echoed back to me from the depths of the well, each one wrapping around me and making me feel even more afraid. Their arms were giant clamps that had my skinny, half-starved legs tightly locked. I tried to fight, but I couldn't, and my tiny body was frozen with terror.

My mother had disappeared into the dark. If she had been there, she would have rescued me. I hated Chi Thoi for not rescuing me; I was alone.

People always warned kids to stay away from the well. A little boy had died when he fell into a well near our house. The rotten stench of the well filled my nose. The smell of awful moss made me splutter and choke.

I struggled to breathe, and it struck me that I may never see my family again. I would be smashed to pieces on the bottom of the well, or worse, be trapped down there for the rest of my life. I was beaten into silence by the horror, and the men pulled me up and carried my now limp body back to the house.

I continued to shake throughout the night, unable to sleep. I heard my mother come home and wash herself for a long time. Each splash of water brought back the smell of the moss in the well that I could never tell her about what had happened to me. I opened my eyes widely in the dark, with tears rolling down my cheeks and a feeling of choking in my throat. My mother was not there to protect me, and neither was my father. I did not know where he was. I just wished to be with him to have his protection. I missed his smell.

❤ ❤ ❤ ❤

Ma worked harder to feed all of us. After working all day, she came home very late, and then she had to take care of my baby brother. She didn't have even a moment to spare for herself. I tried my best to attend to Hung, but often I would have to just sit and bear his horrible cries of thirst and hunger.

One day, I heard a loud and unusual crying from his cradle. His wails were so searing, and the cradle was shaking so hard that I ran to the cot in fear of his life. I was too short to see him. I had to hold the cradle on one side and stand up onto my toes. I saw his face streaked with tears, poo, and turning red. His belly was revealed fully, as his top was pushed up to his armpits. It looked like he was gasping his last breaths. I was frozen and didn't know what to do.

The bottle of milk lay empty beside him, and he writhed on his blanket completely covered in his own poo. The mess was splattered all over his face, and the poor little thing had no way to deal with it. I covered my nose and recoiled in horror at the scene, calling out to Chi Thoi in an urgent squeal. When she didn't respond, I searched the house, but the only people at home were my baby brother and me. I felt such a responsibility towards him, but I didn't know what to do. I knew that I had to think quickly and do something, but I was scared of making everything even worse. I felt unable to deal with the scary situation, so I ran from the house searching for my babysitter.

I found her swimming in the river with some friends. 'Chi Thoi. Chi Thoi,' I yelled at her. 'It's Hung. He is covered in poo! He is crying a lot, and he choked!'

Chi Thoi quickly came ashore and slapped me across the face. 'You left your brother at home? How could you be so irresponsible? Again!' she snapped, loud enough for her friends to hear. I touched my cheek and flushed with anger. *It was you that left us at home while you were playing with your friends*, I thought. But I did not say the words for fear of being slapped again.

'Please!' I cried. 'Come back and help him.'

I was trapped and felt the weight of responsibility towards all of my brothers, despite being only three and not understanding what that feeling was.

CHAPTER SEVEN

WAR AND THE DEATH IT BRINGS

Every time I watch the movie, We Were Soldiers, I find myself crying. The movie always ended with my eyes swollen with tears. Once, after watching it with Minh, he commented on the emotional response I always had to the film.

'You cry every time we watch this movie!' he said. 'You have seen it at least three times. Didn't we first watch it years ago with Hong-An? What year was that?'

'It was 2002,' I answered. 'On my birthday.'

Something else had happened in 2002. It was at the end of that year that my father died of a stroke.

Hong-An was in Year 8 at Meriden School. I asked her to watch the movie with Minh and me because we wanted her to know about the Vietnam War. While watching the movie, everything I'd lived through came back to me as if it had only happened yesterday. The film made me think of so many events in my life. It made me remember so many people. People like Chi Thoi, Aunty Huong, and Aunty Phil.

I also thought of all the horrible things I'd seen in Tam Ky; I felt sorry for my country during the war. So many people died in the movie – Americans and innocent Vietnamese people, as well as Viet Cong.

I remembered the narration, and it made me cry even more: 'We who have seen war will never stop seeing it. In the silence of the night, we will always hear the screams. So, this is our story, for we were soldiers once and young.'

I was not a soldier, but I had seen war at my door, and the colour of it had haunted me for years.

'It was so sad for Vietnamese during the war!' Hong-An commented.

I agreed and added, 'And it was a nightmare to Mẹ too.'

I hadn't told Hong-An the details of my childhood during the Vietnam War. I didn't want to share that sadness with her yet. It was my horrible past, and I did not want to upset Hong-An's happy life by revealing it to her even if the past played a role in our present. No, I didn't want to share that sadness.

I looked out at my front garden, the liquid amber trees swaying with the wind. I felt fresh and lucky; our daughter was safe in this country, and she had the best life that a human being could have. The price Minh and I had paid for Hong-An's and our freedom was worth it! 'We are so blessed to be in a peaceful and free country!' we told Hong-An many times, wanting her to know how we had fought for her happiness and liberty.

I remembered times when my own mother had been forced to make tough choices for her children. I was overjoyed when my mother announced that we were going to move to Tam Ky to live with my father. We packed our possessions and rode in an open-backed truck down the highway. I imagined that we were headed to the jungle, where my father was busy healing sick soldiers, but in fact, we arrived a few hours later outside a neat, terraced house on a muddy quiet street. The house was located only a few metres from the Tam Ky bus station. It was so exciting for me as a four-year-old to step through the wooden doors into a new home. I ran around the house, the big, shared front and backyard and into each room, then around again and out to the kitchen at the back.

We settled very quickly into the new neighbourhood. I felt so much happier knowing my father was close by, and I could see him more often. The best thing about this change was that my mother stayed home day and night with us. She couldn't run her old business there.

Later, when Ma finally got a new job with Aunty Huong who lived at the end of our street, I was sad when I woke up without Ma beside me, I missed her. One day, I woke up early, crying, and said to my mother, 'Ma, stay home with me!'

But she refused, saying, 'You all would not have any food to eat if I stay home. Your father is away.'

This was the moment when I understand clearly that my mother had to work to feed all of us. My father didn't bring home food; he was much too busy helping people wounded in the war.

I did what I could to pass the time and distracted myself from how much I missed my parents. I started to explore my new neighbourhood and was stunned when I discovered that our home was only a few steps from a big, yellow, mouldy place known as the 'Death House.'

Through the grills in the window, a haze of smoke drifted out from the house. The house didn't seem real. It was like I had dreamt it, even though I was awake. I watched the clouds of smoke dance in the air; it rose from the bars of the windows, carrying echoes of the voices inside the house, muffled chants and mysterious sobbing noises. Then I smelt it, incense, but not just incense. There was something else wrapped underneath, something rotten and toxic, like the poison hiding under the sweet, pink coating of my father's pills. It was worse than the smell that came from the old well, so much worse.

You cannot hide the stench of death. Once you smell it, it's like you smell it forever, it lives in your memory, and you can never clean it out.

We had literally moved next door to death. Every day, the army trucks would park outside the building and soldiers with serious faces would carry in bodies wrapped in white sheets. I would watch from our doorstep as family members of the dead would arrive, quiet and puffy-eyed, in their white and black mourning clothes. I saw a lot of kids about my age shrieking terribly and accompanied by solemn adults. Some of the adults, yelling and screaming, rolled their bodies in the dry mud road. I watched them, my mouth wide open. Some of the women in black dresses could not walk, and people had to hold them up. I felt their pain and cried with them; they would step into the Death House, already muttering chants. Inside, the chants grew louder, accompanied by cries and wails of despair, then long periods of ominous silence.

Once, I peeked inside and saw people burning fake money. It was believed that this money would accompany the dead, giving them prosperity in the next life. The smoke blew towards my face, and I stepped away, catching just a glimpse of the shadowy rows of dead bodies stacked inside.

Sometimes, the dried mud road had no room for motorbikes and bicycles to get through because it was full of people in black and white. I was frightened to see more and more people rolling their bodies on the road and banging their heads on the ground. I was concerned they would start bleeding like the man who rented from us in An Hai. As the crying got louder, the foul-smelling smoke from the death house left me feeling miserable and suffocated. I reminded myself never to forget to breathe.

I learned that the Death House was for dead soldiers. I thought of my father and worried that he might be lost to me one day and become just another body in the Death House.

Mum started to pray a lot. I would listen to her whispered words.

'Buddha! Please protect my husband! Keep him safe and bring him home to us! Please keep me safe from the gunfire and bomb. My children need me. Please keep my children safe. We are a family, and we all need each other.'

I watched her arrange fruit and incense on a small shrine in the front garden, kneel down, and say the words that I got to know well. I never participated in the ritual or asked my mother about it. But I was swept up in fear of losing him. The coin of life and death was flipped every day, and each evening, I would wait for my father to come home, hoping with my own internal prayers that he would not be returning wrapped in a white sheet.

'Ba! Come home!' I whispered in prayer.

Continually bathed in the scent of aromatic death, it was impossible to escape my macabre imaginings. At night, the toxic incense would permeate my dreams, giving me horrific, bloody nightmares that did not disappear with the coming of dawn.

I could not understand why my mother prayed for herself until one day, I got the news.

❤ ❤ ❤ ❤

Most mornings, Aunty Huong would stop by our house to pick up my mother. The pair would catch the bus to the army camps to trade American dollars. This was one of my mother's business opportunities that allowed our family to stay out of poverty. Aunty Huong had five children, and I would occasionally play with the younger ones while our parents were away. One day, my mother stayed home because my youngest brother Hung, was sick. That afternoon, we heard crying and screaming out in the street and rushed to see what was happening.

Approaching us slowly was a Lambro, and following it in a huddle of desperation were Aunty Huong's five children. My mother let out a gasp and scooped me up in her arms. As the tuk-tuk passed, I saw the familiar hulk of a dead body, but this time, I realised it was someone I knew. A roadside bomb had hit the bus that my mother and Aunty Huong usually took to the camps. Aunty Huong had died along with many others. I watched as her husband arrived at the scene innocently on his way home from work. His face was confused at first, then wide-eyed in disbelief before collapsing into a disturbing display of grief. He fell onto the ground as if the news had broken every bone in his body. He crawled up the dirt road in the rain in the direction of the Lambro, unable to walk and totally unaware of the crowd of people watching him from their doorways. Everyone cried for him.

'More and more innocents die every day! What is the purpose of fighting?' Uncle Eight swore and screamed. Everyone understood that he was so upset about Aunty Huong's death. I became my mother's shadow, following her around the house constantly. I was scared to lose sight of her. I could not control my father's fate, but if I could stay close to my mother, I could make sure I would not lose her too.

Despite Aunty Huong's death, Ma still woke up early and took a different bus to the army camp for her work. The day felt so long waiting for her to come back. The longing for my mother grew stronger.

As I was just a kid, I was curious about life and exploring the world around me. I found ways to stay busy and entertain myself.

Across the road from our house was a little shop that sold a variety of groceries. To me, the owners were millionaires, surrounded by all of that food. The lady, Aunty Anh, who owned the shop, had a daughter about my age. They would sit outside the shop together when it was not busy. I would watch her brush her daughter's beautiful long, silky hair. Sometimes, both of them would chew gum and laugh at each other's attempts to blow bubbles, making exciting sounds. I could not help but feel jealous of their relationship and jealous of the chewing gum which I had never tried. I wished that my mother would spend that much time with me. I hoped that she would laugh with me and brush my hair.

Eventually, I built up the courage to approach the shop, edging my way inside and admiring the rows of goods. Walking down the tiny aisle, I stepped on something squishy. I pulled my foot back to reveal a discarded lump of gum and stretched between my shoe and the floor. Hopping on one foot, I removed it from my shoe and felt its stickiness between my fingers. It was too precious, too tempting not to taste, even though it had a layer of sand like sesame seeds stuck to it. I put the whole lump in my mouth, expecting heaven, but it did not deliver. It just felt like rubber in my mouth, and little bits of grit and sand from the floor crunched in my teeth.

'Yuck,' disgusted, I spat it right back out onto the floor.

'Gross! She ate gum from the floor!' To my utter horror, the girl with the beautiful hair was pointing at the gum and calling for her mother. I was so humiliated that without thinking, I rushed at her and hit her across the arm. Aunty Anh appeared and observed what was happening. I was frozen, unable to run away or even speak. Then the older woman smiled kindly, walked over to the counter and took out a fresh packet of gum. She bent down and handed it to me with such warmth that I burst out crying with relief. I unwrapped the little package and put it into my mouth. The pair of them watched the look of wonderment spread across my face and laughed. That was the first time I had cinnamon chewing gum that came from America. That lovely smell follows me to this day, reminding me of Aunty Anh's kindness. I learned something that day; kindness could be born from violence.

We all became friends after that. Aunty Anh's house was my heavenly refuge when my mother was away on business. For a while, I almost forgot about the fear and worry I had for my mother's safety.

'If Ha-Le had a different mother, she could grow into a very smart girl,' I heard Aunty Anh tell Aunty Chi about me while I played hopscotch with her daughter.

'She has four children and one niece to feed, and her father and mother are fighting all the time,' Aunty Chi rubbed my hair.

I knew my mother would come home at night, but I did not know where my father was. Suddenly, I missed my father and his smell. If he were home, he would buy whatever I wanted from Aunty Anh's shop.

'Come to my place tonight, Ha-Le,' with my blossoming personality, I began to charm many lonely ladies in the neighbourhood.

'So many people have booked time with Ha-Le,' Hien would tease me with jealousy.

As their husbands were away fighting, they craved a young person to keep them company. They wanted uncomplicated human contact. Or perhaps, in their eyes, I was the child that they had not yet conceived. To my delight, they would bribe me with lollies and sweets to keep them company and even to sleep in their beds at night. Sometimes, despite the lure of lollies, it was too much for me, and I would hide from them.

Aunty Phi was the one who spoiled me the most. She was the one who gave me my first taste of American apples, grapes and butter with bread. Addicted to those things, I agreed with Aunty Phi that she could fix my hair however she wanted, even if it sometimes felt like the skin was being ripped off my head. In return, she fed me what I loved.

Our little heaven was taken away one day when Uncle Viet, her husband, was killed in a battle. Aunty Phi wore black and sat still in front of Uncle Viet's altar almost every day and night. I could see this from my house; she did not smile at me when I went over. I was scared and overwhelmed when she held me on her chest and said, 'I wanted to die with him Ha-Le.'

Since Uncle Viet died, our deal was broken. My hair blew around freely with the breeze, and Aunty Phi's fridge was empty. Her beautiful face had disappeared, leaving two big eyes with dark shadows around them. We had a sad goodbye a few months after that. 'She needs her family in Hue for her newborn baby,' Ma explained.

The war was getting closer; people talked about it on every corner. The big well had fewer people washing clothes, and I did not bother to go there to collect flowers for my pretend play. The neighbourhood was infused with fear and uncertainty. The explosion that killed Aunty Huong was just one of many bombs that the Viet Cong had planted close to Tam Ky. They would emerge from the jungle in the dead of night to quietly lay traps or terrorize the area. As these incidents became more and more frequent, the town mobilized for safety.

I would overhear snippets of conversation that I didn't understand. The war and the Viet Cong were all that the grown-ups talked about.

'We signed the agreement at the Geneva conference. Why does the Viet Cong keep stepping into our Southern boundary? What bastards!' A lot of people were upset.

I heard someone say, 'There is so much bloodshed, many places and homes destroyed! Children have lost their parents; this war has ruined everything!'

One morning, my mother led us out past the houses into a big open field, populated only by a few cows and coconut trees. When we walked closer to the tree line, I noticed rows of carefully disguised green sandbags partially buried into the soil. We stopped, and mum pointed to the ground in front of us, where a hidden trapdoor was currently exposed.

'If there is ever any trouble, come to this spot.' she said.

We all stared into the darkness below the trapdoor.

'We have to go down there?' Hien asked.

'Just come to this spot if there is any danger,' she said. I looked down at the dirt covered in chicken poo. I kicked a little dried piece of poo into the hole, and my mother shot me a stern look.

'But Ma, I heard that two boys died down there when they were playing,' Hiep said. He was the one who knew everything.

'This is not playing, Hiep. It's not a game. Our men are out in the jungle trying to protect us. We need to keep safe,' she looked at each of us, in turn, to check that we were listening.

'We need to stay together but if you can't find each other, come here anyway, OK? Someone will tell you what to do.'

I did not like what my mother said. I hated this war.

A few nights later, I woke up to a disturbing sound. 'Hiep,' I whispered. 'Wake up. Is that gunfire?' my brother turned over and ignored me. The sound came again, closer this time.

Clang, clang… clang clang.

I got out of bed and went to the window. Outside, I saw several men, dressed in black, walking quickly up the street on either side, occasionally pausing to beat a stick on a piece of metal. Viet Cong, I thought.

'Ma! Viet Cong! Ma!' my mother was up in a flash, heard the sound, and then quickly reassured me.

'It's OK, sweetheart. It's the villagers. They are warning us to go and hide. Quickly wake your brothers up.'

A group of local villagers had organized themselves into a home security force to serve the residents of Tam Ky. When they got any sign that the Viet Cong was coming, they would warn us by clanging bits of scrap metal together.

My brothers protested, but within a few minutes, we were assembled outside the house. That night, my father came back home. He had a gun in his hands. I looked up at him in his army uniform, and I felt protected.

'Go!' whispered my father. 'Stay together and don't worry,' he slung the gun over his shoulder and walked off toward the thicket of bamboo near our house.

'But Ba,' I called before my mother silenced me with a hand over my mouth. 'Come on Ha-Le. Your father is needed.'

I watched him slip into the bamboo, disappearing immediately amongst the tall moonlit foliage. My heart followed him.

We began walking quickly towards the tunnel, joining groups of families who had just woken up like us. It was strange seeing so many people, and yet everything was silent. I began to panic as my little legs could not match the pace of everyone else's. I felt like we were walking in a dream. By the time we got to the tunnel entrance, we could hear distant gunfire, real gunfire. I looked back in the direction of the bamboo thicket but was quickly ushered onwards and down into the darkness.

The heat and smell of so many bodies in such a small space suffocated me. There were no concrete or supportive structures, just hardened mud. After a one-legged man had closed the trapdoor with a few swear words, we fell into deeper silence, inhaling the tunnel's strong, musty odour. I listened to the breathing of the people around me and held tightly onto my mother's arm. Above, we could hear the muted sounds of gunfire and an occasional thump of an explosion. In the darkness, my imagination lit up. I saw through my father's eyes, crawling through the trench to a fallen soldier, looking over his wounds and applying a rough bandage before dragging him back to a safer spot. I opened and closed my eyes but could not tell which was scarier. We drifted into restless, noiseless half-dreams until finally, the one-legged man called down to us that it was safe to return.

I gulped in mouthfuls of fresh air as we walked back in the first light of dawn. It was a ritual we would get used to. More and more frequently, we would be woken up in the dark of the night and forced to climb down into the small, dark tunnel. Once, we were not quick enough, and the black-clothed men ordered us to stay inside. My mother made us all lie down together on the bed and cover ourselves with the blanket. Outside, I heard gunfire very close and the footsteps of soldiers running past. We did not know which side the noises belonged to. I felt my mother shaking next to me and realised that she could not protect us. Her strength was no match for soldiers with guns.

We had heard the rumours. People had said that the Viet Cong had stormed into other towns and villages and killed everybody. In the dark of night, they could not tell the difference between soldiers and civilians. Anyone could be shot. We clung to each other under the blanket until we heard the familiar noises of the street strike up again, and somehow, we began our day.

We were always ready to rush off to the tunnels from then on, and at one stage, we would go every night. I began to really appreciate the daylight and the freedom of open space. How quickly I valued these simple things when they were taken away from me.

I now understood what war really was. At least, I understood little bits of it, and I knew that I was a part of it. War was all around us.

~

CHAPTER EIGHT

NEW BEGINNINGS

I grabbed a VB beer and sat in the alfresco, letting my thoughts wander with the breeze. It was a hot Australian summer day. Home sweet home, finally! Home means so much when you have been away. After a big holiday spent in Hong Kong, Taiwan, Macau, and Vietnam, we'd come back with a vivid fresh reminder of so many distant memories of this time in our life. I traced the boat route when it shuttled me so many years ago from Vietnam, through Macau, and then to Hong Kong, where we eventually settled for several years. I also spent time in Vietnam, visiting all the spots that I had remembered in Da Nang. All these memories gave me ample time to reflect on life and on what home really meant. I was again considering writing a book about my life. So many things had happened that brought me to where I am now, happy in our home in Australia. I felt finally settled somehow. I inhaled the fresh air, taking in the view of my gorgeous backyard. How blessed I am! I thought.

We were in the process of moving to a brand-new house, but I was also sad to be saying goodbye to the old one. I had gone from the front yard to the backyard, taking a moment to savour every tree that I could, letting my fingers linger over their bark and leaves, knowing that in only days, I wouldn't be able to do this again. This would no longer be my home; I would soon stop seeing what I saw everyday living here. The front yard and the cul-de-sac used to be Hong-An's playground with us; she had grown up here.

Moving on for the better is great, but sometimes, it's hard to cut off what we are used to.

This house had been an essential part of my journey.

I'd spent so many years of struggle and redemption in this house, and now it was time to say goodbye. I passed by Hong-An's room, with my eyes blurry with tears.

'Awww, my baby!' I cried out, seeing all her beautiful pictures on the walls. I saw her face smiling back at me. She had on the cheerful smile that she was blessed with. I missed my daughter so much!

The new house was filled with gum trees, palm trees, and an expanse of lush, green grass. I had gotten into the habit of sitting outside in the backyard for hours, with a cup of coffee and a book, enjoying the scenery and letting the hours pass me by. In this way, enjoying the new house lessened the pain of missing my old Shackleton house, a house filled with memories of the past seventeen years.

Each experience and each place that I have lived has contributed to who I have become. This life journey has taken me here to this yard and this moment. Growing up in Vietnam, the home was not a safe place. It was surrounded by war, and our world was often filled with pain. I had no one to protect me. As an adult, I took family and home seriously. I wanted to heal the wounds of childhood. The home needed to become a space where my daughter was always protected. I wanted to ensure she lives a life free of pain. I wanted to give her what was taken from me.

Sitting in the yard of my new home with my book and cup of coffee, I was suddenly startled from my thoughts as fireworks started to explode and crackle above. Bright colours filled the sky, it was Australia day, and the people of Potts Hill were celebrating, dogs were barking, and teenagers were laughing.

❤ ❤ ❤ ❤

Whenever I saw fireworks, it brought me right back to the first time that I saw flares shooting into the sky from massive army barracks in front of my house. I remembered feeling a sense of wonder, as they lit up the sky of Chau Lai, but this turned to feelings of fear upon sighting a man wearing an army helmet sitting like a statute in the fort, with his gun and a sharp knife on the top of the gun pointed up.

My father's army camp was at Chau Lai, 30 km south of Tam Ky. When it became too dangerous at Tam Ky, we moved as close as we could to our father and the camp's protection. Our house was directly opposite the large American army barracks. It was a relief to see my father get away from the jungle and the tunnels, but in my imagination, I was scared that the Viet Cong would start fighting with the Americans, and we would all be blown up together.

I watched trucks full of ammunition coming in and out of the barracks. Each bullet, each grenade, each bomb was to be aimed at the Viet Cong. Thousands of potential deaths passed by our house, but it did not fill me with the promise of victory. The Viet Cong probably had the same bullets, ready to use against my father. What we aimed at them, they also aimed at us. I heard people on the street say to each other – 'An eye for an eye, a tooth for a tooth.'

When the Americans came back from fighting, all of the kids would rush down to the road to wait for the convoy to pass. I followed them the first time not knowing what was happening but buoyed by the group's excitement. Those moments would prove to be the happiest I would experience in Chau Lai.

'Try to catch as many as you can,' the kids said, jostling for a position close to the street. I didn't know what they were talking about, but being small, I easily found my way to the front. When the trucks passed slowly by, I saw the faces of the Americans for the first time. Most of them were covered in grease and dirt but were nevertheless handsome and smiling. Their bodies were strong and big-boned but they looked tired. Around me, kids were holding up their fingers in secret communication with the Americans: one finger, two, five fingers. I held my little hands out, mimicking those around me and shouting boisterously.

Into our outstretched hands, they threw small bags of M&M's, chocolates and lollies, cans of dried fruit, pudding and any leftover food from their time on the front lines. They seemed to love children and laughed with each other as they aimed for the cutest kids.

I was five then. I had heard a lot about Americans in my life, and now I had seen them. They didn't have black eyes like us. Some were very white, like milk, and some very dark, like chocolate. Most of them looked at us and smiled.

'If you don't have anything, show ten fingers with a sad face, and the Americans will aim the treats to you,' Anh Hiep explained. I did what my brother taught me; other kids got a lot of lollies, biscuits, and chewing gum, but I got none. I was not quick enough to fight with the other kids for that. Finally, I showed my ten little fingers and made a sad face. It worked, and some of the Americans pointed to me and laughed. They did throw some lollies directly towards me, but I still could not catch any, and it would all fall to the other kids, but it was still fun. It was a chance for me to test my powers and see what I could get as a little girl.

'You were unlucky today. You have to be quick and fight with the kids for what you want,' Anh Hiep said and shared with me some of his biscuits. Life seemed to be all about fighting. Fighting for what we want and fighting for life itself, always a struggle.

The American army supplied its soldiers with all sorts of equipment. The soldiers held their possessions very lightly, partly because they could always get more from the army and partly because, with their friends dying around them and poor Vietnamese everywhere, material things began to lose meaning. The Vietnamese employed in the houses of high-ranked American soldiers would collect items that they were throwing away or even steal them. These goods would find their way to my mother, who was an expert at turning an opportunity into a business.

My mother would put down a mat at the local market and lay out her American goods: shoes, hats, clothes, binoculars, cameras, knives and radios. Anything that she could find, she would trade with a refined entrepreneurial sharpness.

When I found my mother's stall, she would instantly welcome me into her arms. Without my brothers and my babysitter, I felt special and relished the time alone with her.

'Oh! Ha-Le, my darling!' my mother cried out every time she saw me. I was a princess in my mother's kingdom.

I would help her sell her produce, and she would occasionally give me money to buy fairy floss or some other treat. Since I could remember, I had longed to be part of my mother's daytime life and be included in her mysterious world. The world that was necessary: '... to feed the family.' '... to give you nice clothes.' '... so, we will not beg on the streets.' I held onto those moments like treasures. I felt my mother's presence, perceived her smell, and admired the way she chatted to the customers. She was driven by force greater than I understood, and I greedily bathed in its energy.

♥ ♥ ♥ ♥

Right next to our house was a bar that also served as a brothel. I began to recognise some of the regulars Vietnamese soldiers who sat outside drinking, smoking, and laughing. Some of them even knew me by name.

In the house's windows were women, their expressions were animated, responsive to the slightest attention, but somehow also tired and sad, like the pretty dolls my mother sometimes sold at the market. Of course, I did not understand what the women were selling from their windows, but I certainly knew that the soldiers wanted it.

When the soldiers saw me watching, they would wave and call me over to sit with them. I would take turns sitting on their laps, entertaining them with funny answers to their questions.

'What are you doing wandering around here, little girl?'

'Looking for sweets.'

'Well, lucky you!' they laughed and pulled lollies and nuts from out of their army pockets.

'You are too young to be out here, Ha-Le.'

I would munch on their lollies and wrinkle my nose at them. 'You are too old,' I said.

The men found me very cute and funny, and I liked how it made me feel. The women would try to shoo me off, saying, 'This is not a place to play, go away.' But the soldiers fought for me to stay and I began to learn some of their names.

'Hello Uncle Than, Uncle Ung…hey, where is Uncle Van?' I asked one afternoon. The soldiers shifted on their stools and nursed their drinks intensely.

'And Uncle Duy?' I added, smiling.

One of the men left the table suddenly. Another went as if to speak, but stopped, and instead put his finger to his head like a gun and squeezed the trigger. At his action, I immediately saw blood and tasted the toxic incense of the Death House in the back of my throat. I suddenly missed my father. I did not know where he was, just knew that he was at war to care for hurt people. I knew how the war looked from watching the television of our next-door neighbour. War had real gunfire, bombs exploding, and soldiers bleeding.

I needed a haven from the effects of war, but my house, sandwiched between a brothel and the American Barracks, was anything but it. I missed my father terribly, and I never stopped worrying about him.

A recurring feeling of emptiness began to carve a pattern in my life. I did not have the wisdom or experience to know what was missing, but I felt convinced it could be filled with sweet treats most of the time. One day, my older brother came home with a handful of small black dates. I put one in my mouth and looked up at his grinning face.

'Where did you get these, Anh Hiep?' I asked. I had never tasted something like it before.

Anh Hiep pointed to the right side of the house. 'Up in the forest, there are trees. You can pick them right off and eat until you are fat,' he said and poked my belly with his other hand to demonstrate. 'But don't go up there,' he warned. He gave me two more dates and then ran off on another adventure.

I kept the three date seeds in my mouth for over an hour, sucking out all their flavour, in the same way I sucked the marrow out of the bones in my mother's beef soup on the fire. I let my desire for more dates lead me toward the forest. I had never been up there. The houses gave way to a few forgotten fields, and then all of a sudden, I was surrounded by trees. There were no paths that I could see but plenty of space to walk amongst the trees. I ventured further in, feeling the grass and leaves beneath my feet and enjoying the new smells. I turned my attention to finding the dates which I imagined existed in a glorious orchard somewhere beyond the trees.

Suddenly, I heard several loud bangs, and I was on the ground, instantly transported to the tunnels in my mind.

Gunfire, I thought. My heartbeat very fast, filling the silence until I heard another round of shots. I waited a few seconds, then ran behind a tree and crouched again, covering my ears. The guns were close. So close that, when I finally took my hands away from my ears, I could hear the voices of the men firing them. I stood and peeked out from behind the trunk of the tree. In the distance, I saw a group of ten or twenty South Vietnamese soldiers and Americans. There was no urgency about their movements and no attempt to conceal themselves. They were practising, I realised. I had gone looking for dates in a firing range; now I knew where Anh Hiep had collected his bullet shells.

I took a few deep breaths and edged my way backward away from the group, silent as a cat. My survival skills had kicked in naturally. The men were not technically my enemies, but my body knew the danger and acted with animalistic skill. When I was far enough away, I walked quickly along a stretch of grass, keeping close to the tree line in case I saw anyone else.

As my animal fear subsided, my animal hunger kicked in. I became a wild thing, eyeing up every possible plant for its value as food. Amongst some larger bushes, I came across some white berries which tasted a little tart, but definitely edible. I foraged amongst the undergrowth until I had eaten enough to satisfy my belly.

But by the time I had turned my attention to finding a way back home, my stomach began to protest violently. In a matter of seconds, I shed the veneer of pride I had gained from overcoming danger and hunger and was again crouching on the ground, this time with awful diarrhoea.

How suddenly the world can change, I thought, as I shimmied my bare bum on the grass in an effort to wipe it clean.

I had just pulled my pants up when a boy walked out from the trees with a buffalo in tow. I let out a squeal, but the boy appeared more startled than I was.

The buffalo kept chewing on some grass as if nothing in the world could budge it.

'Excuse me, big brother. I'm lost. Where is the road?' he fidgeted with the rope. The boy motioned for me to follow him to the road, where I thanked him politely and walked quickly and uncomfortably home.

When I told Mum as a teenager later, she was shocked, and she also recognised how lucky I was. 'God protected you all,' she said. 'The soldiers could have shot you without guilt when seeing anyone in their practice zone. They could have thought you were Viet Cong.'

I was lucky. But at the time, I knew what I have always known that it was up to me to protect myself as no one else would.

Life kept leading me along with gunfire here and there, with bombs exploding from afar. This was the way I grew up, but through it, I discovered myself. Every step I took, one thing led to another and made me look at life a little differently. Subconsciously, I stored so many tips for survival in my small head. Chau Lai's time was when I knew how to be diplomatic with people and earn love from them. I was growing up fast. I was growing along with the war. My home was surrounded by it, brothels and soldiers as my neighbours and no one adequately protected from it all. This shaped me and made me strong and capable but it also would one day grow me into a mother that would ensure that home was not surrounded by anything but cool grass, big trees, and loving arms. I would grow up into the great protector. I would keep the bullets out no matter what.

CHAPTER NINE

~

THE CHANGE WE FEAR

Often, when I would consider my troubles with Hong-An, I would think about how different our lives had been. Hong-An had seen some hard times when we first moved to Australia, but she had been guarded against sadness and difficulty by Minh and me for the most part. In my childhood, I hadn't been given that luxury. My parents could not have spared me from hard times, no matter how much they tried. My childhood in Vietnam was a far cry from the childhood in Australia that Hong-An had experienced.

Sitting by my father's alter that morning in Vietnam with my mother, I was able to forgive my parents for not being my protectors. I suddenly knew that they did the best they could. There in my mother's house in Vietnam on that night of fights and tears, I had also done the best I could. I was only trying to do more for Hong-An than my mother had done for me. I was doing my best to protect her from that marriage. I was doing what I thought was right, even if all I was left with was tears on the banks of the river.

♥ ♥ ♥ ♥

I had started school in Tam Ky and loved it. It was close to my house, very small and the two teachers were very calm and supportive. Since I was old enough to understand, I was told by anyone who spent time with me that I was smart – the smartest among all my siblings, people would say, giving me grounds to win arguments with them and an extra drive to do so well at school. But in Chu Lai, the school was an entirely different experience.

Unlike in Tam Ky, I had to walk a long way from our house to get to school. Part of the journey involved going through an underpass, which was no problem during the dry season. However, it was the middle of the rainy season on my first day, and the whole area was knee-deep in water. I stood beyond the flooding and watched other children take off their shoes and socks and wade into the water.

Just as I built up the courage to bend down and take off my shoes, I got pushed from behind, and I staggered into the dirty water. Under my hands, I felt slimy weeds tangling and pulling me in further. I remembered, with startling clarity, being upside down in the well and used all my energy to struggle to my feet as quickly as I could. I spun around to see who pushed me. The girl was around my age and chubby, with thin lips now curled into a mean snarl.

'Oh, no. Are your nice new shoes wet?' She laughed. I looked down at my shoes which my mother had bought especially for my first day at school. My mother always made sure I had the best clothes we could afford, and that was a big part of the reason she worked so hard. A stray piece of brown weed was smeared across my left toe. I made an attempt to flick it away, but the girl reached over and grabbed me by the shoulders.

'Not so pretty any more, are you?' she said, shaking me.

'Hey!' another voice shouted from close by. We both turned around to see two other girls approaching, one much taller than the other. 'Leave her alone,' the tall one said. The chubby girl spat into the water and moved off. The three of us stared at her, all thinking the same thing: What inspires such a meanness?

'It's OK,' the tall one said, bringing out a scarf and wiping my shoes clean. 'They still look pretty, don't they, Lien?' the smaller one smiled at me and nodded.

'This is my little sister, Lien. Lien, help her with her bag,' Lien bent down and picked up my cloth bag which had fallen during the scuffle but thankfully, not into the water. She handed it to me and bowed her head gracefully in a greeting.

'Don't worry!' she said. 'It's yucky, but we all do it. Here, I'll help you through.' The three of us took off our shoes and waded through the water together, boldly against the tangle of weeds as a trio.

Lien became my first friend. Her sister was five years older; both of them were very gentle and beautiful. They were from a Chinese-Vietnamese family and owned a Chinese restaurant near the bus station. Their house was behind the restaurant, and every time I went over, they came up with a new and exciting type of food for me to eat. They introduced me to Chinese medicine, which disgusted me at first, but then filled me up with wonder at all of the magical ingredients their parents had handled with such intention and consideration. The sisters were like two angels who saved me from a bully and swept me up into a new world of friendship.

Their friendship made my time at school bearable. The chaos of the war-ridden world had seeped into the classroom itself. No one could settle. When the kids were too noisy, the teacher would bang a big stick on the blackboard to get their attention. The stick was often used on people's bottoms as well. Teachers and students alike were all just trying to get along with life by any means necessary. Sometimes that manifested in violence, mischief, anxiety, and bullying.

I felt protected against the mess of emotions by the salvation of friendship. Lien and her sister were nice to me, in a different way than my family could be, or the men outside the brothel. Lien, the child of her father's third wife, was abused by the first two and had a tough life. But towards me, she was open and loving, and we both really treasured our time together. Friendship, I discovered, was uncomplicated and endless, like pure water from a mountain spring.

It was also fun. My babysitter, Chi Thoi, came to look for me one evening when I was out late at Lien's. I had just finished a big plate of leftover prawn dumplings from the restaurant and hearing her calling my name, I hid under the bed. Lien had a sincere nature and managed to convince my babysitter that I was not there. When Chi Thoi had gone, we laughed very hard, and I felt so protected by my friend. We sat and shared a piece of grass jelly before I reluctantly made my way home.

I paused at the doorway before entering the house. I knew that Chi Thoi would be mad at me, but she would not beat me because my parents were home. In an unexpected stroke of luck, the house in Chu Lai was quite exposed to the neighbourhood, so my babysitter rarely had the chance to lash out at me because of the threat of being witnessed.

Inside, it seemed oddly silent. I tiptoed in and called out, 'Ma? Ba?'

I walked through the main room and into the kitchen. It seemed that no one was around.

'Ma, I'm home. Hello? Chi Thoi?' For a moment, I thought they must all be out looking for me, but then I heard a few abrupt bangs and a raised voice. I raced to Mum and Dad's bedroom and opened the door to a scene that would forever be cemented in my memory.

My mother was on the floor, using her hands to drag herself towards the door, her heavily pregnant belly making the process awkward. Standing above her was my father, trembling with rage, a broom raised in the air. Before he realised I was there, he brought the broom down hard on my mother's back, and she cried out with the shock of the force. He hit her again, and I became paralysed with fear and horror. These were not my parents; my parents did not act like this; my parents were strong and confident; they protected me from danger. Chi Thoi was the violent one, not my father. He was unrecognisable, like an evil guy I saw from the comic books that Anh Hiep had. My mother was sobbing, short bursts of noise halfway between anger and pain. She sat up and clutched her belly, just as my father dealt a final blow across her side. I opened my mouth, but there were no words. My father sat down on the bed, suddenly exhausted, and my mother looked up just as I slid out of view. I wasn't sure if she saw me. At that moment, I lost my hero.

As I ran back from the bedroom, I saw Chi Thoi, my father's aunt, the household helpers and my brothers watching; silent witnesses to this moment of change. Chi Thoi looked at the ground as I passed by.

I jumped into the bed and covered my whole body. I heard my youngest brother start to cry and my mother shushing him through her tears. Nothing in my world was consistent with this picture. I could not reconcile the love I had for my father with the image of him hitting my mother. He was hitting her while she had a baby inside of her!

And a new feeling of wanting to protect my mother came over me like an electric shock. It was not a feeling that I wanted. My body felt like it was hollowed out and stuffed with another person's insides. Ma told me later that it was her fault.

'I'd scolded him on his return from a big battle.'

By that time, my Dad was already suffering from PTSD, but nobody knew.

The next morning, I watched them interact together in an awkward dance of forgiveness. My father washed her naked back, and she smiled gently. The intimacy felt like the greatest unfairness. That my father could beat my mother and then wash her back with tenderness as if he was cleaning away the memory seemed intolerable to me, and I hated them both at that moment. The previous night's memory was wedged tight in my insides, and no amount of cleansing could get rid of it. My father had brought the war into my house and down on my mother and me. But it was me that carried the burden of that fight the most, and to my impressionable young mind, it was greater violence than the one playing out in the jungle.

During this time, I saw a lot less violence from Chi Thoi, mostly because the house was full of people most of the time, which gave me protection. The violence stopped from Chi Thoi but it appeared in my father. I was sickened by this change.

The size of our growing household seemed to have transformed Chi Thoi; she genuinely seemed to be a much happier person. More people now helped her with all of her responsibilities, so maybe she could let go a bit.

But from time to time, I still got scary glares from her whenever I was sulky with Mum and Dad. I looked away from her angry eyes. I wasn't concerned with Chi Thoi anymore. I had a war to fight now, a war inside of myself. I was upset with my father and couldn't stand to be around him because I knew that I would become angry with him. This was the father who had been my hero. This was the father that I loved so much. I couldn't stand the conflicted feelings of love and rage; they were tearing me apart inside.

If he asked me to take a nap with him, I would keep my eyes open the entire time; I couldn't relax next to him anymore. He would hold me tightly under his armpit, and I would panic, feeling suffocated. His smell used to be my favourite smell; now, all I wanted was to get away from him. I couldn't forgive him for what I'd seen him do to my mother.

'Ha-Le has been so aggressive with her younger brothers lately, whining all the time for everything, and she's hardly eating anything,' I heard my mother telling my father one night when they thought I was asleep.

'She may be sick. Get her some nutrition,' my father sounded worried about me. No one knew how I felt inside; my anger and sadness made me tired. Hien didn't want to play with me, and I didn't want to play at Lien's house either. Hating my father made me feel insecure and stuck, I just wanted to be close to my father again. I just wanted to love him and have fun with him again, but I did not know how.

Shortly after that incident, my father moved back to Da Nang. He had gotten a promotion to work in a big hospital there. He took two of my brothers with him, who would stay with my aunt because my father would be busy at the hospital. In truth, I was sad to see him go and was jealous of my brothers even though I was hurt. I knew I'd lost him in that dark moment. My hero had shown the monster inside of him, and it spread like poison through my heart. I was resolved to never look at him with the same eyes. I was left only able to see the monster.

My youngest brother, Hai was born into this mess. I wasted no time in projecting my fears onto him. When I went to visit him in the hospital, I went straight to his cot and pinched him hard on the leg. I felt only mildly remorseful when his screaming filled the room, and my mother scolded me. His crying made me feel guilty for being jealous of him, and since that time, I became his protector.

'Ma, are we going to go back to Da Nang?' I asked her. She sighed and rubbed her eyes as if incurably tired. 'I don't know, Ha-Le,' she said. I knew it was inevitable. We would be reunited as a family soon enough. Even though, in my heart, we were now broken apart.

Despite my many fearful times in Chau Lai, my dislike of school and the endless threat of attack, the one thing I wanted to preserve was my newfound friendship with Lien.

The Lambro took our family of seven members to Da Nang. I just stared back until I could not see Lien and her sister anymore, but her beautiful face and our first friendship have been with me from that moment on. I keep her forever in my heart.

❤ ❤ ❤ ❤

When we went back to Da Nang, we stayed in a hotel as a family. There was a coldness between my mother and father that made the neon-lit room even more barren. They were constantly bickering about things I did not understand, and I felt distant as if I was just one member of the audience in a play of their lives. My father had done something terribly wrong, it seemed, and my mother was scolding him at every opportunity.

I heard bits and pieces of the story: '…I saw you two together… all this time…I went to her house you know…How did you think…And her husband only just having passed away…You bastard'. My father seemed resigned to her attacks, weathering her hot temper with the patience of the guilty.

The pressure built up until one day, I heard screaming from outside the hotel room. I rushed out to see my mother chasing my father with a knife. I knew that knife. I had cut my finger once slicing fruit. A knife meant blood and blood meant death. She chased him down the corridor until my father turned around and grabbed her hand to protect himself. He twisted it back and pinned her to the wall; the knife still pointed at his throat. In my mother's eyes, I saw a similar monster that I had seen in my father and was again shocked at the transformation. As other people came rushing to help, I held back, frozen in fear until she finally released the knife and it dropped to the floor.

I rushed over to her and crouched down, a safe distance from her, overcome with concern but still fearful of her temper.

'Your father is a bastard,' she was addressing me but not really talking to me, but to some other imagined audience.

'I told her, you have five children like me and you stole my husband too. He nursed your husband until he died, then came and took his wife. Give me back that knife, I won't miss this time…'

Her words were icy, but her anger had left, replaced by tears and exhaustion. My father did not retaliate, he just packed his things, put on his uniform and left, and I did not see him for over a year. He was walking out on us again.

♥ ♥ ♥ ♥

My mother had let me down, but somehow the sting of losing my father was worse. It was like a small pebble in my shoe that hurt and stayed with me, but no matter how hard I tried, I couldn't shake it loose. My father was for so long my hero, saving people during the war, in his strong, handsome uniform. He was also my own personal hero for fleeting moments when he would hold me in his arms and give me a slight sense of safety amidst the chaos. He never stayed, even if his smell always lingered. But I lost this image of him that day he beat my mother to the ground. These horrible memories of him and his broken pedestal come back to haunt me like ghosts from the past; they followed me on life's journey impacting my choices along the way.

As an adult, I tried to find a new hero. To heal this ravaged portrait of the man I once adored. I thought I had seen this when I married Minh. I thought I had finally found a man who could live up to this role.

He did mostly. He always tried to be the greatest father to his daughter. But Minh has been unwell a lot, this was not his fault, but it stopped him from being the father he wanted to be. His illness dragged him down and forced me at times to carry his heavyweight. I may have lost my own hero at an early age, but I had high hopes for Minh. I am reluctant to admit it now, as he is still such a constant form of strength in my life, but he failed me a bit with his illness and temperaments. But there was one thing I knew for sure. I wasn't going to let Hong-An lose her hero too. I needed to stop this cycle from repeating. I was the only one who could save us all. I had the strength and I knew what she needed. She needed exactly what I didn't get.

CHAPTER TEN

THE GHOSTS OF THE PAST

The image of my mother chasing my father with a knife settled deep into my subconscious, coupled with the other traumatic experiences already there. But a six-year-old child only wishes to splash on the surface rather than dwell in the depths, and being back in Da Nang provided me with plenty of distractions. When we left, I was only three years old. Now I saw it with more awareness and excitement.

My mother bought us a tiny house on the edge of the city, next to the market. Previously, we had lived in the 'poor' area across the river. Now, although we had the smallest, simplest house in the neighbourhood, we were amongst the energy of the real city.

I would sit and watch the world pass by from our doorstep, fascinated by the motorbikes and bicycles which drove past, the frenetic activity of the shops on the side of the road and the sights and smells of hundreds of different types of food. My hungry mind accepted the stimulation gratefully.

My mother did what she always did best, focusing all of her energy on her business. She would go back to Chu Lai for days, sometimes up to a week at a time. When she left, she would leave money with my babysitter for food and supplies. But with my mother gone, my babysitter now had the freedom to resume her abuse towards me. Instead of buying fish, meat, and vegetables, Chi Thoi invited her friends over and cooked sweets. We were not getting the nutrition we needed, but I was smart enough to know that if I told my mother, she would scold Chi Thoi and it would be my brothers and me who would get the real punishment later. Chi Thoi essentially became our guardian for long stretches at a time, but she did not give us the love and care we needed.

At the smallest of problems, she would release her anger upon us. When she was very stressed, she would lift my youngest brother's arm and slap it over and over again, and when she'd finished, she would give him some coins. It was such a strange and cruel thing to do. It was as if she was paying him for entertaining her. His suffering amused her. I would suffer along with him, suffering from each blow, until finally, I would yell at her to stop. She would stop, but only to slap me or squeeze my cheeks until they burned with pain. It pained me not to be able to protect Hai. I wanted to take him away from Chi Thoi. I wanted him to be safe and happy and loved always. My heart broke when Chi Thoi hurt him. Chi Thoi seemed to be sick somehow; I did not know what kind of sickness she had but even as a child I could tell that something was not right with her.

During this time, I was missing both my father and my mother. My father had been gone for what seemed to me like a very long time. He did send us letters, though. Those letters meant everything to me. My mother would read them to me and answer my barrage of questions. He had moved to Saigon, where an opportunity came up for the hospital to send some soldiers to receive further training. Saigon was so far away, my mother told me. It was a massive city at least ten times the size of Da Nang. He had gone for more training, but also, I believe because his heart was broken. My mother said he was in pain because the other woman would not let him come over any more. I took comfort in knowing that at least my father was safe. He was no longer with the gunfire and the bombs.

His letters proved to me that he did not want to abandon me. He still loved me and asked my mother if there was anything I wanted from the big city. I was very clear; I told him I wanted a pink cardigan and a very big doll. Everyone in my neighbourhood had American-made dolls, and I wanted the biggest, with moving blue eyes. He wrote back to say that my wish was granted, and he would give them to me when he returned. My excitement about being reunited with my father merged with the excitement of receiving gifts. Even though he had hurt me deeply in the past, I missed him and longed to have him home.

I started attending a local Catholic school, despite being officially a Buddhist. Other than the bi-monthly praying for ancestors, my family did not practice much religion. On my first day, we sat on uncomfortable wooden benches and listened to a story about two men called Cain and Abel. The story was about Cain murdering his brother. Cain held a wooden club high and struck his brother with it, and Abel's blood poured down onto the earth. I thought of my father with the broom and smelled the unmistakable Death House incense at the back of my throat. More blood, more violence. There was a Vietnamese saying that black ants are for Buddhists, red ants are for Catholics. I had no idea what it meant, but I imagined Cain and Abel like two ants fighting each other. It was very confusing, and I just wished I was back in Chu Lai with Lien.

'And?' the Father was apparently asking me a question, but I had not heard it. 'What was God's punishment?' he asked, more sternly now.

'Um...' In my mind, I looked at the two semi-naked men, posing in the final act of aggression. It was easy to imagine them as American soldiers, with their white faces and muscular arms.

'God sent them to hell?' I guessed. Usually, I was such a good student, but this class and the thoughts of blood and violence had been too much for me.

The Father let out a small forceful burst of air and stormed down the aisle towards me. Without warning, he brought down his wooden stick across my back. I felt like my whole chest had collapsed. I was on the chair and tried my best to hold my body still, as blows rained down forcefully on my back. I was shaking and didn't know how long I could bear it. The whole class looked at me with pity in their eyes.

'Her family is Buddhist, and she does not know the Bible,' Oanh, my neighbour's daughter, called out, but the Father did not hear her - or he chose not to.

The monster in him was alive. It seemed that there was a monster in all the adults in my life, ready to come out and attack at any moment. I opened my mouth to protest but stopped. It is not right to question authority in Vietnamese culture. It is assumed that if children got a beating, then they must have done something wrong. I got the question wrong that time, but it did not mean I was not clever.

At home that evening, my mother bathed me and noticed the marks on my back. She covered her mouth and called my babysitter over.

'Chi Thoi, look at this.'

They made me tell them what happened, and even though the abuse was inflicted on me, I felt humiliated. My story made my mother cry, but Chi Thoi was not upset.

She was angry.

'What a bastard! Why didn't you tell me? I would have gone and punched him in the face.'

Both of their reactions moved me so much. My mother's tears were a salve for my constantly-longing soul, and Chi Thoi's anger was the first time she had shown any kind of sympathy for me. It was usually her that was doing the damage. I wrapped my arms around my body in the bath, covering the bruises on my back with my hands in a kind of hug.

There were no complaints made against the Father or the nuns who inflicted their punishment in the form of swift raps on our hands. It was simply not possible to challenge that kind of authority. The plan was simply to wait for my father to return to Da Nang and find me a new school. In the meantime, I found a thick black and yellow jumper of Hien's and wore it underneath my school uniform every day. It was boiling hot and, in the humidity coupled with the heat, my back would soak with sweat, but it was an extra layer of protection against the abuse of the Catholic educators in my school. My only defence against the nuns was quiet obedience.

I can't remember learning anything else from that school, other than how to avoid punishment. But I did become an expert at inflicting lethal punishment on red ants. I would hunt them down and burn them to death. My brother Hiep told me I was going to go to hell for killing so many ants.

Maybe I will join Cain, and the teachers at my school there, I thought, undeterred.

Life was pain and suffering, always pain. These beatings from the Father and nuns and from Chi Thoi hurt and left me scars that could not be wiped away, but I took them in and gained strength from them. I ate them up like a meal, fed on them instead of letting them devour me. I ate up those beatings and all the pain that came along with life and let them grow in me like a fire that could not be put out.

As I became an adult, it was this very fire that got me across an ocean to freedom. It is the same fire that helped me build a business in a new country. It is this fire that allowed me to fight off abuse from the small children in my nursery and more than anything it was this fire that would make me fight for my own daughter to have a better life no matter what.

CHAPTER ELEVEN

I GOT SOME RELIEF!

Except for his big army bag, my father came home to Da Nang empty-handed. I had waited all day impatiently for his arrival, expecting my beautiful doll and cardigan. Though I longed for his presence, I think I longed for the presents more, and I eyed his bag greedily. Smiling, he rummaged inside it and pulled out a blue cardigan. Blue. Not pink. I had wanted a pink one, but I accepted it graciously and put it on over my dress.

'Thank you, Ba,' I said, looking at the bag again with high expectation. He made a mistake with the cardigan, but the doll was the true symbol of his love and dedication to his only daughter. My father moved the bag off the floor and onto the table.

'I don't have your doll, princess. I'm sorry. She is at your uncle's house in Saigon,' he assured me. 'Don't worry, one day we can go and collect it,' my heart broke with this news. I had never even touched the doll, and yet, I felt like it had been wrestled from my arms. It was stolen from me before it was ever truly mine.

The best part of my father being home again was that on scorching days, he bathed me. I would sit inside a big basin, and he would get the fresh, cool water from the well and pour it over my head. It was a sensational feeling, and these baths always came with lots of laughing. He scrubbed my back and said, 'My daughter will be wealthy later. You have a black mark on your back, the sign of wealthy people,' I did not understand anything. I just knew that I had the best father in the world.

My deep disappointment over the doll disappeared when my father successfully got me into a new school. I had to repeat grade one, and because of this, for the remaining years of my education, I would always be more than a year older than everyone else in my class. I was always the tallest, and this meant that I was always placed in the back of the class, even though I longed to be in the front. The shame in repeating was brightened by the heaven that was my new school. My teacher was friendly, supportive and never used violence or threats against us. I made friends, built self-esteem, and even enjoyed the long walk to and from school.

Even though my parents were so often absent and Chi Thoi would still abuse me at home, coming back to Da Nang had made my life so much better. For the first time in my life, I could now imagine a world with opportunity and excitement.

That excitement blossomed when we moved out of our tiny wooden house near the market to a much bigger house in a more respectable neighbourhood. The new house was built with big cement blocks. My mother extended a little veranda. Her business had been doing well, and she now had a permanent electrical goods shop in the centre of Da Nang. It was one of the biggest in the whole street, with a treasure trove of second-hand American goods. Her entrepreneurial spirit was developing, and she made money easily.

We had a big kitchen, two American-made beds that we pushed together to make a king-sized one, and a well inside the house. We also had something very special that we'd never had before: a television. It made our family stand out, and our house was like a cinema for the neighbourhood at night. Later, my mother got another TV in the bedroom, and it became my entertainment and also my terror. I could see the war next to my bed, and as I slept, I could hear the destruction of bombs exploding in my mind.

The pride and joy of the house was a big altar dedicated to Linh Un, the female Buddha. It took up around eight square meters of our lounge room and was big enough for me to crawl inside. Offerings would be laid out as presents for our ancestors, bananas, cakes, sweets, and occasionally, bottles of soft drinks. I would crawl inside and imagine it was my personal coffee shop. It was a sanctuary for me. I would play hopscotch outside and hang around the many sweet shops at the start of the alleyway. The houses were all quite close together, but the community was kind and friendly. With the new home, our status improved, and we began to perceive ourselves as moving up in the world. Life presented itself in brighter colours, and I was so hungry for positive experiences that the darkness in my past seemed pushed aside.

Even my babysitter was happier.

'Your sister looks so beautiful and attractive!' the young men from the neighbourhood would say, with their eyes lingering over Chi Thoi. In our new home, many people mistook the two of us for sisters.

'Can I be your brother-in-law?' they would half-jokingly ask. Some of them would even hang around our front gate, trying to get Chi Thoi's attention. My father would scare them away by shouting, 'Leave her alone, or I will get you!'

Chi Thoi had indeed become beautiful. The change happened very suddenly in her. Her lips became thick and red, standing out against her smooth skin. Her full lips were even more striking because they were paired with her burnt red hair.

I once heard my mother say to Chi Thoi, 'Your breasts have gotten so big! You need to wear the right clothes to keep the boys from getting you!'

She went on to say, in a knowing and calm voice, 'You will have a man in your life very soon, a family too. You must behave yourself in the meantime.'

Chi Thoi didn't say anything in response to my mother, but her face took on a strange blush. She tried to hide her smile, a smile that made her look very embarrassed.

But the greatest reward that came with the new house was meeting a new friend: Chi Oanh. At twelve years old, she was five years older than me. One afternoon she rode past me on her bike and asked me if I was new to the neighbourhood. Her calm and friendly nature warmed me. She asked me how many brothers and sisters I had.

'I'm the only girl,' I said. 'And I have four brothers, one older and three younger.'

'I'm the only girl, too!' she said. 'But I always wanted a younger sister.'

Chi Oanh was the youngest among the three. Her father did not want her; he wanted a boy.

She smiled again and raised her eyebrows. I looked up at her on the bike, with her playful attitude and welcoming personality. I had never known I wanted an older sister before, but here she was, right in front of me. She pointed to the house opposite and three doors down.

'That's my house,' she said. 'Everyone in the neighbourhood comes and visits us. You should too.'

I felt very blessed and went over the very next day and then the next. Our friendship blossomed, and her house became my second home. Her mother was just as kind, and I looked up to her like I looked up to the Buddhist lady in our shrine. Her father, on the other hand, was widely feared in the neighbourhood.

He had lost all of his businesses and was now bitter and grumpy. After hearing that he chased a group of kids down the street with a stick, the neighbourhood children were cautious around him. I felt so invested in the family that I became determined to win his heart. Behind his grouchy, cantankerous moods, I glimpsed a more benign spirit, and I spoke to that person with as much charm as I could muster. Eventually, and entirely unexpectedly to his family, he became very calm around me and looked forward to my visits. I got another sense of my capacity to break through barriers and win people over.

In the past, I had charmed a lot of adults, mostly with the agenda of winning some sweet treats from them. But now, I recognised that my emerging talent for charming people had very real effects on their state of mind and their relationships with people around them. It swelled my confidence and gave me a sense of identity that I could not yet name. One day, Chi Oanh's father asked me to sit down and had yummy home-made dumplings for me.

'That has never happened before, with anyone,' Chi Oanh's mother announced with love in her eyes.

I began to feel so comfortable in Chi Oanh's house that I would often prefer to sleep over there instead of in my bed. In the evenings, many of the neighbours would drop in to relax and gossip in the lounge room. It was almost like a private community centre for the street, and I loved the excitement and activity, and also the attention that often fell on me.

One evening, I walked in, and everybody stopped talking at once. Their smiles were a little too forced, their body language a little too exaggerated. I looked around from face to face until my eyes rested on my friend. Chi Oanh looked away and began to pick up plates as the conversation warmed up again. I pretended to go to the bedroom but instead hovered outside the door. The voices then became whispers.

'Do you think she knows?'

'It's unlikely, but it will soon be obvious.'

'She's too young. Don't tell her.'

I didn't understand what they were talking about or why it related to me, but my senses came to life as if fate was calling my name, whispering at first, and getting louder and louder. I lay in Chi Oanh's bed later that evening, unable to sleep. What couldn't they tell me? And why was I too young to know? From the kitchen, I could hear Chi Oanh and her mother cleaning the last of the dishes. When the noise finally stopped, the house grew quiet. I opened the door a fraction and peered out of the crack. I could not see them, but their voices came softly down the hallway.

'Everyone knows that the child is his,' Chi Oanh's mother said. 'But her stomach is not big yet, so the secret is safe for a while longer.'

'But aren't they related? Ha-Le told me she is his niece.'

Chi Oanh's reply made my blood freeze. His niece. They are talking about my father and Chi Thoi. Chi Thoi is pregnant? And my father…

'That is why it is really important that the rest of the family must never know,' Chi Oanh's mother said.

'If her mother found out, who knows what would happen.'

Her words made me imagine the time my mother chased my father with the knife.

'Poor Ha-Le!' Chi Oanh said wistfully.

'Yes, it is not fair on her. She does not deserve this. He only has one daughter, and she will suffer because of it.'

The secret was like a huge cyclone, rising ominously over the horizon and heading straight for my family. But I could not warn them. Chi Thoi was pregnant with my father's child. I had watched my mother go through pregnancy with my two youngest brothers. I knew about the sickness, the pain, and the attention that it brought to our lives. It seemed almost impossible that the same could happen to my babysitter.

I watched Chi Thoi go about her chores as if seeing her for the first time. It was possible that the whole thing was a mistake. Her stomach was as flat as ever, and if she was feeling sick or tired, she was hiding it well. I felt perplexed and began to doubt everything in my life. If this colossal secret was being kept, what else did I not know? What else had my father done?

I did not want to lose the faith I had in my father, so I invested my energy in hoping it was not true, that it would go away. I observed Chi Thoi and my father carefully but saw no evidence of them sharing any secrets or having any sort of relationship. What I did notice was that my babysitter was calmer towards me. Every few days, she gave me money to go to the shops and buy sour dried fruits for her. She was very specific about what she wanted and seemed so desperate that I obediently brought home whatever she wanted.

About a month later, I was woken up by the sound of my mother's shouting. It seemed like every big event of my life at the time was learned by overhearing it from another room.

'Who is the bastard?' my mother yelled. 'Tell me who he is, and I will go and force him to marry you.'

'I can't tell you,' Chi Thoi replied. She sounded as if she was crying. I had never heard my babysitter in a state of distress before.

'I can't say. I can't say,' she repeated again and again as my mum became more and more insistent. I thought I heard Chi Thoi squeal and imagined my mother pulling her hair in desperation. My mother loved Chi Thoi. Her anger was from love, but she apparently did not know the truth; otherwise, the anger would have had a whole new dimension.

For the first time in my life, I felt defensive for my babysitter. She was hurting and burdened by the same horrible secret that I was. We were bound together in the gathering storm and my resolve to keep the secret hardened as if my very resolution could protect us both from the disaster ahead.

CHAPTER TWELVE

~

INDELIBLE FAMILY STIGMA

P olly, my staff was a commanding force on the preschool playground. 'Too loud, children! Calm down!' she said in a loud, firm voice, capturing the children's attention. There were days when, despite our best efforts to calm them down, the kids were just too excited. But that was the reality of working with children, and it was a reality that I loved. Children were such curious and energetic little creatures.

My heart hummed a happy rhythm whenever I heard the joyous shouts and giggles of the pre-schoolers. Those sounds were the anecdote to my stress. Children can compose a beautiful song from their joyful shouts, laughs and giggles, and that right there was the best music to me.

I was full of passion for helping children, and I couldn't imagine doing anything else for my career. Years ago, I would never have believed that I could leave Vietnam and build a career centred on child care. Having built a little haven for children in the faraway land of Australia, it was something that little Ha-Le could never have envisioned.

Hong-An was a big part of the reason that I'd chosen to enter the early childhood field. She was a significant contributor to the decision. Ever since I'd given birth to her, I'd made a vow, both to her and to all children, 'I will be here for you, little people.'

And I have been. My whole life, my entire being, was for them. I made that promise while working with children at Tuen Mun camp in Hong Kong. Devoting my life to children came with joy, but it also came with a pang of sadness. Every time I saw a newborn baby, I would remember Chi Thoi's child. Her child was my half-brother. I never got to hear the sounds of his laughing and playing. I often wonder what he would have sounded like.

I was about nine years old when Chi Thoi had the child. For the period of her pregnancy, I had withdrawn from the world emotionally. When I went over to Chi Oanh's house, I felt ashamed in front of everybody. The shame belonged to my father, but it had settled on me. Amazingly, despite the fact that most of the community knew the secret, they kept it from my family. They even assumed they had kept it from me. I think they all felt so sorry for Chi Thoi that they agreed to protect her. This kind of scandal could ruin a family's reputation in Vietnam, possibly for generations. It was a marvellous gift that they gave to us, but in private, the shame manifested like a weed, taking root in the depths of my body.

On hearing the news of the birth, I was anxious to see the child. Part of me still believed that there was a chance that it did not belong to my father; I wanted to salvage my respect for him. In the afternoon, instead of going home after school, I went to the hospital and found my way to where Chi Thoi was resting. There were many beds in the room, and my babysitter was in the last one. She was sleeping. In the cot next to her was the tiny form of a newborn baby. I peered over the side and found him awake, squirming gently in his blanket and sucking the air greedily. His lips were thick, his forehead was broad, and his nose had a familiar profile.

'Come onto the bed, Ha-Le!' Chi Thoi said.

I climbed up on the hospital bed and sat by her side. 'Does he have a name?' I asked.

Chi Thoi wiped a tear from her eyes. 'No. But he will one day. He…' she paused as if deciding whether or not to continue.

I waited, not sure if she knew that I knew. Her expression was one of exhaustion mixed with incredible sadness. I thought maybe that expression would never leave her now. She would wear that look for the rest of her life. I kept silent, not knowing what to say.

'You were only a baby when I came to live with you,' she continued, looking at the ceiling. 'I wasn't much older than you are now.' I tried to picture her as a girl like me, maybe someone in my class, but it was strange to think of her, not as an adult.

'I had been out in the field with the buffalo. As I walked home, I saw smoke and flames coming from my house,' she paused and closed her eyes, remembering. 'I ran over, but I could not get close to it. It was too hot. I couldn't see anything inside, just broken bricks and smoke. I called out for my family. I called every name, over and over again. Seven names. Seven…' Her voice became too quiet to hear, and I lay down next to her intuitively, hugging her from the side.

A bomb had dropped on her house and killed her whole family. Every single person had died. My mother and father eventually took her in. They had two young children, and my mother had been working to pay back debts my father had run up. They needed help, and Chi Thoi needed a family. She put her arm around me and cried. I listened to her quiet sobbing until she fell asleep. The unnamed baby gurgled, still sucking the air beside us.

At night time, I went to see her with my mother and some of the neighbours. I had a terrible fear that the secret would be revealed by the neighbours when my mother saw the baby. Everyone was happy to touch the baby's face and said that he was handsome. My mother did not notice anything, and no one mentioned a thing. I just stood in front of his cot and stared at him without blinking. That was the second time I saw my brother and, unbeknown to me, the last.

CHAPTER THIRTEEN

MY SECRET HALF BROTHER

I really hope to meet my half-brother one day,' I said to Minh.
'It may be challenging to make that a reality,' Minh explained gently. 'The world is so big, and it has been more than forty years.'

I nodded thoughtfully, absorbing his words.

'I know that you are right,' I said, 'but I still have hope that I will see him again someday. I don't know how, but I trust that the universe will answer my wish.'

When Chi Thoi returned from the hospital a few days later, she was carrying only a bag. She walked inside and began cleaning the kitchen without saying anything.

'Where is the baby?' I asked.

I had been looking forward to having a new brother in the house, even if it was a secret half-brother. I wanted more laughter and fun. I wanted to channel all of the complicated feelings I had into the care and attention I would shower him with. He was so innocent and pure, and I imagined us playing, united in our common bond. I would protect him against the secrets of his life.

'I gave it away,' Chi Thoi said.

She didn't look at me. She kept cleaning, letting her words hang heavily in the air. I felt I now knew her well enough to see through her words. I could feel that she was devastated, but having already suffered so much loss, she didn't want to address her feelings. She knew how to cope. I began helping her with the dishes in an attempt at empathy, but, in fact, I was overwhelmed by my grief. I felt like I had lost a brother. We had held onto the secret for so long. We had struggled and persevered through all the shame, with a little life growing inside of Chi Thoi. Now, we were left with nothing. She had just given birth but, yet again, we were the only family she had.

Much later that night, my mother came home, expecting to meet the baby. I had waited up with Chi Thoi long after I should have gone to bed, and instead of falling asleep in my bed, I had fallen asleep in the lounge room. I woke up to the sound of my mother hitting Chi Thoi across the face. I was paralysed, unable to get up to defend my babysitter.

'Why did you give the baby away?' my mother snapped. 'I've accepted you back in the house, so you and your baby would have a place to live. Who did you give the baby to?'

'I can't tell you,' Chi Thoi whispered. She had no motivation to defend herself physically, but her resolve to protect the secret was as strong as ever. 'I don't want to see him again.'

'It's simple, Chi Thoi. Tell me who the bastard is so that he can take responsibility.'

'I can't, I can't,' she said. She couldn't.

Little did my Mum know that the bastard was in the bedroom, probably pretending to sleep.

'Tell me or get out,' my mother threatened.

I felt so sorry for Chi Thoi at that moment. She already had an ocean of pain and now faced the torture of my mother. Perhaps, in that situation, nothing hurts any more. When you have given away your child, the threat of not having a house to live in is nothing. You are already so numb. Being kicked out into the street does not hurt.

In the morning, she had vanished, but her thoughts remained with me. Many, many times before, I had wished that Chi Thoi would have disappeared from my life. I had even hoped that she would die. But I had new space in my heart for her, and the compassion now had nowhere to go. I had thought that her baby would grow older with me, and I held onto the promise that despite the controversy, our family would somehow find a way to live together in peace.

I watched my father eat his breakfast and tried to read his emotions, but the secret was like a mirror. The more I looked at my father, the more I was confronted with my own feelings about the situation. In that emptiness left by Chi Thoi, a wall began to emerge between my father and me. We lived in the same house, but I could not get close to him.

CHAPTER FOURTEEN

I LOST HER!

On the plane back to Sydney, I thought about Chi Thoi and her face came to me suddenly, and all the memories flooded back again.

Across the aisle was my own daughter, an eye mask on, sleeping peacefully on Travis's shoulder. At that moment, thinking of Chi Thoi's loss, I felt blessed to have been able, at least, to be a part of my daughter's life. I had experienced all of her joys and challenges. I allowed myself a smile, the first in many days, and watched her sleep a little longer. Perhaps sensing my attention, Hong-An stirred a little and settled more deeply into Travis's arms.

The plane engines roared, or maybe it was just the echo of chaos inside my own head. I wasn't sure.

Hong-An had no idea how much pain I had carried with me all of my life. She only saw me as a strong mother. She assumed that nothing would be hard for me. I knew that this was why she had left me alone with my despair.

'It is your fault, Ha-Le!' I chided myself. 'You've never let her see that you are weak. She has only seen you wearing the mask of a brave and strong mother. Why didn't you ever cry out to Hong-An and let her understand who you really are?'

My cheeks were burning hot and wet with tears. I blamed myself more than anything. I felt stupid. I had sacrificed everything for my daughter, and she didn't know anything about the pain inside her mother's soul. Now, I had more pain to carry in my soul. Hong-An was turning away from me and there was growing tension between us. I had lost so many people who I loved so much in my life, I couldn't lose her too.

At some point during the flight, I started to nod off. I don't know how long I was asleep, but Minh's voice interrupted my dreams.

'I am very disappointed in you, Hong-An,' I heard him saying. 'You are not the daughter that we raised. Why have you been so heartless towards your mother? She hasn't been feeling well. She had a high fever when we got to the airport.'

I blinked my eyes open and looked over to where Travis and Hong-An sat. Travis was staring at Minh with hard eyes, although I knew he couldn't understand what was being said, as Minh was speaking in Vietnamese.

I cleared my throat, and the three of them looked at me in surprise.

'Please, leave them alone, Minh,' I whispered. 'Everything comes from a heart. You don't need to remind her to take care of me.'

His face dropped with a disappointment and a big long sigh, but nothing more was said about it.

We landed in Cambodia, and I hoped that we could all try to be pleasant again.

'We should drink a Cambodian cocktail while we are here!' I announced cheerfully.

Hong-An and Travis ignored me. They left the plane without saying a word and walked resolutely to the transit centres. Minh and I wandered far behind them. It was as if we were strangers. Hong-An didn't even look back. She was acting as though I didn't exist. I clearly knew that I had to pay the price for what I had said to Hong-An at my mother's house.

I went to the bar and ordered a cocktail alone. It tasted bitter in my mouth. It matched the heavy feeling in my heart.

When we arrived in Singapore, Minh had asked Hong-An if she and Travis would like to eat with us in the restaurant. Her reply was short. She said, 'No. We are good. We'll come back when it's time for our flight.' And then she and Travis hurried away from us, disappearing into the crowds of strangers weaving their way through the Singapore airport.

Hong-An's words stung me. I wanted to scream out my anger. Why had everything gone so wrong?

'The mess that all of you created is so big, Ha Le. It's all because of your stupid ideas about being a good mother!' I scolded myself again.

I didn't know what would happen, but I could feel the tensions among us rising. It wouldn't be long before those tensions exploded. For the whole flight, we were strangers. I sat silently feeling my heart ripped into pieces. I couldn't bear the feeling of guilt for the things I said to Hong-An.

We went through the motions. Taxi home. Bags in the hallway. Quick showers. Kettle boiling. I prepared a quick breakfast which no one really ate. The air was heavy with one unspoken fact: the holiday that was supposed to bring us together had failed. We were even further apart because of it.

From behind me, I heard Hong-An's voice.

'I'm taking some things now, but I'll be back for more. I'm not going to stay here anymore.'

I turned around, a flowerpot in my hands as I was trying to distract my mind with gardening, but the world just kept spinning around me. The person in front of me looked like my daughter, but she acted like someone I hardly knew. There was nothing left to say. I couldn't stop her. At my mother's house, each word I said to her was like a brick that had built an impenetrable fortress between us. Adding more words would be like adding more bricks, more fortifications between the person I loved the most in the whole world and me.

She turned and went back into the house without saying goodbye. By the time I was able to stand and follow her inside, she was gone.

After Hong-An left home, I was an emotional wreck. I told the staff at the preschool that I needed some time to rest after my long holiday.

'Erin, I need you to make sure that everything runs smoothly for the children, 'I explained. 'I'll be taking a week off.'

'Of course, Ha-Le,' she assured me. 'Everything will be fine. Take care of yourself.'

Erin's words gave me comfort. I felt reassured by her promise to take care of the preschool while I was gone. I really needed to be alone for a few days and sort out my feelings.

Once I arrived home, I went straight to my bedroom and allowed my pathetic body to flop onto my bed. I started to cry. I'd cried so much in the past week. I wondered how my body continued to produce tears.

I remembered feeling very much the same the times that my father had gone. I'd always tried to be his princess, to make him happy, but he still let me down.

I suddenly felt all the events of my childhood all connect together. The longing in my heart is what connected them all. In all these situations, I'd longed for greater closeness and love, and in all of these situations, I'd been denied that. They were all somewhere in the past. So far away from me now.

I felt like the only soldier left on a bloody battlefield, with no one left to fight and no victory in my survival. I walked around our house as if surveying a landscape of destruction. In every room, there were traces of my daughter. I saw pairs of her shoes, university textbooks, a hair-dryer, photos of family holidays on the wall, an old note on the fridge that read: Happy Birthday to the best Mum in the world. Every image stung me with the shocking reality of her absence.

All of the sacrifices that I'd made for my family were nothing now. Years ago, when I'd left Vietnam, I had thought I was leaving the past behind. I thought that I was creating a brand-new life for myself, a life of my own making. I had survived so that I could build the life that I wished for here in Australia. I wanted us to be a happy family, with lots of love for each other. I wanted us to live next to each other forever as a small tribe, a tribe that was born from love. I was somehow sure that love would compensate for all the wounds of the past, maybe even heal them, like a salve.

But the past is done, the present is all that we can control. But I knew that I hadn't done enough to keep my family together when it came to my present situation. I hadn't done enough to keep it from falling apart. I hadn't done enough to keep Hong-An from picking at the invisible scars of my past. She hadn't been there with me when my father had left with bullets flying through the trees and us hiding from the Viet Cong all night, but I could see now that, somehow, my scars had become hers. My wounded heart had created an injured family.

I couldn't escape my past. It followed me, day and night, sometimes in disguise, tricking me into believing I'd rid myself of it for good. It was glaring and obvious now. My past was staring me down, with an ugly and terrible face, scaring me. Hong-An had been at the very centre of my existence for the past twenty-three years. But now, suddenly, she was acting like she didn't need me anymore at all. She certainly didn't want me. She only wanted Travis. She was only happy with him. My worries increased. There either had to be something wrong with the two of them, or there was something wrong with me. I struggled with this thought, turning it over and over again in my brain, wishing that I had an answer.

I just wished that I knew what to do.

I found myself in my bedroom. I laid down on the bed and stayed there for three days. Those three days were among the darkest of my life. My misery was reflected back at me from the full-length mirror on the wall, like a terrible, tragic play with only one actress. I cried until my eyes were swollen and the woman looking back at me became an ugly, pathetic character. She oscillated between different states of pain. Sometimes, she would glare at me angrily.

'What have you done, Ha-Le? You have ruined your life. How could you say those things?' she asked. Other times, she would be more desperate and forceful, pleading with me to find a solution to the mess I was in. 'Call her. You can't just lie there and be depressed. This is your daughter.' In the early morning, she would be more compassionate. 'Ha-Le, you have tried so hard, and all you get is suffering. You don't deserve this.' But late at night, when my insomnia kept me awake in my misery, she was bitter and vengeful. 'She is still a child. She knows nothing about your life. You have spoiled her for so many years, and now she is so ungrateful. And Travis? He took her away from you. He led her astray and changed her into someone who is not your daughter. Not your daughter.'

I pulled my hair, slapped my cheeks, threw pillows at the mirror, but most of the time, I settled into a deep state of depression. The wounds I had carried for most of my life opened up, and a single, clear voice echoed across the decades: 'What the father sows, the daughter shall reap.'

Was this my punishment? Was it time for me to pay back what my father owed Chi Thoi? I was lost in a raging sea of agony. I realised that everything I called success in Australia was nothing but a bunch of flimsy bandages on old wounds – wounds far from being healed. They were not the solutions for all the pain and shame I had endured. I needed something more.

'God, please have some mercy on me!' I frantically prayed in the darkness. 'Help me to sleep and never wake up again. I am done with life!'

I lay in the dark, knowing that I was a coward. I hoped beyond hope that a miracle would happen and my life would end. I needed a gentle miracle to end the agonies that were mine alone to face. I needed some sweet relief. My life had become far too much to endure.

CHAPTER FIFTEEN

~

FATHER SOWS AND DAUGHTER REAPS

My whole world changed when my mother was arrested. This happened not long after Chi Thoi had left. Mum was arrested at the market for selling a stolen loudspeaker system. She had not stolen it – in fact, she hadn't even known that it was stolen and likely wouldn't have purchased it if she had. She had bought the goods from the thief, but that was enough to lead to her arrest. The police arrested the thief first, and then they came for my mother. She was not someone to bow to authority, especially when she was innocent, so she argued with the police right from the start. They took her to the police station and questioned her until her straightforward attitude became too much to bear.

'You police are not very clever, are you? If I were your boss, I would sack every single one of you. You don't know how to look after the community. I know the law well, and you have arrested me without any evidence. I demand to be released!' she shouted at them.

Her anger threatened and enraged the police, and instead of releasing her after questioning, they put her in prison where she continued to berate them for their stupidity.

After my mother's arrest, my father started drinking more heavily. It began the very night of her arrest. He told me the news with a deep frown and then went straight to the liquor cabinet to retrieve a bottle. My young mind couldn't make sense of what I was being told. I thought that only evil people were arrested. Only murderers, thieves, and other dangerous people went to jail. But that wasn't my mother! She wasn't bad. But if she wasn't bad, then why would the police put her in jail? I felt like the world had been turned upside down, and I couldn't make sense of anything.

'How long will she be in prison?' I asked my father through my tears.

'If she can control her temper, then not long. If not...' He gulped down the rest of his drink and waved the bottle in front of his face to check that it was empty. 'Princess, can you go and get me some more of this at the shop?'

I had been buying him alcohol for months already. Whenever it ran out, I would be sent to the mixed shop on the corner. If they had no spirits, my father instructed me to buy Chinese medicinal alcohol. It came in a large jar, filled with all sorts of mysterious herbs floating in it, including sultanas. One day, I dipped my tongue in to taste it and was amazed by the flavour, and the way its warmth spread throughout my mouth and up into my brain. I started having a taste every time that I bought the medicinal alcohol. I loved it, and I would relish the times when my father's favourite spirit had run out, so I could have another taste of the wonderful drink.

On the day my mother was arrested, there was plenty of my father's regular alcohol available at the mixed shop, but I bought the Chinese medicinal alcohol anyway. On the way home, I tried to take another sip; I tripped and got a full mouthful of it, which in shock, I instinctively swallowed. I sheepishly gave the jar to my father when I got home, and he could see that a lot of it was gone. Instead of being angry, he laughed and gave me a cheeky wink.

'That's my girl,' he said.

The alcohol, combined with the news about my mother's arrest, made me sick. My grandmother arrived from Hue in the morning to look after us. She smelt, as always, of Tiger Balm, which she always applied to herself to ward off her many illnesses. I didn't think she would be much help to the family considering her health, and so I readied myself, at eleven years old, to take responsibility for everyone.

My mother would be in prison for six months. Luckily, half of the stolen goods were purchased by a friend of my mother who was the wife of another high-ranking officer. She hired a lot of good lawyers to make a case for both of them. But each time the case was heard in court, my mother was unable to contain her harsh words about the corruption and unfairness of the system, and they would lock her up again.

In the first few weeks without my mother, my life became a constant struggle of making sure everyone in my household was looked after. The pressure felt overwhelming, and I could not see how I could maintain it. My father had an idea for how to keep our household running smoothly.

'Chi Thoi will come back and help us,' my father announced with a happy smile.

I was happy, too. I'd nearly forgotten what had happened in the past. I had almost let go of all the shame his actions had brought me. I found comfort in convincing myself it had never happened in the first place. 'There was no evidence,' I told myself. 'My neighbours made everything up!' This was something that I wanted desperately to believe.

The day that Chi Thoi came back was a happy day indeed. Like an angel, her familiar face appeared on our doorstep.

I used to hate her for how she treated my brothers and me, but everything was different now. I was so happy to see her. She was a comfort to me in an uncertain and stressful time. She was more beautiful than ever before. Her skin glowed, and her hair shined. She wore a beautiful dress to show off her full breasts. She looked cleverer, more confident, and sharper. It had been two years since she had left us, and, at that time, she had become a different person. A feeling of security crept up inside of me as I watched her hug and kiss my brothers. At the time when we needed her the most, she gracefully reappeared. Once again, our clothes were washed, our meals were cooked, and the house was in order and peaceful.

My father was happier again too. Chi Thoi sometimes looked at him and smiled during mealtimes. The looks between them unsettled me.

Chi Thoi and I began visiting my mother at the prison. We would bring her food and talk to her through the barrier. It was hard to see her like that, and I cried each time. She wore no make-up, and her face was swollen from sleeping on the floor. She was thrilled to see Chi Thoi. It was clear there was a certain kind of love between them that had not been destroyed by the prolonged absence or the controversy of her departure.

She instructed Chi Thoi to visit all the people who owed her money and Chi Thoi assigned some of that work to me. One of her debtors owned a shop that sold barbecued pork. Every time I visited them, I would deliver a well-rehearsed speech: 'I'm here to collect my mother's money. If you don't have any, then give me some pork.' I was so shy, and I hated the mission I'd been given, but I rewarded myself with a taste of the meat before wrapping it carefully and taking it to my mother to eat.

The longer my mother was in jail, the more frustrated my father became. Hearing about her arguments with the police officers, he would become angry and vent it on me.

'I can't believe that your mother showed her temper again Ha-Le! At the court today, she asked to see the manager concerning her complaints about the officers. They told me that I have a beautiful wife, but she is a mad lady!' His face was red with sweat.

'Court is court,' he would rave. 'They have full control over everything! Whether your Mum is dead or alive is all up to them!'

'What did she say this time, Ba?' I asked.

'She said no one has a brain in here, and she needs the High Court to solve her case. If they don't know how to do their job, she will help them to make a decision,' my father shook his head, then added, 'Your mother never went to school. The way that she understands things is very different from reality!'

I was upset with my mother, but I also felt very sorry for her. I worried that she would be in jail for a very long time.

But where was her wisdom? Why was she bothering with thoughts about corruption? She should be doing everything she could to get home to her children! We missed her and needed her at home! Fighting injustice was not her job; being our mother was.

Still, I went to visit her with Chi Thoi as often as I could. She was keeping busy in her cell. My heart was moved when she showed me the present that she'd been making for me. She smiled and held it up for me to see. I couldn't believe that she'd remembered how I wanted one.

'Ma made for you a crochet cardigan.'

My mother learned how to crochet in prison, and she made me a beautiful top, which I treasured. It was the first thing that my mother made for me with her hands and love.

At home, Chi Thoi continued to take on tasks that my mother would usually manage, even going so far as to nag my father about his drinking. This was quite an odd thing for a niece to do with her uncle. He was her elder, and she owed him respect. She had no place involving herself in his health habits. Even more concerning, my father listened to her and took all of her comments in stride.

'No more drinking!' Chi Thoi chided him.

'Yes, ma'am!' he responded in a sweet and playful voice that I had never heard him use when speaking to my mother.

I could feel that something wasn't right between them. There was a strange energy in the air between them. But I did my best to ignore these gut feelings because I was so relieved to have Chi Thoi back in the house. I kept on trying to convince myself that the only relationship Chi Thoi and my father had ever had was in my imagination. I kept pushing my misgivings aside, distracting myself or simply not allowing myself to think about it. I couldn't take any more pain in my life. I had to rid my mind of the possibility that the two of them were behaving inappropriately.

♥ ♥ ♥ ♥

One afternoon, I found the two of them together, and what I saw made it impossible for me to continue to deny what was happening. I saw Chi Thoi facing my mother's open wardrobe, the keys still in her left hand; her other hand was resting against the frame. Behind her was my father, his arms were around her body, and they both had exceptional intimacy with each other. I stood there, unable to move, transfixed by the horror of what I saw. My head became dizzy. My vision blurred. Sadness and confusion poured over me. Chi Thoi let out a small giggle and turned around to face him, catching my eye in the process.

The meeting of our eyes was what I needed to break myself out of my frozen shock. My body regained the ability to move, and I didn't just move – I ran. I ran straight out of the house and across the road to Chi Oanh's house. I pushed past her mother and rushed into my friend's room. She wasn't there, but it did not matter. I wanted privacy. Worlds collided. That was my mother's cupboard, my mother's keys in her hand, and my father's hands all over her.

In that wardrobe was my mother's hidden stash of money and gold. That was how our lives were funded while my mother was locked away for six months. That was how my father kept up his drinking and whatever else. I felt as if the universe were falling apart. My father was untrustworthy. My father was a man that my mother could not trust. He was a man that I could not trust. I didn't think anything else could cause my reality to shift so violently. I didn't think anything else could create such a tremor in my soul. I was ashamed to be my father's daughter. I was disgusted by him.

It was late at night when I came home, and by that time, my father had already gone to work. For the remaining weeks, until my mother was released, I avoided contact with either of them as much as I could. I no longer ran to my dad when he came home. I saw the pain in his eyes, but I refused to indulge him with my attention. Only very late at night, if my racing mind were fighting sleep away, I would move to the lounge room where Chi Thoi slept to find some kind of relief.

One of those nights, I crawled in beside Chi Thoi and let myself succumb to a fitful sleep. I woke to the sound of her mumbling.

'What am I supposed to do now? Every time, you make it worse. I had just started to feel better; now it is worse. I miss our baby so much. What you did to me was unforgivable. You are a weak man. You will bring so much suffering. And your daughter…'

My ears pricked up at the mention of me. The air became still, like the moment before a storm, and in their breaths, I heard the sinister winds of fate.

I could not believe when I opened my mouth and asked unconsciously, 'Who is the father of the baby, Chi Thoi?'

'He knows that,' she responded in the dark. 'What you sow, your daughter will reap.'

I shivered as if electricity had passed through my body, and my heart exploded into a frenetic tempo. I clamped my hands tight into the bedsheets and quietly gasped for air. She had said it to my father, but the curse fell on me. Through squinted eyes, I looked up to the towering altar at the shadowy silhouette of the Lady Buddha, but she offered no relief. In fact, her smile remained fixed like a sinister mask. Chi Thoi's curse was my own to bear.

CHAPTER SIXTEEN

AND THE WAR DREW CLOSER

Vietnamese New Year is a time for renewal and mercy. To welcome a new lunar year, families clean their houses, repaint their windows, and decorate every possible surface with cherry blossoms, yellow apricot blossoms and all manner of red and gold decorations. Scrolls and posters with optimistic messages of health and prosperity are hung, and the kitchens become hubs of activities. It is a time for children to receive money, new clothes and indulge in a spread of specially-prepared sweets and cakes. It is also a time where every house in the neighbourhood is open for visitors and the community to come together, embrace, forgive, and enjoy the spirit of unity.

It was also the time that the Viet Cong launched their nationwide attack in 1968. In Hue, a major city near Da Nang, thousands of people were killed. Children and adults were buried alive, we were told. Since then, the weeks around the New Year also brought the fear of another attack. The fear sat uncomfortably alongside the joy of the celebrations. As people ate together, laughing and sharing stories, the televisions would replay news reports from the deadly offensive, reminding us to stay safe and to remember who the enemy was.

My mother was released just before New Year's Eve in a show of mercy by the authorities. Chi Thoi vanished suddenly, before my mother came home, without saying goodbye. That was the last I ever saw of her. She had been my babysitter, my enemy, my abuser, my angel, my protector, and my curse. Now, she was just a memory. My grandmother, who had been forced out soon after Chi Thoi arrived, possibly because of my father's need for privacy, returned to welcome my mother back.

My mother arrived in a house that had been cleared of many valuable things, including gold, jewellery and even clothing. My father had settled into alcoholism in her absence. These were the perfect conditions for quarrelling, and my parents did not lose any time in attacking each other with fierce pent-up frustration and anger. Their battles were long and very public, and I cowered in shame as I worried that the neighbours might hear. In spite of this, my mother never missed a chance to spoil me, and I received new sunglasses, dresses, and shoes and strutted proudly around the neighbourhood, holding onto the happiness they gave me.

We had a safe New Year without any attacks, but not for long. I had stopped going to school. It was impossible because it was full of refugees who had fled from the Viet Cong's steady advance. Our household's population had also slowly swelled to twenty with the arrival of fleeing family members. We were all able to sit and have great big meals together, chatting and comforting one another. Our little house was like a haven, protected from the war, but the war was coming closer. My mother made us cloth survival bags, which we were instructed to take with us at all times, in case the city was attacked, and our family was separated. Inside, some dried food and a bit of paper with our address and parents' names were written on it. An attack could happen anywhere at any time.

One day, my mother returned from work early. Her face was red from the sun, and she wore a panicked expression that I had not seen before.

She looked around the room and then snapped at me, 'Ha-Le, where are your brothers?'

Everyone in the room stopped what they were doing and looked at my mother.

'They are – I don't know – somewhere around the neighbourhood,' I stammered, adjusting to the seriousness of my mother's mood.

'Go get them. Hurry up!'

I raced out the door, even though my legs were already shivering with anxiety. I found Anh Hiep playing cards with a bunch of boys on the corner. He was winning, and his face was flushed with excitement as the group cheered and shouted.

'Mum needs us home now,' I said. 'She's angry,' I added in an effort to make him pay attention. We found my other brothers and rushed home.

By the time we got there, there was chaos in the house. My mother was already packing our clothes into several bags, and my relatives had crowded around, peppering her with questions.

'Who told you?' my uncle asked. 'How do they know?'

'Everyone in the market is talking about it. I don't know how they know, but they know. It's happening.'

'What's happening, Mum?' Anh Hiep asked.

'We are going to Saigon,' she replied but then softened her tone and turned and looked at us. Her five children stared at her in shock and confusion.

'Da Nang will be attacked very soon. The Viet Cong are coming. They have already taken Hue. There is a big ship at the dock that is heading for Saigon,' she touched my shoulder, intuitively aware of my sensitivity. 'We are going to be on it.'

'Quickly! Pack the rest of your clothes children,' my mother said. 'Ha-Le, come with me. I have a special job for you.'

I followed her into her bedroom, and she closed the door. 'Lift your shirt, dear!' she said. Around my waist, she tied a fabric cloth filled with money and gold.

'I wouldn't give this job to your brothers. They would just tell everybody or lose it. You are a good girl, Ha-Le. You can carry this for Ma. I know I can rely on you.'

In the midst of the chaos, I felt delighted to hear my brothers and cousins laughing when the two cyclos made turns and twists along the many different streets on the way to take us to Bach Dang port. I fought back panic. Looking around at my family members, I prayed for all of us to be safe and remain together. I prayed as if I had the strength of will to make this happen despite the impending encroachment of the Viet Cong.

I was always the responsible girl who had the fierce strength to keep life afloat. The one whom my mother could trust to keep the money and gold for her. This character forged amid bombs and war carried me into adulthood and was what made me the mother I would later become.

I carried these memories of grabbing our few belongings and holding them tightly to our chest as we ventured into the unknown. I wore them like dead weights on my ankles as life moved forward. I lugged them with me. When you have few material possessions, the value of family quickly becomes apparent. Nearly all my love that day was in that cyclo with me and I held it just as tightly as I held the gold wrapped around my chest. It was my job to protect us all.

❤❤❤❤

The small child inside me, who had grown into a strong woman, was still holding her back up straight, holding on to the duty of that imaginary gold and the safety of my family. Why couldn't I protect my family now? How had we gotten here?

After the third day, I received a text from Hong-An saying that she would return to pick up her mattress. I had just managed to lift my head above the water, only to be pulled back down with despair. She had left with only one suitcase and huge determination; part of me hoped that she would come back and life would continue as it had. But deep inside, I knew the landscape had fundamentally shifted, and her coming to pick up her bed was the final sign that her decision was not going to change. I could not reply. I could not give her permission to drown me.

I heard a van go up in the driveway and Hong-An's key in the lock. I listened to the voices of her and her friend as they went into her room and carried the mattress out of the door.

We had bought that bed's mattress for her when she was four years old, for her birthday for $400. When we moved into the one-bedroom unit in Cabramatta, the runaway tenant had left a baby cot behind. We opened one side of it and used that as Hong-An's first bed in Australia. Her bed was next to ours, which was also an old bed with a lot of stains. The beds were our good fortune for a new life in Australia. When Hong-An saw her new mattress after coming back from Vietnam for the first visit, it was heaven to her. She jumped on it, giggling delightfully. That picture stayed in my heart forever. It was most of our savings at the time, and it was our commitment to provide a good, proper bed for her little growing body. She had slept on that bed's mattress for twenty years, and it represented nearly her whole life. I didn't know where she was staying now, but I knew her well enough not to have moved in with Travis yet. I pictured her on a friend's couch, wrapping herself up in a blanket and missing her room.

I let them leave the house without a challenge. But when I heard the van reversing down the driveway, I could not bear it any longer and raced outside, yelling, 'Give me back the mattress! Don't you dare take it away?' I didn't care if the neighbours heard me. Hong-An just stared at me as if I had run out onto the street naked, holding a chainsaw. It was just a mattress, and I knew that my love for her was more than just a mattress, but at that moment, it felt like all we had left. The van stopped, and my daughter said something to her friend behind the wheel. That boy had looked up to me as a kind of aunty for many years, and I witnessed his hesitation before he averted his eyes and kept reversing. The truck moved out of the street, and I felt like it took my life with it.

Minh was livid with anger when he came home and saw her empty room, and then I saw his red eyes.

'Nothing else shall leave this house,' he ordered. 'If she needs a bed, she should have bought her bed. If she has no money, then she should have thought about that before she disrespected her parents. She has to live with the consequences of her decisions. She's almost graduated from University. If she wants to be independent, she needs to be properly independent.'

I agreed with his frustration and pain, but I just wanted my daughter home again. All I had wished for was her independence, her freedom to do whatever she set her mind to, but this was not the way I wanted it to happen.

'Her graduation,' I said, suddenly remembering that it was only two weeks away. 'What if she doesn't want us at her graduation?'

'I'm not going to her graduation. I refuse to honour her if she does not honour us.'

'But she has worked so hard. We have worked so hard to give her that education.'

'Yes, and she ruins it all by forgetting that for a boy.'

Travis would be at the graduation, of course. 'I don't think I could bear to see him.'

'Who, Travis? That young man, that boy is not welcomed in our house, and certainly, I will not see him at the graduation because I am not going.' He left the room to emphasise the finality of his decision, failing once again to recognise that I did not want his anger. I needed compassion. I needed rescuing. I had a reservoir inside me filled with love for my daughter, and I was drowning in it.

CHAPTER SEVENTEEN

FINDING LOVE IN DESPAIR

The only ship I had seen until then was in a children's picture book. When the cyclos entered the dockyards, we had to get out immediately because there were so many people shuffling towards the port of Bach Dang. I stood on the edge of the cyclo and looked out over the crowd. Rising above them, almost blocking out the sun, was a huge ocean liner. I had never seen anything that size before, let alone a ship. I could see people swarming over almost every inch of the decks, like ants.

'Yes, Ha-Le,' my mother said, lifting me down. 'We are going to board that ship. Now hold onto me tightly.'

Our little family edged through the crowd. I was too small to see our progress, but my mother's resolve and ability to boss people around seemed to be working. It was so hot, and I thought I might be lost or crushed in the mass of human limbs.

We made it to the edge of the dock without losing anyone, but my mother still counted us off anyway to make sure we hadn't lost anyone. The crowd pressed against us from behind, and two strong men grabbed my brothers and lifted them up onto the plank leading to the deck.

'Go quickly!' Someone said to me, but I was frozen with fear, looking down into the wash of white water below. I was frightened by the height, remembering the time I was dangled in the well by the two men. My whole body froze when a man carried me over the temporary wooden bridge to the ship. Past trauma stays in the body and doesn't really ever leave.

When we were all on the deck and reunited as a family, we quickly realised that the challenge was not yet over. A crush of people was still coming on board, and we were swept onwards in a steady push away from the entrance. There were thousands of people already sitting down and thousands more fighting for a bit of space to call their own. Finally, a young man's voice called out to us.

'There is room here,' he said. Sitting on a canvas bag was a young man about twenty years old, smiling at us. I liked him instantly and sat right down next to him, drawn to his friendly face.

'Hello little sister,' he said. 'I'm Duy, and this is my younger brother Toan. How old are you?'

'I'm eleven, nearly twelve.'

'Wow. Such a cute face for a twelve-year-old!' he teased me, winking at my mother at the same time. 'What grade are you in?'

'Five,' I replied, feeling a bit embarrassed.

The rest of the family put down our belongings, using them to cordon off a tiny part of the floor to claim as our own. It was so small that we could not stretch our legs out, and our bodies were always touching each other. We all sat down and waited for the ship to move.

'And who is this?' He asked, motioning towards Lan, my cousin who was clinging onto my hand. 'Another cutie.'

His brother joined in the charm. 'It's impossible to say who is cuter. But you are too big to sit on my lap,' he said to me. 'But you...' He tickled my cousin, and her face brightened for the first time that day.

Duy kept talking to me, perhaps because he saw I was anxious, and probably because he was too.

'Do you want a biscuit?' Of course, I wanted a biscuit. He reached into a pocket of his bag and brought out several biscuits which I dutifully shared with my brothers. In just a few moments, we made a happy friendship amongst the uncertainty and stress of the environment.

'If you are eleven, how come you are in grade five. Aren't you a bit old?' I liked his cheekiness and the gentle way his brother was playing with my cousin. It made me trust them completely.

'My father moved jobs, and I had to start again in a new school,' I replied. It was a fact that I was ashamed of, but he made no mention of it.

'Where is your father then?' he asked.

'He is a nurse in the army hospital, Duy Tan. I guess he is helping sick people now,' I answered proudly. Indeed, it was his job that made me proud of my father at that time.

Duy looked out across the deck, where the sun was setting.

'That's very important,' he said.

When it became dark, we were hungry and thirsty. Suddenly, there was a familiar voice calling my brother's name. Then mine. 'Ha-Le? Princess?' It was my father. Above us, he appeared like an angel, with an armful of coconuts and snacks wrapped in banana leaves.

'Ba! Ba!' we yelled, leaping up and clinging onto his clothes. 'You found us. How did you find us?'

'I just looked for the naughtiest kids on the boat,' he teased.

My mother had tears in her eyes.

'You came,' she said, moved.

He handed the food over to her but then looked away nervously. 'I am not coming with you. I can't. The hospital needs me.'

My mother took a sharp breath in.

'Your children need you,' she said, then looked at him squarely as if she wanted to say, 'I need you, too.'

My father touched her shoulder in a rare show of affection. It was so crowded that he already had a large audience of people within earshot.

'The Viet Cong will take Da Nang soon. You should go with your family,' a man said.

'If the Viet Cong takes Da Nang, there will be a lot of wounded soldiers who need help,' my father replied, but it was not an argument he could win. After a long pause, he added, 'I can't be a deserter. I can't. I just wanted to come and say goodbye, for now.'

My father ruffled his sons' hair and kissed my forehead. 'Look after each other, you little rascals.' And then he was gone.

My heart was broken. What if a bullet or a bomb killed him? I watched his back as it got smaller and smaller and then disappeared in the crowd. I wondered if we would ever have a regular family meal together again.

I couldn't drink the coconut juice. I just sat and felt sick with grief and worry. Duy kept chatting playfully, and my grandmother began to lather her body in Tiger Balm, as she always did to relieve her many aches and pains. The body odour of thousands of people mixed with Tiger Balm made me want to retch. My mother just sat and stared at a point on the wall near us, lost in her thoughts.

The light was fading fast, and I could see there were still countless thousands of people waiting to board the ship. It seemed like a hopeless endeavour, considering how crowded it already was. I could not lie down because the handlebar of someone's bicycle was digging into my back. So, as the darkness set in and the boat quietened down, I rested my head on my new friend's lap and tried to sleep. Duy sang a mellow pop song over and over in an effort to help me sleep. I felt protected and nurtured by his gentle masculinity in my father's absence, but it did not soothe my anxiety. The night went by despite my restless sleep.

♥ ♥ ♥ ♥

In the morning, the ship was in precisely the same spot. All around me, a mountain of people were waking and attempting to stretch and reorganise their possessions in the limited space. It was a despairing picture. Duy and Toan were already standing and saying their goodbyes. They had located some of their family on a different part of the ship and were moving.

'Can I come with you?' I asked Duy. It had been cold last night, and he had hugged and patted me as I came in and out of sleep. He felt like the only secure thing I had to hold on to.

'No, sweetie,' he said. 'And it is dangerous to try and find me. You could get lost so easily.' He knelt and gave me another biscuit, secretly, so that I did not feel obliged to share. But I'd lost my protecting angel, and the biscuit turned to bitter dust in my mouth.

Suddenly, all around us, people started groaning and fighting. The ropes tying some of the possessions were cut, sending items crashing dangerously into the water below. So many possessions, how could people want to take so much stuff when we were running for our lives? I thought.

Men in white uniforms were trying to clear the crowd away. The final scramble was becoming more and more dangerous for everybody. Families were still flinging over ropes to the sea below so that family members could scramble up. I thought I heard a few people fall off. I thought I heard screams of pain too.

The ship's horn blew like a bolt of lightning through the crowd, and the engines started. We were moving. I still had hope that my father would change his mind and appear like a hero on board at any minute.

I stood at the railing and looked down at the chaos below. My hope in seeing my father tempered my fear of heights, so I clung on tightly and scanned the vessels one-by-one. Joining the mess of boats were hundreds of huge floating bamboo baskets as simple means of basic transportation. People were using any means to get close to the ship in order to have a chance to be lifted to freedom.

Some of the hopefuls were soldiers, escaping in plain clothes, so they were not revealed as deserters. They had guns drawn and seemed to be shooting back at the sailors who were shooting at them in a failed attempt to disperse the crowd.

'Get down!' my mother yelled. My family ducked, but I stuck my head out through the lowest rung of the railing and kept looking for my father. He still had time.

I heard a blast from the horn, and smoke began to rise from the funnels. Very slowly, the ship started to move, and the people began paddling madly. I saw a man launch himself up at a dangling rope, miss, and sink into the water. I saw a woman passing her child up to an outstretched hand, as the infant reached back to her, wailing. Then I saw my father.

For several long seconds, we yelled and screamed at him. He stood in the middle of one of the baskets, pointing and shouting instructions at the woman paddling.

'Go back!' my mother yelled. 'It's too dangerous!' But he did not hear. Then, a larger boat obscured our view briefly, and we lost him. I stood up and craned my neck for another ten minutes but could not see him anymore. Exhausted from concentrating, I collapsed back onto the floor and cried.

But I need not have worried, just an hour later, and my father found us. He made it! When I saw his broad shoulders and smiling face appear above me, all the shame and resentment that I had felt towards him disappeared. I only had room for love.

We were together again as a family. The future was uncertain, and our lives were at the whim of the gods, or the Viet Cong, or the ocean, or some other powerful force. But we had each other, so my heart felt lighter.

'You're here!' my mother gasped in surprise.

'You were right,' he murmured, wrapping his arms around her. 'It isn't right for me to leave you alone with five young children. I can't leave you all to face the war alone. I couldn't stop thinking about what you said. It doesn't make sense for me to rescue strangers. I am the one who needs to rescue my children. We need to stay together.'

They both looked beautiful to me at that moment. I liked that, and I didn't know why.

'There were so many casualties at the hospital,' my father told us. 'Many people are badly wounded. The Viet Cong will be here very soon.'

My father had deserted after all, but it was for very good reasons. The Viet Cong would soon entirely overtake the city. All that we could do was try to make it out alive.

My father must have really fought with his sense of duty. There would have been immense pressure to stay and treat wounded soldiers and fight to protect our home. He could have literally been saving people's lives, but he chose to be with us. He chose the duty he had to his family over his country, and even as a child, I was overcome with gratefulness. I needed him.

I had been searching for a united family for as long as I could remember. I certainly had not imagined finally experiencing that kind of togetherness on an overcrowded ship, escaping from war. This fight for a united family was one I would eventually continue with my own grown family. But for now, this moment was like salve on an open wound. It was the first time I had ever been into the open sea, and I felt a new kind of freedom bursting in my body. The breeze whipped up and around us, blowing away all my anxiety, and leaving only peace. I sensed the significance of our journey. Schools of flying fish came alongside the hull and launched into the air. 'You are free!' they seemed to say. 'Good luck!' I closed my eyes and felt like I was flying with the fish, completely at the moment. All the sad and horrific memories were replaced by excitement for the new adventure with my entire family.

♥ ♥ ♥ ♥

Despite the cool breezes and my optimism, the ship never made it to Saigon. Perhaps that was never the plan. It belonged to a rich man who, we were told, had generously donated it to help us escape. When the speakers came on again, they announced our imminent arrival at Cam Ranh Bay, a port only halfway to our final destination. It seemed that the ship was booked to take rich people away from Vietnam from Cam Ranh to Hawaii – that was what I'd heard from people. The benevolence of the ship's owner only extended halfway to freedom, and we felt betrayed and disappointed.

When the ship docked, we were ushered off ashore. There, we climbed into hundreds of waiting for army trucks and succumbed to whatever fate would bestow upon us.

'The Viet Cong are in the surrounding hills here,' someone said.

'We are being taken to our deaths,' said another.

I clutched the survival bag my mother had given me tight to my chest, feeling the layer of gold and money safe around my body, although it constantly sagged with the weight, and I had to hitch it up regularly. After a longer than expected drive uphill, we arrived at an old army camp in the middle of nowhere. Thousands of people were already there. It was crowded and chaotic.

The Viet Cong operated at night, and we felt very exposed on the hilltop. We set out trying to find water that we could mix with the dried, cooked rice that we carried in bags. My mother looked at each of us and rubbed our hair with tears in her eyes when each of us tried to get rice by our little hands to feed our hungry tummies. My father did not say anything, but I knew he was sad and worried for his five little children through his eyes.

Our family slept huddled together on the rough surface of the floor to a terrifying symphony of bombs and gunfire in the distance.

'How far are the guns, Ma?' my little brother asked.

'Too close,' she said. 'Too close.'

Before dawn, my mother woke us and told us to get our survival bags. 'Let's go before it gets any worse!' she said.

We snaked through the crowd, most of whom were still asleep. The few that were awake watched us in bewilderment. Why were we leaving so early? I had the same question in my mind, but I was trained to be alert and to follow my parents' orders without complaining.

In the valley between two hills, we found a road. My mother and father stood in the middle of the road to stop any traffic, while the rest of the family waited in the dust. Just as I was falling back asleep, my father yelled, 'Hey! There, in the distance. Lights!'

Sure enough, two headlights lit a fitful path towards us. It was a Lambro. The driver stopped and got out.

'Thank God!' he said. 'You are not hurt. A few kilometres back, I passed a car that a roadside bomb had blown up. They were all still bleeding.'

He was panting and had a wild look in his eye. Fear, I assumed, and I felt fear with him too.

'We need you to take us with you,' my father demanded. 'Wherever you are going, we will go. We can pay you.'

The driver shook his head. He was clearly worried about our safety.

'There are bombs everywhere along this road. If we are lucky, we will make it through to Phan Thiet, but no further,' he said with his eyes darting from side to side.

We had no choice. We went with him.

The rest of my family fell asleep very close to each other, but I stayed awake with the driver, my eyes piercing the scenery for any threats. I did not really know what to look for, but my fear kept me poised for action, like a tiger ready to pounce. Dawn began to define the shadows around me. I began to make out trees and abandoned huts along the side of the road.

As the sun rose into the sky, the road became peppered with people walking miserably in the same direction as us. I had seen this image on television. Lines of refugees carrying their belongings and fleeing for their lives but apparently in no rush. Everyone had chosen to leave their homes or were simply forced out. They looked resigned to any danger as it had become part of daily life. The evidence was scattered occasionally on the side of the road; smashed bikes and carts, boots, and clothes and, sometimes, something looked like dead bodies. Once or twice, we would hear an explosion from up ahead, but it did not stop people from walking on. They had nowhere else to go.

'Who wants sugar cane?' my mother suddenly called out. In the middle of this catastrophic scene, how strange to find a makeshift shop selling sugarcane sticks. I nodded eagerly, and my mother reached up to my shirt, expertly liberating a banknote and handing it over the side.

I munched on a stick of sugar cane, and the heady rush of sweetness eased my worries and set me off to sleep, soothed temporarily.

When I woke, the sweetness was replaced by the putrid aroma of rotten fish. We had gone as far as we could by road, and the final stretch would have to be done by sea. We walked along the edge of the shoreline at the Phan Thiet harbour, the main city, for fish sauce in Vietnam, and I listened to the shells crunching under my feet.

My father led us towards a small boat that was rocking like a see-saw on the water. This was what was meant to take us to Saigon. Compared to the ship we had just been on, this boat was not much more than a floating shoebox. It rocked dangerously as we stepped on the deck from a precariously thin plank of wood.

A deep-seated fear of drowning replaced the beauty of the vast ocean I had experienced momentarily on the big ship. I realised that it mattered very much how close you were to the waves. The diesel motor spluttered into life. My grandmother started to apply her Tiger Balm, making me instantly queasy. The only light came from a single bulb attached to a long pole in the boat's centre. I watched it sway from side to side, marking the arc of our undulating passage and the occasional outline of a massive wave that crested the side of the boat. My heart could have stopped right there and then, and I would not have been surprised. I was so sick and weak that it would have been very natural just to fade into the blackness of the ocean myself.

I guess I was half dreaming for most of the night. I felt the heavy rain on my upturned face and heard thunder rolling and cracking around us, along with the sounds of people being sick over the side of the boat. They clutched the edge to hold on as they rode the waves of nausea. I felt the bump of another boat coming alongside us and the triumphant gasp of the engine starting again. I was so sick myself that I could barely move and felt desperately alone as each of my family members tried to hold onto life and each other by a thread. Ma had Hai, and Ba held Hung. I, on the other hand, only had myself for comfort. I was terrified of the possibility of being dragged into the ocean by a strong wave. But I also knew that if this happened, my parents wouldn't leave my brothers to save me.

I only became aware of being truly awake when a stranger lifted me onto dry land and gave me sandwiches and a soft drink. We had arrived at Vung Tau, the closest port to Saigon. The people helping us here seemed different. They wore more fashionable clothes and spoke with a slightly strange accent. They were city people, I was to realise. We were only a short distance from the last safe corner of Vietnam, Saigon.

~

CHAPTER EIGHTEEN

ENDLESS TORMENT

Hong-An had always been an outstanding student. I had always understood the value of education, despite the bad experiences I had at an early age. Minh was a leading scholar of English in Vietnam and came from a well-educated family. We did whatever we could to ensure she had the best opportunities, and she never took them for granted. She was always diligent with her homework, serious about studying, and fully engaged in the classroom. Hong-An was the benchmark for academic success in our community, and we were always very proud of her.

She had always been interested in just psychology but instead opted to study law and psychology at university. Now she was about to graduate, and Minh, the greatest supporter in her studies, had just said, unequivocally, that he would not attend the ceremony.

I was torn, indecisive. I was angry at my daughter, but especially at Travis. I just could not shake the feeling of disrespect he had towards us, but I also loved my daughter more than anything in the world. I pictured what would happen if I was forced to meet Travis, and I could not imagine coping at all. I really did not want to see him again. Hong-An had worked so hard for six and a half years to reach this point, and I had struggled along with her in sympathy. Her success was also my success, and I wanted to participate in it. I wanted to feel part of it. I wanted to make her a unique dress and take her out for a pre-graduation celebration dinner – something we'd planned for many years. We would laugh a lot, review all the memories from her study life. She would ask me what she should wear, which earrings and shoes as usual. I could kiss her hair, as much as I wanted, to let her know that I was so proud of her in everything, like when she graduated her Year 12.

Most of all, I desired to see Hong-An with her head held high, walking out of her house where she'd lived since year four. I imagined walking her to her graduation ceremony with both of her parents by her side. I longed for that moment since she entered university and had no doubt that part of her drive to study was to make the most of the opportunities we had given her. Now, just as the time arose to celebrate her epic journey, I didn't even know if she wanted me there.

'What she did to us is unbelievable. She does not deserve to have us at her graduation!' Minh kept repeating. He was so upset.

I was also in a great deal of pain and felt sorry for Hong-An. Her beloved father was so hurt and disappointed in her. He was planning to be absent from an important milestone in his daughter's life.

Minh was so close to his father when it came to academics.

For Minh's whole life, he shared the honour of all of his academic achievements with his father. Minh's wish surely must be that Hong-An would do the same with him. He might miss all the years of looking after Hong-An, with all of his heart and abilities. He would likely miss the countless times he picked her up, dropped her off at the station, and rushed her to the university in the car when Hong-An needed to hand in her assignments on time.

'I can't believe that I finished my law degree in the same university as you, Ba! Do you remember when I wore your PhD hat and gown on your graduation day? I was in Year 4 at that time!' They both laughed, and I couldn't recount how many times they repeated the same story, always with joy.

The years went by quickly, and now it was Hong-An's turn to graduate, except she didn't have her family with her to celebrate. This should be a day that the three of us were looking forward to together!

'We all lost a lot already, Minh! And the pains have been already so huge. I don't want to create more wounds that we will feel later. Let's go to Hong-An's graduation and celebrate her success. It is our success as well!'

I tried to reason with Minh, but he was much too hurt to listen.

'She disgraced our family tradition. It is time for her to show gratitude for our sacrifices for her!'

'She must take on that responsibility. Our responsibility is as her parents, and we should show our unconditional love for her. I don't want to be remorseful and blame myself later!' I insisted through my tears.

I ran my dilemma past a few Asian friends of ours. They understood the complexities of expectation amongst immigrant families and had a few Australian in-laws themselves.

'You have to go,' our friends, Sue and David said. 'It happens once in a lifetime. Attending with shame and pain is better than regretting not going. You have spoiled Hong-An by being easy on her in the past. Her fiancé is not purposely disrespecting you, but young people these days are very relaxed about culture. Hong-An is normally such a respectful girl. It was her responsibility.'

I felt like trying to explain that Hong-An had changed so suddenly, that her disrespectful behaviour was so new and unexpected, and that I was troubled about her well-being.

Hong-An sent me a text message with the date of her graduation.

'My graduation will be on May 28th. I hope you both will join me, Ba, Mẹ.'

I re-read it many times, searching for the emotion behind it and found nothing. No call. No dropping round to personally invite us. I stared at my phone and pictured her face as she wrote it. Was she concerned that we might not come? Was she resentful in having to invite us? Was she calling out for help? Or was she just stubbornly keeping her distance despite a deep pain inside her? The message offered no clues.

'Thank you, darling. Ba, Mẹ will be there XX.' I replied carefully. I deleted the hugs, but after thinking it over, I added them back defiantly.

However, Minh was still resolute in his decision. I could see underneath he was in tremendous pain, so I persevered with my campaign to convince him to go. Eventually, he agreed.

Minh spent a few days being very quiet. Then he came to me, and he said, 'You are right! We only have one chance to celebrate Hong-An's very first success in academia. We have all worked so hard for this moment. We need to celebrate together, irrespective of what is going on. This is what matters most!'

I smiled and threw my arms around Minh in a hug. My eyes were filled with tears. He was making the right decision to support his daughter.

I patted Minh on the back and told him, 'That is true unconditional love for Hong-An.'

I was relieved, but this was still no great victory for either of us. Our hearts swelled with love and pride for our daughter, but they also ached with a profound disappointment and emptiness. Our two hearts were conflicted, and I could see no end to our torment.

CHAPTER NINETEEN

~

NEW PERSPECTIVE AND BREAKING BARRIERS

'It's called the Pearl of Asia,' my father said to me as we entered the outskirts of Saigon. I looked down from the bus window at the streams of people walking alongside the bus.

'It's hard to believe that now,' he added wistfully.

I beamed with excitement. In my mind, I was crying out, 'Saigon! Yeah!' This was a mystery city to all kids, like Japan to the world. Seeing it on television, I dreamt of coming here when I grew up.

As we edged along, the traffic became more and more congested. There were refugees and soldiers all around us, all of them looking equally worn out and dishevelled. Saigon was so crowded. There were a lot of people who ran from the other cities to escape to Saigon. They wanted to escape the war. They all had one thing in common, the soldiers and the refugees. Despite their differences, they were unified by the same tired look of panicked desperation. You could even see some of them crying on the streets. I suddenly wanted to cry with them too.

My mum's eyes were already red. 'Oh war! How terrible it is for all of us!' my grandma whined. There were a lot of soldiers on the streets and on the cars. They had their guns pointed up to the air in a casual fashion as if they were merely holding an umbrella. They had kind eyes despite their weapons in hand. They all seemed to look too serious but a bit sad and somehow in a strange hurry at the same time. There was a sombre feeling in the air giving an impression that something terrifying was about to happen.

The war had taken its toll on all of us.

'Why do they call it the Pearl of Asia, Ba?' I asked my father.

'Because it is one of the most beautiful, modern, rich and sophisticated cities in Asia,' he replied, but it sounded like he was repeating a story he'd been told. 'Or at least it was...' he continued.

Although the pearl had certainly been tarnished just a bit, it was still a vibrant and fascinating place for me. I had never seen so many buildings, parks and shops. We transferred from the bus to a taxi, which took us through even more tree-lined streets and out to the suburbs, where my mother and father questioned people on the street. 'Do you know this address?' They asked, holding out a small piece of paper, again and again. Finally, after circling around and around, a man pointed up the street and told us it was only about half a kilometre away.

When we arrived at my uncle's house, he ran towards my mother and embraced her for a long time. They both cried, and I cried along with them. 'I've seen it all on television,' he said. 'It's terrible. Please stay with us. It will be crowded, but I'm so relieved you are all alive and well.'

Twelve people sat down to share a meal that night. I watched my mother chatting playfully with her cousin and felt a momentary sense of security wash over me. But as the days turned into weeks, I knew that war was approaching. The television was constantly blaring in my uncle's house. It displayed images of dead soldiers, mixed with rousing music and long parades of tanks and marching battalions and the Viet Cong. The news reports transfixed me, and for the first time began to connect some of the information to my own experience. But it was overwhelming, and a lot of the pictures scared me. I preferred to spend my time exploring the brand-new neighbourhood and visiting as many sweet stores as I could find. Exciting new experiences and different types of people created a brittle veneer of happiness in my otherwise-daunting life.

♥ ♥ ♥ ♥

When I got head lice, I was marched off to the hairdresser who treated it and cut it short into a bowl cut. At first, I protested vigorously. Although I almost certainly looked like a boy, I loved the freedom and the coolness of short hair. As we relaxed into our new life, one by one, we got sick, as if our bodies had held back all this time against the ongoing tide of threats against us and we finally let them go. I had to pay a visit to the doctor when my cough got too serious to ignore. He looked down my throat and then got out his stethoscope and asked me to remove my shirt. I looked at my mother for support.

'Go on, dear. Take it off. What's the matter?' she said indifferently.

I wrapped my arms around myself protectively, and the two adults waited. In the last few months, I had noticed my shirt getting tight around the chest. One morning I looked down to see that my nipples looked swollen and the contour of my body had changed. I was developing breasts, but I wasn't sure if anyone had noticed other than me. Indeed, no one sat me down to talk about the changes in my body, so I kept it to myself with a mixture of curiosity and shame.

I seemed to be all alone in this change. I had observed my friends at school and all of them were still flat-chested. I was changing in so many ways. To my friends' surprise, I stopped playing hopscotch and skipping.

'I need to put this against your skin so that I can listen to your heart,' the doctor assured. So I lifted my shirt and exposed my chest to him. I wanted to chop off my head as he examined me. I was looking at my mother the whole time; I noticed she didn't react, and nothing more was said.

I didn't know why my mother had no reaction to the changes happening in my body. I was confused about it, but I didn't dare ask her. Somehow just brining the topic up made me feel uncomfortable. I knew she loved me dearly, but somehow, I couldn't open up to her.

When I raised Hong-An, I tried to compensate for this lack of words from my mother. I allowed her to talk to me about anything she wanted. I encouraged her to talk about her thoughts and feelings as early as she was able to. There was nothing that she hid from me, nor I from her. We used to be like B1 & B2 from the Australian children's show.

'Oh Hong-An, why did we fall apart? Mummy loves you as always! Tell me what you have in your heart and we can work together for the solutions,' I whispered to myself with both regret and guilt.

I blamed myself for bringing up the problem when we all were vulnerable. We were tired and away from home. I wished so much to be able to take all of it back, rewind time somehow, but I couldn't. I wanted nothing more than to talk to her about what was truly in our hearts. I wanted to talk about her relationship when we were back in Australia where we could have more time to think. I somehow imagined if I had the right peace of mind, I might just be able to search out just the right words to heal our wounds. I wanted our words to flow freely again; this was the gift I had always been able to provide her.

❤ ❤ ❤ ❤

Saigon was an island in a sea of war. My uncle's house was an island of security in the big city, and I was an island within it. I felt my mind and body adapting to a new way of life and a new set of expectations. It was both exciting and threatening, challenging and rewarding at the same time. But, despite the crowded house, I mostly felt alone in my journey. My four brothers amused themselves with their own games, and my parents were preoccupied with their problems of adapting to this new reality. I could only dream of the big doll my father had promised me before we had left and which I had never gotten.

Because of the crowded house, it started to become evident after a few weeks that we needed to find our own place. Mum found us a new accommodation. We began sharing an apartment with a family that we would never have associated with before the war. The owner of the apartment was a single mother, a gambler and quite possibly an alcoholic. She smoked heavily and dressed like a prostitute, and although I was scared of her, she was very kind when she was sober. She had five children who also lived there.

I made good friends with one of the girls in the family who was about my age. Our friendship helped me to forget the war from time to time. Her name was Tam, and I felt an instant and intense connection with her. My heart sang, and my joy soared whenever she called out to me to come and play. Life was an absolute mess, but with Tam, I still found moments of sweetness. 'The play' was my antidote to the disease of war that hung in the air.

Then one day, the news came. Every television began reporting the same thing over and over again. Every conversation flipped instantly to one subject. The Viet Cong were here. Saigon was about to be washed away. Almost straight away, the bombs began. I was out on the balcony with my friend, chatting and watching the world pass by, when I heard two massive explosions. Instinctively, I raced inside and hid under the bed with the other kids. Sirens began to wail, and more explosions echoed from further away. My cradle of safety was gone. The Viet Cong had surrounded Saigon and were shelling it indiscriminately.

'Where is Hung! And Hien, where is he? Hiep, go and find your sister,' my mother kept on shouting and shouting. Her voice was filled with panic as she ran around trying to locate everyone in the family.

'If things get worse, you should all run for your life and look after your children!' Grandma told her. 'Don't worry about me. I am old and cannot run very quickly, so don't waste time bothering with me. I will only slow you all down.'

I heard her words with deep sadness. It was like I was hearing her say her last goodbyes, and my heart couldn't take it.

'No, Ma!' my mother shouted. 'We all run together! You are my mother, and I will never leave you behind.'

They were both sobbing now.

'I am the man of the family,' my father insisted. 'I will carry you on my back. I will look after you, Ma.'

'You must worry about your children first,' Grandma gave her firm order. 'Your children are still very little. You have to focus on them. They need you to take care of them.'

Outside, the sounds of bombs and gunfire filled the air. The explosions rattled the ground beneath us.

The bar across the street from our apartment had been transforming over the last few days into a battlement. Sandbags had been piled on top of one another, and soldiers with bullets and grenades strapped to their bodies swarmed the area, getting ready for the inevitable gun battle. The next morning, from the relative shelter of our apartment, we watched as a tank rolled down the street and positioned itself right outside our front door. I'm not sure if it made us feel more secure or more frightened. My mother's words were unsettling. 'If they fight here, we will become hamburger meat, and all the building will be smashed!'

We kept the television on the whole time. I saw, to my alarm, images of Da Nang and Hue with communist flags emblazoning the streets that I knew so well. I realised with a shock that I might never be able to go home again, but the thought refused to lodge in my brain – as if it was just a dream. I could not keep watching the screen. I had seen too much blood and misery on the television in the last few months and my imagination was already inundated with horrific scenes of my death. Later this evening, I imagined, I would be thrown up into the air by a bomb. I would crawl across the blackened rubble, bleeding from a massive wound in my stomach, trying to find my family. One by one, I would discover them, dead, dead, dead, dead... I would become like Chi Thoi: a girl with no family, making her way through a miserable, meaningless life.

I preferred to watch from the balcony, where my imagination was restricted by the stark reality of the outside world. My father called out to the household any information he learned from the news reports.

'They are saying there are 100,000 Northern soldiers... the biggest helicopter evacuation in history.'

'The Americans have abandoned Vietnam.'

'The 18th division is putting up a fight.'

'...impossible.'

'The president has resigned.'

I heard helicopters in the sky but could not see them. I imagined them crammed full of people, just like the ship we were in. I imagined them being shot down and crashing into the sea.

At lunchtime, my mother took out all of the food we had, including the special treats, and laid it all on the table: BBQ pork, some mangoes and mung bean sweet soup; all of these foods were usually treats for special occasions. My brothers and I would all shout in excitement when we saw that Mum was preparing these foods. But none of us was smiling now. We did not have our usual watering mouths.

'We may as well eat all of this now,' my mother said.

I finished her sentence in my head: '...because we are all going to die tonight.'

We sat around the table and gorged ourselves, but no one was really hungry or satisfied. After the dishes were cleared, we settled back to our macabre waiting game.

We had all seen enough news coverage to have a good idea of what was going to happen to us. The black and white pictures of bloody corpses had prepared us well for this eventuality.

Mum made sure that each of us had our own survival bag.

'Don't forget it!' she commanded, looking each of us in the eyes to ensure we understood.

'Hiep and Ha-Le!' he continued. 'You both need to watch out for Hung and Hai if Mum and Dad get lost or killed.' And then she turned to Hien and said, 'Don't get naughty and run around everywhere playing! You need to stick with your big sister and brother at all times! Remember this!'

She looked at Hien to ensure that he understood how serious this message was. He nodded with widened eyes. He looked as if he did understand. It was vital that he understood the dangers of war. She stared long and hard into my eyes. She was clearly deeply concerned. I remained quiet. My mind was whirring. There was a horrifying picture forming itself slowly inside my head. I saw the five of us, lost and alone in a big city filled with bombs and gunfire. A city full of smoke and riddled with debris and dead human beings strewn about the streets. I reached over and grabbed my youngest brother's hand, I gave it a squeeze. I felt so small and scared at that moment.

This small scared child would live inside me forever. She had been frozen at that moment somehow. The taste of fear lingered on my lips could not even be sweetened by the mangos we ate. That fear would remain a part of me, embedded deep in my heart. It would never really leave.

As a grown woman, I wanted to protect my own daughter from hardship. I wanted to spare her this suffering I had had. I tried to protect her from any pain, but somehow despite all I had done to get to this seemingly perfect life in Australia, I could never really shield her.

I cooked for Minh a version of the mung bean soup that we had eaten all those years ago in Vietnam. The smell reminded me of all that waiting, waiting for our impending death. But now, much like then, I left it cold on the table of our big empty house. We were still waiting somehow. I didn't want to eat and neither did Minh. We both missed Hong-An so much. We missed our happy time together. I missed her laughs and her jokes.

We did not have any friends to come and visit, to distract us from this mess. There were no weekend parties to fill the rooms full of festive noises. We had nothing more than just an empty house to rattle around in. In only a few short weeks, we had all transformed somehow. We had become different people. I could never have imagined that my life would go like this. I had fought so many battles since I left Vietnam. Hong-An walked away so easily after getting upset with me. She wanted to be with Travis. It hurt. She would never know my sacrifices. She would never meet that small child inside me. How could she know what her father and I went through to build this family? And how could she know how hard we work together to give her a life without having a taste of fear in her mouth?

♥ ♥ ♥ ♥

Despite those nights of waiting with uneaten food on the table, fearing that death would come, the inevitable battle to end all battles never arrived at our door. The new acting president saw the reality of the situation and simply surrendered Saigon to the Viet Cong. The loss of life would have been too much for the country to bear.

We had lost the war. The Americans had disappeared, and the city opened its doors to the enemy. The 30th of April 1975 was marked as the darkest day in the lives of us Southerners.

My grandmother was relieved.

'No more war,' she kept reiterating. She was certain now that she would be reunited with her husband, her son, and the rest of her family. My father was despondent. He had been recruited as an undercover Viet Cong agent, he had been caught and made to spend time in prison, being tortured by the South. He had then fought hard to get in the Southern army, and spent his career attending to the wounded from both sides. He had abandoned his post just days before they needed him most. His loyalty, in the end, was to his family and we had all survived. But the result of all that fighting, upheaval and pressure, was only surrender. My father was now a target, and he knew he would pay the price for being a Southern soldier.

I watched my father go through the house and collect all of his clothes and belongings that could identify him as an ex-soldier. He made a pile on the balcony and then threw them off one by one onto the pavement. I looked down at the street and saw that there were piles of belongings outside every building as far as I could see. People were getting rid of army clothes, boots and hats – even medals and certificates. I walked a little further down the street, but when I heard gunfire in the distance, I rushed home. Apparently, there was still some resistance.

When I saw my father being so miserable, my heart melted for him. I could not think of anything I could do to ease his emotions. The previous week we'd visited my great uncle, and I'd discovered that there had been no doll for me. My upset about that now melted with my love for my father.

The next morning, still confined to our apartment, we watched the Viet Cong march down the street. They walked alongside trucks, smiling and waving at us. I was surprised that they did not look like the murderous monsters in my imagination. They were almost all young, both men and women, and they wore beautiful black and white checked scarves and hats in the colour of banana leaves. I waved back, automatically, but my mother stopped me.

'From now on, you must wear dark clothes. No colours. No nail polish or make-up,' she spoke wearily and with no clear emotion on her face. 'No more fun. No more business. We'll be working hard in the fields soon.'

No one replied or challenged her. We were all lost in our thoughts. These friendly-looking people were the same people that had planted bombs on the side of the road. They were the same people that had forced us out of our home. The same people that had killed all of Chi Thoi's family, Aunty Huong and Aunty Phi's husband.

CHAPTER TWENTY

~

WAR BEGETS UNEXPECTED ENEMIES

Hong-An came home from school one day and opened her textbook on the kitchen table. She had just started year nine, and she looked very grown up in her new uniform. We were very proud. We had sent her to a private school called Meriden.

'Look!' she said. 'We'll be learning about the Vietnam War later this semester.'

Characteristically, she had skipped ahead and perused the whole history textbook. The page she had opened up to was filled with pictures of the evacuation of Saigon.

Minh turned the textbook towards him and skimmed through a paragraph. 'You know the Vietnamese don't call it the Vietnam War.'

Hong-An had already asked about our lives in Vietnam many times, but her motivations seemed different this time. Perhaps, because she was the only Vietnamese-Australian in her class, she felt a certain pressure to understand the topic in a more academic context. 'What do they call it?' she asked. 'The American war?'

'Well, not only that. The government officially calls it 'The Resistance War against the American Empire to Save the Nation. But the American War is easier to say.'

Hong-An nodded, taking in all of this information.

'But that's what the people who live in Vietnam now call it,' Minh explained. 'For the people like us, people who fled Vietnam, we've always called it the Communist War.'

I nodded my head in agreement with Minh. 'The Communist War' was a fitting title for the war we'd lived through. The North had attacked those of us living in the South of Vietnam. Our attackers had broken the Geneva Agreement. I'd always been told that the Americans said they were in support of the Southern government, but they were really involved because they wanted to test weapons on Vietnamese soil, weapons like the firebomb and the orange bomb. These bombs caused a great deal of suffering for the Vietnamese people. I was not sure about the facts that people talked about the war in Vietnam, but I was sure that I hated it. I hated seeing my people killing each other, and there was too much blood!

Hong-An's next question made it seem as though she had read my thoughts. 'But why did the Americans get involved? I mean, I know they were scared of communism, but wasn't it obvious pretty quickly that they were going to lose?'

It was a big question, and we both looked at Minh for a serious answer. My husband looked as though he would start a long description of international politics, but then he shook his head.

'Politicians play their games of power, soldiers follow orders, and innocent civilians suffer. In the end, it's hard to see the logic in it all. The Viet Cong believed they were creating a better world, but they had no idea how much of an international challenge that posed.'

'And they won. They are still in power, right?'

'Yes. Though their communist ideals appear a lot like capitalism now,' Minh said ironically. 'War makes enemies out of normal people, but the lines are often blurred. Ask your mother. She was a communist once.'

'Yes,' I said, laughing. 'My friends called me "The Little Bolshevik". I would wake up at four in the morning and walk around the neighbourhood banging a drum in the name of communism.'

'Really? What? Why?'

'Communism, especially under the regime of Uncle Ho, valued physical fitness in children, so I took it upon myself to wake the kids in the neighbourhood. I'd lead them down to the beach for exercises. For two years I did that,' I said with a deep belly laugh.

I noticed a little glance between Hong-An and Minh. 'Wow! Full-on.' My daughter said, her eyes opened wide in disbelief.

'Not much has changed,' Minh teased.

Hong-An laughed, and I laughed along but with less enthusiasm.

'Now she just bosses us around,' Hong-An said as she stood up and hugged me. 'Just kidding, Mẹ. I'm glad you boss us around. You do know best.'

'Little Bolshevik,' Minh teased again.

'No, but seriously Mẹ, I thought our family was against the communists.'

And then, after thinking, she asked me something that made me choke with laughter when I translated it into Vietnamese.

'Tell me if Uncle Ho is a bad guy or good guy!'

'He was your Mẹ's idol,' Minh said with his mouth wide opening with a loud laugh.

'Some people say he was good, some say he was awful. I'm confused.'

'You can say he was bad in here,' Minh said seriously. 'But when you go to Vietnam to visit your grandparents, keep your tongue still, ok?'

'But I want you to tell me what kind of person Uncle Ho was so that I can tell my friends at school. They are confused too.'

'You'll have to do more research to find out and draw your own conclusions,' I told her, leaving her frowning while I thought of the statues in Cabramatta. 'Do you remember seeing the statues when you were playing by the fishpond as a little girl? They were statues of Vietnamese and Australian soldiers.'

'No, I can't remember that! Really?' Hong-An said. 'Did a lot of Australians die in the war, Mẹ?'

'Let me check,' I said. 'I don't really know.'

I went to the computer and looked it up, returning with the information a moment later with shock and sadness in my heart. I still could not believe that had happened to Australia.

'Yes,' I told her. 'A lot of Australians did die in the Vietnam war. Australia lost five-hundred and twenty-one soldiers!'

'Wow,' Hong-An replied with wide eyes. 'That's so many.'

'America lost many more,' I added. 'Over fifty-eight thousand American soldiers died.'

'What a big loss!' Hong-An gasped.

I was also surprised by the information I'd just found. I was thankful that my father had not been counted as one of the dead soldiers. I knew that he easily could have been one of the many casualties of the war. I felt a sharp chill running up my spine as I thought back to all that I had gone through in that war as a child. I'd always wondered why the American soldiers had allowed themselves to suffer such losses. I had vivid memories of the American soldiers. They had always looked so strong and rich, whereas the Viet Cong didn't even have enough rice to eat. I watched them on television; when Southern soldiers caught them, they all appeared so skinny and tired.

Hong-An and the rest of her young generation had a responsibility to learn about the past. They should know all about the events that had occurred. They should know the history of the world but no matter how much they learned, they would never truly understand what it was like to live through it. Even if she desperately wanted to, my daughter could never truly understand this piece of me. No one could understand the terror and despair that filled our souls. Only those of us who lived through it are capable of fully comprehending those feelings. The ties joining our past to our present are powerful and lasting in each of our stories.

I told her more of our story for the rest of the evening: parts she already knew and some she had forgotten. It felt good to share with her the history that had defined the trajectory of our lives. But despite all that, I told her I would always hide the really grim details of daily from her. She was still my daughter, and I didn't want to contaminate her mind with too much pain despite being happy that she wanted to learn about my past.

I told her how Saigon fell. 'Your grandfather was a nurse in the army, but he was educated as a communist when he was a teenager,' I said. I told her as much as I could remember about those weeks in Saigon when the whole country flipped surprisingly quickly into a new regime. She listened with such earnestness that at times that I burst out crying, not at the memories, but with a sense of pride at the wonderful character of my daughter. Hong-An had been a blessed girl, growing up in this peaceful and beautiful country that all three of us now called home. She was not haunted as I was by the shadows of the war. Memories of pain and suffering did not pollute the ground that she walked on. For this, I was eternally grateful.

The past had led us to the present, so for this I was willing to accept all of my struggles to have arrived now at this beautiful life. A life I could give Hong-An.

CHAPTER TWENTY-ONE

ENCOUNTER WITH VIET CONG

My mother had returned to Da Nang without telling us to test if it was safe to go back. I felt concerned for her safety but was preoccupied with other things. My father had taken to drinking heavily at the apartment in her absence which was one of the few dark shadows of my time in Saigon.

My mother did eventually return safely. She came back with stories of decimated roads and dead bodies along the way. But Da Nang was safe, and our house was as we left it because my grandpa and my relatives had kept the house so well. I didn't want to leave Saigon. I had reinvented myself there and let go of so many of the bad memories from my past. But I had to say goodbye, of course, and after little more than two months in the city, we moved back home. The fear and anxiety that had been so close to the surface during the war now vanished almost as quickly as the Viet Cong had taken over Saigon. The war was over. My family was not going to be killed. We still worried about my father's safety, but it was not the same terrifying, uncontrollable feeling that rose like a nauseating tide at the sound of gunfire or the flash of a picture on TV. We were under a new regime, but we were no longer running for our lives.

I did miss Saigon. I had gotten comfortable with city life during my time there. I had gotten to know some of the soldiers. I had returned every evening to visit the same group of soldiers who always welcomed me with shouts of excitement. I imagined that these men had families and sisters of their own backup North, and to them, I represented family and home. My presence seemed to be healing to them – and me as well. I decided that I had been wrong to be afraid of the Viet Cong. They were all so kind and friendly to me. These weren't the monsters that I had imagined at all. After moving back to Da Nang, I missed these conversations. I missed the hustle and bustle of city life as well.

❤❤❤❤

Our neighbourhood had already begun to organise itself around communist structures.

'Ten families were assigned to be in a group that would support each other and report back any problems,' Aunty Seven explained.

She had become the group leader of our neighbourhood. Young people were required to join one of three groups, depending on their ages. My world was changing fast, but I felt ready to take on these sweeping changes in a way. Having just returned from Saigon, I had more confidence than when I left and a lot of energy for socialising.

From each suburb, a few special young people were selected to be Uncle Ho's Honoured Children. A close friend of mine, Thanh-Van, had already been selected, and I believe she wanted some company in her role. On the way home from school one day, she asked me if I would like to join. I thought of the young men I had met in Saigon and said yes straight away. She put a word in with her big brother, a Youth Leader, and before I knew it, I was one of Uncle Ho's Honourable Children.

I bristled with pride. Uncle Ho was the founder of the communist movement in Vietnam and the leader of the independence movement against France. I didn't know much about politics, but I knew him to be a hero with no wife or children. There were many stories told about his life and sacrifice for his ideals, it was all very inspirational to me. He devoted his life to Vietnamese freedom and peace. Freedom and peace were exactly what my heart had been longing for. I ached for this feeling deep in my soul for as long as I could remember. All the years of pain and suffering had built up in me. Chi Thoi's beatings and the heavy burden of pain my family had bestowed upon me were something that I carried around like a heavy backpack. These were all feelings that I wanted so badly for someone to take from me. I liked Uncle Ho. He had worked so hard for what I really needed for so long. He gave me the feeling that he had the power to lift this heaviness from my shoulders, to carry the burden for me as I walked through life, making me lighter and free.

On the anniversary of his death, I was admitted into the Honour Group in a ceremony that made me feel very blessed and privileged. Blood rushed from my heart to my head with pride, and I made a vow to be faithful to Uncle Ho and serve the country dutifully until my last breath. I had found a new sense of myself that I didn't know existed.

It was not a decision that I ran past my parents, so when I came home that afternoon with an official red scarf tied around my neck, my whole family stared at me in shock.

'Ha-Le has become a Viet Cong!' My big brother exclaimed dramatically. My mother smacked him hard on the back and looked around.

My father looked stupefied and kept shaking his head in disbelief.

'What did you do, princess? What is this?' he asked. And then he burst out laughing and left me with my confusion.

But I didn't care what my family thought. I took great pride in wearing the red scarf around the neighbourhood and was blind to anyone's disapproving stares or what they said about me behind my back. The scarf gave me an empowering feeling and a sense of belonging to something.

My political awareness grew along with my identity as a young woman. I took to wearing hippie tops and short skirts along with the infinitely-robust but stylistically questionable rubber flip-flops known as 'Uncle Ho Sandals.' Chi Oanh had helped me strap my rapidly-growing breasts with material so they would not show through my clothes and bounce around when I was marching in parades.

'Ha-Le, you should be showing them off. Most girls would love to have breasts your size, including me,' she said as we looked at the mirror to check her work. 'Lucky you keep wearing those sandals or the boys would never leave you alone!' Then she added, with a loud laugh, 'Please change your shoes when you go to the movie with me'.

Most of the other youth leaders in my group were sixteen years old, four years older than me. We met at sweet shops or in homes to talk politics, learned rousing communist songs, and had parties at night or on weekends. I discovered Marx and Engels' theories and how they formed their ideas about how to reinvent society by uplifting and empowering poor people. I loved their premise that everyone was equal. How beautiful was that? I had already helped so many poor kids and old people by giving them my mother's money, food and rice when they knocked on our door. How beautiful it was that people could love, care, and be equal to each other. My naïve mind was dancing with my thoughts. My friends convinced me that the Southern Government had strayed too far from the wholesome Vietnamese way of life along with its Western influences. Not only had they lost touch with good traditional values, but they had also become morally corrupt, and the same virus touched everyone associated with them. 'We are all equal,' I would say to myself every day.

One of my responsibilities was to go to rich peoples' houses and find any material related to the old government. 'Old music and literature are contagious to people's minds,' I was told. We would filter through the contents of a house, selecting records, books, papers and clothes and put them in a pile outside and burn them. The youth leader gave us this command. My mother and Chi Oanh told me to stop doing it, but the liberating feeling I would get was too good to give up. I would watch the flames rise higher and imagine all of the pain I had experienced before 1975 burning up with it.

It was like burning up my own pain. I had suffered a lot in the time of the last government, and not only was I helping the country, but I was healing myself. I was healing all my old wounds. I felt like becoming a new person and being in the group strengthened my resolve and sharpened my awareness of myself.

But as the months continued, it was not enough for the authorities to destroy people's contraband belongings. They started to take their houses too. Every family that had worked for the government or the Americans were identified, and a statement was delivered to each of them, giving them a few hours' notices to vacate their house. A piece of paper was then displayed in the front of the house saying: THIS HOUSE BELONGED TO A GROUP OF BAD PEOPLE. IT NOW BELONGS TO THE GOVERNMENT.

I turned a blind eye, but my faith in the party began to dwindle slowly when it happened to my friend. Late one night, the authorities arrived at their house to take it over. The next day, she did not turn up at school, and I heard they had had to move cities to stay with their relatives. I understood that it was for the good of the country, but it also seemed like a contradiction. They were just a typical family, living a relatively simple life. Maybe we were not equal after all.

I started to consider my own family and our vulnerability towards the government. Could they come and take our house? The thought felt like a storm inside my head.

At our group meetings, I would boast about how comfortable we were, thinking only of how our family were lucky and prosperous under the new regime. I mentioned how my mother stored some of her American goods at our house and had an abundance of rice and fabric. My comrades were jealous and would often come to my house and look around as if it was a museum. In fact, it was a relatively simple house, but we were wealthy in comparison. My friends often ate rice with fillers of corn, sweet potato or full oat for the animals from Russia because they could not afford it. They were often hungry and lethargic and spent much more of their time helping their parents with the chores. I had more energy and motivation mostly because my physical needs were generously met.

Luckily, I did not boast to my friends about exactly where my family stashed our gold because, inevitably, the authorities arrived at our house with guns. I was shocked that they had come. They swept through the house and took all of my mother's fabric. But they did not find most of our valuables thanks to my mother's ingenuity. Our dinner table was a massive piece of wood resting on top of a container full of rice. Our gold was in plastic bags in the well and sewage system.

We survived the purge, but it had dislodged something which, until then, I had complete faith in the regime's integrity. By invading our house, I began to think of them more like thieves, who ransacked people's houses and sent the valuables up north to fund their political agenda and the lifestyles of the high-ranking officers.

My enthusiasm for the regime slowly turned into despondency.

Minh-Anh, one of the boys in my class, lost his father when a falling tree crushed him. I cried when I saw him and his mother weeping in front of his father's new altar. And then I overheard my father tell my mother, 'Ha-Le's classmate's father was a high-ranking official in the old government. They killed him for his concern for the country's future.'

They thought I hadn't heard that, but I had, and it made me think.

Chi Oanh, my mentor and idol, had been laughing and teasing me about my allegiance to the regime's ideals. As the pieces of the puzzle started to come together for me, I began to see a much darker picture of communism than the one I had aspired to. I realised that Chi Oanh's playful teasing was actually a compassionate way of telling me she disapproved and was genuinely worried about my views. She was a good friend in so many ways and would often come by to take me out.

'Let's go to the movie! Chi Oanh called out to me from my front gate. I walked down the steps to greet her. I was dressed for being seen, sporting my new black mini skirt which was just short enough to make you look. I had a tight sleeveless top, which was red with flowers that showed off my newfound curves.

'Wow! Your new shoes are beautiful. I like them,' Chi Oanh commented with a big laugh. She was cheeky, of course, and she knew that I had thrown away my Uncle Ho sandals. My new shoes were a political commentary of sorts and she had noticed.

I had begun to channel my faith and rebellious spirit away from the communist party and into myself. Wearing a mini skirt and proper shoes was one way for me to proudly show that I was not a conformist.

I had a new identity. I was not a communist anymore. I was not one of 'Uncle Ho's Good Children.'

I was just me. I was a rebel.

CHAPTER TWENTY-TWO

~

ANGEL? THINK AGAIN!

By grade ten, I had fully shed my commitment to the communist party. The political problems I had hoped to tackle with my fiery enthusiasm collapsed in the face of the painful reality of personal and family issues. Our family had moved to a bigger house in a more respectable suburb. With the bigger house came a higher status for our family. Even within the constriction of communist structures, there was always room for social mobility. My mother needed to protect her wealth in property rather than in plastic bags stuffed into the toilet basin.

Along with the big house came big problems. My parents had moderated their fighting in the last neighbourhood, partly because the consequences were so dramatic. Diligent community members reported dysfunctional families, and drawing attention to your family was not a good idea, especially if your family had secrets. Their anger was bottled up instead, and in the apparent privacy of a bigger house in the suburbs, they let it loose with new and unprecedented volatility. However, in the spacious rooms, their shouting was actually amplified, and certain overly-punctuated words like 'Bastard! Whore! Bitch! Thug!' could be heard right down the street.

My mother vented all of her upset feelings to me. 'Your dad accused me of being a money-making machine and neglecting him. He does not know how hard I work for this family.'

'I was accused by your mother of being a useless drunk, with no sympathy for her hard work. Yes! I have been useless my whole life. What can I do now?' my father got angry when expressing his feeling to me. I was in between and did not know how to react to either of them. I learned how to wear a mask that hid my emotions behind a stoic face to get by in the world.

For the first time in my life, I had my own room. It was such a privilege and a rarity for teenagers that my friends would come to my house, like tourists, to see it. Occasionally, boys would linger a little longer than what was appropriate in my bedroom, but nothing ever happened. I was proud of our relative wealth and the privileges it gave me. I had no shame in flaunting it, and to many, I appeared to be a successful, confident young woman but that was only one side of me. To cover the dark and painful side, I lived a life where my inner and outer worlds did not match.

The identity I presented to the world was outgoing, self-assured, vivacious, ambitious and often cheeky. But this identity was like a veneer, a sweet outside layer that hid my bitter internal struggles. It was like the fancy house that hid my dysfunctional family.

This illusion was something my father shared and used to his advantage. After the war, he did not work for a long time, relying, as we had for most of our lives, on my mother's business skills and superior management of money. He languished in a depressive state, drinking heavily until my mother used her contacts to essentially buy him a job as a secretary in a bicycle factory. They sent him for training in the city, and he became very good at his role. He focused more on his work and drank less, but his problems ran much deeper than that.

My father was very generous. I would be the first person he would give money to, and he would go out of his way to buy me sweets. One day, he told me, 'I am going to the market to buy twelve eggs for you to bake a cake.' Baking a cake was considered an activity of only the most affluent families, and the gesture really showed the extent of his will to give me what I liked. He knew the limitations of his abilities as a father, and it was like he was trying to prove his worth to me through overly generous acts. I accepted them regardless, without too much questioning. However, when he was leaving the house, I noticed he was carrying a large bag full of antiques from around the house. When he saw me, he tried desperately to look natural, further accentuating this guilty demeanour.

Suddenly, the pattern of his behaviour became clear. For a long time, things had been going missing in the house. My mother had opened the cupboard one day to serve tea to guests and yelled, 'Where is all of the good china?'

My father's wage was barely enough to fuel his alcohol habit, let alone buy his daughter expensive treats. I watched him tie the bag sheepishly to his bike and ride off toward the market, a thief from his own family. I felt distraught but also sorry for him, which could only crystallise into burning bitterness. Each time I baked a cake, I dropped many tears in it.

My complicated feelings towards my father became more and more intense. His generosity, it seemed, was also funded by loans from other people. His debtors would sometimes appear at the house, and my mother would be forced to pay them off to avoid losing face.

Sometimes, mysterious ladies would visit the house too, and my father would treat them with the type of kindness and affection that he never employed towards my mother. As the man of the house, people often assumed the wealth was his, and it became clear that this gave my father considerable leverage to charm beautiful young women. His absences and expenses began to point to the fact that he was not just enjoying the attention from women. He was having affairs with them.

Someone told my mother about one particular woman, and their fighting intensified. My mother had no motivation to consider her business and stopped working. She was like the mafia and believed in an eye for an eye, and a tooth for a tooth, so I waited in anticipated dread of what she would do to him. I could see she was planning something and that my younger brother Hung was going to be involved. I had seen her chase my father with a knife and had no wish for it to happen again.

One of the weapons that Mum invented for chasing bad women was detergent mixed with very hot dried chilli. Much to my dismay, she created this weapon for a relative before Saigon's fall. 'When they taste this,' she declared, 'They will not bother your family again.'

When Mum left home at that time, I sent a prayer that my mother's terrible idea would not hurt any woman.

'Oh Ma!' I cried out. 'Stop it with these wicked ideas!'

I was so upset with her. This was the part of my mother that I hated the most. It made me feel scared of her and what she might be capable of. I could imagine how horrible it would be for any woman who encountered my mother's homemade chilli bomb.

I could feel the heat coming from the concoction as my mother mixed all of the ingredients. The burning hot chilli powder mixed with condensed detergent would burn the eyes and face of anyone it was used against.

'No one deserves to have this on their face!' I said to Hung.

My mother gave me goose bumps when she announced, 'They are just lucky that acid is illegal now. The chilli bomb is nothing compared to what I could have done to them!'

My mother's words shocked me. An angel could become a devil in no time at all. My mother had grown angry and bitter from all the pain and jealousy that she was feeling.

'Just pretend to do whatever she asks of you,' I told my brother when seeing my mother's weapon again. 'Don't actually do it.' I was so concerned that I stopped studying to keep an eye on the comings and goings of the household.

Each evening, my father returned late, ate the food that I had prepared, and went to his bedroom. The house felt like a prison, and although I was innocent, I felt I was locked up in solitary confinement, with no one to talk to. Usually, I would have had Chi Oanh to console with. She knew all my secrets and was often an antidote for my loneliness but Chi Oanh had been caught trying to escape from Vietnam and was in prison. Her prison had real bars, but mine felt almost as restricting.

One afternoon, my mother and brother followed my father to a coffee shop after work and observed him sitting with a woman and chatting intimately. Hot-tempered and never afraid of a challenge, my mother watched for a while and then stormed over.

'You never smile at me like that,' she snapped. Moments later, she attacked the other woman.

'Ba had risen, picked up a chair and was about to bring it down on Ma's head when I stepped in.' Hung told me with panic still in his eyes. This event proved that my father had an affair and also proof that my parents' relationship was officially a complete wreck.

'Your parents' relationship has ruined your life!' Chi Oanh commiserated with me. She was well aware of the problems that could come from drama and strife in the family, and she felt a great deal of sympathy for me.

❤❤❤❤

In Vietnamese culture, if your family is a wreck, then it is assumed you are too. I was always tired and unable to concentrate on my schoolwork. I had been accepted into the selective class, where I studied with the smartest people in the school, but the talent which got me accepted started to wane because of the troubles at home. I lost face in front of my classmates. My assignments went undone, I went to school late, slept during the class, my friends looked at me and wondered how I got into a selective class at all.

Many years later, I would sometimes open up to Hong-An, telling her about the hard times of my teenage years but I would only tell her about the things that happened, describing them like details of a news article. I would never really explain how these events made me feel.

My friends began to comment on how skinny I looked. My mother always tried to feed me to help me put on weight, but the food made me feel weaker. I felt like I was in a pressure cooker, along with every negative emotion I had collected since I was in my mother's womb. Every interaction I had with the world was framed through the lens of my problems. I was just waiting for the pressure to blow, like a grenade, and destroy my whole family. Even the confident persona I projected to the outside world lost its fire. My yearning for experience, passion, ambition, and capacity for laughter disappeared, along with my spirit.

I started looking for something new to fill my heart. I needed a distraction, something new to entertain and uplift me. In the midst of depression, and without any role models to advertise the merits of relationships, I nevertheless developed a severe crush on a boy named Thanh. He was two years older than me and in his first year at university. I had been hanging out at my friend Thuy's house, my favourite place to go to avoid being at home when he dropped in to visit her. Thuy and Thanh were next-door neighbours, and they'd grown up together.

'Whatever you do, don't fall in love with him,' Thuy warned. 'We may be friends, and he may look a little bit like a Greek god, but I know his true character, and he is not husband material, OK?'

Greek god was just about right. He was tall and strong, with broad shoulders and a Western nose similar to my father's. She was also right that I would fall for him.

For this brief moment I was happy. I was more than happy. I could feel all of the burdens and distress I had been carrying melting away. My heart no longer had room for sorrow. I only had room for love. This was my very first taste of love as a young woman. I was treasuring and savouring it. But it wasn't love that was reciprocated. All I did was wait for him.

I waited and waited some more.

I waited and waited for him to confess his feelings to me, but the moment never came. I kept waiting until the silence became more and more uncomfortable. At first, I decided he was just shy, but then another more complex thought occurred to me. Perhaps he knew about my situation. Perhaps he knew, through Thuy and probably others, that my family was dysfunctional. Maybe he could tell that I carried with me a curse and that even extending his hand to me would be welcoming disaster and ruin into his own life.

Finally, I told Thuy, 'I've decided I can't wait any longer. I want to write to Thanh a letter telling him I love him and want a relationship with him.'

'No girl does this, Ha-Le,' Thuy said to me. 'Don't be silly!'

'Do it for me!' I commanded. Thuy was unhappy and reluctant, but finally, she gave in, hand-delivered the two handwritten pages to him, and then gravely reported back what he had said.

'She is a silly little girl,' he said to Thuy. 'She should be focusing on her studies rather than falling in love.'

Silly little girl? Thuy's words shocked me with deep hurt and shame. He had shown so many signs of liking me, and yet he'd rejected me. He wasn't the man I thought he was. It was very confusing, and the love story I had built up in my imagination began to fall apart. His reproach felt like a physical blow to me, knocking out all of the little energy I had and opening up all of the old wounds I already had inside me. My body was broken into little pieces, and so when he saw me again, the girl who had expressed her unrequited romantic notions indeed did appear like a silly little girl. These were my first feelings of love, but it was also my first broken heart. But in some ways, this broken heart was also a gift; it set the tone for what I would later look for in a husband. After that horrible dismissal of my feelings, I knew that a Greek god was not the best man to care for my tender heart.

My broken heart, combined with all of my other anxieties, led me to terrible marks at school. My situation, and my marks, only deteriorated further the next year. Everyone was studying madly to get into university, even though we all knew that our career prospects in communist Vietnam were bleak. I had no focus at all, and though I placed the blame squarely on Thanh's rejection, it was the accumulation of a thousand different forces which had been at work in my life.

I was not surprised when I failed the university exam. I couldn't forgive myself for wasting my academic opportunities. For what? What did I have to show for all the struggles I had endured? My classmates were singing and writing in each other's journals. I read what they had written in mine later that evening. It was all very positive and encouraging, and I was moved by how much they liked me. But I also felt guilty for failing. Every other person in my class had gotten into university. I, however, had no university acceptance. All that I had was uncertainty. I had dreamed of becoming a biologist. Biology was the subject I enjoyed the most, and I imagined myself helping to develop crops to stop people from going hungry. I had to admit to myself that I was not equipped to look after myself, let alone other people. I fell into a deep, lonely depression, which in those years in Vietnam had no name and no cure.

When facing the external war, I had my whole family with me, but I was completely and utterly alone when I was dealing with the internal war inside myself. No one could help me escape. I had no other choice but to carry this burden. My family's slow destruction carved out my path in life. This was the path that I followed as a young girl, as a teenager, and now as a woman. This was, perhaps, what had led me to my strong feelings for Thanh, as I had my first dance to the rhythm of love. This attention enriched my youth and added a new depth of feeling to my life. My soul expanded with that experience, even if my pride was wounded and my heart fractured in the process. I kept moving forward in life, taking it all as a learning experience. I stored it up inside of me.

CHAPTER TWENTY-THREE

~

HE IS FAMILY TOO?

As I walked with Minh through the university car park, the sight of happy families made me almost unable to keep going. Sydney had delivered another beautiful day for Hong-An's graduation ceremony, but inside of me, it was cold and raining. I waded through the flood, past beaming daughters who walked arm in arm with their proud mothers and fathers. Their smiles, their laughs of excitement, and their intimate conversations all seemed to be aimed at me.

Minh looked sad and miserable, walking beside me. I had to handle my pains as usual, but I also had to try to comfort Minh. He had no idea how much I needed him to lift me.

I suddenly remembered what I had told Thuy and the rest of our group of friends years ago when they'd asked me why I had accepted Minh's proposal of marriage. 'I chose him to protect me,' I said.

I also recalled the words that Minh had spoken when he'd made his poignant proposal. 'You will be in my arms, and we will laugh every night, Ha-Le.'

One thousand stories had never happened. They were still in my dreams.

The area outside of the auditorium was peppered with balloons, and triumphant classical music whispered from somewhere within. I was reminded of the many trips to the library we had had together throughout her life. We would walk home together, our carefully selected books heavy in our arms. When she was very young, we struggled through children's books in English together, but it did not take her long to surpass my abilities. After that, it was Hong-An who would be dragging me to the library and explaining all of the amazing things she learned back to me in Vietnamese. When Minh began his PhD research, she travelled with him to the university library after school and on weekends. She happily browsed and wandered through the shelves of books.

She had been so proud on the day of Minh's graduation, and now the tables were turned, except our pride was a lonely pride.

Oh! This university brought me back so many memories. Both sweet and painful.

On Minh's PhD graduation day, I could not walk properly due to my severe insomnia and anxiety. My preschool was at risk of closing down after only two months of being opened. Poor Minh! On his special and important day, he had mixed feelings of worries and joy. I was his biggest supporter, but I was very ill and could not share his great academic success with him. There were only three of us together to share Minh's graduation. Now Hong-An had her turn, and our family was divided into two groups.

We approached the hall and joined the last of the thousand-strong crowd as they made their way inside. We had just made it on time. When the fanfare began and the graduates entered from the back of the room, I scanned the procession earnestly for Hong-An. Minh, who had been sad for days, joined me in my search, the flame of his motivation suddenly back to life with the hope of seeing his daughter. We had almost given up, and for a second, the horrible thought came to my mind that she had chosen not to attend. But there she was, tiny in her graduation gown and hat, like a thinner, paler version of the girl we knew so well. Even from a distance, we could see that her skin was unhealthy and her cheeks hollow. Her plump lips and beautiful smile had become dry and sullen. The clothes hung off her. She was nothing but a withered core of the fresh apple that she'd been only six weeks ago, the last time we saw her.

'Where are you, and what are you doing now, Hong-An?' I wondered.

I remembered my mother's panic, counting each one of us when the bombs and gunfire ripped the city of Saigon apart. I'd heard her maternal fear, her absolute torment at the thought of losing one of her children. I felt that same torment now. It was wrenching me apart. I was living in another war now, a war of separation and disappointment. This was an exceptional moment in my daughter's life, and I hardly felt like I was even a part of it. I was losing her; I could feel it.

My knees went weak at the sight, and I burst out crying.

'Are you happy crying or sad crying?' Hong-An would say to me when she was young enough not to know the difference. It was sad. Pure sad. People around me started to cry as well, moved by my unintentionally emotional performance. I think they thought I was overcome with joy, and perhaps somewhere in my emotional state, there was some joy. But it was entirely overshadowed by a brutal, visceral pain so encompassing that I found myself on my knees, shaking and unable to breathe.

Minh pulled me back up by my arm.

'Stop embarrassing everyone,' he snapped, though I could see he too was holding back tears. His upper lip trembled.

I calmed myself down when they were finally seated, and the proceedings began. 'Minh, she looks five years older than when we last saw her,' I whispered, tugging at his blazer.

'Be quiet!' he replied, twisting away from me. 'It's beginning.'

I heard almost nothing of the ceremony. Instead, I sat and composed my speech to my daughter. 'Congratulations, darling. We are so proud of you. I know things are tough between us, but everything that has happened is now in the past. It is time for you to come home. Let me cook for you and look after you. Let me bring you back to health and happiness. We can build everything again together and let the past go.'

A past graduate delivered her final remarks, and a few of the words drifted into my reverie '...bring together all of your knowledge and serve the world.' How could my daughter serve the world if she was not healthy herself? If she was exhausted by caring for her unwell partner.

'I have no more room in my heart for anger,' I continued in my imagined speech. 'Just love for you and for Travis too,' I shook my head. It was the right thing to say, but I know I did not mean it. I had no love for Travis, and the thought of seeing him in the foyer after the ceremony made me bristle with anger and resentment again. I did have room for anger towards him, so it seemed, but not for my daughter. If I could have flown across the auditorium and lifted her, I would have done it straight away. I would have carried her across the city to our house, where a feast would be waiting. I would have carried her across oceans, again, just to save her from the life she had before her.

But I could not fly. I just edged closer as the graduates were leaving the room. I caught her eye briefly then, but the recognition was cold, and she did not smile or wave. She just pointed outside as if to say, 'Calm down Mẹ! We'll meet outside.'

Outside was the madness of champagne, flowers and happy families, and Travis, no doubt. Minh nudged me and whispered to remember our agreement. We would persevere with Travis's presence in order to see our daughter, but we would not acknowledge him at all. We would act as if he didn't exist, in an icy display of rejection. However, when I saw him from a distance, I was instantly upset. Just before they saw us, I realised that Hong-An was the only girl in the room without flowers. Travis had empty hands too, and the thought of my daughter with nothing was too much to bear. I took a slight detour to buy the biggest bunch of flowers available and a surprisingly expensive teddy bear with a graduation gown on.

Travis greeted us, but we had eyes only for our daughter. Hong-An did not open her arms to hug us and only accepted my flowers reluctantly.

'Sorry, I forgot to get you something,' Travis said to Hong-An, who immediately neutralised his error with a smile and a shrug.

'Your presence is all I need, darling,' she said.

Her words fuelled my anger. How quickly you forgive him, I thought, and how stubbornly you punish your parents.

The four of us stood in awkward silence, staring at the bear in Minh's hand.

'Your mother bought you this,' Minh said finally, absolving himself of any responsibility for the gift that Hong-An clearly did not want.

'OK. Thanks, Mẹ.' she said quietly.

Better to regret going than to not go at all, I reminded myself forcefully.

'Let's get graduation photos done,' I announced.

'No Mẹ, it's expensive. Don't waste your money,' Hong-An pleaded.

Nothing was too expensive if it meant that we could salvage this moment and wrangle it into a positive memory, I thought.

On the way over to the photo room, many of Hong-An's friends greeted us. I wished that I had a mask. I could not bear their polite greetings. I was sure they all knew about our situation.

As we took our places in the line, I turned to talk to my daughter.

'Please come home with us, Hong-An. I can cook you anything you want. All of your favourite food,' I said, summoning up my confidence.

Hong-An kept her eyes forward in the line. 'It's OK. I'm tired. I think I will just go back to mine and rest,' she said. She looked tired, but I could tell that she just wanted to avoid the significance of agreeing to come home.

Travis took the opportunity to score a point. 'I'll cook for you then.'

'Oh, thank you, darling. That is very thoughtful,' she replied, unable to manage the now-obvious battle being waged for her approval.

Thankfully for everyone, it was then our turn, and the photographer took control.

'OK, just the graduate first. Thank you. And where are Mum and Dad? OK. One on either side. Beautiful. Now the whole family,' he looked around, and

Travis was the only one left. Minh and I froze quietly in our already-contrived smiles. The whole family? Travis was not yet our family, and we hoped that he would never be. But Hong-An beckoned him into the frame and, under the gaze of the strangers around us and the weight of civility, we did not protest.

We returned home without my daughter. Just the two of us. We walked through the front door and immediately to separate rooms, Minh to his study and me to Hong-An's bedroom. The house felt so big, and I felt a cold wave of realisation that this could be my future. Without Hong-An to glue us together, we were just two people living separate lives, struggling with our various problems. I went to my daughter's wardrobe and smelt her clothes again in an effort to invoke her presence, but all I found was the sobering scent of detergent. Her room was exactly as she left it, in every precise detail.

On the wall hung a picture of the three of us, with Hong-An looking so pretty. Her beautiful smile with sweet plump lips tore at my heart. I just wished that I was dreaming and would wake up finding my happy family was still the same, but, in reality, my daughter was gone.

I had suffered so much in youth, and this was what caused me to work so hard to keep Hong-An safe from suffering. My mother had never known what I needed as a child. I hadn't had my emotional needs met. How could I give my daughter something that I'd never had? Maybe it was impossible.

I had hoped that by finding the strength to attend her graduation, I would mend something that was broken. I had imagined that we would return home with our collective wounds safely wrapped in the past, with no intention to open them again. But in the end, all that effort to swallow my pride and stand smiling for photographs was without any real payoff. Nothing was healed. The pieces still laid shattered on the floor.

I had allowed myself to imagine for some time that with my daughter graduating from university, she would have more time to spend with me. This was something she had promised me since year ten. This was what we had always talked about. It was time to see her get out into the big world, working as a successful woman with my job as a mother with a contented smile. It was time I cried out, 'Whoo-hoo!' to celebrate our victorious journey together. It was time for me to see her hand-in-hand with a healthy boy and then a beautiful, fairy-tale wedding. I now had to settle on the realisation that there was a new future ahead, one that I had never imagined.

CHAPTER TWENTY-FOUR

HANDSOME MEN PHOBIA

Hong-An never knew how she had trained me to be a good wife to her father.

With Minh, it was not 'love at first sight.' In fact, when I first saw him, I thought he was weird. He walked into the classroom like some kind of short, long-haired alien. He was completely different from anyone I had ever seen before in my life.

I had been taking evening English classes mostly as a distraction to keep me motivated and going on with life. In school, I had always received good grades in English, but in reality, I retained nothing except a passion for the subject. The classes were filled with postgraduates and young working people, and it offered more socially than it did academically. People joined to make friends and even to find boyfriends and girlfriends. I was one of the youngest in the class, along with my neighbour Huong, the two of us enjoyed lots of attention from the wandering eyes of the male students.

The class was a new community for me, an open field for socialising. It gave me a fresh start to reinvent myself, as nobody there knew about my family situation. I acted like a spoilt, hard-to-get princess and was treated the same way in return.

Huong liked to poke fun at me, and upon seeing Minh, she started making jokes and trying to get a rise out of me.

'He's the perfect one for you, Ha-Le,' she whispered with a giggle. I whacked her on her back.

I observed the funny little alien again, who, it turned out, was not a student but our substitute teacher for the evening. He was very short and hunchbacked, with thick glasses. He was oddly proportioned, but his stature did not limit his expressiveness. As he taught, he jumped around like a spring, demonstrating words and sentences like a comedic character in an amateur theatre production. Periodically, he would shift his glasses up, and they would slide down his nose again with the force of his jerky movements. He looked like someone who would never find a girlfriend, and I felt sorry for him.

'Him?' I replied dramatically. 'Never! Not Ever! How could you even think that?'

'But he's that guy. He's the famous English teacher that all the university students are in love with and you're both the same height,' she teased.

'Why don't you take him? He's a little bit taller than you,' I retorted.

'He is definitely for you,' Huong affirmed, giggling again.

I looked again at his long curly hair and oversized head. This time he caught me observing him and smiled. This was not the hero of my imagination. Not even close. How could he be the catch of the university?

That night, he made the English class come alive, and we had a lot of fun. Nobody wanted the lesson to end. Everyone talked a lot about him and his academic qualifications and could not wait to have him again.

But it was true. Minh was the centre of attention amongst the female university students, and, as the stories went, he could pick and choose one among them. He came from a good family, and he already had a good reputation in the academic world. His teaching style was second to none. I was impressed by his teaching but didn't really think any more about him until I saw him at a Christmas party hosted by one of the students. It was on the rooftop of a fancy house, and we had been having a great time for hours already. I was wearing a beautiful white dress and felt like the special girl at the party.

Minh walked through the crowd like he was a rock star. Everybody wanted to greet him and spend time with him outside of the classroom, and he was generous with his attention. I estimated he was at least five years older than me, but it was hard to say.

I watched his progress around the party and how the girls acted cutely around him, flashing their eyelashes and playing with their hair. With remarkably executed charm, he gave every girl at the party a lolly – every girl except me. I pretended not to care, but as the night went on, everyone else seemed to be having fun and laughing while I had become anxious and grumpy.

In the end, it was me who approached him.

'Where is my lolly, sir?' I asked as he walked over to me. 'How could you have missed the prettiest girl at the party?'

I had intended to sound cross, but the words came out with the same flirtatious undertone I had observed in the other girls. Wow, I thought. Maybe he really does have special powers.

'Oh, I'm sorry, I just didn't notice you,' he teased, allowing his eyes to travel down the full length of my dress to my naked legs. 'Hey, I remember you. You were the girl in that class who looked at me with disapproving eyes.'

Luckily, he had not seen my tongue out at him when he turned his back to write on the blackboard.

His confident manner of speaking affronted me but didn't put me off. His voice was very warm, and the way he spoke hinted at multiple layers of meaning as if he had a whole dictionary inside him and was playfully flipping through the pages.

He continued with a smile, 'I remember you put up your hand to answer my question, but I pretended not seeing you with a purpose of teasing you.'

The cheeky girl in me, who had all but disappeared in the last few years, returned on cue. 'Now, my lolly, please.'

I held out my hand, and he looked at it with a mischievous grin. He reached inside his corduroy jacket, which was several sizes too big for him, and pulled out a lolly.

He winked and leaned in a little closer, so only I could hear and said, 'I have only one lolly left for you. You are the most beautiful girl here, and ignoring you was the only way to get your attention.'

I covered my mouth automatically, embarrassed at his flirtation. He bowed and left the party, leaving me standing alone, wishing that the conversation had not ended.

During the Vietnamese New Year, in keeping with tradition, my English class visited each other's houses as a group. Someone suggested that we include Minh's house on the tour.

'He's so fun to be with and talk to,' they reasoned. I disagreed.

Minh lived with his parents in a big house. On that day, I wore a red dress, and he stared at me when our group went in.

'I saw you all from outside, and my older brother Bao told me to try to get the red dress girl,' Minh confessed later. He had not prepared much for the New Year but made up for it with an energetic conversation, and our group livened up in his presence. He then joined us on our travels from house to house.

My house was the final stop on our New Year tour. We had saved the best for last. My family had gone overboard with New Year preparations, and my friends gorged themselves on the food. Minh engaged everyone in conversation vigorously, and as the crowd left, it became apparent he was not in a hurry to leave with them.

'You are welcome to stay longer if you'd like,' I said to Minh politely. It was customary to extend a generous welcome and good luck to the family hosting someone of his reputation. In truth, I had remembered feeling lifted by our last conversation at the party and wanted to experience it again, just the two of us.

'If it pleases you, then, of course, I will stay,' he said, saying goodbye to the last guest who gave us both a quizzical glance.

The house was suddenly tranquil.

'What do you think of my flower arrangements?' I asked, gesturing for him to sit down. Minh studied a nearby bunch intensely as if it carried within it the secrets of the universe.

'The break from tradition shows a rebellious nature and a creative flair. But the attention to detail gives away your respect for order and form. Still, there is something haphazard about it. It's like you have so many thoughts in your mind that compete with each other.'

He looked up from the flowers and directly into my eyes. 'Taken together, there is a striking beauty, but one composed of complex, even troubled, parts. Am I right?'

I felt exposed before him as if his deconstruction of my flowers had also removed my clothes. For a moment, I almost told him everything: that my parents were planning to get a divorce, that my younger brother had gotten into gambling and had started to steal gold in order to support his habit. I almost told him that I failed the university entrance exam and even studied a second time and felt like a failure for not getting into university. That I carried within me as pain. That it wore me down so much, I felt tired all the time and yet was unable to sleep at night. That I had been seriously considering this New Year as my last New Year and had fantasised about ways I could take my life. I almost told him everything, but I stopped myself.

'You were right about the beautiful part,' I said, but the way he looked at me revealed that he knew he had been right about it all.

'I assume that someone so beautiful already has a boyfriend?'

I thought of Thanh, who had all but abandoned me but still represented the man of my dreams.

'No, I have hundreds of admirers, but no one has stolen my heart.'

Somehow, although there was no physical attraction, Minh had the ability to inspire flirtatious conversation in me. The attraction was a multi-layered phenomenon, I realised. The feelings stirring around this strange man were more profound, as the mysterious and slightly dangerous undercurrents in a river.

'Very interesting,' he said. 'So, what are you looking for in a boyfriend?'

It was the kind of question Chi Oanh would have asked me. Her being in prison had left a big hole in my life.

'Someone at least five years older than me. Someone who I can respect and admire as a mentor. Someone who can inspire me in the good times and protect me in the bad times...' I left off the bit about being tall and strong because he had risen in his chair with each listed attribute and I did not want to deflate him. Minh was charming and smart, but he had the features of an awkward teenage boy trapped in a man's body. His greatest physical attribute was indeed his head, but only because it housed his remarkable brain.

'Very interesting. Well, perhaps the universe has arranged it already.'

'Maybe a doctor. I'd like someone to look after me when I am sick,' I said. Even as I described my perfect partner to Minh, I was thinking about Thanh. Minh was growing on me. My interest in him was growing stronger, but I still held onto my feelings for Thanh. He was so different from Minh. Was it possible for me to be attracted to two men who were so entirely different from one another?

'Well, if not a doctor, then a man who can carry you to the doctor in his arms,' Minh replied. He melted my heart at that moment; he showed me that he would care for me with these simple words.

Minh had a way of asking questions that inspired openness and more in-depth conversation, and he asked plenty of them.

'I wonder what it's like for you, being the only girl in your family. What do you enjoy about your studying, and if you could meet yourself in ten years' time, what would you say?'

I felt like this man could be my counsellor. A wise, trustworthy guide and supportive friend in a world often felt like it was too much for me to bear. He was the most exceptional man I met in my life. Our conversation only stopped because I could hear my mother and father downstairs in their opening stages of a fight that would soon rattle the floorboards and expose too many of my family troubles.

Minh brought me twenty-one roses on the morning of my twenty-first birthday. My brother had opened the door and invited him in, but Minh had insisted that he did not want to see me. One rose was expensive at that time. Twenty-one was too much. There was a note attached which read, in English:

'Happy Birthday. Even twenty-one roses are no match for your beauty. Sorry I cannot make it to the party. P.S. Please excuse my inferior flower arrangement.'

It took me ten minutes with the dictionary to work out what he meant.

I had thrown a party for myself and invited all of the people from my English class, including Minh. He had decided not to come but offered a very expensive gift as an apology. I did not see it as a, particularly romantic gift. Part of me blindly insisted that this man was destined to be a mentor, not a lover.

My type was still Thanh, tall, strong, and handsome like my father. Minh was precisely the opposite, and yet he left me with a strange desire. I was captivated, almost against my will, by his manner and his apparent ability to listen to me and understand me.

At the party, we played a game where each boy took an Italian biscotti and went across the room to invite a girl to share it with him. In Vietnamese culture, it was about as risqué as we got in public. It would have been the perfect gesture for Thanh to show me, without words, that he was now ready to take me as his girlfriend. In slow motion, I watched him offer his biscuit to Thao. She gave me a genuine look of shock, which spread around the group like a cold shiver, leaving me publicly rejected at my party. The tiny threads that had kept my heart from failing completely broke the instant she took the biscuit. All of my friends looked at me with pity in their eyes.

I made a decision at that moment. I would stop yearning after handsome men. I wanted a man with a beautiful soul, a man who would cherish and appreciate me. I needed a kind heart to rescue me from the deep darkness in my life.

The one person I thought of who might console me had not even come to my party. When everyone had left, I looked at Minh's roses, one for every year of my life, as if they were painful reminders of all the losses and heartaches I had endured. At that moment, Thanh and Thao and all my other friends seemed so young, carefree, and ultimately shallow. I felt like I was drowning alone in a sea of sorrow, but there was a small, broken piece of wood that, if I could hang on to it, might just keep me afloat.

That piece of wood was Minh.

~

CHAPTER TWENTY-FIVE

I FOUND SOMETHING TO LONG FOR

Minh and I had been through so much together. We had struggled through an incredible life journey, clinging to each other as we fought to escape Vietnam in search of a better life. I thought back to the tumultuous beginning of our relationship.

I remembered the rainy season in Da Nang; the humidity builds throughout the day, making everything progressively hotter and more laborious. Just before the water tumbles from the sky, all the neighbourhood dogs start to stir, barking at the change in pressure or some other invisible force that humans have forgotten how to sense. Then, with only a few seconds to spare, an abrupt cool breeze whistle through the city, signalling the street vendors to lift their umbrellas and the motorbike drivers to stop and magically whip out hidden raincoats. The heavens open up and flood the partially-drained roads, and for a mad hour, it seems like the world is ending.

The years I stayed in the bigger house were like a gathering storm that never broke. The layers of pain, fear, and stress built up like humidity that could not be released. The pressure increased each day until finally, I was one hundred per cent ready to explode. I spent countless nights, unable to sleep, imagining that if the storm inside me broke, it would flood the whole city permanently, and everyone would drown with me.

My mother had stopped doing her business completely, swapping it for a full-time job and scolding my father at home. My father spent more and more time in the village where he grew up, promising us that he would use some of our gold to start a farm. In reality, my mother said, he was just setting himself up to drink with his cousins and uncles.

It was a hopeless relationship, and one day my father announced that he had submitted a request for divorce to the court. I was one signature away from being a girl with no future. The fight my parents had that night could have been their best performance ever, but I was avoiding it in my room. I had given up thinking that I could save them from themselves. They were engaged in a battle of their own destruction, and I did not have the willpower or the strength to intervene.

After a lull in the shouting, my mother burst into my room, crying.

'What can I do?' she snapped at me. 'Your father wants to take half our possessions. I hate him, but I don't want him to stop being your father. If we divorce, it won't be long before another woman steals your father. He'll have another life. Another family even, and he will forget you and your brothers. No one will want to marry you if you have a broken family. Everyone looks down on girls without a father.'

Her anger was for my father but seemed to be directed at me, and I felt it transforming the pain inside me to a white-hot rage. I thought of Chi Thoi and my father and her fierce curse.

'The damage is already done,' I said coldly. 'No one will ever marry me anyway. The whole world knows who I am.'

'Well, you can thank your father for that.'

The rage was like a volcano now, and my mother's words exposed a break in the surface.

'Mum, you have to wake up!' I yelled. 'The problems come from you too. Dad drinks and has affairs, but you have your own problems.'

She glared at me, daring me to continue.

The lava came up in a blistering explosion of fire. 'You left us alone when we were young. You never stopped Chi Thoi from beating us. I had to live in two different worlds in confusion, a princess to Dad and you but a slave to Chi Thoi. You are a mother, but you never knew the pain and shame I felt within our family. You...' I paused briefly. 'You two should never have been together! All you've ever done is fight and be horrible to each other! There has never been any improvement in your relationship. If you finally divorce, at least my brothers and I can have some peace!'

I let all of these angry words spill out of me. The volatile words shot out of my mouth like gunfire. I let loose of all the rage and shame that had been burning me from the inside out.

I remembered clearly in my mind the horrible night that the two men held me upside-down in the well. My mother never knew about that. I'd also figured out through my parents fighting that, on that terrifying night, my mother went out to sell herself to feed us and to buy a house for us. Those secrets stayed festering inside me, giving me horrible pain, and my mother never knew.

It was too much. My mother reacted as anyone would when the secrets of their life are spit back at them. She slapped me hard across the face and dragged me by the hair off the bed. I fell onto the floor. The shock silenced me and brought me back from the furnace. That was the first and only time that my mother had ever struck me.

When she saw me on the floor, her anger gave way to tears, and we both cried in silence. She took a deep breath, and her face settled into a miserable, bitter expression.

'You are on your father's side. You don't even love me!' she shouted. 'All I have done is sacrifice for this family, and what do I get for all of my hard work? I get to stand here and be insulted by you, Ha-Le?! Why don't you appreciate all that I've done?!'

'Your sacrifice doesn't take me anywhere, Ma. All it does is press me into darkness.' I intended to say but decided to be quiet. I did not want to hurt her any more than I already had. I watched her, shaking with rage, her hands clasped tightly at her sides. I didn't reply, and a moment later, she turned on her heels and marched out of my room.

If her words were designed to make me feel guilty, they didn't. They brought up my anger again, but the volcano had closed over, and it had nowhere to go. I had spent my whole life loving my mother. I knew she loved me, but I rarely felt compassion from her, and the longing for the fruit of our love was one of the only constant things in my life. For her to deny me was unforgivable.

The anger and hurt burned in me for the rest of the afternoon, searing away any remaining tenderness I had for myself and my family. All that was left then was one brutal reality: I could not continue living. I knew, with blinding clarity, that my life could not get any better. The joys I had experienced so far were all in the past.

The pain I had experienced would just grow and grow until it overtook me and spread to the people around me. My life was over anyway. I knew what I needed to do. There was nothing else left for me. I knew that I had to find a way to kill myself. I had lost so many people that I loved throughout my life, and the people who remained in my life, my mother and father, continued to let me down, over and over again. But it wasn't just my family, the friends that I loved disappeared from my life, and Thanh had rejected me. I was starting to see who the actual problem was.

The problem was me.

I was unlovable, and no matter how hard I tried, I would always end up abandoned and alone. I felt powerless to stop this cycle. I remembered every loss and rejection, going all the way back to the time that I was three years old. I had stored up each of these rejections. They were brewing and bubbling over inside of my heart. I could see now what my place in the world was; it was a cold and lonely place, and I didn't want to stay there for the rest of my life. I didn't want to fight for survival any longer. I couldn't. I felt weak like there was no more fight left in me. I was ready to let go. I was prepared to let go of everything. This world was not a place I wanted to remain.

I decided that killing myself was not a selfish thing to do. It would be good for everyone. I thought that my suicide would be the wake-up call my parents needed, and they would change to become better parents for my brothers. They would love each other and be fair to each other. They would wholly devote themselves to our family. My suicide would bring everyone closer together, and through it, I would free myself from my pain as well. Yes, this really would be best for everyone.

Calmly, I considered my options. Poison, hanging myself from one of the big trees outside in the garden, jumping from a bridge, cutting myself. If I had a bottle of pills by my bed, I might have swallowed them all right then. My mother would find me in a few hours with my tongue rolling out of my mouth and my eyes staring lifelessly at the ceiling. She would scream and rush over, shaking me and hugging me, regretting right then and forever all of the sufferings she had caused me.

It could be that my little brothers would find me. No! I loved them dearly and didn't want to hurt them. That made me more tearful and uncomfortable, so I stood up with a new sense of determination. If I was going to die, it couldn't be tonight, and it couldn't be at home. I had to leave immediately.

My younger brothers looked so sad when I told them I was leaving. I had been responsible for their well-being all their lives, but they were not happy. I had failed them. Maybe it made no difference if I looked out for them. Perhaps they would be better off without me, I thought.

I told Hai to go next door and tell my friend Huong to open her window. Then, I packed a bag of clothes, threw it into her bedroom from my window, walked calmly out the door and into her house. I was running away from home, but it appeared that I was just going next door to my family.

Huong took one look at me and started crying. Perhaps she sensed my resolve or felt my frustration and was overcome with a protective concern for me. She gave me my bag, along with some money, and told me to be careful. 'Where are you going?' she asked.

I had no plan at all other than leaving my house, so I just said the first thing that came to my mind.

'I'm going to ride to teacher Minh's house.'

Minh was surprised to see me at the door. He had tried to visit me over the last few weeks since my party, but I had been too miserable to accept him into the house. For a moment, he did not seem like the famous, charming teacher I knew and was just a man opening the door to a stranger.

'Sir, I have come to say goodbye,' I said.

'Goodbye? How about you start with hello?' I did not smile or laugh at his words, and he realised the situation was serious.

'What's the matter? Come in, please. Leave your bike against the wall!' He said, taking my bag and ushering me into his house.

I didn't even sit down before I started talking. 'It is all too much to bear. This is the best option. To be free.'

Minh shook his head. 'To be free from what?'

He wasn't getting it.

'From life, Sir. Honestly, there is nothing left for me in this life. I have no future.'

Minh rubbed his eyes as if trying to shake away a dream. Then he looked at me again with concern.

'What you need, at this moment, more than anything is sweet soup.'

I had been crying, I realised, and despite my resolve to end my life, he was right. Somehow, amidst my despair, that was exactly what I wanted.

He took me to a nearby dessert shop, ordered me the biggest dish and leaned across the table.

'Everything has a solution,' he said. 'Whatever you are going through can be worked out. It doesn't mean it will be easy or that you won't need help from other people, but you will work it out. Trust me.'

He spoke with such sincerity and wisdom that I did trust him, but I was sure he didn't understand my situation.

'Sir, I'm not the girl you think I am. Everyone thinks of me as a beautiful, lucky young woman with lots of promise and opportunity.'

'But it's more complicated than that,' he said, finishing my sentence. 'People are more complicated than that. Families are more complicated than that.'

Any restraint I had from exposing my family's secrets had evaporated in my anger earlier that night. In that sweet shop, I told him all of my problems. I even told him about Chi Thoi and my father. He listened carefully, nodding his head and adjusting his glasses. Occasionally, he took his glasses off to wipe tears from his eyes. He did not cut me off or offer any advice. When I stopped speaking, we were the only people in the restaurant.

'You must be embarrassed to be here with me,' I added.

'Firstly, let me say that I am sorry that you had to go through all that. You didn't deserve it. And secondly, I am not embarrassed in the slightest. In fact, I am the opposite. I already did my research on you. I could see your suffering through your smile almost instantly, but it only drew me towards you. I have heard every rumour about you and your family from your schoolmates. Some seem to be true. Some are definitely exaggerated, and some are even more controversial than expected.'

I swallowed hard. Had he done his research? My friends had exposed everything they knew. What rumours were going around? Did they tell Minh that my father chased my mother with a hammer?

'Before you freak out,' he said, 'I want to tell you that none of that makes me feel ashamed to be here with you. Every single person I know has shameful secrets that they carry around, especially since the war. Almost none of them are responsible for it.' He took a sip from the iced tea that had, until now, remained untouched in front of him.

'I'm not any different,' he continued. 'I'm not saying you have not suffered incredibly. Clearly, your suffering has led you to the absolute edge of your perseverance. If I could take away all your burdens and have them as my own, I would do that right now. It's not up to me to give advice. Trust me, I am no angel of wisdom. But I will say that you have to think about the people who care for you in situations like this. Your brothers, for instance.'

I knew that he was right. I couldn't give up and abandon my siblings. I missed my two younger brothers dearly. They also missed me a lot too.

What I thought about, across the table from Minh, was that I had finally found the big brother I longed for. He already knew all my secrets, and yet, he was not put off by them. Instead, he reached out to me with protective energy that I had not felt before. This small, strange man suddenly appeared to me as an unlikely hero of strength, and from that moment, I wanted to spend as much time with him as I could.

Minh cleared his throat and paid for the dessert. 'But right now, we must attend to practical matters. Like where you are going to stay if you are running away from home.'

'I want to go to the countryside to focus on studying for my university's exams. To get away from the city. My father's relatives will look after me if I go out to his homeland.'

Minh pulled out a few large banknotes and pushed them across the table. 'This should cover the bus fare, although it's late now. Perhaps you have missed the bus.'

I had. There was only one bus a day, and it had left in the morning. 'Do you have any other relatives in town? he asked.

I remembered a cousin, the eldest daughter of my father's sister, and we rode to her house together in a flash. My aunt was there too, and they welcomed me in and convinced me not to go to the countryside.

'There is no electricity there,' they said, 'and there are no sweet shops.'

For the second time that night, I felt protected and understood. Minh stayed for a little while until it was clear that I was comfortable.

'Is he your boyfriend?' my cousin asked when he had gone.

Her eyes were alive with the promise of gossip.

'No. He's my teacher. But also, kind of like my big brother.'

I looked her squarely in the eyes and saw she did not believe me.

'He's just a friend,' I confirmed.

'Well, he likes you. No man chases a lady like that without a purpose, so if you don't like him back, don't give him hope.'

I laughed and then yawned, the trauma of my day fading into tiredness. 'It's not like that. He's just an open and caring gentleman,' I hugged my cousin goodnight.

'Of course, he is...'

In the dark of the night, I was feeling a renewed sense of hope. I had a glimmer of motivation. Through my pain, I'd found something to long for. Maybe I could overcome this after all. Perhaps I was much stronger than I knew.

CHAPTER TWENTY-SIX

~

I DON'T AGREE WITH HER

Later that evening, Hong-An's graduation was still playing out in my mind, getting out of bed to cook dinner for myself, and Minh took all the strength I could muster. What would happen, just once, if I did not cook for him? I asked myself.

I was so exhausted, both emotionally and physically, that getting up to cook gave me feelings of absolute misery. All that I wanted to do was shut out the world and sleep, but my duty as a wife led me to cook his meal, even when I had almost no motivation. I was miserable, but I didn't want to neglect a family member because of my negative feelings. I had to push through and do what was right.

So, I cooked for Minh, hoping to comfort him with my food. I knew that he needed a distraction from his feelings of missing Hong-An, just as much as I did.

I watched him eat and tried to remember him as a younger man. In those days, when he was courting me, it seemed his life goal was to be attentive and supportive. He would regularly appear at my cousin's house, with snacks and presents, and take me out to cafes and restaurants. He would sit and listen to my troubles as if just the sound of my voice satisfied his hunger. He knew all about my family history and, while other men would run a mile, it brought him closer. I looked forward to his visits at my cousin's apartment. I lost my desire to kill myself and found comfort and inspiration in my conversations with him. Our relationship had progressed from there, and over the years, we'd come to understand each other better. There were still some aspects of our relationship that could be strengthened, but overall, my life with Minh had been good.

I thought about my daughter and her future husband. Was it possible that Hong-An and Travis might be the same as Minh and I? It's true that our marriage wasn't perfect, but was there even such a thing as a perfect marriage? No couple had a perfect marriage, but that's what made marriage so special. It was a commitment, a commitment to hard work and understanding. Maybe I could come to accept Hong-An and Travis's impending nuptials if I kept this in mind.

Hong-An was an adult now. I couldn't protect and guide her forever. Just as I had chosen Minh, Hong-An had the right to choose her partner. I didn't agree with the way the two had treated their engagement, not following Vietnamese tradition, and disregarding our feelings, and most of all, Travis's mental health made me worry about Hong-An's future, but I couldn't hang onto that grudge forever. I had tried my best to recuse the situation, and it didn't work in the way that I had wanted. I loved my daughter, and I wanted her with me again. Whether I liked it or not, Travis made her happy. I did want my daughter to be happy, and indeed, this tension between us was making her unhappy. She must be feeling the same unhappiness that I was. One of us had to make the extra effort to make peace. I was the mother. This was my bridge to mend. I couldn't leave it as it currently was, slowly smouldering to the ground. I didn't want my love for my daughter to be reduced to ashes. Our relationship was on the line, and I had to work hard at acceptance with so much at stake. I had to make sure Hong-An knew that I'd come to this decision. She had to know how much she meant to me and that I would do anything for her, even if that meant accepting that she was making a choice I didn't agree with.

As we sat together in silence, I remembered all of this with our daughter now gone from our home.

I sat on the couch, sorting through my feelings, trying to formulate a plan of action. This couch was where Hong-An and I used to sit together. It was one of our favourite spots, and the two of us often sat here when we had long chats, hugged each other or watched television. I missed her terribly.

She had changed so much and in such a short time. I imagined how hard life must be for her right now. She had left behind her childhood home. She was in a new place, separate from her parents who always protected and cared for her. I knew that she must be having an awful time adjusting to independent adult life, all while facing strain in the relationship with her parents. I had to do my part to make things easier for her.

I remembered how hard life had been for me when I'd run away from my parents' home. The time that I'd spent at my cousin's house was a huge adjustment. I was away from my comfort zone. I was missing my family. Even though I'd had my cousin to take care of me and comfort me, it had been difficult, and Hong-An did not have any family by her side now, so I knew that however difficult it had been for me, it was much more so for my poor daughter.

'I have to get Hong-An to come home!' I said to myself. 'I must do this! I must do this!'

I went to Minh and explained my thoughts. 'We have to accept Travis,' I said to him.

His mouth popped open, and his eyes widened. I could see that he was wholly shocked by my announcement. Before he could say anything, I continued, with tears streaming down my cheeks.

'At least, Hong-An chose him from the heart! This is the very core of what love is!'

'But what about his mental health problems?' Minh argued. 'His life is always going to be hard, and this means that Hong-An's life will be hard too.'

'I know,' I said. 'You are right about that. But the more we resist this, the more problems we will cause. We can't stop them from marrying. They've already made up their minds to do it. We can't change Hong-An's mind. All that we can do is accept this for what it is and show her how much we love and care for her. Minh, we have to do this! Just go with the flow! Let love connect all of us! I am so sick and tired of the fighting. I don't want to do it anymore!'

Minh was quiet as he pondered my words. I could see that he was still feeling hurt by Hong-An's actions. He was also very worried about Hong-An's future and well-being. It was going to be hard for him to put his protective feelings aside and learn how to accept what we could not change.

But I was ready to move forward. In my heart, I no longer harboured any resentment for Travis. All of the resentment I'd previously held onto came from a place of fear. I was scared for my daughter, and this had twisted into anger towards him. It was time for me to let all of that go. Family was more important than anything. I'd already let this conflict continue for far too long.

'Just listen, Minh,' I said. 'If we aim to accept Travis, we can have Hong-An back in our lives. If we can all get along, we may even be able to convince them to live very close to us. We need to be welcoming and supportive of the two of them. We can support him in his sickness and make life easier for both of them. With our support, maybe life does not need to be so challenging.'

Minh nodded his head, suddenly seeming as though a chord of inspiration had struck him.

'We could also think about renovating part of the house for them,' he said. 'It will be bigger than a two-bedroom apartment. They might consider taking us up on that offer. They could have their own little kingdom. It would be close to us but have its separate entrance and plenty of privacy.'

He sounded excited. I loved seeing this side of him. He always had good ideas when it came to his daughter. He loved Hong-An with every bit of his heart. He was a wonderful father, and this was a blessing to me as a mother.

All that I wanted was to have Hong-An and Travis in front of me, so I could hug them and kiss them. I needed them in my life very much. It was time for me to put my ego as a Vietnamese mother aside.

I took the leap, and texted Hong-An, pouring my heart out. I asked her to forgive me, so that we could all make amends and move forward.

'Ba, Mẹ have missed you so much! Come home to have a meal with us! Family means no one is left behind!' I ended my text to Hong-An with our favourite quote from 'Lio and Stick.' Hong-An usually used this quote to make me laugh when I was upset with her.

Hong-An came home two days later. Minh and I were so happy to see her beautiful face at the door. It felt just like she was coming back home from the university as usual. Sometimes, ordinary things were so precious. I hugged her and kissed her hair and felt like a millionaire. I was elated to see her enjoying my cooking as usual. My heart expanded with joy as Hong-An conversed and laughed with us. It was just like old times again.

'Let all of our fightings become the past, Hong-An! Come home so that we can move forward! Let's all be together as a family again.'

Hong-An listened to what I had to say and promised that she would think about it.

'I will consider this and let you know later,' she said.

My heart was filled with hope. I wanted our family to go back to being what it used to be. I wanted peace in my home and my heart once more.

CHAPTER TWENTY-SEVEN

~

JUST SKELETONS

While I was staying at my cousin's house, my parents' divorce was heard in court. I was still cross with them and did not attend but heard about it through my aunt, who must have talked to them or heard the rumours around town. My father had remained steadfast in his resolve to proceed, but my mother had changed her angle on the divorce. I'm not sure what exactly was motivating her, but she stood up in the courtroom and made a passionate appeal, saying that her children needed their father. He could live his own life and follow his path, but she would wait for him at home and remain his wife. Apparently, everyone, including the judge, wept at her performance, and the divorce was denied.

My mother appeared at the gate of my cousin's house one day, and I pretended not to see her. I just kept on walking along with Minh. I think she had been keeping an eye on me and possibly even giving my aunty money, which she left under my pillow anonymously.

A few days later, she returned, and I hid in my room, pretending not to be home.

'I know she is here.' she said, loud enough so that I could hear. 'I have heard about that man that is pursuing her. I suppose she wants to be with him more than her own family.'

Her guilty trip did not work for me. It only sharpened my resolve. A few days later, both my mother and father appeared together as a united force.

'We have been talking,' my father began. 'And we have decided to stay together, for the sake of everyone's future, especially yours.'

Maybe they thought that Minh and I were a couple, which in my mind was not yet confirmed as reality. Perhaps the fact of me leaving home had triggered some real love between them. Either way, I did not believe in their ability to moderate their fighting for my sake. I had given up hope in them. In fact, I had lost faith in marriage altogether.

'We don't think about ourselves anymore—just you. Only you,' my mother said. But I heard other statements in her words, echoes from the flashbacks of the violence and misery of our household. I refused firmly.

But as the days and weeks passed, I began to miss my friends in the neighbourhood. I also missed having my own room and the privacy of a bigger house and all the comforts it contained. One morning I woke up and wished so much to be back in my bed that I packed my things and rode my bike home.

I felt like the prodigal daughter returning. Thankfully, I had so much credit in my neighbourhood that any shame I had earned from my actions was overpowered by their relief and happiness everyone felt to have me home. I was too old to forgive my parents easily, but my stubbornness became muted, and life resumed in a more subdued, stable fashion.

I was more relaxed and had time and energy to focus on preparing for my second chance at the university exam. But thanks to my depression and distraction, I had done no studying up until that point, and my head was almost entirely empty of the knowledge I required. My reputation was still that of a smart girl, and my vanity prevented me from admitting that I would probably fail again.

My father, inspired by my coming home, announced that he was going to give up alcohol. It was a huge statement, and for him to even reach the point of committing to trying was so meaningful to the whole family.

'I'm doing this for you,' he told me privately. 'You are now a young woman, and your future depends on our family being strong and formidable. I don't want to see your suitor scared off by a drunkard father. I want to do better for you and help you prepare for your future.'

I didn't want to disappoint him by telling him I wasn't sure if I was going to marry Minh. I felt very close to Minh. I knew that I cared deeply about him. But as to whether or not I loved him, I didn't know. How can such a young person know something like that? With these things in mind, I kept quiet. I wanted to encourage my father's efforts at becoming sober. It was the right thing for him. It was the best thing for his health and happiness. I had to be a good daughter and do whatever I could to encourage his efforts, even if that meant keeping the whole truth from him for a time.

It was tough for my father to stop drinking. It took a great toll on his physical health. One might think that ceasing an unhealthy habit would strengthen him, but it didn't, at least not at first. His body was so used to a constant supply of alcohol, and he became sickly with the withdrawal.

His skin lost all its colour, and his lips were always pressed downward. He lost his appetite and walked around the house like a wounded animal. He was physically and mentally battling his demons.

I was frightened to look into his eyes. They were sad as if he'd been crying. I could see a well of sorrow in them. I honestly preferred seeing my dad's drunk eyes. They were always happy and smiling. Sometimes I wondered if it was in this version of his eyes that I could see his truest soul. Was that the real and genuine version of him?

Then, magically, he appeared at the dinner table, happy and full of vigour and energy again. He kept talking through the whole meal. It seemed like he was back to his old self. But it was too sudden a change. He had flipped. I could smell the alcohol on his breath, and even though he had returned to his normal character, his 'normal character' was the one running away from his true self. He drank so that his true self, with all its trauma and pain, did not come out and terrorise his life.

It was a big gift to me, and though he was ultimately unsuccessful, I was very grateful for the gesture. His problems were too deep to resolve by taking away the one thing that made them manageable. I asked myself, what else can you expect of a man who grew up an orphan? Who lost his family at only three years old and grew up with strangers who hardly gave him any love at all? I knew that my father's drinking was like a salve for his inner pain. Perhaps, he could have dealt with all of his primary issues and emotional pains from the past and been able to kick his habit as a result. But no one had access to that kind of wisdom in Vietnam at the time, and he certainly did not have the tenacity to face them.

Minh had been coming to my house more and more often, and I kept going to meet him after his classes. Rumours flew around the university that he was in love with me. Girls shot me jealous eyes, and I enjoyed the pride it gave me, even though I was not yet ready to admit it. I still thought of him as a mentor and friend. I didn't have any physical attraction to him at all.

I enjoyed the attention, without obligation, until the evening when Minh touched my hand. I used to ride around town with him on the back of his old bike. On that day, it was strangely cold, and I rubbed my hands together to keep them warm.

'Are you OK back there?' he asked.

'I'm just so cold,' I replied.

Minh reached back with his left hand and found mine. He clasped them together and held them firmly. It was the first time any man had touched me before, and I started shivering, not from the cold now but from the significance of his touch.

'Is that better?' he asked.

I realised that Minh must really like me. It was such a simple gesture, but it was a public signal that he wanted to be more than friends in Vietnam. My response to his question was 'tears.'

'Happy tears or sad tears?' He asked, hearing me sniff. I had so much respect for him, and the softness of my heart stopped me from taking my hand away.

'Not happy. Not sad,' I replied in English, to simplify the situation.

I surrendered my heart at that moment. I longed for a man who would protect me, and that is precisely what Minh was. He'd done something for me that no man in my life had ever done before. My father and elder brother had never protected me. They had never been the pillars of strength and fortitude that I needed them to be. Minh was the very first man to treat me in that way. He opened up his arms and his heart to me, and he shielded me, allowing me to hide inside of his protection while I trembled with the pain of my family struggles.

I held Minh's hand all the way home. Not pulling away was like saying yes to his unasked question. In one simple touch, the relationship had turned upside down, and I could no longer hide from the fact that Minh was pursuing me as a potential partner. Unless I came back to him with a firm refusal, I had given him the sign to continue with his advances. It was traumatising. I felt so confused. If Chi Oanh had been around, I would have accosted her to help me through my decision-making process. But she was still in prison, and I was left to make my own decisions.

I kept asking myself if I loved him, and the answer was always an emphatic 'No.' But it wasn't enough of an answer.

Why didn't I love him? He was a successful, polite, respectful gentleman. He did nothing but to support and encourage me. He lifted my spirits when I was down. He saw past my family problems. Thanh was tall and handsome, and I could read that he loved me, but he calculated too much about his love to me and then ran to Thao. My father was also tall and handsome, but he could not bring happiness to my mother. He could not bring happiness to any of us.

Minh was the exact opposite of all of them. I kept trying to figure out how to react to Minh's advances. How should I act the next time that the two of us were together? These questions swam and spun about in my head, making me dizzy with all of the possibilities. I didn't want to make the wrong decision.

Then a funny thought occurred to me. What if all of the men I'd known were stripped of their features, no eyes, no hair, and no skin - just skeletons. Then they would all look the same. Which man would I choose then?

The answer came to me easily. It was exceedingly simple.

I would choose Minh.

I imagined re-attaching Minh's face to the skeleton. His individual features were actually not that ugly. I would choose Minh for who he was. I would pick a beautiful soul.

The thought experiment helped me to isolate the fact that I simply was not attracted to his physical appearance. It made me feel very guilty. On top of that, I had to admit that I would feel shame to take him as my boyfriend. Outside of the narrow, luxurious world of academia, he was very far from a catch. Everyone would think I was mad for choosing him.

And yet, this weird little man was in my life. I had welcomed him as a confidant and friend and enjoyed the benefits of his compassion for months. My pains were a bridge that connected us to one another. Everyone thought I was a princess who should marry a prince. But despite my outward appearance of vanity, I knew very well I was no princess. Who was I to refuse the attention of a man who understood me and loved me for who I truly was? Minh comforted me that his parents would be OK with my background.

It took me more days to decide, and, respectfully, he did not try to visit me. I rode to his house last evening, and he greeted me at the door as if nervously welcoming his destiny. He knew I had come with an answer. I suggested we go out for sweets, and we rode down the street without holding hands. I asked him to stop, and we parked the bike. We walked along the footpath until we stood in relative privacy, under the shade of a tree. Then I began to speak.

'I know that you love me, and I love you too.'

Simple. Clear. Precise. I said those words with certainty but not with passion. Honestly, it felt like an obligation. I felt like I owed it to him and that he could not live without me offering my love to him. He was overjoyed and pulled me gently into his arms. Then I kissed him on his forehead with my nose; my naive thought was that this was the best place for me to kiss my lover. I felt so shy and bashful after doing this. Still, my body tingled with the new frontier of our romance. We were taking fresh, new steps together.

I relaxed into his body. I let the finality of my words wash over me and gave myself over to the quiet submission that my life would never be the same again.

CHAPTER TWENTY-EIGHT

~

A COMPROMISE

After Minh and I had resigned ourselves to our daughter's engagement and decided to be more accepting of the life Hong-An and Travis were creating together, life started to move towards normalcy. I had begun to admit that my reaction to their proposal had been unfair. Now I was trying very hard to make sure that everyone got along. I wanted happiness and peace in my family forever. I would never again let our differences tear apart the strong ties that bound us together.

Travis started to warm up to me again. He was slowly forgiving me and began to trust me again. He and Hong-An started spending time at the house with Minh and me. I was filled with joy at the progress we had made.

Then, one day, Travis and Hong-An made an announcement that weakened my ability to stay out of their plans. I had to strain to bite my tongue. I just could not believe the decision they had made.

Hong-An and Travis said that they wanted their wedding to take place at the surf club in Maroubra. It was another terrible blow to my expectations. The venue was neither the romantic setting for a life-changing event nor the kind of place that could cater to the needs of the guests. I imagined our Vietnamese family turning up to a place where the waiters wore T-shirts, and the customers were barely out of their swimmers.

I had been to the surf club before. It was a fun and casual atmosphere, and there was nothing wrong with that, but while the setting might be appropriate for a relaxed dinner with friends, it certainly didn't suit a formal and important ceremony. It wasn't right to have a wedding there.

I tried to discuss my worries with Travis's mother through Skype.

'A wedding is an exceptional milestone in a person's life!' I exclaimed. 'It can't be in the surf club, Travis!'

I'd hoped that Travis would share my concerns and that maybe the two of us could team up to talk the young couple into a more appropriate choice, but she didn't seem to view their choice of location as a problem.

She only smiled and shrugged, saying, 'Kids nowadays are so simple. You know, I was the same. My wedding was held in my parents' garden.'

'I had my wedding at my house too,' I said. 'But that was our time. Life has changed so much since then. If I could have Hong-An's wedding in my front yard, then I would. But it isn't done that way anymore. No one has a wedding at home anymore. I don't know why they would insist on the surf club. I'm more than happy to cover the expenses for a proper venue.'

Travis and her husband, Tom, listened as I talked through my concerns.

Then I remembered the red suit. When we were in Hoi-An, Travis told me how he had made a custom red suit for the occasion. His description sounded more like something out of the Anchor Man movie than formal wedding attire. This sounded like a sign of his poor mental health as it seemed improbable that anyone would want to look like a newscaster on their wedding day.

Even as I heard myself describing this concern to Travis and Tom, I could tell that it sounded bad. I was interjecting myself where I shouldn't, once again. I was acting like this was my wedding. Was I making the same mistakes all over again? Was I still the old me inside?

'OK! No worries, Ha-Le! I will have a talk with Travis,' Tom reassured me with his laugh.

I threw a beautiful and elegant engagement party for Hong-An and Travis. More than seventy guests attended, and all of our friends and family loved it. Even the people that came with Travis commented on how unique the party had been and how nicely everything had come together, especially the fourteen-course meal I'd prepared. Everyone appeared so happy and enthusiastic about the party and the young couple's engagement. I had decorated many of the rooms with beautiful photographs on all walls, and I heard many exclamations of 'Wow!' as guests came out onto the veranda, where I'd hung pictures of Hong-An and Travis as children. There was one picture of Hong-An at only a year old, and next to it, a picture of Travis at two years old. I had paired with these baby pictures a lovely handwritten note from Minh that read: Travis asked, and Hong-An said YES!

The guests also appreciated the front yard that I'd decorated exquisitely and festively. There were colourful and charming Vietnamese lanterns hanging all around, mixing with elegant candles. The guests lingered in the space, taking in all of the decorations. I was so happy to see how much everyone was enjoying the party. I truly wanted to make this important milestone memorable for Hong-An. I wanted her to cherish these memories forever. Minh had worked hard, helping me to shop and plan, in the days leading up to the engagement party. This party was our chance to mend all broken ties with Hong-An and Travis. This would show the two of them that we really had accepted and loved them unconditionally and wanted no more bad blood between the four of us.

I also hoped that this engagement party would show them that I could help them plan the wedding if only they would listen to me. I decided to share my honest opinions with them. I would wait until the perfect time, and then I would explain all of my misgivings. Maybe one day they would be grateful for my suggestions. Perhaps I could save them from having a much too casual wedding, and years from now, they might laugh and say, 'Thank you, Mẹ! Our wedding would have been so silly, but you were brave and talked sense into us!'

The other huge shock that I received was the frighteningly close date of the wedding. I struggled through my words as Hong-An told me the news over the phone. They were going to be having the wedding in November. Now I had to worry about both the casual venue and the time frame, which was much too short. There wouldn't be enough time to plan a proper ceremony!

A few days later, I brought my concerns to Hong-An over the phone.

'In my experience, sweetheart, it should take around a year to prepare for a wedding. Not just because it is a lot of work, but to test the relationship.'

I heard Hong-An sigh over the phone as if she was patient with a small child who did not know any better.

'We want to have it in November. We've already talked about it a lot, and we don't want to drag it out. It's our wedding, Mẹ. It's what we want.'

I was getting used to being shut out of my daughter's life, but that did not make it hurt any less. My Hong-An had never spoken to me in that way before, and the fact that she was so curt over something so small pained me very much.

'Your father and I waited a year. It's a good amount of time, that's all.'

'I think it's a bit different, Mẹ,' Hong-An replied. She might as well have said, 'Are you really using your marriage as an example here?'

I felt a shadow come across me, like that of a plane in the sun. A cold, hard glitch in my logic would have made any further arguments hypocritical. Then it was gone, and I remembered with blazing certainty the rationale I had carried with me ever since I found out I was pregnant. My life with Minh was for my daughter. I had made my decision to be with him, and from that decision, Hong-An came into the world. Nothing could touch the resolve with which I'd maintained my marriage. It was all for the benefit of my daughter. And the challenge that my own marriage had been was the main reason I was so concerned about Hong-An's decision.

I said none of that of course. I just said that I hoped she would consider us in her decisions and that I hoped to hear back from her after she had spoken with Travis.

I also tried to discuss my concerns with Travis. I attempted to talk to him about the upcoming wedding.

'Travis,' I said, 'I have to be honest with you. I don't think the surf club is the best choice for your wedding. It isn't a good match for our culture. Our family would never expect Hong-An's wedding to be held at such a casual place. I want to ask you to respect our culture. Not only that but to respect your wedding. I think that you and Hong-An need to choose a decent place. You could choose an upscale Chinese restaurant. I'm sure that your Australian friends and family would enjoy Asian food too.'

'I'll take that into consideration,' Travis answered. 'I promise to let you know.'

I kept quiet and didn't say anything else about it. I tried to be patient and wait for the results that I wanted. It had been so hard to convince Hong-An to come back home after her graduation. We were still trying to heal our relationship after all of the fightings that took place during our holiday to Vietnam. Then there had been all of the inner conflicts that Minh and I had suffered through. It had been incredibly difficult for us to accept that this wedding was going to happen. We'd both had to work very hard to accept that Travis was going to be joining our family.

In the end, they made a compromise. Or perhaps, they just realised that November was actually too close, and the Surf Club was actually too casual. A booking was made at The Phoenix Chinese Restaurant (with the fancy table settings) on January 25th. Travis announced their decision on one of his visits to our house. It was a small win for me, but I took no pleasure in it. I had to admit to myself that it didn't matter where they chose to marry or what Travis was wearing; it was still him. In my mind, he was still a threat to my daughter's happiness. I would not be ready to accept it, even if the date was two years into the future.

I began to shift my thinking from complete despair to an active acceptance, but the change felt awkward and inauthentic. I wanted, above all, for my daughter to be happy, but I also didn't want to lose her in the process of protecting that happiness. The next few months stretched out like a rope between two tall buildings, and I would have to take one step at a time, hoping not to fall. I found my mantra. I told myself over and over again, 'Let it be, Ha-Le. When you cannot change something, then all you can do is let it be.'

I reached in, deep down inside myself, searching for strength. I had already tried to change Hong-An's mind, and I had not been successful. It was time to stop fighting it. I had to accept the situation for what it was.

'Let it be, Ha-Le,' I said to myself. 'When you can't change something, it is best to let it be.'

CHAPTER TWENTY-NINE

~

TWO CUTE LITTLE SPARROWS

In Vietnam, people kiss with their noses. The way that Minh kissed me was different.

When he kissed me on the lips, it just felt weird. Then it became uncomfortable, as he started to do something that I'd only seen in movies. He pushed his tongue into my mouth, moving it around. He was giving me a French kiss! It placed strange and unsettling feelings in my gut. His French kiss was so far removed from the kind of kisses that I was used to. I was used to being kissed with a nose, not with a tongue!

I talked to my friends afterwards, and they laughed at my predicament so hard. None of my friends had ever French kissed, and hearing about my French kiss with Minh gave them quite a lot of entertainment. They laughed and listened at the edge of the seats as if they were watching a movie. The rumours circulated about our strange romantic behaviour. But there was nothing romantic about it, and I did not like that kiss at all! I had my own fantasies, of course, but none of them fit in well with the man I had chosen. My fantasies were mostly playful and fun, a type of tender intimacy, not the racy passion or strong desire that Minh had hoped to evoke in me. I had tried to use my head to choose Minh as a partner, but in the end, romance is a language of the heart.

When the upheaval of my family wounded me, Minh was my saviour. Now, my family had normalised into a kind of truce, and I had come back to myself. My expectations in life were different now. I waited for Minh outside of class most days and still got shocked every time I saw him. Every time I built up a pleasing picture of our future in my imagination, it was shattered when I saw his modest, awkward frame coming towards me.

'I am his rescuer now,' I said to myself. I carried this affirmation in my mind.

The longer we spent together as boyfriend and girlfriend, the more difficult it would be to break it off. My family had done their research on Minh. He had been moved up two grades during school and passed with honours as the Dux of his university. His mother came from royal blood, and his father's side were all respectable teachers. He also came from a famous Duke's family descendant from the last king of Vietnam. Even though the new regime did not value academia, he held a high position as the youngest university lecturer in Da Nang. As my family regained their reputation, Minh and his family would give us even more status. Our future was starting to look much better.

But Minh also had grey hair already and did not appear to be a healthy and strong man. He used a lot of Tiger Balm, like my grandma, and that made me wonder if something was not right in his well-being. He never knew how that smell affected me. It depressed me. He had told me he had a brown belt in Kung-Fu, which my parents held onto as evidence of his strength, but I knew better...

When Chi Oanh returned from prison, I told her about my predicament. I showed her a picture of Minh, and she laughed so hard she nearly doubled over.

'He's a perfect match for you, Ha-Le,' she said ironically. 'Are you sure you love him? Are you sure you can spend the rest of your life with him?'

'Yes. I love him for his internal traits, not his external look.' It was a noble thing to say, but she saw the holes in my thinking.

'Well, let's hope his internal traits get better with time because his external looks certainly won't.'

She was not mean. She was honest, and that is all one can wish for in a true friend. She had not seen me for a year, but she could still see my true colours better than anyone. Behind the laughter and jokes, she was saying, 'Don't do this, Ha-Le. Don't do this!'

And somewhere deep in my mind, I was shouting the same. I was shouting this to myself because my heart had not yet found the rhythm of true love. My head and my heart were not communicating. They were completely separate entities, and my head could not get my heart to listen.

I took Minh to meet Chi Oanh. She really liked Minh and enjoyed talking to him. Minh could be very charming in conversation.

'He is nice, but his appearance is a bit odd, and he lacks health to protect you,' Chi Oanh commented. Chi Oanh's mum looked at us and said we looked like two cute little sparrows. Indeed, we did, but it was really an eagle that I wanted beside me.

My family moved to a new house that was only a five-minute drive from the university where Minh worked. This proximity ensured that Minh and I had a lot of time to spend with each other. Minh was very proud when he would hear of students passing by my house, just so that they could see what his girlfriend looked like. Not only was Minh spending more time with me, but he was also spending more time with my family. He would come over to our house for coffee, watch movies, and eat meals with my family.

But as much time as we were spending together, I still felt that our relationship was not really progressing. I started to feel a gap growing between us. One day, in an effort to get to know him better, I began to ask him a lot of questions about himself, and he surprised me with how open and forthcoming he was. He ended up telling me all about his childhood and his struggles with his poor well-being.

'When I was young, my mother neglected me for her work.' he explained. 'She didn't do it on purpose, but because of this, I had many problems with illnesses. I always had lots of headaches and episodes of dizziness. Because of these terrible headaches, I never read very many books when I was young.'

I was moved by his sharing this with me. It made me feel like he must really trust me and care about me.

But in general, I did question how much he cared. Something that always bothered me was that Minh had never sent me a handwritten letter. This was something that I truly craved from the man who said he loved me. I thought this was a sentimental and romantic gesture that all women should experience.

Sometimes Minh would joke about this. He would say things like, 'I got this princess without ever putting pen to paper!'

He had no idea how his words carved into my heart. He made me feel unappreciated and stupid.

When I saw the full box of letters that Minh's sister-in-law treasured, a collection of love letters sent to her by Minh's brother, I was terribly jealous. I wanted my own box of love letters to treasure.

To me, a love letter was a connection between two souls, a connection that Minh and I did not currently have.

I was resentful that Minh didn't care enough to be romantic with me. I wanted tenderness and romance. I wanted the man that I was with to spend time trying to make me feel special. I was getting none of this from Minh.

Minh's role in our relationship was that of a counsellor, and that was all. I strongly felt that I needed more from the man I intended to marry. He needed to be more to me than only a confidant – that wasn't what a romance should be about.

It was during this time that we started quarrelling all the time. Our fights were about all kinds of different things, but in the end, it didn't really matter what we fought about. The result of our fights was that I started to have less and less feelings for Minh over time. I wasn't even sure if I loved him anymore. My feelings were not clear at all, but I didn't want to confess this to him or anyone else. I didn't know what to do, and so I kept all of my feelings locked away inside. All I could do was wait for a greater sense of clarity to come over me. But as much as I longed to love him properly, his lack of health and well-being and his general apathy towards life left me incapable of giving him my heart the way I knew I should. I would force myself to try, but his lack of strength made this so hard.

I knew that I had to end the relationship before it became too hard to walk away. The honeymoon period of our relationship had ended, and we could now see what the future of our relationship would look like. We'd had enough fights for a pattern to emerge. It could be clearly seen.

Minh would have periods after a fight where he avoided me for weeks. I felt like an abandoned toy. He would call me headstrong and spoiled and then disappear.

I would forgive him, and then this pattern would repeat. Whenever things got tough, he would withdraw from my life, perhaps as his way of punishing me for the limitations of my character. It felt wicked, and yet, every time, I chose to see past it and welcomed him back into my life. I imagined a future where this pattern repeated over and over again and resolved to end it firmly and cleanly. I wondered if I was recreating my parents' marriage model, I could see so many similarities.

'No!' I thought to myself, I didn't need to repeat the history of my parents' relationship. I needed to end this.

On the day that I planned to end our relationship, I asked my brother to invite Minh to our house. Minh arrived at the appointed hour, slightly bewildered and anxious about what was happening.

I had rehearsed my speech over and over and knew exactly what I was going to say. I delivered the news calmly, without regard to his emotions. I had done a lot of thinking, and I refused to be swayed by any arguments or excuses he gave.

'Minh! We are not right for each other. We have so many differences. You and I will suffer a lot if we stay together.'

I don't think he thought me capable of such seriousness, and he looked shocked and miserable after my delivery. It was over so quickly that I didn't know what else to say without opening the door to his rebuttal. I allowed him to hold my hand for a short time, but he dropped to his knees when I tried to stand up.

'Ha-Le. If tomorrow you received the news that I was dead, would you cry for me?'

For some reason, the thought that someone so well-known in town would be willing to die if they couldn't have me really moved my emotions...

My whole body got goosebumps with his tone. I already felt in charge of his life. I cooked food for him, made his clothes, and seemed to occupy most of his waking thoughts. I had opened myself to him largely because I felt I owed him the respect of my affection. I had been serving his needs over my own for so long, and now he was threatening to make me directly responsible for his very life.

I did not sleep that night. Minh appeared very balanced and together, but I knew that his family had not looked after him well, and I worried about his capacity to flip completely into a dangerous state of mind. In the morning, I rode to his house to check on him. There was no answer when I knocked on the door. I knocked again and again, getting increasingly worried. On the fourth knock, Minh appeared, smiling.

'I knew you would come,' he said. 'Only a stupid person would end their life for a loved one.'

I was upset by his flippant words but was so jubilantly happy that he was still alive that I let them slip away. I knew that in this single moment that my action of coming to him had locked me into a lifetime duty of being responsible for Minh's life. From that moment on, I took on the obligation of caring for a man outside of my family. I knew that I would care for him with the same seriousness and tenderness I'd always taken when caring for my brothers and the rest of my family. Minh had rescued me from thoughts of suicide in a dark time in my own life. Now we were bound together, the tables turned. I became the rescuer.

The hero who had rescued me was gone, and in his place, there was a poor and unhealthy man, asking me to love him. I accepted that challenge. I gave everything that I had and everything that I was to him. I devoted all of myself to him, and in the process, I forgot all about myself.

Later, I would have to admit to myself that these were the origins of my lack of acceptance of Travis as a partner for my daughter. Even though I of course, grew to love Minh very much, there always remained a small bit of doubt in the back of my mind about his strength as a man. I sensed in Travis this same weakness that I felt in Minh. I wanted Hong-An to have the strong hero that I had not chosen for myself.

CHAPTER THIRTY

A SERIOUS RELATIONSHIP

I gave up my quest for an academic life, which set me further apart from Minh and his family. However, the new regime did not favour those with university educations. I witnessed professors marrying businesswomen in order to help feed their families. Minh took me around to all of the famous people he knew in the business community and introduced me to them in order to find me a job. I was not interested in any of the careers offered. Like my mother, I was drawn to entrepreneurship. I wanted to start my own business. Because this was my goal, I decided instead to work as an apprentice tailor for Minh's sister.

I committed to three years as an apprentice working in her shop, but I showed so much talent that she let me leave after three months to start my own business. My mother bought me the materials I needed to set up the tailor shop. She also helped me in growing my customer base. Since I looked so young, she talked to the clients and easily gained their trust. I did all of the creative work, and with her help, the business began to flourish. Soon, I was earning what would be considered a good income for anyone.

Minh had been honest with me halfway into our relationship, admitting that although his family seemed well off, the war had left them with very little income. He told me that he had to sell off a lot of his possessions, just to buy me the sweets I liked when he was courting me.

I was surprised and moved by his love and honesty. That was what I needed from a man. Instead of running away from this unpleasant truth, I felt much closer to Minh. What I wanted most in my life was a beautiful and honest soul, and Minh was showing me that this was precisely the kind of soul he was.

While his honesty moved me, a big part of me felt anxiety around his financial situation. Vietnamese culture expects the man to look after the woman. The imbalance in my parents' income had led to many issues in my own family.

I knew how to handle it. I worked hard to earn some money and look after Minh. I had learned how to do this from my mother. I cooked a lot of food for him, made nice shirts for him, and became the university's most stylish man.

One day, my parents came to me and said 'Ha-Le, we think it's time you begin a serious relationship with Minh.' 'Serious?' I thought. What could be more serious than providing money, food, clothing and emotional support for someone? But when I thought about it further, I knew the answer my parents were looking for, it was marriage. 'You want me to be Minh's wife?' I said attempting to casually glance at the floor even as my mother's serious and stern eyes were looking right at mine.

My parents had spoiled me all my life, to the best of their abilities and at the mercy of their limitations. They did not want to force me to do anything, but the obligation had grown like a forest around Minh and me, and we couldn't see our way out of it. He was not the same man I had first met. He had abandoned the charm and the tenderness he once lavished on me when I was single. His attitude towards me had been so unbearable at times that I had recently jumped off from the back of his moving motorbike and walked home. He always apologised eventually and sincerely, and I always forgave him, but we had entered into a toxic partnership.

I could not summon the rebellious spirit to let my parents down. My family had only just recovered their reputation, and my rejection of Minh would send them back into a spiral they may never recover from. My reputation would suffer as well. I would forever become the girl who spent three years with Minh and then refused to marry him. Everyone would assume that we had slept together, and my dignity would be ruined. My duty to my parents bound me, and the pressure from my culture to marry a man who I had no romantic attachment to, no physical attraction to, and often, no particular interest in.

I had lost my sense of self as it was being wrapped up in my duty for family. But who was I, and what did I actually want? Did I even know? I was the daughter of parents in a toxic relationship. I was the daughter of a woman who did not have a clean past and a man who was worn down by alcohol and adultery. Who was I was to ask for a perfect man to marry me anyway?

Instead of unburdening myself from this, I chose to wear a mask to prove to everyone that I was fine. I could simply present the image of the blessed wife-to-be to this well-known man. This would help me to save face with the outside world. This would bolster my reputation. I lived with these two faces and accepted them as I kept moving down the path that life had set me upon.

Despite our challenges, I got along well with Minh's parents. They had done everything that I wished Travis's parents would do, or at least wish they had considered, given our background. Although I had spent a lot of time around Minh's family, I had kept a respectful distance from them, as was the culture. His father was a school principal and was very friendly, a stark contrast with his wife, who maintained an elegant and distant air. We had never had a personal talk about Minh or our relationship. That conversation was reserved for the formal meeting with my parents in preparation for our engagement.

They were to arrive at our house at 7 pm, bearing gifts of wine and sweets. My mother cleaned the house and wore a special dress, Dad refrained from drinking, and my brothers kept their distance. Usually, the girl would be shy and anxious, but I was not. I had been around Minh for three years already, I came to his house quite often and knew everything I needed to know, including all of his dark sides. Minh knew everything about me, and though I wasn't sure if he had told his parents about my family, it was not the environment where anything would be revealed.

First, the parents exchanged our dates of birth in order to analyse our compatibility. Neither side took this very seriously, but the tradition was sacred and important.

On hearing this, my mother looked at me privately and widened her eyes slightly. Somehow, even though we had celebrated each other's birthdays, I had never known how old he was. I had just assumed, as had my parents, that he was five or ten years older than me. I quickly calculated the dates and returned her surprised look. He was just about a year older than me. He had been put ahead two years at school, and I had been kept back two years. It made sense now. I had been blinded by my desire for a mature, experienced man.

The news of his premature birth accounted for his strange proportions, and a wave of concern flowed through my parents and me as we imagined our future children and grandchildren at risk. This was no Kung-Fu hero. This was a sickly boy – a boy with greying hair, with constant headaches, and with a lot of Tiger Balm. I felt sorry for Minh and also for myself.

More than ever, I could see that our characters were not compatible, but it was too late. Once the parents had visited a girl's house, you already belonged to their family. I did not want to dishonour either side of the family, and my pride kept me from speaking out against it. The train was in motion now, and nothing could stop the momentum.

My mother spent a lot of money on the wedding on my side. There were so many guests that we had to have two events over two days, one in the morning and one in the evening for my side, and Minh would do the same for his. It was a great success except for one thing: Minh woke up with food poisoning and was so sick he could hardly move for the whole celebration. As part of the Buddhist tradition, the man would lead a long convoy of people, bringing gifts to the woman's house and laying them on the altar to ask permission for him to take me away. He arrived with a ghostly pale face and asked my mother straight away if he could go and lay down. It was not a good sign, but I persevered, alone, through what was supposed to be the most important day of my life.

My father, in contrast, had the energy of a little boy at Christmas. He was drunk, of course, but also joyfully happy. Possibly, he felt vindicated from the suffering his actions had caused. The curse that had been placed on me, his only daughter, looked as if it was finally over. Minh was a reputable, educated man who, in my father's eyes, could bring me the happiness and fortune that he could not.

I distilled all the remaining energy I had into a hope that Minh would recover by the end of the wedding. I still longed for my hero to carry me off to the bedroom and make love to me on my wedding night. It is every girl's dream and every couple's expectation that such a momentous occasion should be consummated with love and affection.

Minh was asleep before I even got to the bedroom. The romantic desire I had cultivated for so long burnt like a flame in me. I was a passionate young woman with a hunger for experiencing life to its fullest, but my wedding night was a profound disappointment. I stayed awake the whole night with many thoughts racing in my mind, keenly aware that I may never be truly fulfilled.

CHAPTER THIRTY-ONE

THE SMELL OF THE SEA

I begged Hong-An to go on the last holiday with us before her wedding. Just the three of us.

'It will be just like old times.' I suggested. Just like The Three Musketeers enjoying time together before she was married, but my daughter refused, saying that she had too much to organise before the wedding.

'I can help you when we get back,' I said. 'The two of us can work together to make it an amazing day.'

'I don't need your help, Mẹ,' she replied as if it was just a fact and not a kick in the guts. 'I want to make all the decisions with Travis. You go and enjoy your holiday with Dad.'

In only a few months, our mother-daughter relationship had changed dramatically. She still had not forgiven me for what had happened, even though I had tried to move past it all. I had tried to leave my hurt feelings and apprehension behind. I was trying my absolute best now to start anew so that I could support them both in the challenging journey that lay ahead. The number one priority on my mind now was Hong-An's and Travis's well-being. My daughter did not look well lately, and her mood had become so unpredictable.

'Let it be, Ha Le! Stop making more of a mess of the situation! You tried your best for your daughter, and it's time to let her make her own choices.' I repeated this mantra in an attempt to suppress how I really felt inside my heart. I knew that I needed to accept whatever came with her choices.

Minh and I signed up for a cruise. I hadn't been out on the open ocean since I'd escaped from Vietnam all those years ago. I had been on the sea only twice, and both of those times had been huge events in my life. I suddenly remembered that Hong-An came to me when I left Vietnam, and now she was about to leave me for the man she loved.

We stood in a line waiting to check in for the cruise. Years back, I'd been like a beggar on a tiny boat. Now, I was about to embark on the ocean once more, only now it was for a luxury cruise, and I was not fleeing for my life but taking a trip for the sheer joy of it. The changes that had occurred in my life had been momentous. I had grown and evolved, changing as time sped along.

To have gotten to this point of my life, I should celebrate and give myself a pat on the back, shouldn't I? I thought.

I looked over at Minh, the man with whom I'd shared the majority of my life. We had seen and shaped so much of each other. We had so many shared experiences. Despite this, time had not brought us any closer, and yet we were still together. I tried to figure out what I could say to Minh to start a positive conversation. I wanted us to have a good time and enjoy each other's company.

'Thank you, Minh.' He was surprised at my acknowledgement.

'Thank you for what?'

In my heart, I wanted to start something new with Minh on this trip, something that could bring us together by ourselves. I wanted us to be together because we wanted and needed to be, not only because of Hong-An. 'Thank you for doing your best in helping me raise Hong-An,' I answered.

'That's because of my love for her and you.' Minh was honest as usual with his expression.

On so many occasions, he had spoken to me from his heart, saying, 'I love you so much Ha Le,' but I could not feel that love. Was I hard to please, or did he not know what I wanted from him?

I had no answers, and I felt sorry for myself. I thought to myself, 'I've never received the things that I wanted most from a man. Everything I've wanted in a romantic relationship I've never gotten from Minh.' I pondered these thoughts for a moment, mulling them over and considering them from different angles.

Sometimes, when Minh and I argued, he would say, 'The ideal man you are looking for does not exist! You are looking for a man from a movie or a novel. No real man will ever meet those expectations!'

This joke of Minh's made me upset.

'You never even asked me what I'm looking for in a man!' I would argue back. 'How can you know that? You have never even tried to give me what I need!'

Hong-An had always been the glue that held us together. Without her between us, I worried we would drift further and further apart. I feared that the time for us to strengthen our bond and grow our love was gone. We had always been so focused on Hong-An. It occurred to me now that we had never taken the time to focus on our relationship. Now, with Hong-An slowly disappearing from our lives, seeing her less and less often, we could no longer distract ourselves with our mutual concern for her. The fissures in our marriage were glaring now. They could not be avoided.

'I also thank you for the shopping, cleaning up, and the times you had to wash clothes for me,' I said.

I meant what I said. I knew that I was lucky to have a husband who was such a great help in keeping the household. I had thanked him for his contributions many times before, but I still felt it was important to express these sentiments now. I wanted to forge a more in-depth understanding with Minh. He had been my partner in life for so long. It wasn't right for the two of us to have such separation between us. Minh had been great at helping with all of the household chores. He'd always tried his best to support my tired body after working. After a long day at the preschool, I hadn't wanted to expend energy shopping or doing laundry, and Minh had been understanding and supportive of this. He'd pitched in often, allowing me to have some rest. I could have managed this by myself even if I needed it. I wanted to create a space with Minh that had a purpose, a purpose of having something to connect us apart from Hong-An.

'You have done so much more for our family than I have,' Minh mumbled.

I knew that and had heard that too many times from him. I started my conversation with him, talking about my new hope of a better relationship for us. We'd had so many hiccups after Hong-An moved out of the house. I just wanted to give him a hint, so we could begin building our romantic relationship. Minh didn't seem to understand what I yearned for. After such a long time of being co-parents, all that I wanted was to be husband and wife. I wanted to hold him in my heart for such a long time.

'I hope we will have a good holiday,' I reached out for his hand, taking it in mine as usual. We had always held hands for intimacy. Since we were young, we had always done it, starting years ago when he held me tightly the first time I was on the back of his bicycle. That occasion marked the very first time I had welcomed a man into my life officially. I wanted to try to recreate that same feeling. It hurt me that I was the one who had to take this initiative.

Why was I the one reaching for Minh's hand? Why wasn't he reaching for mine? Thinking back to our first dates, it struck me that Minh had changed in the way he treated me. I wondered why men did that. Why did men only put in effort in the earliest stages of dating? Why did they not continue trying to woo the woman they loved? Why did men move on to take their women for granted? I wondered if all men were like this or if it was my bad fortune to have a husband who had stopped trying to make me happy.

♥ ♥ ♥ ♥

We boarded the cruise ship, and at first, I only had eyes for the other families on the boat who walked around, showing off their love for one another. There were happy scenes of mothers and fathers talking and laughing with their kids in every corner of the vessel. I missed Hong-An so much. It still felt strange, having this rift between us. It was as if it were the first time we were having a holiday without her. If she were with us, she would have run around to check everything. Then she would have run back to me, laughing as she reported her findings.

I went to the open balcony, and as I looked at the sea, I was transported back to the time I held my parents' hands as a child. We had watched the flying fish as we sailed away from Da Nang to flee the Viet Cong. I had felt so free and so connected to my own family, but the vast ocean had taken on an entirely different meaning when we fled the country the second time. Just the sight of the undulating waves brought back sickening smells, hunger pains, and images of miserable faces. I experienced many things with many people, but I will always wash up as a Boat Person on the shores of history, and the ocean will always be synonymous with that part of my life.

'I want to go for jazz music tonight,' I told Minh when we passed by the entertainment area.

'Wow! The cruise has everything, and it's so luxurious!' he beamed.

'Well, it's worth our money,' I responded with a smile.

'I'm going back to the room to rest. I feel dizzy,' Minh said.

These words from Minh wiped the smile away from my face. Minh had developed his old terrible headache once again. He comforted himself in bed under blankets and covered in Tiger Balm. That strong smell brought back unpleasant memories that made me feel sick. An unpleasant sensation settled in my gut as I recalled my grandmother using that same ointment to ward off her own ailments. That smell had accompanied some of the darkest moments of my childhood, and yet somehow, I'd married a man who made that smell a consistent and wholly depressing part of my daily life.

I had the feeling that all of these realities were somehow mixing together like a soup of discontentment in my psyche. My grandmother, Minh, and now Travis. I had to admit to myself that it was all somehow connected for me.

I wanted so badly for my daughter to have a strong, healthy man by her side. I wanted her to have only the happiness that I had never found. I had wanted Minh to be this man for me. I had even wanted my grandmother to be this for me at one point. I longed for this source of strength to lean on. How was it possible that two of the most important people in my life had succumbed to only Tiger Balm and dark moments spent hiding under the covers, and now somehow, my daughter would be left to endure the same with Travis. I recalled my grandmother's battle with depression. At so many moments when I had needed her most her depression dragged me down and became part of my own mental struggles. I felt Minh also weighing down my happiness, like an anchor dragging a ship that only wished to blow free with the wind. Oh, how I wanted more for my daughter than days spent madly escaping ointment and sadness. I fought so hard to give her that freedom and that right.

When I went to the balcony to be with the sea again, the blue colour soothed my heart and gave me some relief from my stress. I wanted to release the vision of Minh's reality, let it drift away with the wind that blew in my hair, but all I could do was to relive the scene that had just played out over and over again in my mind. I thought through my conversation with him once again. How could he be so unwell, even on holiday? I felt the growing sense of disappointment that always arose in me when Minh fell ill. I thought back over our conversation.

'Sorry, Ha-Le! I couldn't go for jazz tonight,' Minh coughed. 'Sorry for being too sick and making you sad!'

'It's OK. You rest,' I replied as I had for the past twenty-six years.

I had gotten used to Minh's well-being as I had accepted it before we got married. I knew that his poor well-being would be a part of my life with him. I was sure that Minh knew the main reason he made me sad was his personality.

I'd always heard people say that when a couple is made up of two people with opposite personalities, they complement each other. People said that opposites attract. In my case, I had found that this was not true.

But I had chosen him, and I had chosen this life with him. I considered why I would pick someone who was so different from me. I had grown up among my parent's tumultuous romance. It was unstable and hot-headed, but there was always passion when they reunited; even if threats of violence still lingered in the air, there was still a passion. Had I chosen this man for safety? Had I sacrificed passion for the vapid smell of Tiger Balm and a weak cough? I wasn't sure I could admit this to myself, but I considered that this was possible.

Minh and I were so very different in so many ways. He was a linear problem-solver, while I was a big picture sort of thinker. When I wanted to leap, Minh wanted to walk. While I loved spending time in big, open spaces, these places usually gave Minh a cold or irritated his sinuses. Minh was dogmatic. I was pragmatic. I liked soft and sweet romantic movies. Minh loved violent action movies. I could go on. If I were to try and name all of the differences between the two of us, the list would be very long. These differences didn't bring us any closer together. We didn't complement one another. We didn't fit together, like two opposite puzzle pieces. We didn't meld together neatly. We clashed and butted heads often.

'Our marriage has survived despite the odds,' I thought to myself.

There were times when I wondered how my life might have been different if Minh and I had never gotten married. At times, I wanted to be free, but I was bound by duty. I was bound as a mother, as a wife, and as a Christian. Although I wasn't always happy, I stuck by my husband in order to make the best situation for our family. I knew that I had made the right choice. I always knew this, even on days when Minh's behaviours pained and upset me to no end. My family of three had clung together through it all, making a brand-new life, in a land far away from Vietnam. But wasn't this life the chance for new starts? Isn't this why I had come here, so my daughter didn't have to suffer my life?

I knew if Hong-An married Travis that she would be repeating so many of the sorrows I lived through with Minh. Like me she would end up looking after a weak, sick man who would not be able to give her the love she needed. This fear was like a monster that resided in me and would rise up at unexpected moments. I wanted to keep her from this fate with every part of my soul. All the loveless suffering I had endured was locked inside of me and was what drove me to try and keep Hong-An from suffering my own fate.

I had a secret that I had never spoken aloud to anyone, a secret that ate at me like a cancer from the inside out. Minh's illness didn't just rob me of his time, it robbed me of his affection as well. It removed any ounce of passion he had to give. His illness stole passion from us like a thief in the night. It wasn't only our wedding night he was unable to fulfil my needs as a woman. It was our whole life together. I was left with the tedious task of keeping my passion bottled like a soft drink that had been shaken and was longing to be opened to releases the bubbles. I ached for a man that had a lust for me and who couldnot allow me to let out mine.

I never shared this secret with my daughter as it was a private matter, but I knew that Travis's mental health had the capability to rob Hong-An of this right that every human has to unbridled passion and lust.

Now, here on this ship watching Minh struggle through illness, I began to miss my daughter again even more. When her father was unwell at home or on holiday, I usually spent time with her. When I set my foot on the cruise, I had imagined that Minh and I would go around, hand in hand, enjoying the music and everything else that the cruise had to offer. I had tried my best to mend our relationship by getting closer to Minh, but it seemed the chances came and went. We had been getting to know each other for the past twenty-eight years. I still zealously longed for a true love from Minh to touch my heart. I wanted the love that he had promised me! I wanted him to take me in his arms and protect me. I wanted him to make me smile and laugh always. This was what I truly wanted, a marriage filled with love and laughter. I felt a poignant emptiness. I was still waiting for the wedding I had envisioned to materialise.

I walked around by myself and saw many different families enjoying the cruise together. I was in a large crowd. I was surrounded by people but felt so alone. To avoid the painful displays of affection, the only place to look was out to sea, and so I did. This went on for days. There was so much room to move about and space to spread out, unlike those long ago trips escaping Vietnam where we huddled together out of necessity.

I walked to the balcony and sat there watching the breath-taking colours of the sunset. The smell of the sea, the dark blue of the water, and the aroma of diesel took me back to the past. Back then, the story had been different. Back then, the story was still being written, and it still had the chance to become anything it wanted.

CHAPTER THIRTY-TWO

DETERIORATING

We were not the first people to decide to leave Vietnam. Ever since Saigon fell in 1975, the whole of South of Vietnam, including my hometown, had been awash with stories of people trying to escape. Many had already been successful. I had already done some undercover research before I got engaged to Minh, but this ended very badly.

Most people escaped via small beach-side villages, where they were less likely to be seen or reported. I had heard about one of the villages from my apprentice tailor and visited it under the pretence of seeking a weekend nature retreat from the city. I attended the church and visited many locals, asking questions and determining how safe it might be. I returned a few times and eventually met people I trusted. I gave them some gold to invest in the building of an escape boat. It secured my place, but ten days before we were due to depart while swimming in the river further upstream, I slipped from a rock and badly hurt my knees. The cuts were so deep that I could see my tendons and fat, and the wound spewed out blood like a hose.

I had no choice except to wait until I could walk again. It took two weeks, and although the escape group had promised to wait for me, they didn't. I received an excuse-filled letter from Hong Kong from one of my students who had gone without me. It was an embarrassing and discouraging first attempt, and I gave up any thoughts of escape for a long time. By that time, Minh and I were still dating, and my mother was willing to pay the fare for him to go with me.

I knew that we needed to escape; it was not a life for us. As poverty and disillusionment increased, crime and gangs of bored youth began to roam the streets at night. Sometimes I would encounter them when I walked to Minh's house. They would bully, provoke me, and touch my private parts. Once I had to use all my strength to stop myself from being abused. I ran away and cried in shame, angry at the violation and mad that there was nothing I could do about it.

But I kept going building my life as if escape wasn't always a possibility lingering saliently on the horizons. I persevered with my tailoring business, expanding into embroidery and employing my students to work for me. It was creative and lucrative work, but I was unfulfilled. I still longed to study more and follow my creative passions further, but there seemed to be little point in pursuing that in Vietnam. People who had escaped to the USA, Canada, and Australia were sending pictures to their families documenting their abundant new lives of freedom and happiness. I had no future in Vietnam. We had all the things that money could buy, but not freedom and education.

As it turned out, you could buy freedom. We would soon learn that the price of freedom was four big pieces of gold per person. Minh and I had spoken with his neighbours, who had witnessed their three children escape to Hong Kong safely. We arranged a meeting with the wife, Aunty Bich, who knew the organiser of an escape. I met her alone on the beach. She liked me straight away, and we quickly began to trust each other.

I didn't tell my father about our plan. He could not be trusted with the secret because of his drinking. Also, his devastation at the news would probably have stopped me from going, and in my heart, I was committed. We were not abandoning our families. The plan was the same for everyone who wanted to escape. If we made it to another country, we could earn better money and send some home. Eventually, we might be able to sponsor some members of our family to come and join us. My mother saw the opportunity for the family, despite the danger. My father lived much more at that moment, and the idea of my absence in his life would have been too much for him to bear.

I packed our things. It didn't take long because we had to appear like regular rural people rather than wealthy urban escapees clutching oversized suitcases. Men were not allowed any luggage, and women were only allowed one small bag with only one pair of clothes. As the day approached, I became nostalgic for my home country and felt melancholy at the thought of leaving my friends and family. Nevertheless, we were embedded in the decision and were swept along with the tide of logistics.

I could read Minh's emotions. He was sad and quiet; he could not say goodbye to his family. His whole family was against his decision because Minh's actions could jeopardise the future of every member of the family.

On the night of the escape, we put on our rural clothes, said goodbye to my mother, Hung, and Hai, and rode to the spot where we were told to gather. I had not anticipated how far away it was. The village was called Dien Ngoc, and it was a four-hour ride on the bike. The whole country knew it as a Viet Cong Hotspot. It had produced many of the army leaders and had a massive network of tunnels around it that were used to protect the Viet Cong during the war. It was safe to say that it was still full of communists and, therefore, a surprisingly unlikely place to hold a mass escape. No one would expect it there, we were told.

The man who greeted us and led us to a small hut near the river turned out to be someone who worked for a Chief of police – a Major, no less, who controlled the police force in the whole area. We were either very well protected or extremely exposed. We were told to wait in the house until we were called one by one to the boat. If their illegal enterprise were discovered, the police would point the finger at us without a thought. Or maybe the whole thing was a ploy to trap us, and the police were about to arrest us all. We huddled together like pigs in a pen, awaiting our slaughter or our freedom. The coin of life and death could be flipped at any moment.

After a few hours, whispered voices ushered people out one by one. Minh was led out first, and then I was led out a few minutes later. The moon was the only light, and I could just make out the tree line and the boat's outline as we approached the river. It seemed impossibly small. It looked like a floating toy in the darkness, not a boat capable of taking us across the ocean to Hong Kong. The sight of it made me want to run back, but I knew the police would probably tackle me to the ground and suffocate me if I threatened the whole operation. The safest thing to do - the only thing to do - was to keep going towards the boat.

I crouched down where I was told, next to two strangers. We were no longer pigs in a pen; we were sardines in a tin can. I wasn't sure how many people were on board, but I could smell the acrid, garlic, onion smell of body odour. I covered my mouth. I had not felt fear like this since I was a kid during the war. I watched a small light blinking on the front of the bow and counted the seconds as if they were my last.

A baby started crying, which set off a few muffled shrieks among the other passengers, and a flurry of activity ensued to silence it, lest it gave us all away. There was a long period of silence, interrupted only by the roar of the engine.

The sound cut my heart into a thousand pieces. We were moving. This was it. I might never see my family and friends again. I might never walk through the city that I loved. We all sat, transfixed in terror, sadness and nostalgia silently running through our thoughts as the boat gathered speed and made its way across the river.

Then, all at once, the boat stopped, and everyone let out a collective gasp. We had hit a sandbank. In the small time it took for that fact to register, people began jumping off the boat onto the riverbank. I called Minh's name out under my breath and then felt his hand grab mine and help me off the boat. People were all running for their lives, and we began to run with them, pulled along by the cumulative fear of the group. Dogs barked, and Minh started to freak out. I took control and stopped us.

'Let's go in the other direction Minh,' I whispered. 'If we all stay together, we are more likely to get caught. Come on!'

We had jumped out without shoes, and my feet were cut up from running across the rough ground. We slowed to a walk and began to act more natural as if we were local villagers out for a stroll. But no one went for a stroll in the dead of night, and especially not without shoes. We had no idea where we were, except that we were extremely far from home.

We found a dirt road and walked along it blindly until I heard the familiar rattle of a Vespa in the distance. We instinctively hid off to the side of the road, but then we thought better of it. If we were caught, we might be tortured, imprisoned, or killed. It was wiser not to act guilty and pray the bike would just speed by.

As it got closer, it slowed and then finally stopped in front of us. Its headlight shone towards us, obscuring the identity of the rider. Minh was sweating and breathing hard; he nevertheless addressed the man with a competent version of a rural accent. 'Nice evening to be out and about.'

The man on the bike had no time for pleasantries. He just mentioned the woman who had introduced us to the organisation. My heart froze, and I risked a look at the rider's face.

It was the Police Chief.

We were saved. It was a miracle that he had found us, and we jumped on the back of his bike and drove all the way back to Da Nang. We cruised through the familiar streets of my hometown in the early hours of the morning while the whole city was sleeping. I felt the cool air on my face, and a swell of relief rose in me, making me feel safe and secure. I was glad we had failed and even more delighted to see my mother and brothers answer the door. My brothers checked the street up and down to see if we'd been followed. The danger was not over. If others were caught, they might reveal the identities of the others in return for a reduced punishment. We had played the game of escape and lost, but I was not disappointed.

CHAPTER THIRTY-THREE

THE IMPOSSIBLE AND LIFE-CHANGING DECISION

Aunty Bich visited us the following morning to check that we were safe. She told us that some people were caught and warned us to stay alert. Minh went back to work as if everything was back to normal, but it wasn't. Our names and addresses were now registered with a secret organisation. Even if we decided not to try again, we were still on the list of traitors. We had shot the arrow and now had to go along with it to its target. There was no turning back to a safe life in the current regime. We were renegades either way and for the next week, we lived in fear of being caught and bringing our families down with us.

We were doing everything we could to prepare for an escape. We had a bag assembled with all our important documents. I had even started to take the contraceptive pill to manage my cycle and ensure there were no accidental pregnancies at such a difficult time. I wanted to make sure I was at my physical best for the journey.

At first, I tried the Russian variety, but the side effects were dramatic, making me so queasy that I felt like vomiting. I then tried the French version, which was much smoother, but the timing did not seem to match. The period it was supposed to induce never came. But I had to imagine working and doing its job to protect me from a child would make this journey even more difficult.

We knew we had to keep trying for an escape. We were finally contacted again with the news that the next boat would leave in a week. It had to happen quickly because soon, storms would start pounding the ocean and make the trip a suicidal mission. The relief I had felt coming home did not last, and again, I was torn between the horror of braving the escape or committing to a life in Vietnam that felt more like a prison sentence than a real life.

We decided to try again. This time, we knew what to expect, and I built up my energy in preparation. Waiting in the hut, we heard lots of dogs barking, and it activated everybody's fear in the same way that gunshots did during the war. Again, we were led to the boat one by one, but this time I made an effort to locate and sit with Minh, if there was any trouble. If we had to run away again, we would almost certainly not have the same luck as the last time.

Outside, it was dead silent as we waited for the engine to start, but inside my head, I heard the funeral music. It didn't feel right, but we had no choice except to continue. I had made a strong effort this time to transform myself into a rural person. I messed my hair up, donned Uncle Ho sandals for the first time since my Little Bolshevik days and darkened my skin with makeup. I had practised walking and talking like a farmer, but I could not change my attitude or subdue the inevitable fear in my eyes.

'You have got to act well and perfect your attitudes and accent, as people will recognise your city face easily, Ha-Le!' Minh reminded me again and again.

We travelled further than the last time, and I felt lighter and lighter as the distance between the Viet Cong village and us grew. Then, again, we stopped in the middle of the river. The engine was still running, but we were going nowhere. I heard frantic whispers from everyone on board, and we waited a long time before finally we were given instructions.

'The boat is caught in a net. I'm sorry, but you now have to jump into the water and run for your lives,' the boat's captain said. He was barely a man, and his voice sounded terrified.

We had failed again. We were at the hands of an inexperienced boat captain. Surely, it was not that hard to sail down a river, I thought angrily.

People were less quick to obey. Most of us could not swim. Luckily Minh could, and he jumped in the water and encouraged me to join him. There was no time to help rescue the others. Everyone knew they were in it for themselves. The water was deeper than my body. Minh and I scrambled clumsily to the side of the river, rushed up the muddy banks, and ran frantically into the night.

We were soaking wet, and again, we had no shoes. A little further on, we heard people yelling and dogs barking. They were being chased. We ran across fields and skirted around tiny villages looking for a road. It felt like we were going in circles, but finally, we found one. Along the way, we were joined by a boy with a shaved head who had followed us at a distance. At first, we thought he could be a local Viet Cong informer, but as it turned out, he had been on the boat as well. He walked ahead with Minh for some time before I told him to make his own way. I explained that it was safer if we split up.

We ran around and around in the dark as if we were in a matrix. I was out of breath but tried to keep myself alert. I looked as hard as I could for the direction, but we came back to the old spot with our panic. I heard the clash of prison doors in my mind. I was so afraid. I didn't know how much longer I could keep my fear contained.

As day broke, farmers started to walk into the fields and tend the rice. We could not hide from them, and I could sense them looking at our feet with intense curiosity. Eventually, we built up the courage to ask for directions. We told them we were visiting relatives in the area and had gone for a walk to get some exercise. I wasn't sure if they believed us, but they pointed us in the right direction.

We found the road and followed a group of people carrying market goods towards a shelter that we hoped was a bus stop. We assumed that everyone around us would be connected in some way to the Viet Cong and tried to act calmly as if it was entirely normal to get on the bus with dirty faces, no shoes and nothing in our hands. The bus came, and we boarded it along with the group.

We had to sit in the aisle, and I covered my naked feet with a chicken basket to stop people from noticing. When I saw people looking and whispering to each other, I pretended to laugh and joke with them, telling them we had run so fast to catch the bus we had both lost our shoes. We knew we were only one stroke of bad luck away from being turned in. There was no cash reward for turning in traitors, but some people considered it an act of service to their country. In a culture of fear, people easily turned against each other. The authentic morals that country people had always been known for, we had to assume, were a thing of the past.

Eventually, we got back to Da Nang, and Minh quickly secured a covered cyclo so that we could obscure our faces. Even now, in our hometown, suspicion would be aroused if we were seen out of context in rural clothes. With our appearance disorder, the cyclo man knew what we were up to and supported us. He covered us quickly, something everyone knew was only for the rainy season or for taking a very sick person to the hospital. Luckily, I judged him to be the right person. Through the cover side, I saw my friends, Minh's friends and colleagues on their way to work. I just hoped that we had covered ourselves well and nobody saw us.

I worked out where to go to and gave the order. 'To Noi-Ha, please.'

We went to Chi Oanh's house first, fearing that the police might already be waiting for us at my house. I had not told my friend about our planned escape, but she took one look at me and knew. After we had washed and eaten, I sent her niece, Bo, over to our house on a bicycle to check and see if it was safe. She came back with good news, and we returned home.

My mother had been praying all night and could not believe we had failed again. Minh and I collapsed on the bed, emotionally and physically wrecked.

Suddenly, I bolted upright and shrieked at the top of my lungs, 'The bag! We left the bag.'

It had hit me all at once, the realisation that our bag of important documents had been left behind. We hadn't brought much with us, but we had made sure to bring our most important identification documents. This was in case we died during the voyage, whether by police or by drowning. Then, we could be identified, and our families would not have to wonder what had become of us. They would know, with certainty that we had perished. Not only did the bag contain our identifications, but the identities of our families as well. There were the addresses of our relatives from overseas, as we hoped to have their support when we arrived in Hong Kong and needed to know where to find them. We had been prepared with all of these papers because we knew we had to be ready for anything. In the chaos, the bag had been abandoned somewhere. This was very dangerous for us. Minh looked at me gravely. It was direct, irrefutable evidence leading right back to our families and us.

I burst out crying. It was all too much. We were trapped in a cycle of fear that we could only escape by escaping the country itself.

Over the next few days, any loud noise or knock on the door sent Minh into a panic. I could barely leave the house. I felt so tired and sickly like something was not right with my body. The escape season was almost over, and I worried that we might have lost our window of opportunity. Nevertheless, a week later, we received our next invitation. The boat would leave in three days. It was our last chance, but my body felt unable to take on the challenge.

Minh took me to the doctor to try to understand the problem. They asked me a lot of questions and then had me complete a urine test. Moments later, the nurse, who was also my evening classmate and one of Minh's students, came back with a big smile on her face.

'Congratulations! You are pregnant.'

My soul left my body at that moment. I was an empty shell awash on the beach. Waves pushed me up and down against the sand, but I felt nothing. I was not there.

When the shock wore off, our minds raced with questions. How was it even possible? Why now? What about the pill? Did it not work? What does this mean for our future?

We had no answers, only deeper, darker questions. I had heard and witnessed countless terrible stories of babies being born with deformities due to dodgy contraceptive pills. Prostitutes during the war would overdose on the same contraceptive pills to try and kill the foetus, but it often did not work, and the baby would be born with no legs or arms or only one eye. What if the drugs I had taken had already damaged the child? Remembering the time, I had a glass of water and pills in my hand, a cold chill ran up my spine.

Minh took me home. I lay on the bed and stared at the ceiling for hours. I had imagined having a family when we were safely in another country. I was not ready to welcome a child into the world, especially if that world was full of fear and anxiety. I was born into such a world, and I would never wish that on any living being, let alone my own child.

I mentioned to Minh the possibility of having an abortion. It almost seemed more merciful, given the circumstances. In my mind, the child would either have physical deformities or live a life of misery. If we continued to live as fugitives in our own country, the safety of my child would never be guaranteed. If we escaped, they could die with me in a storm in the ocean. We did not want to suffer for our whole lives. These are the things that I told myself in order to ease my guilt. I was torn by indecision.

Minh said he trusted my intuition but clearly was overwhelmed by the thought of having the child. I tried to reconcile my competing thoughts and think clearly and logically about the situation, but it was impossible. I drifted in and out of sleep. My bed felt like a little boat, braving the ocean, and I clung on for dear life.

In the middle of the night, I woke in a startle and knew straight away what to do. My unconscious had spoken to me clearly and firmly; I would have the child. Whatever it took, I could not destroy its life. I was already responsible for its future, and it was up to me to guarantee that it was a future worth living for. I did not know if that meant staying or escaping, but I knew that my choice would be determined in service of the child inside me.

'You deserve to be a human,' I told my child. 'Mum will be with you, my baby.'

Minh was teary when I told him, 'He or she is our baby, Minh. This is now our love and someone we need to protect.'

'Stay back,' my mother advised. 'Stay back with the millions of other people. If they can survive, so can you. You will be around your family who can help you. I will look after the financial side of things.'

Mum was right! My baby deserved to have many loved ones around. This was such an essential part of Vietnamese culture. Her advice was echoed by others that we sought advice from.

I visited Chi Oanh. She knew me better than anyone, including Minh. She stroked my hair and told me that it was my decision, but if I decided to go, then she wanted me to take her niece, Bo.

Her request surprised me. Bo was a girl with a beautiful soul who was ten years younger than me. If she came with me, I would receive a bonus from her family and the organisation I worked for. I said I would consider it. That same afternoon I was visited by another friend, Le. She had heard that I was pregnant and came by to congratulate me. She could tell that I was distracted and confused. I already knew she had tried to escape a few times but had given up. I opened up to her, mentioning that I had one last attempt in a few days but torn with indecision. Like Chi Oanh, she did not offer direct advice but stated emphatically that if I decided to go, she wanted to come with me, with her niece and nephew. Of course, she told me, she would pay the bonus.

In the end, the impossible and life-changing decision that I was faced with was tipped by the simple, practical offer of the company and financial relief. I would have people to help me through my pregnancy, and the money would ease the burden for my mother, who, despite her outward confidence, was struggling more each day in her business and well-being. I agreed to her offer on the spot, and all of a sudden, we were again committed to escaping.

Two days later, while we waited to be picked up by the policeman, my father pottered aimlessly around the house, utterly ignorant of the significant events unfolding around him. It grieved me that, about to leave the family, he never knew anything about me. Before he started drinking, I called him into the kitchen. I was already dressed in my rural clothes, but he did not seem to notice the change.

'What's the matter, princess? Do you want some food? Let me find something for you.' He went to open the cupboard, but I put my hand on his arm to stop him and pulled him into a hug as I cried.

'I just want to say goodbye to you, Dad. I'm leaving the country tonight.' I buried my face into his shirt and perceived his smell. Instantly, it made me remember him in other times before he started drinking and fighting with my mother, before Chi Thoi and the mess of the war. The time I was on the boat across the river, tugging at his uniform and looking up at my hero. I felt him crying and pulled back to speak to him directly.

'This is not the last goodbye. When I get out, I will send money and sponsor you to come too.'

'Don't go,' he said feebly. He was not used to giving advice, having doubted his value to me for most of my life. 'You have a child inside of you, and it's not safe. What if something happens to you on the sea? Stay back here where we have each other.' His eyes fluttered with panic, and his lips trembled.

I was silent because there was no answer.

'They are coming soon,' I said. I hugged him again briefly and then left the room as if to prove that it was not goodbye forever and carried his smell with me.

CHAPTER THIRTY-FOUR

~

TRAVAILS

I took a deep breath, staring down at the mobile phone in my hand. I'd been trying to reach someone I hadn't spoken to in a very long time. I'd already attempted to contact him a few times but to no avail. I decided to try reaching him once more. Redialling the number on my mobile phone, I hoped that Anh Hong would pick up.

'Hello! Who is this?' a man's voice asked.

My entire body electrified.

'Is this Father John?' I asked. Even though he was speaking English, I could recognise Anh Hong's voice.

'Yes, it is me,' he replied. 'Who is this, and how can I help you?'

'This is Ha-Le. I'm Minh's wife. Do you remember us?'

'Yes, I do!' he said, switching to Vietnamese. 'Wow, it has been a long time! How many years has it been already?'

'It's been at least twenty-five years since we met in Bankstown,' I answered. 'Maybe longer. So, what can I call you now: Father John or Anh Hong?'

He laughed. 'Just call me Anh Hong – Same as before.'

'Wonderful,' I said. 'So, listen Anh Hong, the reason I am reaching out to you is that I need your help. I am writing my memoir. I've finished all of the parts when we were on the sea, but I feel like I missed something. I thought that you would be the best person to give me every detail of our dangerous journey. I'm so thankful to have gotten back in touch with you.'

I paused here, taking a breath, and then continued.

'Two years ago, Le came here from America, and we flew to the Gold Coast and searched for you, but we were told you were away. Thank God we have reconnected now!'

'I don't know how much I can help, Ha-Le!' he said. 'I am a Father, and I have a lot of work to do.'

'I know! I know!' I interjected. 'I understand that you're very busy, and so that's why I got straight to the point with my question about our voyage. Do you have time to help me with this?'

'Sure!' he replied. 'But I only have about thirty minutes to talk now. We will have to finish chatting another time.'

We planned a time to meet, and Anh Hong gave me invaluable information for my book. I listened to what he said and took notes with blurred vision. Tears dropped onto the back of my hand as I jotted down each sentence. His insights made everything so much clearer. He helped create vivid scenes, bringing my past to life. Events from years ago played out in front of my eyes as if they had only happened yesterday.

The first thing I heard was the sound of people cheering. It pulled me out of my sleep and the dark dreams I had been having.

'That's right. We have just escaped the jaws of the shark.' A young man's voice seemed to cut through the air and dim the cheers with his words. The reaction was immediate. There was a bout of nervous laughter that erupted all around me.

'It may seem like I'm joking, but really, a school of sharks followed us for a few hours back there.' The people around me indulged him with another bout of nervous laughter before someone else decided to speak up.

'Just tell us if we are out of Vietnam or not.'

This time, the voice belonged to a woman. I wanted to know the answer to her question, so I brushed away the material that covered my face. The bright light that surrounded us hit me like a ton of bricks, triggering a pounding headache, accompanied by a wave of nausea that caused me to shield my eyes. That didn't help me a lot, though. I still felt sick and miserable in the cramped boat.

Once my eyes adjusted to the light and my body started to move past the headache, I took stock of my surroundings. The young man who spoke first sat up, seeming pleasant and full of energy for a man stuck on an overcrowded boat in the middle of the ocean; his dark hair was slicked back from his face as he chatted with another passenger. I couldn't help but dwell on where we were and how we had gotten here, we had feared that the dogs barking after us would catch us. The moments when the boat's engine seemed like it was malfunctioning. Our boat got caught in a fishing net sometime during the night. We had waited with bated breath when it seemed like we would be captured by a group of fishermen no less!

The fishermen had taken one look at us and known that we were trying to flee the country; luckily, we were able to buy their silence with some money and jewellery.

'Hey, everything is going to be OK. We made it and we are out of Vietnam.' The voice of a woman pulled me out of my thoughts. She laid a gentle hand on my arm and helped me wiggle into a sitting position. It was harder than it should have been because of how tightly packed we all were.

The voyage had been long and arduous. As it neared an end, I felt like I was leaping over an enormous hurdle. This trip had been dangerous and unpleasant. Minh and I had both dealt with a great deal of nausea and illness throughout the journey. Minh had especially struggled throughout this trip. His well-being deteriorated quickly. He had debilitating headaches and suffered greatly. I was tasked with caring for him, as well as myself.

From here, the memories seemed to rush back. I remembered the shock I had felt when the boat sailed through the centre of Da Nang and how I had been able to see the streets one last time through a gap in the tarpaulin. I had been able to see the stone chairs where I sat with my friends for many years, fire trees, and buildings that I knew so well. I wished for the boat to move slower, even though I knew it wasn't wise to linger; I wanted to look at everything, experience everything one last time before I left my beloved city.

My heart sang a sad goodbye song, and my eyes blurred with loss. I wanted to take everything in; I wanted to keep the sight of my home in my heart because I didn't know when I would be back to see my home and my loved ones. Sometimes we think we are capable of something, but then we attempt it, and we find ourselves truly challenged. Still, it is these challenges that create our strength.

I hadn't known leaving would be so incredibly hard. I felt torn. A part of me had wanted to go, and the other part wanted to stay, but I didn't have the luxury of waffling in indecision. I had chosen to go, and it was too late to reverse that decision. I had to take responsibility for the path I'd chosen.

I didn't know that we were heading for the sea; I merely assumed that we were going to take a less obvious path. It was as daring as setting forth from a Viet Cong village. Although no one would suspect a small fishing boat to be laden with refugees, it was still a risky move. In some ways, it was a brilliant idea. In others, it was pure madness.

'Goodbye, my Vietnam.' I whispered. My heart was heavy, and my vision blurred with tears.

❤ ❤ ❤ ❤

The trip had a rough start. Our captain was hardly an expert. In fact, he didn't even have the necessary equipment. Turning to the crowds on deck, our young captain asked us, 'Now, who has a compass?'

There was a horrified silence that followed. It stretched out between us, straining between the passengers and crew. I refrained from looking over at Minh. He had straightened his back and was standing tall and serious as if the captain's words had sealed our fate, and all that was left to do was to brace ourselves for the inevitable.

'I do,' a young man answered. 'I have a compass.' He retrieved the compass and passed it up through the crowd. It moved from one set of hands to another until it reached the hands of the captain.

'Great, thank you. Now, who knows how to work it?' the captain said.

His words were without a trace of humour. Minh almost laughed, thinking it was some kind of a joke, but then he realised that the captain was serious, and he stepped up, admitting that he knew how to read a compass.

Minh's admission drew the attention of the people around him, but it was his identification as a professor of English by a young man who had given the captain his compass that got everyone's attention. My husband's academic prowess just might be the ticket to America for everyone on board. They were also shocked because they knew that he was taking a higher risk by escaping.

His punishment would have been severe if he was caught.

♥ ♥ ♥ ♥

Our captain came from a small fishing village in Da Nang. He had no formal training. All he knew about sailing was what he'd learned by watching other sailors and by going through the process of trial and error. His family had sent him to a Catholic monastery with plans for him to become a priest, but he was naughty and got expelled before he earned his qualification. After the war, he became a fisherman to support his family; he had no formal schooling after grade six. Captaining the boat was an opportunity to get out of Vietnam, and he seized it as soon as it was offered to him.

His name was Anh Hong, and he would later become a priest in Australia.

He had decided to captain this ship to get out of Vietnam; however, when they showed him the boat, he predicted that it would last three days on the ocean. To be fair, I thought that he was too generous with that estimate. The boat was small and seemed to be made with a mash of second-hand parts of other similar boats. To make things worse, he had agreed to do it as long as the people on board didn't exceed fifteen, only to find out that the boat would carry fifty-four passengers. All of these people were now depending on him to get through this ordeal with their lives intact.

'We were all on a suicide mission.' Anh Hong laughed as we reminisced years later.

♥ ♥ ♥ ♥

The stuffiness of the cramped space made my nausea flare up every time someone applied Tiger Balm or Singapore Green Oil. It always reminded me of how my grandmother used to use these same treatments to retain her health. The overpowering scent of diesel didn't help either. It brought back vivid memories of the Phan Thiet trip with my family before Saigon fell. Slowly but surely, the combination of those two scents made me feel sicker. Other people retched over the side of the boat continuously, contributing even more to my nausea.

There were sick people all around me. Next to me was a girl who kept trying to cling to me for comfort. Her face, red with spots, made her look like an abstract painting. She cried out all the time. 'Water! So hot!' she would yell. 'Please let me jump down to the sea.' She begged. A couple of girls dragged her back next to me when she tried to move over to the edge of the boat. The next day, her face turned from very red to as pale as a sheet of white paper. Her messy hair was covered in a bit of her own vomit. I felt sick when I looked at her. She looked like the dead people I had seen on the roads when escaping from Da-Nang to Sai-Gon. Somehow, I was scared to be close to her even as she was alive and needing care, and I just wanted to look the other way.

The sun beat down on us aggressively, a constant reminder that we were alone and exposed in the middle of the ocean. I tried to feel grateful for just being alive and free; however, the main feeling I had was of incredible hunger and thirst. My throat felt parched and dry, so I asked for a cup of water. The water tasted foul. I spat it out and inspected it. It was murky and full of strange particles. It was obviously river water, but rather than hand the cup back to the burly looking man in charge of the water rations, I drank every drop and stifled the urge to vomit. The taste of the river water lingered in my mouth for a while, but I knew I couldn't afford to be picky. I sent Minh to ask for food, but he returned empty-handed. The man in charge of the rations made it clear that we were all to receive our meals at a specific time, and I had to wait until then. I began to panic, thinking of the baby growing inside of me. I felt the baby tossing and turning, and each time I panicked, I realised the baby was panicking too. The child inside of me would share every feeling that I had. I tried to calm down. A futile endeavour because I had never experienced hunger in my life, and I felt even worse with concern for my unborn baby.

I watched two women try quite frantically to keep a small fire alight to cook rice: despite how much they rearranged their belongings to shield the fire, the wind still found a way to extinguish the flames. I was afraid that the wind would upturn the wood stove and condemn us to a fiery death. After a few hours, they produced a partially cooked nugget of rice for each passenger. I really had to force myself to swallow it and keep it down for the sake of my baby. We had been told that the journey would take seven days, maybe ten if the wind was against us. I didn't think I could last one more.

There was a point in time when one of the crew members thought he had spotted Hainan. My husband was called over to help them figure out where we were. He took one look at the compass, spoke to the captain and crew, and shuffled over to continue lying in a fetal position. His seasickness had him in a tight grip, but he was able to inform me that we hadn't reached Hainan yet. We were in a delicate position; we were close to the island of Hainan, but we were also close to North Vietnam. If the wind changed, we could be blown back to the country we had run away from.

We soon caught sight of some mountains, which brightened everyone's spirits, until we got caught in the force of a strong wind that seemed to be pushing us away from land. The captain tried his best, but in the end, we were at the mercy of the winds and the sea.

The violent waves of the ocean made everyone's seasickness much worse. I turned onto my side with retching and moaning all around and did my best to block it all out. I slept a fitful sleep until the voice of the captain roused me.

'Listen up!' he said. 'I need to ask you all to remain very still. If you need to go to the toilet or throw up, do it very slowly and carefully. We are in the middle of a reef, and we don't know what is down there, so please, no sudden movements, OK?'

Anh Hong tried to set us at ease. He told us being in the middle of a reef meant that we were close to land. He sounded positive about us reaching land, as long as we didn't capsize the boat. I didn't have a lot of strength left, so I marvelled at the way he leapt around like a jungle cat as he steered us away from dark masses underneath the water. However, as the sun went down, it soon became too dangerous for Anh Hong to continue steering, so he decided to turn off the engine.

'God, I tried my best, and now I leave everything in your hands,' our captain said.

He was obviously trying to keep us from hearing the terror in his voice. We weren't all Christians on the boat; some of us were atheists, Catholics, or Buddhists, but we were all united in our fear that day. There was a little boy, Cu Do, who kept shaking so badly because he couldn't hold back his sobs. My heart ached for him. He had tried so hard to be brave for his mum, but he could no longer keep his fear at bay.

At one point, we saw a Chinese boat passing by a few hundred meters away. Everyone yelled at it to stop, but if they heard shouts, they ignored us. China and Vietnam were not exactly great friends at that time, politically and culturally.

The boat suddenly lurched as it hit something, making an awful screeching noise as it seemed to drag against the reef, and for one heart-wrenching moment, it seemed like our boat was about to capsize. However, our luck wasn't that good, and according to the captain, we had lost the boat's propeller and rudder as a result of our collision with the reef. The silver lining was that we soon were close to land, and Anh Hong was able to get down and start pulling the boat towards the shore.

'I was in pain as I had so many cuts on my feet, but I tried my best for the fifty-four lives on board,' Anh Hong recalled later.

Other than Minh and me, only a few men offered to get out and help Anh Hong. Like Anh Hong and the rest of the men, I suffered many cuts to my feet when I got off the boat. The sand rubbed my cuts raw. When we were done, I limped to the shore and buried my feet in the sand to stop the bleeding.

I was unbearably exhausted and fell asleep quickly that night.

I slept for several hours before I woke up to the sounds of commotion. Minh informed me what had happened. We had lost a passenger. It was a young woman named Tu. It was the girl who had laid next to me when I was at the heights of seasickness. She had been just as ill as I was and had fallen over onto me many times. In irritation and misery, I'd shoved her aside. I had treated her so callously, and now she was dead. I sobbed in guilt and sadness. In normal life, perhaps Tu and I would be good friends.

That night I looked up at the stars. I regretted leaving already, and it was only the second night. I missed my family. I missed the comforts we had left behind at home. Fear reinforced these thoughts. We had already lost a passenger. I knew that we were exposed to nature's whims, and without proper food, we could die. I touched my belly and apologised to my baby, as I wondered if it would ever be able to see the stars.

'Sorry, my dear child! Sorry for bringing you to this tribulation!' my face got burning with tears.

CHAPTER THIRTY-FIVE

~

HANG IN THERE!

When morning came, we were asked to pool together the gold we had to buy replacement parts for the boat and some extra supplies. We couldn't object. We were much too concerned with our survival. There was a small town nearby, and a group was assigned to walk there in search of the goods we needed. I decided to go along, mainly out of curiosity, but when I saw how comfortable the locals' homes were, I was struck with longing. All that I wanted at that moment was to have a shower.

I followed that longing with a single-minded determination. I walked from house to house, miming my request. Because I couldn't speak Hainanese, I think most of them thought I was crazy, and I was shooed away from each house. Finally, I met an old woman who waved her hand to stop me from gesturing and led me to her outside well to wash. The water felt velvety smooth on my skin, and I marvelled at how a shower without soap felt like such a luxury to me. The dirt and smoke from the engine turned the water black as I poured it over my hair. I almost couldn't believe that all that dirt was coming from me.

We returned to the camp. We had decided to stay in unenclosed fishing storage shed nearby with some supplies. That night, we ate instant noodles mixed with vegetables. We had gotten them from the market, and we devoured them like they were a New Year's treat. They were the best noodles of my life, and I sucked at each string with unashamed delight; we were too relieved to pretend otherwise. However, the relief didn't last long, as a group of teenage boys from the village gathered around the shelter, staring at the pretty girls in the group, making loud comments in their language and snickering to themselves. Le and I joked that they were spellbound by Vietnamese beauty as a way of lightening the mood. It worked for a while, and we were able to put the boys out of our minds.

We shouldn't have bothered because the boys returned later that night, this time with more men. They moved through our camp quietly and started rifling through our personal belongings. We thought they were after our gold, and we didn't want any trouble, so we let them search. Eventually, they ran away when one of our men stood up and yelled at them. Later, some girls told us that the boys had laid their hands on them. When I heard this, I wished that we had stopped them sooner. There was a feeling of helplessness that surrounded our camp for a while. The men rearranged themselves into a circle to protect the women. The boys did not return. I am not sure we would have survived if the villagers had decided to turn against us.

Our travails had made us stronger as a unit. We were no longer strangers who didn't care for anyone but ourselves; we had formed a bond. It was sad that our newfound unity couldn't take us back in time to save Tu. On the fourth morning, the winds cleared, and Anh Hong finally gave us the go-ahead to leave; however, before we did, the Buddhists insisted that he should apologise to Tu so that her spirit wouldn't curse the boat. I developed more respect for Anh Hong that day because even though he was apparently uncomfortable with the idea, he still apologised to her in his own way for the circumstances. We were all happy to leave the island behind, even though we didn't know what was waiting for us once we left.

I said my prayers from the boat; I felt sorry that she never made it to freedom. The fact that she had died so young, having seen so little of the world, added to the sorrow weighing upon me. The only thing I could do was pray for her soul and pray that no one else would die on this journey with me.

❤ ❤ ❤ ❤

We were in good spirits when we passed the reef and made it to the open ocean, but even that was short-lived. Suddenly, our boat's engine stopped. Despite the best efforts of Anh Hong and his assistants, the engine refused to work, and so we were left to the mercy of the winds. The possibility of reaching Hong Kong seemed to be slipping through our fingers like fine sand.

We floated aimlessly upon the waves for a while, and it seemed like we would soon join the legions of people who had been sucked into the sea's embrace. If not by the winds that tossed us around, then by the waves that lapped close to the edge of the boat, or by the rains that bore down upon us. It was hard not to admit that it seemed like a watery grave was inevitable. I caught many glimpses of sunken boats beneath the water's surface. I didn't know how many people had died already, but I knew that I didn't want to join them.

We were like that for two days and nights, being tossed around by the wind, afraid it was taking us back to Vietnam but powerless to stop it. The hunger and thirst hit us all hard. Food and drink were restricted because we didn't know when we would see land again or where we would end up. I recalled stories of people lost at sea who were forced to drink their own urine and eat human flesh to survive. My baby seemed restless within me, and one side of my stomach felt hard. I began to panic for my baby's survival.

'Be alive with mum, dear child. We will fight together for our survival,' I kept chanting. Later that night, a man named Anh Binh offered to help with the engine. He was a strong man who used to be a boxer. We hoped that brute strength would be enough to start the engine, but we had no such luck.

Then, some of us slept. I did not dream of death. I only dreamed of food – Papaya salad, dried squid, steamed fish and spring rolls. Mountains of fresh salads, endless miles of beef jerky, and steaming hot bowls of Pho danced in my mind. It was more torturous than the threat of drowning or being lost at sea. I shed tears of guilt for my unborn baby. I felt so hungry and fearful, and I knew my baby did too. My mouth kept watering with my imagination of the foods I was craving for. Never before had I starved to that degree. Hunger and burning emotions tightened their grip on us while the little boat with its dead engine lulled relentlessly in the ocean.

My body longed for food like it was a drug, and I was an addict. I was crazy with particular cravings that I knew could never be satisfied by the mouldy rice and the raw dried potatoes we had on board. The sun was not yet up, but I could make out the outline of Anh Hong, still staring at the engine. I shuffled closer to him and asked him if he was OK.

Someone tried to get the engine to work every few hours, and the men painted a large S.O.S in charcoal and tied it up facing east. That couldn't stop us from drifting, but twice we saw a boat in the distance, and we tried to get the passengers' attention. We yelled until our voices were hoarse, but there was no response. The poor boy who had sacrificed his shirt for the S.O.S got a bad sunburn. Others also took off their shirts to write S.O.S messages. Five men lost their shirts to the wind. Despondency began to set in even more, and we were beginning to think about the option of a quick death, as opposed to the drawn-out affair the ocean was promising. But Anh Hong was hopeful. According to him, God was looking out for us.

Suddenly, Anh Hong's voice broke the hopeless silence that had settled in like the foggy mist that surrounded us.

'Land! Land!' he yelled.

After two days and nights of seeing nothing except water, we almost didn't believe him. He was right, though. Through the morning fog, we saw what we believed to be China. It looked like a smudge of brown on the horizon. Soon the fog cleared enough for us to realise that we were closer to land than we expected. We could make out the silhouettes of trees and buildings.

There was an obstacle between us and the solace that land offered: the engine. The waters were too dangerous for us to make it to land without an engine, and the distance was far enough that we would drown if the boat capsized. We saw no way to get out of it until Anh Ha, a man who usually kept to himself, spoke up.

'Let me try to fix the engine. I used to work on motorbikes a long time ago. Please don't get your hopes up.'

He spoke softly, as if he was afraid that we would lash out at him. He was not wrong; his words angered us all. If he could have fixed the engine, why did we have to suffer all those days? We got our hopes up, though. How could we not?

When he finished, we looked at the engine that seemed to carry all our hopes, and waited with bated breath as the boxer, Anh Binh, cranked the shaft. Once it started, the rumble of an engine had never sounded sweeter to me. The other passengers agreed, and we cheered in unison, an action that almost capsized the boat. Our joy was short lived. The engine stopped a hundred metres before we reached the truly rough waters. The boxer started it up again, and this time, the captain proceeded with caution. I wish I could tell you that it was smooth sailing from there, that the engine behaved, and we passed through the rough waters without a hitch, but that would be a lie. The engine stopped, and Anh Binh started it again. This was a process that repeated itself, a process we didn't understand but feared.

'Ten minutes. The engine goes for only ten minutes at a time,' Anh Hong announced.

'What does that mean?' someone asked. A quick look in the speaker's direction revealed that he had dark hair, a face smudged with dirt and a wild look in his eyes. I think we all looked that way.

'It means we have ten minutes to cross that stretch of water,' Anh Hong said carefully. Minh and I looked at the vast expanse of water between us and the land that seemed to stretch out like an insurmountable obstacle.

'Is it enough?' I asked the captain. Anh Hong didn't answer me. He simply warned us to hold on and be prepared to charge the turbulent waters.

We hit the water fast, and the boat groaned under pressure. There was no time to slow down, so we skimmed across the tops of the waves. Each wave made the boat bounce a little, and soon it seemed like we were dancing to a frantic beat that could consume us if we made a wrong move. It would have been fun if we weren't scared for our lives. I held my belly tight, hoping to keep my baby safe.

CHAPTER THIRTY-SIX

~

THE PRICE OF FREEDOM

The rhythm stopped as quickly as it had started. The boat settled in the calm water, and Anh Hong breathed a sigh of relief. He looked to the sky as he prayed. We were so proud of him, and we joined him in celebrating the miracle. The now gentle waves took us to the shore. All of the women jumped down as soon as the water was shallow enough, paying no attention to the men who demanded to know what we were doing. We hadn't been able to pee in days, as the danger wasn't enough to convince us to pull our pants down and pee in full view of everyone. We peed through our pants then, and the sense of relief grew stronger. Strong enough that we ignored the Chinese people who shook their heads at us as they walked by. We all understood what we had done, and soon the knowledge had us giggling, happy, and relieved. It made me a little uneasy, but we just didn't care when compared with the last few days. We had already passed through the most difficult challenge of the journey. We now sat on the shore and recovered our spirits. We had just faced a major ordeal. Nothing could take the feeling of relief from us.

'We are safe now. I am alive, and I will see you one day soon,' I said to the baby in my stomach. My words were full of confidence and hope.

One of the group leaders went around collecting the rest of our gold to buy a new engine, but we had already given ours away in Hainan, so we had nothing left to give to him. However, some people had held on to their stashes selfishly. Now, their selfishness was helping us, and we found ourselves glad for it.

I saw countless sea snails lying on the shore. My eyes lit up with joy and anticipation. I knew that snails were excellent protein for my baby. I felt like I'd found a pile of gold on the street. How ecstatic I was!

I bent down and picked one up. These snails were the favourite snack of poor people in Vietnam, and my babysitter had shared them with me once. She fried them with coconut and lemongrass. They were delicious. I went back and borrowed a large pot and collected a few hundred for dinner. While we waited, I gathered sea snails and boiled them. At first, people looked at me as if I was doing something disgusting, but they realised they liked it after they tried the food.

The night grew cold and windy, a change that would have killed us for sure if we were still out on the ocean. We took shelter in some mangroves and cut branches to lay over ourselves. It was the only way we could keep ourselves warm. My body became itchy through the night, and I had to throw the branches away to keep from itching. I wrapped my hands around myself in a tight hug. I wanted to keep my body warm for my baby, but I kept shivering all night from the extreme cold.

Minh examined my body in the morning and found tiny red spots all over me; bites from fleas or sand flies could have caused them. Another possibility was that I was allergic to all of the sea snails I'd eaten. However, there was yet another dreadful option that I didn't want to consider. As my heart rattled away in a fearful and frantic rhythm, I recalled Tu, the woman who had died on the boat. I remembered seeing tiny red spots on her skin just before she'd died. I hoped and prayed that I hadn't caught something from her, some dangerous disease that would bring my unborn baby and me to our untimely deaths.

Later that morning, we learned through Linh, a woman who spoke Chinese, and acted as our interpreter to the richly dressed couples who walked past, that there was a five-star resort nearby. Minh and I decided to walk up the beach to get some exercise, and as we walked in the sand, there was no mistaking the way everyone was looking at us. Our clothes and faces were dirty so that I couldn't blame them, but I was struck by the reality of how far we had fallen. I could not believe that I was a real beggar, perhaps one of the most impoverished beggars in the world.

We marvelled, with heavy hearts, at how quickly we had lost our status. Our families had fought and struggled so hard to gain and retain their reputation in society. Ours was stripped to nothing in a week. The price of freedom was so high!

When we returned, Linh informed us that they had traded the gold for Chinese money to buy a new engine, but they couldn't find a suitable one that morning. Instead, they brought some barbecued duck back, and it was divided evenly among us all. My mouth watered at the thought of delicious barbecued duck. Minh gave his portion to me, as did Hung and Tram.

'For the baby,' they all said in turn. I savoured every morsel and even ground up the bones with my teeth for calcium.

The news that I was pregnant spread like wildfire through our group. No one wanted a pregnant woman on a long and dangerous journey. The group leaders gave us all a bit of money to buy whatever we wanted, and I immediately knew what I wanted - more barbecued duck. We went into the beautiful little town, and I bought myself half a duck and very hot chilli sauce with my money. I ate it like a ravenous lioness while my Le, Bo, Na, and Bi cheered me on.

The police were already at our camp when we got back. We didn't need an interpreter to know that they wanted us to leave. Even if we'd wanted to cooperate with their request, the waves were too choppy, and we still had no boat engine. We were more afraid of death than whatever the police planned on doing to make sure we left. One of the policemen faced down our captain and kept pointing at a map.

'The wind is too strong. Unless you want to give us one of your nice speedboats, there is no way we are going back in the water. You may as well shoot us right here.' He gestured to prove his point before walking away from them. The policemen erupted in a fury, and once again, we didn't need an interpreter to explain what they were saying. We understood perfectly.

That night, the terrible itchiness returned with a vengeance. This time it was accompanied by painful shivers and a high fever. Minh examined me in the morning. He had studied some medicine in school. He looked at my skin. Each red mark now had pus coming out of it. I could not move without a searing pain shooting down my spine to my legs. He told me that my condition was severe. If I did not get medicine, I would die of infection within twenty-four hours.

The news of my illness spread through the camp very quickly. No one wanted a pregnant woman to die on the journey, as they believed the trip would be even more cursed if that happened. So, people came to visit me. Some brought ginger and garlic for me to chew to ward away the fever; others brought sweets, duck and anything else they had for me to eat.

Hung took control and dispersed the gathering crowd, telling them that I must be taken into town immediately. He lifted me into his arms and took off at a fast pace, with Minh and Linh hurrying behind us. I felt like I was taking my last breaths, and I had to tap Hung to put me down after a while. The jolting had made me nauseous. Although releasing a stream of foul-smelling vomit made me feel lighter and even helped me breathe easier, Hung still insisted on taking me to see a doctor.

Luckily for us, we were able to find a doctor willing to treat me in a beautiful, clean villa. He gave me some medication, and it took me four days to finally recover.

We had secured a new engine but were still waiting out the bad weather. Every day, I took a walk along the beach to get some exercise. I needed the fresh air to get stronger.

Sometimes, when I took my walks, I would look at our forlorn group from a distance, huddling together to stay warm, and I understood the disdain of the wealthy, Chinese couples. We were pathetic. No one, save for that kind doctor, cared if we lived or died: our existence was of no value to anyone. There was also the fact that our families had no way of knowing if we were safe. We were like the sea snails – scattered, with nothing more than the clothes on our backs, nothing to protect us from predators. We had only a boat to serve as our protective shell, while the ocean's unpredictability threatened us.

I thought then that if I could magically transport myself back to Vietnam, I would. By that point in time, I would rather have lived under the regime. I would rather have lived in discomfort that I understood and could count on than continue to deal with the jarring uncertainty of our untenable situation. But alas, that fantasy was not possible. We had cast our lots the minute our feet left Vietnamese soil. When we boarded that boat, the arrow had been shot. We were now swept along in that arrow's wake. All that we could do was hope to stay alive and hope that our arrow landed somewhere favourable.

CHAPTER THIRTY-SEVEN

~

A HERALD OF DOOM

'Yeah! Last day of school! See you later at Sydney Town Hall!' Hong-An called out cheerfully.

She was wearing a dark, navy blue blazer, covered in numerous pins and medals. It was the day of Hong-An's assembly. She was graduating from Year Twelve. My daughter was beaming with excitement, and my own heart was swelling with pride. We had made it through her high school years together. She had worked hard and studied hard, and I had been right behind her, cheering her on throughout it all. This was the last day that my daughter would wear her high school uniform. I was filled with love and bittersweet feelings for my daughter.

She clasped my hands. 'I made it! I can't believe I'm finally done! Thank God!'

Happy tears streamed down my swollen face. I was undergoing treatment for my thyroid cancer, and one of the symptoms was the current puffiness of my face. It wasn't an ideal situation, but I was OK. I was still alive and sharing a crucial moment in my daughter's life. I had so very much to be grateful for. I had survived for my daughter. I was still able to work, and between myself and Minh, our income was enough to send Hong-An to one of the best schools in Sydney. I was so blessed to have been able to give my daughter the best education possible. I couldn't ask God for more. Between my daughter's love for me and her academic success and bright future, I had all of the blessings that a mother could ask for.

'My friends and I are all going to tear one of our dress uniforms in a few days. We are going to tie the strips of torn fabric into our hair and around our waist to celebrate the end of our school girl life!' Hong-An laughed. 'Won't that be silly?'

'Go for it! Why not?' I laughed along with her.

I watched Hong-An's face, alight with laughter and joy, looking so happy and blessed. I knew that I had made the right choice when I decided to risk everything and escape from Vietnam. I remembered all of the horrors that I'd seen take place during that voyage. I recalled how I had clutched my pregnant stomach in fear, wondering if my child would make it through, wondering if he or she would be born healthy and go on to live a happy and prosperous life. Well, all of that had happened. My child had been spared and had grown into a beautiful and vibrant young woman who had a bright and lucrative future ahead of her.

I thought back to the journey that had brought us to where we were today. There was still a shadow of terror in my heart as I recalled the most horrific night we spent at sea.

'Yes! We made it together! I can't believe that we have finally come to this point in our lives! Thank God!'

❤ ❤ ❤ ❤

After we refused to leave, the police came back with double the manpower and triple the aggression. They had the look of murder in their eyes. They held leather straps so tightly that it seemed to cut off circulation from their hands. Many in the group ran away when they saw them coming, but I was still weak and recovering from the infection so that I couldn't get away. I only managed to stand up before they raided the camp and started hitting people with leather straps. I fell to the ground, unable to defend myself, and the police took advantage of that and kept hitting me.

The new scabs on my body started bleeding. The sight of them beating me enraged Minh. He screamed and tried to charge at the police, but others held him back in our camp.

'You are hitting a pregnant lady!' Many people shouted at them. The voices rose together, amplifying as others joined in. Everyone was horrified by what the police were doing to me. The police then backed away, and I thought people might try to get their revenge and attack them. Luckily, they didn't; otherwise, the police might have beaten some people to death. I had no doubts that the officers would take it that far. I lay there, with sand in my hair, clothes, and wounds, crumpled and defeated on the ground.

The policemen finally left us alone when we started packing our things and making our way back to the boat. Even then, they watched us like hawks, ready to descend upon us with their leather straps, if at any moment it seemed like we were going to change our minds about leaving.

The wind had not died down. It was just as intense as ever, and it was whipping the waves into a frenzy, a warning to anyone who dared to brave the waters that day.

'You are sending us to our deaths!' Linh kept repeating a final plea to arouse compassion. But the police had no empathy, or if they did, they had put it aside when it came to their dealings with us. We were like vermin in their land. They wanted to exterminate us. Sending us back to the sea was the sea's problem and not theirs. They did not care what that meant for us. Our lives had no value to them. We were nothing to them, so they didn't feel bad about sending us to our deaths.

It was challenging to get the boat out to sea again. It was like a suicide mission again. The wind and the waves were violent rioters, joining forces to torment us, constantly provoking and pushing us around. They bullied us, splashing water over the edges of the boat just as fast as the men could bail it out. It was all that we could do to keep afloat. The ocean was determined to sink us. All that we could do was hang on and hoped that we survived.

We were all soaked through. My body was on fire with pain as my new wounds absorbed the sting of the saltwater. We pressed on against the wind, exerting pressure on our new engine until the camp was only a dark haze in the evening light. Nausea hit us all hard. Everyone vomited, either on themselves or into the sea. We pressed as close to the edge of the boat as we dared, still afraid that a random wave could pluck us out of the boat. During a crisis, people usually turn to faith, and this was no exception. The sounds of prayers and feverish chanting echoed through the air. Everyone appealed to the force that they believed in. "God, please have mercy on us!' they prayed. Buddha, be with us.' they chanted. You could hear these words overlap as they echoed through the wind.

Ounces of Tiger Balm and Singapore Green Oil were smeared over every available surface of the exposed skin in the vain hope that it would ward off the chaos. It didn't.

I had convinced the crew to save the fuel bottles for the women and children that could not swim. These would help them float, and hopefully, survive long enough to get rescued. In the growing danger, Minh whispered in my ear, telling me to lunge for them as extra protection if the inevitable happened. No one mentioned it, but we all kept a close eye on the empty diesel bottles. We all knew that the chances of being rescued were slim, so those diesel bottles wouldn't really be of use. Anyone who took a bottle to stay afloat was likely to die of starvation and exposure. That didn't matter to us. We all saw those bottles as our one slight chance at survival, and we wanted to take that chance, however small it might be.

'We might have killed each other for those bottles.' Anh Ha would joke later, but it would be a joke with a deadly truth behind it. We had gone past the point of unity. The feelings of camaraderie we had once felt had dissipated in the mad desperation for survival.

As the night wore on, the rough weather graduated into a furious storm intent on punishing us for braving the sea. Raindrops smacked violently against us. The mix of fresh water from the rain and saltwater from the sea kept my body in a perpetual state of pain. The rain landed hard enough to undo whatever healing my wounds had achieved, and the splashes of saltwater stung – a process that repeated itself over and over again. I held on to the side of the boat and hugged my knees to my chest, to protect myself and the baby. The boat wobbled as if preparing to offer us to the sea.

Surely, I thought, this was it. We had been bailed out by God too many times already, and we were at the end of our journey. It would be a dramatic way to end our tumultuous trip. We all prepared ourselves for death, with the taste of saltwater in our mouths and a flood of water filling our noses and lungs.

We each began to grieve for our impending death in the same way. Everyone held onto their last moments of life with regret. We regretted ever setting foot on that boat. We regretted ever undertaking such an enormous risk. We had known before going into this that we were putting our lives at risk. Now, we were going to pay for taking that chance.

The tiny boat carried fifty-four tired and worn bodies through the rough giant waves that dark night. We feared the boat might be broken into pieces at any time, and my heart almost popped out of my chest every time the boat slid down from the top of the giant waves. I called out to my parents and my brothers. I wished I could see their faces just one last time. I knew in my heart that I would never see my hometown, my Vietnam, again. It would be my last night with Minh, and my unborn baby, and the fifty-four other terrified souls on board.

'I'm so sorry, baby. Sorry for getting you into this trouble,' I said, holding my belly tight. I was filled with guilt. It was not myself that I was sad for, but my unborn child. I regretted subjecting my child to this horrific experience. I was saddened not for the impending loss of my own life but for the fact that I might never bring my baby into the world.

Fifty-four lives, with fifty-four different stories, were all facing death as one. There was no more hope. No one prayed anymore; they didn't see the need to. The boys yelled and worked together to bail water out of the boat, but it felt like they were just barely holding back something inevitable. Some were already extremely exhausted. They no longer fought fate. They no longer held onto the edge of the boat. They almost seemed to relish the thought of being swept away. I held on for my life and watched everyone as if it was my last chance to observe the people who had been with me for the two weeks of this intense journey. I whispered my prayers; that was all that I had in my power to do. That was all that I could do for my baby, my husband, and myself. Death had already spared us many times. I didn't expect him to be kind enough to spare us once more. Minh held my hand tight. We both understood that if we died, we went together with our baby.

But God and nature were the same force. That force nearly broke us into tiny pieces that night. But then that very same force cleared the sky and settled the sea by the morning. Much to my surprise, I woke to the whir of the engine and the sound of birds, hardly believing that we'd survived. I'm sure the other passengers felt the same way. It was a miracle. Not only had we not been consumed by the sea the night before, but we'd also woken up to beautiful weather, better weather than we'd seen on our journey so far. I took a breath of air, and it was fresh and rejuvenating. All traces of despair from the night before had vanished. It was as if they'd been washed away by the rain. I touched my belly instinctively to see if my baby was OK. I was now two and a half months pregnant. I could feel the mass changing inside me, an evolution I felt blessed to be a part of. The little being was still barely visible from the outside, but I could feel it waking. I could feel that little being demanding life.

We'd fought to stay alive and afloat all night, and in the midst of all that, we'd lost direction completely. Nobody knew where we were. All that we saw, from every angle, was the vast and unforgiving sea. We needed to reach Hong Kong if we wanted to gain our freedom, but that freedom was still so far from reach. We'd already come so far; we'd already given so much, and yet, we still had no way to find our destination. We were powerless. All that we could do was turn our lives over to God's will. Our fate was in His hands now.

I wasn't sure if I had the strength to hang onto my life. I'd already gone through so much, overcoming scabies, hunger, beatings, illness, fear and despair. Was it possible that my baby might be giving me the strength that I needed to fight for both of our lives? I leaned into my love for my unborn baby and held onto the amazing experience of a sacred and powerful love amid a fight for survival.

The two of us fought together. And we lived.

CHAPTER THIRTY-EIGHT

~

LANGUISHED

Have you been crying, darling? What has happened?' Le asked. 'Nothing. Just felt overjoyed after talking with Anh Hong again.' 'You have both chatted?'

'Yes! I just want to confirm with him that everything I remembered was correct. We were so lucky, Le! We have been alive in this beautiful world! You have built your life in America, while Minh, Hong-An, and I have built lives in Australia! The people from our boat have all survived and now live all over the world. Our fates were the same once, but now we've all gone off to live out our lives across the globe. It's truly beautiful.' I said to Le, holding my breath.

I was so filled up with gratitude. I felt the intense joy of my many blessings. Back when we'd been on that boat, we all could have easily vanished without a trace. Each of our stories could have stopped there.

People from our boat are everywhere. We have all survived and are still alive. 'You are quite excited today!' Le said, sounding puzzled by my words.

Our journey happened over thirty years ago. The memories seemed to fade for the others with each passing year, but they were still very fresh and vivid for me. Maybe these memories were another blessing. Remembering the rough road I'd travelled had helped me to truly treasure the life I have. There had been fifty-five people in that boat. Fifty-five people and fifty-five stories. Surviving the sea and then surviving Hong Kong, these experiences became a legend in my mind, and I lived that legend.

Le's next words cut into my thinking.

'So, are you ready to come to America, Ha-Le? Only three more months till that day arrives!'

'Yes!' I replied enthusiastically. 'I surely am! We have been waiting for this celebration for the past thirty years. America is calling me!'

'Make sure you make Australia proud of you, in front of more than 600 refugees from all over the world!' she said.

'I surely will,' I replied with a happy laugh.

That journey of years before was indeed an accomplishment to celebrate. We went through so much. There were so many times that I didn't think we would make it.

♥ ♥ ♥ ♥

The boat kept on going. We rode the waves without direction. We were at the mercy of the sea. Mother Nature was our navigation system now. Although my heart was filled with worry, I still couldn't help but notice the endless beauty of the sea. The panoramic ocean view, its changing colours, and the space where the horizon met the sky were the only images I had to mark the passage of time. I stretched my eyes out as far as they would go. As far as my vision stretched, there was nothing but sea, and it was gorgeous. It was terrifying and breathtaking all at once. If I hadn't been in such danger, I could have mistaken this moment as one of being on holiday. If not for the dread and sickness pulling at my gut, I could have really enjoyed myself. I have always loved nature, and the inspiration that it draws, so even in these moments, the ocean gave me a sense of overwhelming awe.

From the outlook of the sea and the sky, the world was nothing more than a grand performance of colours. From the pitch-black night, the light of the sun seeps slowly into vision before it finally appears, eroding the charcoal sky to a wash of pale grey. If there are clouds, they are set on fire first, sometimes with a crisp, bed sheet white and other times a pale lemon.

High above, the brilliance of the sky becomes almost brown before maturing into its reliable, crystal blue. In between its intensity and the horizon is the natural canvass. Here the clouds are like brushes that slowly work the shades of blues and greys throughout the day, preparing it for the final act of sunset.

I counted those final days after the storm by the sunsets. Seven. Each sunset lifted us for an hour or so in admiration of the elements as we made our way along the Chinese coast to Hong Kong. The food and water we had secured at our last landing were rationed out with more and more moderation. I was not starving like before, but my cravings were constant. My baby was crying out for nutrition, and all I could give it was small portions of rice and noodles. Yet it grew inside of me, floating along in its own tiny universe.

After the third day, I was allowed to stay permanently under the shade. The young men had all lost their shirts, and their skins were baked by the sun. Their reddened and peeling skin made their faces unrecognisable. I felt sorry for them, but by this time, the world had lost all of its subtle social niceties. I was engaged full time in a delirious battle of endurance. Minh was also catatonic and constantly seasick. He sat hunched over exhaustedly beside me while the younger men kept the boat going.

I was awake and felt lethargic again and again for many days on end. In my dreams, all I wanted was to have something to eat for both of us, my baby and me. Saliva kept dripping out of my mouth because my body was crazily craving for food. I never ever had such a desire before in my life.

By the sixth day, I was not sure if I was awake or not. I relived countless scenes from my youth in an endless series of disconnected hallucinations. Each vision was like the story of someone I once knew but had long forgotten. I watched as my younger self-struggled, laughed, and cried.

Our boat never made it to Hong Kong.

♥♥♥♥

I woke to the sounds of people shouting.

'We are saved! We are saved!' they cried out.

I felt the boat being nearly capsized and I heard a roaring of a speedboat coming towards our boat. I looked out to the side and saw two imposing speedboats, heading directly for us. They bore Hong Kong Royal Police flags, flapping triumphantly in the wind. When I saw them coming, I thought they were coming to rescue us. I believed that we would soon have a nice feast and a warm, dry place to sleep.

'Minh!' I whispered. 'It is your time to shine.' My husband, who had languished in a depressed, sickly state for weeks, suddenly came alive like a spring. The entire crew looked at him as the police boats pulled up to either side of our boat.

He stood and waved to the men staring us down.

'Good afternoon, Officers. We are so glad to see you.'

The rest of the boat, not understanding, turned to the police in expectation. They had no time for pleasantries and began barking orders at us in English while Minh translated.

'Sit down. Turn off the engine. Do not stand. Your boat will be towed to a police boat. Leave everything behind,' Minh added an extra sentence to make us laugh. 'We are robots. We have no hearts.'

We didn't laugh. We had expected a warm welcome. We expected empathy and congratulations on having made it so far.

As the two speedboats towed us towards the larger ship, we said our bittersweet goodbyes to the vessel on which we'd weathered such an adventure. The organisers of our escape had taken our money and given us the skeleton of a barely seaworthy boat. They had hired an inexperienced captain and sent us off into the dark. Except for Tu, we had all survived, against all odds, for twenty-five days. One hundred per cent of our group determined that the organisers would not get the rest of our money.

When we arrived at the police ship, we were brought to the ship's deck and made to stand like cattle in one long line. We watched as they made holes in our boat and sank it. I cried, along with many others. We had hated that boat, but like a sick old donkey, it had persevered and muscled its way through, only to be sent to the bottom of the ocean.

Police officers examined us while holding their noses. When they saw my red scabs covered with mucus, I was singled off and separated from the rest. A few minutes later, a female police officer came towards me with a strange machine. It looked somewhat like an industrial vacuum cleaner. She made me lift my shirt and then sprayed me head to toe with white powder. I had not expected it, and I choked with surprise. It took me back to my childhood when we would come back from playing with white powder all over our body. Chi Thoi would order us to take our clothes off and scrub us clean. The powder was some kind of chemical that the Americans had sprayed on the forest. Looking back, I shuddered to think what damage it had caused me.

This powder, I guessed, was some kind of disinfectant against whatever disease I carried. I stood there like a chicken dipped in batter, completely humiliated and stinking of chemicals. Minh kept shaking his head but had given up reasoning with the officers. We were powerless.

They counted us again, and then several of the police officers rolled out a large sign and displayed it before us. It was in Vietnamese:

'Hong Kong has been closed to refugees since June 16th. You are now captured as illegal immigrants.'

There was to be no feast for sure. We talked amongst ourselves frantically and tried to work out what it meant. Minh asked them a few questions and then turned to address the group.

'I'm sorry. This is not good news for us. This really is the worst news.' The spirit he had regained was now depleted once again, but he maintained his composure for the sake of everyone else.

'Hong Kong government made a new law. Too many people came from Vietnam, and the host countries have reduced their intake of refugees. If they kept the door open, Hong Kong would be overrun by the Vietnamese. They can't handle that. They don't want to.'

'So, what does it mean for us?' Anh Hong asked. 'Are they sending us back to Vietnam?'

His question caused everyone to gasp and groan with anxiety. Minh turned to the police officers and asked another series of questions. When he was finished, he looked for a long time at them. I knew that look would mean one of seething anger, but he remained controlled.

'We are going to be detained. We are going to a detention camp.'

I rubbed my belly, and a sense of guilt ran through my whole body from head to toe. I got frozen!!!

CHAPTER THIRTY-NINE

~

ILLEGAL MIGRANTS

I sat on the couch and looked through the window to the front yard on Boxing Day. I wondered how Hong-An felt when she had her first Christmas without Minh and me. I suddenly remembered that just last month, Hong-An and I went over to Vale and Thomas' house to pick up some furniture they gave to her and Travis to use in their new home after the wedding. I didn't like the idea of the two of them starting their lives with second-hand goods, even though they were expensive, but Hong-An had convinced me that this was the best thing to do. She said she wanted to save their money for other things. I disagreed, but I respected her choice. She had changed so much since coming back home from her graduation day, and I didn't want to do anything that would cause any issues with her.

The week before, I'd gone to her with an offer.

'Ba, Mẹ will buy all of the furniture for your new home!' I'd said.

I had heard that they were planning to take Vale and Thomas' old things, as the two of them were giving away their stuff before leaving for Africa for their mission trip.

Hong-An wasn't having any of my suggestions.

'No way!' she insisted. 'It's time for me to be independent.'

I felt myself growing exasperated with her. She wanted to be independent, but she did not understand that an independent life had to be built step-by-step. She had to do things one bit at a time. Transitioning from childhood to adulthood was not like flipping a coin!

Walking through Vale and Thomas' yard, I noticed all of the gorgeous trees and the oranges that grew on them. Every branch was heavy with plump and juicy spheres. With Hong-An at my side and me feeling quite dejected by her choices, we walked beneath the trees, making our way towards the house. The toe of my shoe nudged one of the fallen orange fruits, lying bruised on the grass.

Hong-An looked down and then looked over at me.

'That's your favourite fruit, Mẹ,' she said. She smiled, letting me know that our relationship really was warming up again. I smiled back.

'Yes, that's right,' I said.

I blinked then, looking away to hide my tears from my daughter. She had never known why I loved oranges so much. Oranges meant something very different in Vietnam.

♥ ♥ ♥ ♥

Leaving Vietnam had been a momentous occasion. It had indeed mapped out the trajectory of the rest of my life. Our trip had lasted twenty-five days. We had risked everything to leave the hell of Vietnam for the heaven of somewhere else. We had thought that reaching Hong Kong was all that we had to do to gain our freedom and happiness. That dream kept us going. It kept us focused on overcoming the extreme conditions of our journey. We watched the spectacle of Hong Kong city materialise in front of us as the boat approached. It was like a jewel set between beautiful green hills. This city was to be our paradise, the completion of our odyssey, before the final victory lap of settlement in a third country.

'I hope we will stay in one of those tall buildings,' Bo said. 'In a nice bedroom of my own, with a view of the whole city.'

I looked at the hundreds of skyscrapers shimmering in the heat like a fairy-tale city. We were heading straight towards them, and I allowed myself the final hope that she was right. This business about not accepting refugees was a mirage. Minh would use his superior English to negotiate a quick and easy onward journey to America or Australia – somewhere I had no idea about. Our situation was different, special. Soon enough, we would be eating dim sum on Hong Kong's streets and planning our future.

But the boat stopped far short of the skyline as if the city itself was a mirage, docking on the pier of a small island in the bay. It looked like there was nothing much on the island except for high barbed wire fences, and as we neared them, our hopes came crashing down. It looked just like the prisons I had seen in American movies. We soon arrived at Green Island.

One by one, we were signed in. They took our photos and our thumbprints and made each of us wear a gooey cap to get rid of head lice. We didn't argue; we were all in a state of shock. Our expectations for a welcome arrival had built up and crystallised during our epic journey to the point where we could not believe anything else was possible. Surely, after the paperwork, we would be informed of the real story. That, even though Hong Kong had officially closed its doors, the humanitarian agencies, the UN, the foreign governments - someone - would secure our safety and freedom. We were not in a communist country anymore. The officials were not corrupt and uneducated idealists.

But there was no briefing. We were just ushered indifferently to a large room, where thousands of Vietnamese people were already sprawled out in a human display of chaos. There was nothing but the bare floor and our bodies. Our boat stuck together and found a relatively free space on the ground. I collapsed on the floor as I was emotionally and physically exhausted. I could not move. All around us, I heard Northern accents. My head began to swim. That night, I was dimly aware of people around me, rubbing my body with coins and pulling my hair to keep me from passing out. I felt like I was still at sea, drowning in the anarchy of humanity around me.

In the morning, we were given baked beans, biscuits, and condensed milk, which was a completely alien food for Vietnamese people. The smell alone made me want to throw up. An officer came over to our section and asked if anyone spoke English. Minh put up his hand, but Le was quicker, and they led her away.

She came back in the evening with a box of rice, two American navel oranges, and the ghost of a smile on her face. She had been taken to the hospital to help with the treatment of a Vietnamese patient. The UN, she told us, are still looking out for our health and safety. If anyone is sick or pregnant, we would be transferred by boat or helicopter to an excellent hospital. It was a small relief in an ocean of disappointment, and we were not motivated to celebrate the news. We just stared greedily at her box of rice, having been fed baked beans for lunch and dinner too. I asked her for some orange skin, suddenly overcome with a craving, but I was not the only one to request it. We secured a thumb-size piece of orange peel, and I nibbled on it like a rat until it was gone.

'You have to go, Minh.' I demanded. 'I absolutely need an orange for myself and the baby.'

Minh was selected the next day but returned with only a box of rice, which I could not eat, and he shared it with someone else. He had failed at getting me my orange but was wildly successful at proving his translation skills. He became an instant favourite amongst the officers.

After a few more days of morning sickness and my stomach refusing the only available food of baked beans, biscuits, and condensed milk, my craving for oranges had transformed into a wild desire. Minh used his new contacts to arrange it for me, and it felt like a drug deal. I was told to wait in one corner for the guard with the glasses. He looked friendly and responded compassionately to Minh's explanation of my pregnancy needs. He smuggled the orange to us, and I cradled them like they were made of gold. The taste was good, but the real prize was the brief window into true humanity that I had witnessed in the guard. It proved to me that there was still some dignity left to be preserved. Despite the vast inequality before us, there was still true goodness in people that would shine through.

I divided up the orange peel to share with some of my fellow boat passengers. I felt like a priest giving bread during mass. Everyone sniffed and sucked on the peel as if it contained the last shred of happiness in our disintegrating worlds.

After seven days, the baked beans were replaced with rice. A victory cheer went around the room. I watched everyone chewing their rice with wild and frantic pleasure. I didn't share in their joy. The guards still marched around outside, treating us like we were animals, and in turn, we acted like them. The toilets were dirty, and some people just pissed on the floor. Men spat and snored and farted. We wore the same clothes that we had travelled across the sea in, no doubt absolutely reeking.

Most of the people in the room were poor Northerners, who had lived very simply, many in slum conditions. They were used to living this way. Usually, they would spend their days fishing and fighting for food. Here, they just had to wait. Many were perfectly happy with this situation.

But for me, everything was upside down. I could not eat or sleep. I grew very skinny. Minh insisted that I eat, but I could not swallow anything. The loudspeakers periodically broadcast the message we did not want to hear: 'You are illegal migrants. After screening, expect yourselves to be returned to Vietnam.'

CHAPTER FORTY

TO CATCH A FERRY TO PRISON

I went to shopping with Minh to pick up something for our Christmas. Our fridge was almost empty as I thought we would spend our Christmas on the Gold Coast with Hong-An and Travis's family. I stood in the queue, with an enormous yearning for my daughter, waiting to check out at Woolies. I could see that I was going to be here for a while. The line was very long, and every person in front of me had a trolley full of food. Australia was such a rich country, where the people had everything they needed.

The woman next to me was muttering and complaining to herself.

'I can't believe they don't have prawns here!' she huffed in disgust. 'They should have prawn in here for Christmas! It's such a shame I can't complete my party list. It's so inconvenient!'

She looked over to me for sympathy.

'Well, you could make something else,' I suggested. 'Or you could check the other market nearby and see if they have it.'

She shook her head and waved her hand dismissively, seemingly annoyed by my comments.

'I'm not going to do all of that,' she said shortly. 'I'm not going to bother.'

I looked away, feeling suddenly quite saddened. People in Australia had so many advantages, but they didn't even realise it. They didn't understand the struggles of people from other countries. Countries that were not nearly as wealthy such as Green Island in Hong Kong, where Minh had been forced to beg and barter just to get me an orange to eat during my pregnancy. In those days, filling my belly had been a blessing and one I wouldn't have dreamt of taking for granted. In a way, my hardships had been a blessing too. I saw life through a different lens. I was filled with gratitude for everything my family had.

♥ ♥ ♥ ♥

I always carried the days of struggle with me. I carried with me all of the fear and uncertainty of our fight for freedom. After arriving in Hong Kong, we were all so sure that someone would help us despite everything they said. They must've had an idea of what we'd gone through to make it to their shores. Surely, they couldn't be so heartless as to turn us right around and send us back to the place we had fled from. I dreamed that they would save us. I dreamed that they would help us start new lives on new shores.

I kept this fantasy alive when, after two weeks, we were put onto a ferry and moved towards the glittering city of Hong Kong. But I knew it was wishful thinking. I knew that our troubles were likely far from over. Hong Kong, I learned, consisted of hundreds of islands, and to my dismay, we arrived at another seemingly uninhabited island. In different circumstances, I would have been overcome with its beauty. It was almost entirely covered with trees and rose from the water like the top of a submerged mountain.

As we neared the jetty, I read the sign: 'Hei Ling Chau Island'.

I tried the words out a few times. 'Hei. Ling. Chau. Hei. Ling. Chau,' I repeated as we walked in single file along the jetty to a line of prison trucks.

The trucks drove up a hillside towards the centre of the island, finally pulling up outside a tall, metal gate. Above it, there was another sign. It read: 'Hei Ling Chau Detention Centre'.

'What does detention centre mean?' I asked Minh.

'It's a polite way of saying prison,' he said. 'It's a prison for people who are not criminals.'

The fence stretched for a long way on either side of the gate and was capped with razor wire. Inside I could make out rows of white and grey buildings with small windows. It certainly looked like a prison, and we certainly felt like prisoners, as the guards herded us through another series of administrative procedures and led us to our new accommodation.

'Sit down!' they yelled, pulling their batons out, whipping a few people, and forcing us all to resume our positions quickly.

As the people at the front collected their supplies, the guards, laughing now, made us shuffle on our haunches like slaves begging for mercy. If you tried to stand up, they would hit you again with the baton. It was as if we were dogs shuffling around obeying their commands for fear of punishment. The discomfort mixed with the shame brought tears to my eyes. These guards had no respect for our human rights, and it was clear they enjoyed the power it gave them. I wanted to shout, 'You are bastards to our poor people!'

We had been robbed of everything, and now, that included our humanity. They had stolen from us all of our dignity. We had nothing left.

♥ ♥ ♥ ♥

Over the next few days, it became clear that Northern Vietnamese gangs controlled our new home. The man who'd spat in front of me was the leader of the most powerful gang. They were constantly fighting amongst themselves and against Southerners to keep control.

'What are they fighting for?' I asked Minh. 'We are all in the same position. They are fighting to have control over nothing.'

'It is in their nature,' Minh replied. He had already been identified for his English ability and had been approached by guards and gang leaders to take advantage of his skills.

'Probably one-third of the people in here were already criminals before they escaped. Real criminals. That's what they say anyway. I wouldn't be surprised if it were true.'

I considered Minh's hot temper and warned him to keep his head down and never talk back to or provoke any gang members. His English ability turned him into a valuable asset for everyone. Minh became the camp's unofficial news interpreter. When updates were received through newspapers, guards, officers, or overseas volunteer aid workers, he would translate the news to everyone. Initially, there was not much news to report, other than the repeated warnings that we would be sent back to Vietnam.

When his T-shirt was stolen, Minh walked around the camp topless, looking for it. Within fifteen minutes, one of the gang leaders visited our bunk and delivered the T-shirt.

'If anything else happens, report directly to me, and I will have it fixed,' he said.

I recognised him as one of the thieves from our first night but nodded gratefully regardless. We needed protection, and he was offering it to us.

We settled into a strange and uncomfortable lifestyle. I could hardly sleep at night after witnessing the robbery, even though the gang had offered us protection. Minh was often unwell, and I struggled through every meal in an effort to give myself and the baby sustenance. The only meal I enjoyed was chicken and fried little mackerel, which we got once a week. The rest of my group always shared theirs with me, and I ate every morsel, including bones for the calcium. At least I could do that for my growing human.

♥ ♥ ♥ ♥

At some point, an announcement screamed over the loudspeaker, 'All pregnant women must go immediately to the hospital in Hong Kong for a routine check-up.'

I was excited, even though the other women who had already had check-ups moaned about the difficult boat trip and the discomfort of the whole experience. A lot of them hid from the authorities in order to escape from the compulsory trip. I thought they were crazy and signed up for it straight away.

On the boat over, I immediately understood their reluctance to go. From the top of the island, the water looked calm and inviting, but it was cold and hostile on the surface. I clung onto the railing with intense nausea as the other women collapsed around me. If my baby were OK at the camp, it would definitely not be by the time we got to Hong Kong. But my excitement to experience the city of my dreams kept me upright with my eyes open. I watched the buildings get larger and larger until we arrived at the pier.

Stepping onto the dock felt like stepping onto the moon. I could not believe that finally, I had set foot in the place we had longed for, albeit as a detainee. I stood for a few moments, transfixed by the activity around me. Hundreds of people in suits moved around, stepping on and off ferries and looking terrifically busy.

In the few minutes it took to walk from the ferry to the waiting prison truck, I breathed in the freedom like it was oxygen. The rest of my observations of Hong Kong were through the metal gate of the prison truck window. I poked my nose through it and gathered as many images as I could to store in my imagination and report back to Minh and the others at the camp.

The hospital was the biggest I had ever seen. Inside it felt so luxurious, clean and high-tech, and the staff were very professional. I felt almost uncomfortable to be treated so differently than at the camp—the contrast was so huge.

I went through the same procedures as any of the other patients would have, but I sensed the doctor's ambivalence. He knew I was a detainee, and although he was not rude, he extended no compassion or sensitivity toward me. By the time my tests were finished, the Vietnamese interpreter had already gone home for the day. The doctor kept pointing at my stomach and speaking the exact phrase in English that I did not understand. I began to panic, thinking that he was perhaps trying to tell me there was a problem. They did not release me along with the other pregnant ladies from the camp that evening. I stayed overnight, fretting and worrying about the health of my baby. Maybe the baby was deformed, just as I had predicted in my greatest fears.

By morning, they must have deemed us both fit enough for release. An officer escorted me back to the truck, and we drove, I had assumed, towards the pier. However, our destination ended up being a large, heavily fortified brick building.

'What is this place?' I asked the officer, but he did not seem to understand my English. Or perhaps he did not want to tell me.

We had arrived outside Victoria Prison.

I saw the sign on my way in, and as soon as we got into the reception area, I began firing questions rapidly. In my mind, they had made a mistake. I repeated my camp's name repeatedly, and the staff just nodded and tried to silence me with their hand gestures. Thankfully, we were joined by another group of pregnant Vietnamese women, and they calmed me down.

'Relax. It's OK. Yes, this is a prison. Yes, for real criminals. Wow, your belly is so small. When are you due? You must be scared. Don't worry; we know how you feel. It will all be OK.'

They explained that I was just in the office to clear some paperwork, but that one month before I was due, I would return to the prison and stay there to be close to the hospital during the final weeks of my pregnancy. I looked at them as if they were joking. It could not be true. Were they going to keep heavily pregnant women in jail? Did they not trust us at all? Did they think we would run away when our child is about to be born?

Oh, how inhumane! I cried in my mind. Why should we be tortured before giving birth to our babies?

When I got back to Hei Ling Chau, I told Minh the news. We asked around to get confirmation and found out it was, in fact, true. Surely, pregnant mothers should be treated with more respect during that critical time. We were already prisoners, but to force us to sleep in jail, with rapists and murderers down the hall?

It wasn't like our camp was exactly a haven either. The fighting had increased, and a faction of people from Hue had been split off and locked themselves in a separate room. Their comparative wealth made them targets, and their feisty political opinions made them resistant to back down.

One of their group leaders, Quang, turned out to be the son of Minh's old lecturer. He confronted us one day, concerned about our choice to stay in the main building.

'You are one of us,' Quang said. 'We can't let these uneducated Northerners boss us around. They threaten and fight to keep control, just like the Viet Cong. This is what we ran away from. Come with us, and we will look after you.'

We were polite and respectful, but honestly, we just wanted to stay in the middle of the groups. Our only concern was having the baby and surviving long enough to get processed. We already had protection from the Northern gangs, and they made up ninety per cent of the camp population. Quang was compassionate towards us but affronted by our refusal to move.

We kept our heads low. I became, like almost all of the other women expecting children, a Pregnancy Fugitive. None of us wanted to make the nauseating journey to Hong Kong Island or face the reality of the inevitable stay in Victoria Prison. Every week, our names would be read or reread over the loudspeaker for our monthly check-up appointment. If someone came around looking for us, word would spread quicker than their progress around the camp. We would hide in the toilet or in someone else's bunk.

Then, after a series of huge gang fights, stabbings and stand-offs, the Hue faction decided to strike. As a group, they walked to the basketball court to camp out until they were granted their demand: to be moved to a separate camp for their safety. Minh and I reviewed our options and, fearing a backlash from the northerners if they found out our connections with the Hue leaders, we decided to join them on the court.

Winter was coming, and it was excruciatingly cold. Not many people had thought to bring blankets, and I lay on the freezing ground, instantly regretting that we had agreed to join them. I looked out across the dark expanse of water to the twinkling lights of the city and missed home. I missed my parents and brothers and the warm weather of Da Nang. I shivered and cried and moaned until I fell into a fitful sleep. I told Minh I did not think I could last another night. He looked at me gravely and touched my belly.

'We can't go back now,' he said. 'The Northerners will think we have betrayed them. I can't guarantee our safety.'

When you have almost no options, the answer is sometimes obvious and rarely ideal. We could be striking for weeks, and I feared not only for my safety but the baby's too. I had to go somewhere away from all of the danger. I had to go back to the hospital and check myself into prison.

When I appeared at the office to surrender to the health check, the translator joked with me to lighten the mood.

'There you are! We have been looking for you for a month now. Thank you for listening to us, sister. This is a good decision for your baby and yourself.'

He escorted me back to my bunk bed to get my belongings. I was worried about my safety, but the Northerners were very concerned and compassionate for my well-being. 'It's cold out there,' they said. 'Tell Minh to come back and be with us. No one will hurt you.' Even the gang leader reassured me directly.

I went to say goodbye to Minh and informed him of the promises of the group inside. The stereotype of the Northerners that I had maintained throughout my time at the camp had started to fall away. They were good, wholesome people, I told Minh. My husband held me for a long time, and I felt the bump of my belly pushing into his body. The next time I saw him, I thought there would be three of us. A rush of anger rose in me then, at the unfairness of it all, that my husband could not come with me to soothe and protect me in the most crucial time of our lives.

We said our goodbyes with wet eyes. Alone, I walked towards the prison truck to catch the ferry to prison.

CHAPTER FORTY-ONE

~

TEAR-SMEARED RICE

I could hear cars and motorbikes from my prison bed. Sometimes, very early in the morning, I could even hear footsteps and voices speaking in Cantonese as people walked past the prison walls, getting on with their daily lives. Our room was close to the street level, and the sounds somehow found their way over the wall and through the small window, fuelling my imagination and my hope that one day I would be out there too as a free person. I would buy BBQ duck and pork and rip the meat off with my teeth like a lion satisfying my craving for food. I would sit for hours and enjoy my coffee with beautiful music to ease all my suffering.

An officer led me down the quiet corridor, her footsteps echoing through the building. After going down a flight of stairs, the walls became thick and damp, and I started to feel claustrophobic. Finally, we arrived at my new home, a small wing of the white and yellow-painted brick set with a dozen steel barred doors. My heart leapt into my throat, and I hesitated in the entranceway. Then I heard Vietnamese voices, laughing and teasing each other, and I took the courage to enter the cell.

'Don't worry,' one of the women said to me with kind eyes. 'I've been here two weeks, and it's fine.'

The other women affirmed her words. They could see fear and uncertainty in my eyes; I had no doubt they felt it themselves. I sat down on one of the beds, and they laughed as they saw me react to the hard and cold plastic panel.

The first meal made me want to vomit. I stared at it in my plastic plate while other women ate happily. It was a forlorn piece of pork belly, mostly fat, smothered in a mysterious dark sauce. Just the smell made me nauseous. My pregnancy was reacting badly to the food. I tried just to eat some of the rice, but the horrid sauce had infiltrated almost every grain. I gave it to others to share, telling them it must just be my weird pregnancy appetite playing tricks on me.

To my dismay, the same thing was served for dinner, and again, I could not bring myself to eat it. Even the smell of the others' dishes was too much for me. The ladies promised they would try to get me plain rice in the future.

A couple of days later, as I was making my way back to my wing from the TV room, I bumped into an Indian woman dressed in an officer's uniform. I thought she would flash me a scowl like some of the other officers, but she surprised me by smiling at me. She raised her hand to her mouth, indicating a spoon, and I shook my head, pulling a grimace, and we both laughed.

'Do you speak English?' she asked.

'I can speak a little bit,' I said.

I had never seen an officer smile like her before, and it warmed my heart. The ladies had managed to get me some plain rice back in the room, and I ate it gratefully. I cried into my bowl, letting go of a thousand mixed feelings. To my delight, the tears added a salty flavour to the rice, making it easier to eat.

Over the next month, the Indian woman became somewhat of a silent friend, smiling and greeting me in simple English phrases. I slowly learned more English and some Cantonese phrases from the television dramas we watched on TV. I practised my budding language skills on anyone I came into contact with. With my natural skill for language, I picked up English very quickly. I felt confident speaking it with the officer and felt so proud about that. These were small exciting things that entertained me in the mists of depression.

Two times a week, we were transported to the hospital for check-ups. I learned that the mysterious illness I contracted during my journey was scabies. I also understood why the doctors were concerned last time. Someone along the line of medical bureaucracy had mistaken my due date to be much earlier than it was. Although my belly was swelling rapidly, I was barely out of my second trimester. I prepared myself for an extended stay in prison.

❤ ❤ ❤ ❤

I tried my best to do whatever was in my hands to protect the tiny human inside me. I tried to stay positive and to stay sane. I took walks and tried to eat as much food as I could, given the circumstances. My every waking thought was focused on my baby, but I still felt like a terrible mother. I couldn't give my baby everything that he or she needed. I was not giving my child a strong start in life, and the guilt of knowing this kept me tossing and turning every night.

During this time, I missed my family so much. This gave me a great deal of pain. I knew they would be worried for me, Minh, and our unborn baby. We did receive a letter from my father during this time. Minh sent this letter to me at the prison, and I learned that my family was in trouble. The police kept coming to my mother to demand money. Le and Bo's family had decided not to give my mother the money to give to the police. My mother had to face this responsibility alone, and unable to come up with the funds, the police threatened to arrest her. She ended selling our big house only four months after Minh and I had left Vietnam. Our home was gone now. It was the only way that my mother could escape this trouble from the police.

I felt racked with guilt, somehow helpless to save anyone I loved. We had worked so hard to escape but for what? I wanted to give my baby the food she needed, and I only wished I could help my mother too.

I had no choices or power over my situation. My only hope was God, and that was what kept me going from one day to the next.

I didn't know what my future would be like. All that I could do was make it from today to tomorrow and then wake up and do the very same thing again. I had to contend with an ice-cold bed keeping me prisoner in sleeplessness, fighting to intake enough calories each meal, intense and persistent nostalgia for my home and my family, along with every other pain and emotion that burdened me. I kept going, step by step, inching along through life, praying that everything would be better very soon. I remembered back when I was in the Lambro, moving from Cam Ranh to Phan Thiet with my parents and brothers; I had made it through then, and I would make it through now. Thinking of this and the tiny life growing inside me, soon to be born and make me a mother, gave me the courage to keep going. These thoughts gave me a small glimmer of peace and made the passing of the day much easier.

One day, a woman arrived from our camp, bringing a special surprise to me from Minh. Her eyes were alive with excitement as she handed over a small cloth package. Inside, wrapped in plastic, was a small ball of shrimp paste. I let out a cry of joy. I had been eating only tear-smeared rice and dry biscuits until then, and the shrimp paste was like caviar in my hands. I refused to share any of it with my friends and rationed it out over the next week of meals. Each bite was like heaven to me, as if I was somehow restoring my dignity and pleasure for life in the very act of eating the glorious substance. Minh had gained so much credit in my eyes through this beautiful attempt to please me. I believed that he must have had to put down his ego to ask for the shrimp paste. This thought warmed my heart even more with each bite.

The women started to tell me I looked very pale and tired, and I began to worry more and more about the baby's health. How could he or she grow on my diet? I was only surviving on rice and the few M&M's we smuggled from the Chinese women next door? I still had months ahead of me. Every night, I began to fantasise about the possibility of returning to the camp to have my baby. My mother had told me countless stories of women who had had safe births at home. People would surround me, and Minh could be part of the journey. If something went wrong, I could always be taken by helicopter to the hospital, I figured.

My imagination came true when one day I was informed, without an explanation that I could travel back to the camp if I wanted to. I accepted it immediately, bursting with excitement, and was escorted on the ferry to Hei Ling Chau.

I returned to the camp triumphantly, feeling changed inside after my experience in prison. Minh looked so happy to see me and cheered along with many others when I stepped back into our building, my belly now bulging out in front. I just wanted to breathe the comparatively fresh air and spend time with Minh. Even if our marriage had a few bumps at the start, I now had a new perspective on Minh. He was now for sure my best friend, and I would relish every moment with him for the rest of my pregnancy.

'I pretended to be sick,' Minh told me. 'And went to see the camp doctor. I gave him a letter with the hope that he could find a way to rescue you from Victoria prison, and he did.' This little information Minh had shared with me would make me feel grateful for the rest of my life.

The camp had changed quite a lot in the month I was away. The air sang with the cries of newborn babies, and there seemed to be many more couples than before. Girls and boys walked around the camp in fashionable clothes, flirting and joking with each other. It had become a happier place. Men and women from many different countries had arrived as volunteers to teach us English, monitor our health, assist women in family planning, and give us administrative and legal advice. The most meaningful guests for me were the missionaries, who were motivated by the grace of God to come and spend time sharing the gospel. It was a wonderful time for me to reconnect with a sense of spirituality that had been pushed aside by so much stress and anxiety. Every Sunday, I felt the spirit enter into me, mending all the broken parts of my soul.

However, this happiness was short-lived. It ended the moment a body fell from the top of my bunk bed to the floor with blood pooling underneath it, right in front of me. We had been sitting on our bed chatting when we heard shouts from somewhere beyond our area. The screams were followed by a few loud bangs and the frantic sounds of people being chased. Suddenly, the bed shook, and we heard a short, sharp yell and a flurry of retreating footsteps. In the few seconds of silence that followed, I opened my eyes and pulled myself from Minh's protective grasp. The body fell to the floor and started squirming like a worm stuck in the sand. For a moment, I was frozen with fear.

I let out a terrified scream, and several men rushed over to help the fallen man. I recognised his face. It was the gang leader that had spit on me on my first day at the camp. He had been stabbed in the stomach. There was blood everywhere. The news tore through the building like a wild wind. The stirrings of a dangerous kind of chaos began to occur. A storm was coming, I thought. This was bad. This was very bad.

Minh closed the curtain of our bed to hide us. I shut my eyes and prayed for our safety. Children were screaming, and the sound of running footsteps went back and forth like rounds of ammunition.

The next day, preparations for war began. The Northerners split into rival gangs and began to take pieces of metal off the beds to sharpen into crude knives. One of our connections found us a larger space away from the epicentre of the danger, near the toilets. It would be a good space for us when the baby arrived, they said. It was bigger for sure, but over the next few nights, we realised why it had been left vacant. It was right next to a window that invited the freezing air directly into our bed and into our bones.

'It's OK, it's a good place for my newborn baby,' I told myself. This was also much better than being in prison, but it wasn't, and the danger looked like it was increasing by the day.

Minh was always ill, and I worried that he would not be able to protect me in an emergency. I played out the scene of my birth in my mind. I would get contractions, and then the helicopter would be called on the UN bankroll. It was crazy to be given such expensive emergency healthcare and yet to live in squalor in the middle of gang warfare.

In the middle of this horror, I received a letter from my father. I smelled the letter as if I could smell my father. I missed each person in my and Minh's family.

Our lives had been an epic upheaval of constant battles. We had fled Vietnam to avoid the very things that plagued us in the camp every day. We were no freer, no safer, and had no more opportunity than the day we left the country. More than ever, I just longed to be back with my family.

CHAPTER FORTY-TWO

BITTER WITH EVERYTHING

I put fifty dollars in a red envelope for Hong-An, as I always did for the Lunar New Year.

'I am too old for this now!' Hong-An laughed, but I just shook my head.

'You might be almost twenty-two, but you will always be my baby,' I said.

I gave her a wink and then a kiss. We hugged each other like a mother koala and her baby. Time flew, and my love for her had grown bigger by day, just as she had.

'Did I tell you yet that I love you today?' I asked her.

Hong-An teased me back as usual, 'No! Not yet!'

The Lunar New Year always brought me back to the very first Lunar New Year I'd spent away from Vietnam.

For four weeks, I tried to settle back into the routine of prison. There was an entirely new group of pregnant women there, and we quickly became friends. Twice a week, I had medical check-ups, and on the way to and from the hospital, I observed the city transform with the preparations for New Year. Lanterns and streamers were hung from many lampposts; shop fronts were ablaze with brightly coloured fruit and red and gold adornments; posters and scrolls were hung on doors and windows. There seemed to be some evidence of New Year coming on every corner, and each image brought back so many memories of my family in Vietnam.

I missed Minh, the prunes and Coca-Cola from the Hei Ling Chau Camp so much. They'd all been heaven-sent to me. Every sleepless night, I lived another life in parallel, imagining myself back in Vietnam doing my usual preparations for New Year. Just undertaking those simple tasks of buying and preparing food and arranging flowers would have satisfied my soul. My brothers would be fighting to help me, all wanting to be the most helpful they could for their pregnant sister.

My mother would fuss about, giving me advice on what to eat and how to ease the pain in my back. My father's eyes would shine with pride as he watched me putter around the house, getting ready for the celebrations.

But this was not my life. My family was not with me, helping me to prepare for the birth of my baby. They weren't with me to celebrate the Lunar New Year. Each morning I would wake up to prison life, and the cold rush of reality would sink in, like the stale freezing air of the room itself.

The time I spent sleeping, or rather trying to sleep, was when I was the most afraid. I was attacked from all sides by my terrified thoughts. I lay on my back in my freezing bed, wondering why I had chosen this path in life. Why had I left behind my beautiful life in Vietnam? Why had I left behind my family? I had traded in everything that I needed for a life of only fear, frustration, sadness, and depression. The heaven that I had dreamed of reaching was still so far away, and I had no way of knowing what was going to happen to me, Minh, and our baby. I was stuck in this prison, counting every day that went by. I could see the world moving forward without me, but I could not move with it.

'Be strong for your child, Ha-Le!' It was the only command that I could give myself. It was all that I could say to keep myself moving forward, in a daily battle, with no end in sight.

When I came back to the prison, the only familiar person was the Indian officer. She raised her eyes in surprise upon my appearance. Seeing her eyes wander over my body and fixed on my tummy, I said, 'Soon!' and both of us laughed together.

By that time, my English had improved a great deal as I knew how important it was for the baby and me to communicate outside of Hei Ling Chau camp without Minh. We chatted for a while about different things in front of the inquisitive eyes of my Vietnamese roommates. Seeing me walk around the narrow alley for the usual exercises, the Indian officer put two thumbs up for me with a broad smile. I saw her every two nights, and it was one of my favourite times of the day. I became my group interpreter, requesting extra blankets and called the prison officers when one of the ladies got her contractions. I felt useful for so my people.

I kept observing as life went by in prison. None of us were happy. We came for different reasons but somehow found ourselves the participants in one grand play: a performance of prison sadness.

I came back one time and realised that some of the girls in my room had black beans for their afternoon tea. My mouth was watering, and I understood clearly from my bodies craving for this that the black beans would be so good for my baby.

'Illegal trade, the Chinese really want our biscuits to fill their tummy. It's a good deal, and we both got what we want,' I was said in broken English.

'Like trading M&Ms?' I asked my roommate, Chi Phuong.

'Yes! But we have to be super quick, or we get to trouble with the prison officer. She is a bitch,' she said, pointing to the Indian officer at her desk.

'She is very nice, and I like her,' I said.

'No! You don't know her yet,' Chi Phuong insisted. 'You are so honest and, and you are not quick enough to run back to our room. I will do the deal for you if you want.'

I was moved by her kindness and felt protected. She gave me a tablespoon of her steamed black beans in my palm. I picked them up one by one and enjoyed their familiar flavour. Something I had tasted already countless times back home. Black beans were my favourite mixed with creamy coconut milk.

At night time, I tossed and turned around many times before I could finally find sleep. My mind was churning with the thought of half a cup of black beans I'd get to have the next day.

The deal was successful, and I understood why my roommate said we had to be super quick. We couldn't pretend to chat, do the deal, and then hide the black beans. It was liquid and in a prison cup, so carrying it would be evident to everyone that we were breaking the prison rules. It was my dream meal, and I enjoyed every small piece of black beans I tasted with a heap of nostalgia. If I were home, it would typically be so easy for me to enjoy, even if I didn't need it for my diet, black beans back home were commonplace, but here they were like pure gold.

'We really had a good meal today, my dear. It's enough nutrition for a day,' I rubbed my belly contentedly and thanked my roommate several times.

'Do it again tomorrow!' Chi Phuong urged me, her cheeky eyes sparkling. She reminded me to slow down my eating, and we both laughed. I couldn't wait to have it again tomorrow.

'You have to be very careful, Ha-Le. Find somewhere to eat, as the bitch is here today. She is very quick, and we will be in big trouble with her if we break the prison rules.'

I was half reluctant to do the deal but gave my biscuits to Chi Phuong. The craving tortured me inside, and I wanted to eat the steamed black beans for my baby's nutrition.

Chi Phuong ran back very quickly with the mission completed. I found a corner and turned my back out to the door to prevent anyone from seeing me doing something illegal.

BAM! With no warning, I received a very hard slap on my face. Shocked, I almost fell off the slippery plastic bed. Blood rushed to my face when I saw my favourite girl in front of me. She looked at me, her eyes simmering with anger, then took the cup from my hand and threw it into the bin. My mouth was full of black beans, and I had only one choice – chew it and swallow it down as if eating red-hot charcoal. Hurt and humiliated, I stared at the blank wall in front of me.

'Ha-Le never commits a crime in here, but she was the first one among us to get a slap from that bitch.'

'That was my fault!' I responded.

'No, Ha-Le, someone informed her, and the trouble fell on you. We did it so many times, and nothing happened. We just try to survive and exchange what we need. We didn't harm anyone.'

'But we broke the prison rules,' I reasoned.

The room was quiet, and I only heard chewing sounds from my roommates.

I dared to leave my room and did my evening exercise routine, even though I was offended by the Indian officer and still really hated her for what she did to me in the afternoon. Our friendship was done. I didn't greet her as usual and walked around as if I didn't see her at her desk. Through my peripheral vision, I could see she stared at me when I passed by her place. The words I'll never forget what you did to me swam in my mind.

I didn't eat that night; my heart was much too heavy and full of sorrow. I became very bitter at everything. I was away from all the people I loved, and one of the few people who treated me warmly in this cold and lonely place had turned against me. When she slapped me, she took something that I desperately needed at that time: warmth and human compassion. I was furious with her for taking that from me and for reminding me that, even when people smiled and were kind, that didn't mean that they could be trusted. It could always be an act.

The night before New Year, I ate my usual salted plain rice and M&M's and was staring sadly into my empty bowl dreaming of Vietnamese desserts. An officer appeared at our door and told us to come to the office quickly. Anxiously, we walked as a group up the stairs to the administration office and to our surprise, our husbands were waiting for us.

Minh was beaming in the centre of the group. It had been his idea, and he had staged a war of correspondence with the authorities to make it happen. We all burst into tears, and I hugged my husband with relief and tenderness. I had not seen him in two months, and though he looked pale and weak, he stood straight and proud.

'Happy New Year, my darling,' he whispered in my ear. Then he pressed his ear against my belly with wide eyes. 'You are so big now; I can't believe it.' He looked at the clock on the wall. 'You have three more hours of the Year of the Dragon left. Otherwise, our baby will be a Snake!'

'What's wrong with a Snake?' I asked, not seeing that he was joking.

He hugged me again. 'Nothing. A Snake is perfect. Perfect.'

Minh never knew that I was scared to death of snakes, and there I was, sure that my baby would be born in the year of the snake. Whatever animal he or she had, I still loved my child with all my heart.

We were only allowed thirty minutes with our husbands before they were led away. We had not talked much; it was too overwhelming, and I had no real news for him. He told me that we made the right choice in sending me back to prison. There had been a lot of fighting, and someone was recently killed. I was so sad to see Minh go but grateful for his amazing effort to visit. There was still plenty of heroism in him, I thought fondly.

My body kept trembling, I felt very cold inside the whole time, and I did not know why. It was overwhelming for me to have such a surprise visit from Minh; it was surreal. It was like a miracle to soothe my heart in the midst of nostalgia. It had been perfect timing. If they had not come, the sounds of the New Year celebrations would have broken my heart in two. I listened to the fireworks at midnight, and their colourful reflections lit up the cell like the light from a television in the next room. I felt the explosions deep inside my belly and wondered if my child was startled or excited by the sound. Minh would see the same thing from his cell, and I wondered where they put him. We were so close in the distance but could not reach each other when the New Year of the Snake arrived. When the fireworks finally died down, the vibration in my belly did not stop. Was that my baby kicking? Or was that my heartbeat? Or…?

Suddenly, I felt a warm discharge from my body. I stayed very still for a few minutes, unsure of what to do, and then I felt a wave of pressure rising into a painful cramp.

It was happening.

'It's happening!' I said. 'It's happening!' The women around me began to stir, and when they realised what was happening, someone summoned the guard. Chi Phuong packed a bag for me, and another woman rubbed my back. We had developed strong bonds, and though I didn't think of it at the time, this would be the last time I would spend time with them as a group.

Two tired prison officers escorted me through the corridors to one of the trucks. It felt like I was walking through thick, murky water the whole way. They did not offer help to support me but walked ahead purposefully with their footsteps echoing through the prison. Each step exacerbated my pain and loneliness in the middle of the dark, freezing night.

'My husband might still be here,' I told them when we neared the truck. 'He was just here. Maybe he is still waiting to get back,' I said to the guards in Vietnamese.

They just stared at me blankly.

'My husband,' I said in English, wishing that I had tried harder to learn the language. 'My husband. Here. Where? We get my husband.'

I knew Minh was here, locked in one of the cells. He might have a good sleep as usual. The night was so cold, and soon I started shivering and crying.

'Minh, where are you? Don't you know that I am about to give birth to your child?'

I just wished for a miracle, wished that Minh would suddenly appear to go to the hospital with me. Miracles had happened for Minh and me a couple of times already, and I hoped it would happen again this time, the time that I needed it the most.

Then I realised that I was a prisoner.

'Stop dreaming!' I shouted to myself. I moved my heavy steps to the prison truck, barely managing to pull myself up the truck's stairs. I pitied myself when the officers stared at me without providing any help or support. There was no traffic at night; hence, the truck took turns without caution and somewhat dancing on the road. I struggled to keep myself from falling off the seat.

'Yes, yes. Relax. We'll be at the hospital soon,' the female guard said, apparently having no understanding of what I was going through.

I had no energy to argue. At this moment, I was totally alone. I could not lean on anyone. I had no choice but to search helplessly for any lost shred of strength I could find. I needed to dive deep inside myself and recover my inner dragon, even if we were now in the year of the snake. The guards talked amongst themselves in Cantonese as I held onto the metal grill bracing myself as we went around corners. I desperately held on for dear life to those cold metal bars, praying for strength for me and my baby. I knew it was all up to me now. I had to be my own source of power and will. In Vietnam, I would be treated like a queen at this moment. I would be the most important person in the world. In the back of that truck, I had to find a way to be my own queen, find the power within me to birth this baby alone among strangers.

CHAPTER FORTY-THREE

~

MY DAUGHTER

Congratulations, Erin! I typed out. I clicked the button to send my message.

Just two days ago, I'd hosted a baby shower for her at my house. I had cooked a huge meal and invited the entire staff from the preschool to join us. Erin was new from Canada to Australia and had always been such a great help to me in my business. The preschool wouldn't be what it was without her, and I wanted to show her how valued she was. I wanted to show her how much we all cared about her and wanted to support her in her new journey of motherhood.

I had shed tears many times, watching her belly swell bigger and bigger as she played with the children. They would place their tiny hands on her stomach to feel the baby inside. Watching moments such as these play out reminded me of my pregnancy. I was happy for Erin and moved by the love of the community around her, even though her entire tribe was still in Canada. There was also a part of me that felt sad for myself. I'd had to go through my pregnancy in loneliness. I wished I'd had the privilege of going through the pregnancy of a typical woman in normal circumstances, but that had not been the path the universe had in store for me. Instead, I'd gone through my pregnancy in various states of discomfort and detention.

'I am so happy for you, Erin,' I had said to her on many occasions. This is what I said outwardly. Inside, I was saying, 'You are so lucky. I wish I had the experience that you are having.'

Erin had everything that I had wished for when I was carrying Hong-An inside me.

'Suggesting that she should stop working to get ready for the baby is the right thing to do,' I said to Polly. 'Otherwise, she could end up having the baby at our preschool!'

The impending birth was triggering all kinds of painful memories in me. I was trying to keep them at bay. I reminded myself of my blessings, despite everything, beating all odds, Hong-An had been born healthy. I had praised God and shouted my gratitude many times. My Hong-An was a miracle. I thought back to my younger self and gave my young, new mother self a salute. I still don't know how she endured all that she did. Even more unbelievable was that that young, resilient woman, who had undergone all of those struggles and trials, was me. I was that young woman, and everything I'd gone through had given me greater depths of resounding strength.

♥ ♥ ♥ ♥

I remembered the night of Hong-An's birth and how lonely and afraid I'd felt, having no idea what to expect. That night had been a whirlwind of fear and joy, pain and love. The mixture of so many different emotions was overwhelming and beautiful, and it still left me in awe.

When we arrived at the hospital, there was a stretcher waiting for me. I drifted in and out of awareness, hearing the sounds of other patients in pain around me. Nurses checked my pulse and examined my whole body. I felt too weak to speak. Even if I could have, I would have been unable to communicate as fear and despair made me forget every word of English. I was at the whim of the professionals around me. I allowed myself to be poked and prodded as the waves of pain washed over and enveloped my whole being.

I must have fallen asleep because I woke up early the next morning screaming in pain. A woman was patting me on the shoulder and comforting me. She was not a nurse, so I assumed she must be another patient. I spoke to her in Vietnamese in the drowsiness, but she just shook her head and asked in English, 'Where is your husband?'

'I am boat people.' I said. I felt her hand pull away slightly and then return with added compassion.

'You look so Chinese,' she said. 'Such beautiful pale skin. I'm sorry you are alone.'

She kept soothing me, and I heard her cry a little in sympathy for my situation. I called out for Minh, for my mum and dad, and my brothers. I kept on feeling the consistent rhythm of warm hands patting me on the back. An angel had appeared unexpectedly in my life, and her sweet love dissolved some of my bitterness.

For the rest of the day, I swam in a river of pain, submerged into the depths and waking up gasping for air. I was desperately hungry, but the food they brought for me was always removed before I was conscious enough to eat it. My body was so weak. I could not imagine how it could handle giving birth to a child.

My contractions became more and more frequent in the middle of the night until my whole body felt like one vessel of pain and discomfort. I screamed and tried to catch my breath, using every last drop of my energy to push when they told me to. I was not aware of time. I felt like I was being taken by a massive wave and continuously pummelled into the rocks. Each time, I could not believe it was possible to experience any more pain. Then again, the whole process would be repeated. It was an unbearable nightmare, but like all nightmares, it eventually ended.

Exhausted after two nights and one full day of painful contractions, I remembered feeling my baby's head arrive. I remembered hearing the firm voice of the female doctor: 'Push your baby out! Push your baby out! Push! Push! And push!'

I obeyed her like a soldier following her leader's commands, and after a few moments of straining, the baby came out. The doctor took the baby by the legs and lifted it. Overwhelmed like never before, I looked at the baby's absolute perfection. How could this be? Checking her entire body quickly in case she mysteriously disappeared, I cried out, 'Oh! My daughter!'

It took me a while to realise what had just taken place. I was finally meeting my baby. I was finally meeting my daughter.

'So, tell me, is your baby a boy or girl?' the doctor asked.

I was confused. What was the point of the question? Later, I learned that they wanted me to confirm my daughter consciously for the record. It was a procedure for all mothers at that time.

'It's a girl,' I answered firmly and without hesitation. I had no strength to sit up, but I wanted desperately to hold her in my arms.

'You will see her tomorrow,' the doctor said. A nurse took her away crying. My heart went with her, and I wanted to insist they leave my baby with me. I wanted to demand to know why I couldn't have my baby, but I didn't dare to ask. I was a prisoner, and I knew well that I had to listen and obey. In this egregious situation, even with my freedom and autonomy long gone, with no clue of when they might be returned to me, that night, I was overjoyed. My daughter had been born, and she was perfect. She was healthy and physically perfect.

'Thank God! Thank God!' I chanted again and again.

My joy made me feel nothing until the male nurse announced, 'Finished! Good girl! You bore the pain so well.'

I realised that I hadn't been paying any attention, and hours had passed as he danced around me with the needle in his hands, suturing me up. I'd sustained significant tears from pushing my daughter out.

Joy flooded through my being. My daughter, nothing mattered now but her. She was going to be my everything from now on. I felt myself become someone new. I was a mother from that time on, and everything that I did would be for her.

CHAPTER FORTY-FOUR

GRACE FROM GOD

Being back out on the ocean on the cruise with Minh brought the memories of my escape from Vietnam back to the forefront of my mind. Some things were the same, like the sky and the stars, the lapping of the waves against the boat.

On the previous trip, I'd caught scabies, fought hunger, and watched a fellow passenger die, along with countless other horrors. My biggest problem was the emotional distance between Minh and me and how to spend my leisure time enjoying the selection of the decadence of food available.

It was as if the sea had stored all the emotions of my escape from Vietnam, and now those same waters were releasing them back to me in an overwhelming torrent.

I wished Hong-An was with me. There was a time when she relished my stories, and here I was, rediscovering memories that had been buried for years. I longed to tell her the larger story of the events leading up to her birth. I wanted to say to her how straight after her birth, they made me wait twelve hours before I could meet her. I had collapsed in the shower because I'd pushed the wrong button and been soaked with cold water. I wanted to tell her how I counted down the minutes until she was brought to my side. When hearing the other infants crying in the baby room, I just prayed it was not Hong-An that I was hearing. Even if those cries were not hers, I desperately wanted them to stop. I did not want the cries from the other babies to keep my daughter from sleeping or cause her any distress. I did not want anything to bother her in the first few hours of her life.

I waited and waited for that magical moment when I would finally have my baby in my arms. When the magic moment came, I stared into the baby room. There were so many bundles of newborns. I knew I would see my daughter soon. When it was about noon, I started feeling anxious. Nearly twelve hours had passed. Then I saw a nurse carry a white pocket with a baby in it. My eyes instantly became wet, and my heart began to flutter as I knew that the baby she held was mine.

'Here she is,' the nurse said, handing her to me.

I sighed loudly. My daughter! I sniffed – she smelled beautiful. I gave praise to God as tears fell from my eyes. At only 2.4 kilos, she was so soft and exquisite.

I decided to choose another name for her. She needed a name that would remind me that she was born thanks to God's miracle for the rest of my life. I tried to find a name that would remind me of my gratitude to Him at all times.

'Hong-An! I name you Hong-An,' I whispered, kissing her. Hong-An means 'happiness, luck, and peace,' and for Christians, it means 'Grace from God.' Indeed, Hong-An, my daughter, was a grace from God.

I sat on the bed and watched my daughter as the time passed. I couldn't stop looking at her. The vast store of love was already filling me up. I patted her and whispered Vietnamese lullabies to her when she moved her body and was about to cry. I never knew I could love anyone that much. In that high emotional moment, I made a vow to my daughter.

I will lay down my life, with every breath to raise you, Hong-An.'

I opened my heart with curiosities for all solutions that I did not yet know. The moment Hong-An entered my life, it changed.

I could tell you were going to be smart from the first glance, I thought. You were tiny with beautiful soft skin and a wide forehead—room for a big brain. I just held you and hugged you, thanking God that you were healthy and happy.

No one told me what to do with you, so I gave you my nipple when you started crying. Oh, sweetheart, you chewed on it so hard, your little mouth felt like sandpaper, but I couldn't bear to stop. Even when, hours later, my nipples became red and infected, and I developed a fever, I refused to let you go hungry. Throughout the night, you squirmed and sucked and slept, and I watched you with wonderment. The nurses came in the morning and scolded me for not giving you the formula, but I had no idea. I just wanted to please you. To give you everything you desired, and my breast was the only valuable thing that I could offer to you.

I held Hong-An in my arms and turned my tear-stained face towards the wall whenever the other mothers would have their families in to visit. I couldn't stand to listen to the happy and cheerful sounds in Cantonese. I understood some of them. I had never missed my family that much, and I knew that they would all jump up and down with joy when seeing Hong-An. We had no happy visitors to come and see us, bringing smiles and gifts. We had no laughter or happy news at our bedside. I felt like Hong-An, and I was in the strange big, vast world on our own.

All of these memories spun about in my harried mind for the duration of the trip, and by the time the cruise ended, I was still feeling transfixed by the past. It had a hold on me that I couldn't shake.

The day that Minh and I returned from the cruise, we sat at Lidcombe station, waiting for Hong-An to pick us up. She and Travis had been staying at our house while we were away. I was aching to talk to her about everything that had been on my mind. I knew that while we'd been gone, Hong-An and Travis had been working hard at planning for their wedding. They had joked that they were also having a holiday, but theirs was a 'holiday at home.' I hoped that she'd had a nice rest and an enjoyable time getting everything ready for the wedding. I was looking forward to spending some quality time with her and opening up more about my past. She grew up and old enough to learn more about who I was, who I had been before her birth and everything that had brought me to where I was today.

I wanted to tell her more about her birth, what it had been like for me, and how lonely and afraid I'd been.

I was brimming with emotions and excitement to see my beautiful daughter once more. But when Hong-An arrived at the station, she looked grumpy. She was irritable and tired, like she hadn't slept. I decided to keep my memories to myself for the time being.

In the car on the way home, I realised our recent disconnection was still very raw. My own emotional journey, across the ocean of our lives, was not enough to bring us close to each other. In fact, it only made the distance more obvious. All the happy memories of her birth twisted into anxieties, considering the kind of trauma she had gone through inside me and as a newborn. Had my life choices led to the inevitable deterioration of our relationship?

'I missed you,' I said.

'Me too, Mẹ,' she replied, but her answer did not fill the hole inside me. I wanted to hug my daughter and kiss her hair, but, seeing her unhappy, I kept quiet. I didn't want to end up pushing her away. Our once-strong relationship was already so fragile, fractured, and weak.

When we got home, I sat on the couch.

'Sit with Mẹ for five minutes,' I asked Hong-An.

'I need to have a quick rest and then drop Travis off at the airport,' she replied, reminding me that Travis was flying back to the Gold Coast that day.

I was confused but accepted that Hong-An needed a rest.

We still have late afternoon and the whole night together. I reminded myself.

She went to her room, and I heard them chattering. I had not seen her for over a week. She could not grant me even one sentence, yet she could happily chat with her fiancé for over an hour, even though she had spent the whole time with him while we were away. The pain in my heart was sharp and unwavering.

After our dinner, I still wanted to sit down with Hong-An for mother and daughter time.

'Sit here with Mum for a little while,' I invited her over with a cup of tea in my hand.

'I am tired and need a rest,' Hong-An replied. Indeed, she looked tired. She also had a sad and strained look on her face, as though she was disappointed in something.

Hong-An went to her room, and I had a shower. I could hear her talking with someone from the bathroom, and then I heard Travis's name. Under the cool water, my head started burning. I became upset with Hong-An.

'She said she was tired but would happily talk to Travis for ages,' I mumbled.

I came out of the bathroom, and the conversation was still on. I became more and more upset with Hong-An and felt a fit of stabbing jealousy. How could she be so happy to spend time with Travis and not miss her mother at all? Didn't she even care about me anymore?

I was angry and sad and altogether brimming with mixed emotions, and before I knew what I was doing, I had stormed into Hong-An's room. 'You don't want to even take a moment with me? Do you prefer to give all your time to Travis? I am your mother!'

The words came pouring out of me before I could stop them.

'You demand so much,' she said with exasperation.

'Do I, really? Five minutes is too much?' I said without thinking. 'If I demanded so much, I would never accept a son-in-law with a mental illness, no job and no promise for his future. If I demanded so much, I would never allow the pain, the worry, and the hurt to torture as it has since I met Travis. If I demand so much, I should ask Travis's parents to follow our culture for the wedding. If I demand so much, I should talk to Travis and ask him to give you a good life. I gave you a lot of freedom and allowed you to do whatever you wanted. I allowed you to become who you are today. Is that demanding too much? Huh?'

My hands were on my hips, and I spoke rapidly, with the speed and violence of a machine gun.

As my daughter cried and cried and called me a horrible person, I realised that I had done it again. It was a pattern. I could not deny that the feelings rising in me were real and essential, but the way I dealt with them wasn't helping anything. I was only hurting my daughter more and more.

I knew that all she could see in front of her was her furious mother. She saw nothing more but for me and my anger. But what was invisible to her and what I wished she could have seen were all the ghosts standing behind me. She couldn't see the ghost of Chi Thoi, with her angry words pouring out like a river. She could not see the Indian guard with her furious slap or my own mother filled with rage for everything my father had done to her. Even more invisible still were the army of people who have spat at me, whispered insults, or treated me as nothing more than a common animal.

Hong-An had no idea that when she faced my rage, she was battling this army of painful traumas. The harder I tried to forget these ghosts, the more the tides of my anger rose inside me. If only Hong-An could see them herself.

I went into my room and buried my face in my palms, my tears burning through the skin. Inside me was a beautiful soul full of love and compassion, but the angry, spiteful Ha-Le had knocked down her daughter again. I was hurting myself and my own daughter when all I really wanted was to see her have a happy life.

Minh came into the room and reproached me. 'What did you do? You are normally wise with your words.'

Minh was hurting too. There were no winners in this fight.

'Do you remember when you first met Hong-An?' I asked him, staring out the window.

Minh was silent for a few moments, and I watched his reflection in the glass. 'Of course. It was so long ago.'

'It was twenty-three years ago.'

'I remember waiting for you behind the prison fence for hours. When you got out of the truck, you looked so weak I was so afraid you would drop the baby.'

'That's right. I had to get someone else to hold her on the ferry because I couldn't stay upright.'

We both sat for a few minutes in comfortable silence, like the eye of a hurricane, remembering how Minh had taken the little bundle in his arms and spoken to her with the tenderness I remembered from our courting days.

❤ ❤ ❤ ❤

'You are so beautiful, my dearest daughter Trang Dai. I am your father. I will love you forever. Do you know that? Forever,' Minh held Hong-An for the first time as a father while saying his sweet words to his newborn daughter.

I said to him, 'I changed her name to Hong-An to give thanks to God for His miracle. Sorry for not asking you.'

'I like that name,' he said seriously, then roared with a laughter, rocking Hong-An in his arm.

'When Hang came back to the camp before you and told me that my daughter, Hong-An, looked healthy and beautiful, I told her that the baby was not mine.'

Minh and I laughed on the way to the office to register Hong-An. He spoke to her all the way to the office where she was signed in as a new detainee. Her number was 14397. Minh's was 4917, and mine was 4918. She was only a week old and already a prisoner, a fact she would joke about when she was old enough.

From that moment on, Hong-An was like the super glue that bound us together as a trio. The gangs were still fighting, but there was a new dynamic in the air. The screening for refugee status had started. It had electrified everyone, but the energy had nowhere to go. There was nothing else to do but wait. The verdicts kept coming down one by one. Denied. Denied. Denied. Not one person had been granted asylum yet. People hoped and hoped, in full awareness that the odds were against them.

The three of us struggled to make a comfortable family life, but all we could do was focus on surviving the challenge. My arms became Hong-An's bed and were so weak they turned to iron. I could hardly move them. Minh had to spoon-feed me because even when I put her down, my arms would shake uncontrollably. It was still so cold, and no one had given us extra blankets. Day and night, I sat, holding her to keep her warm on the edge of exhaustion, patting her back to help her sleep amid the loud noises that frightened her.

I lost my appetite but forced myself to eat so that I could make milk for Hong-An. Minh organised to get me extra cow's milk and pressured me to drink it all. Mealtimes were torture for me. I put on weight that tired me out. I was carrying new, unwanted flesh.

'I suppose these days they would call it Post Natal Depression,' Minh said, breaking our reverie.

❤ ❤ ❤ ❤

Now, years later, with our lives and our freedom intact, I sat on the edge of my bed, staring at my reflection in the mirror on the wall. My family had been through such a long journey. We had overcome impossible situations and impossible challenges. This should be the time of our lives when we were celebrating. We should be rejoicing and enjoying each other.

But that wasn't the reality at all, and the state that my family had come to was tearing me apart with regrets and pain. Why had I fought with Hong-An again? Why had I said all of those hurtful things to her? Why? Why? And why? It was like I was addicted to a version of me that I just couldn't let go of.

The regrets were like a cyclone in my mind, and I couldn't take the spinning vortex any longer. Loud sobs burst forth from my throat, racking my body with their intensity.

How could I survive with this much pain and guilt in my heart? How would my family ever recover and become the loving and united family we had once been?

My heart was slow and felt heavy as lead. Maybe it wouldn't. Perhaps we would never be the same again.

CHAPTER FORTY-FIVE

~

INNOCENT

I sobbed again and again over the next few days. I cried at home and my office. I sobbed about the words that I threw at Hong-An without thinking. I felt so remorseful. It was not in my character to act that way. The horrible person I was acting as was not the true Ha-Le, and I couldn't figure out where this person had come from for the life of me. I kept trying to come up with some kind of a solution.

This was my family. This was my daughter. She had been my daughter since the very first moments I'd felt her growing inside of me. She would always be my daughter, the love of my life. I had to make things right between us. I remembered when she was a baby, and I was just starting to get to know her. Being a new mother had given me something to hope for in the camp. Without Hong-An, I don't know how I would have kept ongoing.

♥♥♥♥

Hong-An became so important in my life. My newborn baby counted on me for everything, including protection, and I took my new role as her mother very seriously. I started to understand what unconditional love meant as a mother. I chose to focus on my daughter only and kept myself strong for her. My target now was to raise her to the best of my ability. I had to do everything that I could for her. I was surprised by how my newfound unconditional love guided me. No one taught me to be a mother, yet I found this new sense of self when I held my daughter in my arms. 'What a miracle love between a mother and a child is. It's like nothing else that I could ever describe!'

I tasted the sweetness of motherhood. It was sweetness beyond all of my imagination.

To me, the time in Victoria prison had trained me to become tougher with perseverance. I overcame what had tortured me and transformed it into my strength. I carried it with me through my next unknown battles in life. I saluted myself for the endurance that I had acquired in difficulty, pain, discomfort, discouragement, and fear. All of these torments I had passed through and borne to the end without quitting. My mother would have been pleased to see me become so independent. She would be proud to know that I could take care of myself and raise my child. It seemed like whatever challenged me before became a ladder for me to step up on to become a mother.

'Mẹ love you so much Hong-An,' I whispered to her. 'Mẹ will lay down my life for you and will be with you forever.'

I smelled my daughter over and over again. She smelled beautiful and healthy. I was so thankful that we were both alive, and I was holding her in my arms now. She was all the blessing that I could ever want from the universe. God had truly smiled upon me.

Raising Hong-An together with Minh was an excellent chance for us to mend our relationship. I could see Minh was both a great father to his newborn baby and good to his wife. He tried his best despite having no experience looking after people. He was the youngest, and it seemed he never had any responsibility for anyone. I felt so appreciative of his efforts toward Hong-An and me.

'The water's so cold, and my hands froze while washing the clothes for you and the cloth diapers for Hong-An.' My heart throbbed with love and understanding, and my eyes welled up with tears as I heard these words from Minh's. I forgave him for all the sad moments that I'd experienced from him in the past. I felt proud of Minh for helping so many people in the camp. He'd also given people hope with his translation. In front of thousands of people, my husband looked like a star, and for sure, Hong-An would be very proud of her father too. She brought us together in a way, the united force of loving her. Our mission was to try our best to raise our daughter every day, in and amongst the challenges we faced as detainees.

'Let the past go, and we can start a new journey as a trio together. Isn't that right, Hong-An?' I nursed my daughter with a new love and hope for Minh and me.

Minh opened the blanket curtain of our bunk one afternoon. Hong-An was sleeping, and I put my finger to my lips in case his entry woke her up. His eyes were full of excitement.

'Look,' he said, handing me a folded piece of paper.

It was filled with English words, and I shook my head. 'I'm too tired.'

'Look at the other side. I translated it already. Just read the top bit.'

I turned it over and concentrated on his neat handwriting.

'A refugee is someone who has been forced to flee his or her country because of persecution, war, or violence. A refugee has a well-founded fear of persecution for reasons of race, religion, nationality, political opinion or membership in a particular social group.'

There were lots of other statements and words underlined and circled. Hong-An stirred, and I patted her gently on her back.

'Can you just tell me what it means for us?'

'Well, OK. I've been talking to Julie – you know, the volunteer from America? Anyway, it turns out she has a law degree. I asked her so many questions, and she let me read through all her legal documents on the UN law on refugees. Wow, it's complicated, but I've been studying them. Basically, we just have to fit the definition of a refugee to get accepted. I don't understand everything yet, but I will.'

I thanked God that I had married a professor. Most people in the camp would not even think to ask about the definition of a refugee, let alone study the legal documents. My pride and faith, and love for Minh was growing stronger every day as I watched his efforts to support us as a family.

Minh got a notebook and kept it with him everywhere, even when he washed the diapers. He wanted to learn by heart how to respond correctly to the interview and write everything accurately. Minh held his notebook and walked around the football field all year, practising for the interview. My heart followed him with love and appreciation.

I looked again at some of the words he highlighted: Persecution. Violence. Religion. Political Opinion. 'Well, the Chinese Government make all these things pretty impossible. It's obvious, isn't it? Why do they deny everyone?'

'It's complicated. I guess they have to make it difficult; otherwise, too many people would leave their countries. A lot of Vietnamese are what they call Economic Refugees now. It's not enough just to want to escape the war. You have to be directly persecuted and in danger by remaining in the country and have demonstrated that you have been trying to avoid it. Don't worry, we qualify. It's just we have to know how to prove it.'

'OK, so if we –' I began, but Hong-An started crying, and I became distracted, calming her down.

'Look – leave it to me. I'll make a plan and if we get called for an interview, just let me do the talking and agree with everything I say.'

Hong-An was five months old when they finally called our name for the screening interview. Minh had been so prepared, but the night before, Hong-An developed a very high fever, and her skin went the colour of charcoal. It looked as if she was about to die, and there was nothing we could do. The clinic would open at 9 AM, and until then, the door would remain locked under all circumstances. We stayed awake all night, sobbing and praying. Our daughter's mystery fever tore at our hearts, and I was afraid to lose her. By the time we rushed her to the clinic, her fever had died down, and the nurse told us not to worry.

Minh nearly fainted when they called our number. He had no energy left after our sleepless night.

'We are going to fail,' he stammered. 'I... I have no... My mind is so cluttered. I can't think of anything...'

We sat outside the office and watched the people exiting with devastating looks.

'So many questions,' they warned us. 'We couldn't answer any of them.'

When the official called us up, Minh asked not to have a translator.

'I would like to answer the questions in English,' he said. It was a good strategy. To fit the English definition, he would use the right English words. 'My wife and baby are both sick,' he added. 'Please allow me to speak on their behalf.'

I waited with Hong-An outside the room for longer than expected. When Minh finally came out, his face was pale as a ghost, and his neck was glazed with sweat. Hong-An let out a delightful and surprising laugh, and the officer came over and played with her.

'Glad to see you are feeling better, little one,' he said.

Then we all smelled something unpleasant coming from Hong-An's diaper. The officer walked away immediately, and I burst out laughing. 'It is a good luck sign, isn't she my beloved daughter?' I asked, Hong-An giggling as I spoke.

We walked back to our building, and people flocked around. 'How did it go? All of us will be in the same boat. Rejected! Rejected! Rejected!' they all said, and teased Minh.

'As good as expected,' Minh replied.

Everybody knew his capability. If anyone was going to get accepted, it would be us.

However, the answer did not come to us that day or the next. We waited a week with no reply. Hong-An started to crawl and experiment with a few words. After a month, Minh started to act more and more concerned.

'It's too long,' he said. 'Too long!'

At the end of the second month, we still hadn't heard a word.

The waiting was intolerable. All I could think about was my daughter's future. No one on the outside could tell what was happening inside of me. I was on my own internal journey. I began to transcend from the person I once was to the person I knew I had to become. There was no clear direction of change. I only knew I had to keep going to arrive at a new destination. I had to rely on the warrior inside of me. It was a long battle for a full year with many unknowns, but the warrior inside me was so faithful to her owner during that time.

'We have a new fight, my darling girl, we'll fight together!'

I kissed my six-month-old baby with tears streaking my face. I owed my daughter a good life, but I had yet to deliver the life that she deserved. She did not know this. She was only a baby and didn't understand. She looked back at me with her bright, innocent eyes, having no idea of the hell she and her parents had been through. She smiled back at me with beautiful, red lips and laughed an innocent and joyous child's laugh. There was so much in the world that I wanted to give to my beloved daughter.

CHAPTER FORTY-SIX

NO CHRISTMAS TREE

I finished writing my email to Hong-An with blurred eyes and an aching heart. She was right to be angry with me. I had been a horrible mother to her. I am trying to make changes in how I act with our family, I wrote. I keep on taking baby steps, and that's why I keep falling. But I am going to keep trying. I will learn from this fall. I will pick myself back up again. I will be wiser, stronger and more determined moving forward.

I poured out my heart in my email, and I hoped that Hong-An would understand my reasoning. I hoped she would forgive her poor mother and give our relationship another chance. She would never truly know what I had gone through in my life or what she had gone through in her infancy.

I clicked the Send button and hoped that everything would be better soon.

We had planned to travel to the Gold Coast together to spend Christmas with Travis's family. It was meant to be a peace-making mission leading up to the wedding. I had written a long letter to Travis's parents while Minh and I were on the cruise, explaining why we were unhappy about the wedding preparations. I'd also explained some of our expectations for the wedding and delved into our concerns for the well-being of Travis and Hong-An, as they progressed in their relationship. Minh had checked it and added some thoughts, and I sent it with a heart full of openness and vulnerability, but between the lines, there was a lot of disappointment. We had wished that they would have made some time to talk with us. We'd hoped they would be open and willing to understand our cultural expectations for the wedding.

Their reply did not address the pressing concerns we had raised. It left us feeling misunderstood. They seemed so casual about the wedding as if it was something that Travis and Hong-An had under control. We rose above our disappointment and committed to the Christmas visit. In person, it would all be smoothed over, and we would discover our common expectations and respect our differences.

On the day of the engagement party, Minh and I tried our best to have an impressive blend of Western and Asian styles. We hoped that, through this, both cultures would understand each other better and build the foundation for a strong family relationship. We were all becoming one family, after all.

I waited and waited, but I didn't receive anything back from Hong-An. Minh told me that she would come around eventually.

'You are so brave,' he told me. 'And you love Hong-An so much. She is upset with you now, but she will get past it. You'll see.'

I tried to believe him. I tried to keep everything glued together, but I felt as if everything was cracking apart. And the cracks between Hong-An and me were only growing bigger each day. Would we ever be close again? Would I ever have my sweet daughter by my side again?

Was all of this my fault? Was it me who got worse? Or was this all happening because of the wounds inflicted on Hong-An when she was young? Hong-An had stored up emotional wounds just as I had, and now, the emotional cuts were beginning to show. We both needed to be healed, and I needed to do this first.

'You say sorry, and you do it again. I won't trust you anymore,' Hong-An scolded me when I asked if she had read my email. I was fired up with her attitude but tried to calm down for her wedding. It would be taking place in about one month.

'Everyone makes mistakes, in fact, this is just a normal part of being human. The main thing is we know how to correct and change it for the better,' I tried to reason with her.

'And then you do it again and again,' Hong-An mocked me.

I couldn't help but agree she was right, even if I wanted to argue. It does seem to be true that so often, cycles become patterns that repeat over and over again. Humans tend to make the same mistakes until they become ingrained habits of behaviour, and I was no exception. I wanted to close my ears to her words, but I knew what she said was true. I started to realise the power of the pause. I just needed to find the strength at that moment of frustration when I wanted to repeat these old patterns to simply pause and take a breath. Breathe out the frustration and find the courage to choose a new path.

I pleaded once again for my daughter's forgiveness with humility, but it was too late. Her heart was not open to her mother's words.

Hong-An walked to her room without saying anything. She looked exhausted. It was not my usual Hong-An. It had been over a year since we had gotten upset with each other, said we were sorry, and then could all laugh again, back to normal. What was wrong with us this time? Why couldn't we fix things?

'I really didn't want to go to the Gold Coast when you suggested it last month, but I agreed to go as you were so insistent. Now, with Hong-An's attitude, I want to cancel the trip,' Minh said, with a tired yet decisive voice.

I knew what made Minh say this. I kept quiet and stared into the night.

I was in the bedroom in the morning when I heard Hong-An wheel her suitcase across the floor. My heart was cut, knowing that she was preparing to go on her own to the Gold Coast after work.

'Let us bring the suitcase for you later,' I said, trying to rescue the situation.

'No! I will go by myself,' Hong-An answered me with a shudder in her voice.

She went downstairs and wheeled her suitcase without asking Minh to take her to the station as she usually would.

'Let her go!' Minh snapped. 'I don't want to go anyway.'

'The ticket is already booked.'

'It's OK; I don't care.'

I sat down and didn't know what to do. In this family, when I stopped thinking, everything became paralysed. It couldn't be that way. I had to find a good solution. I had to clean up the mess as the wedding was so close.

Minh went shopping, and I decided to get help from Travis to rebook the tickets and then insisted that Minh go to the Gold Coast with me.

'You were horrible to Hong-An again, Ha-Le!' Travis said when he answered my phone call. His voice shook with emotion. I felt like a giant balloon had popped in my face.

Travis's words stabbed sharply into my heart, and the anger rose in me again.

'No Travis, there was a misunderstanding. I did say sorry to Hong-An! Please let me explain....'

'I don't trust you anymore, Ha-Le. You are a liar!'

Enough was enough. I couldn't tolerate Travis's rudeness anymore.

'You are so blind, Travis! You only listen to Hong-An. With all that I did for you, how you cannot see that I was trying to love and support you. I can't believe the way you talk to me! How can you say such things?'

I cut the conversation off and sat down with tears, anger, and hopelessness. 'No one understands my good intentions,' I mumbled.

I had taken another baby step and fallen yet again, only this time, I was severely hurt and bruised.

'I'm sorry, Ha-Le. I have never seen Travis rude to anyone like that,' Travis's mother said to me later on the phone, sounding regretful about her son's behaviour. 'Come over, and we can celebrate Christmas. We'll talk and get to understand each other.'

'No,' I said, 'I've decided not to come. I don't want to see Travis anymore, and Minh never wanted to go to the Gold Coast from the start.'

On the morning of Christmas Day, I saw many texts from Travis, and I spotted the word 'SORRY.' I acted without thinking, deleting all the text messages from him. In my heart, I was determined to remove Travis from my life for good.

This was the first Christmas that our family would be apart. There was no Christmas tree, and the presents that I had chosen and wrapped so carefully laid there untouched under the tree. I remembered Christmas last year, when our two families came together, with plenty of love and laughter. The sweet smell of Christmas that I had remembered turned to an unpleasant stench with everything that had just happened. Sydney was sunny and warm, but I lay on the couch and felt cold, like the day Hong-An received her university graduation. I thought and thought again, trying to figure a way out. I could not stay stuck like this. Her wedding was in a month. I wanted to cry, but I did not. I had no tears left to cry and no energy left to shed them. My eyes were dry, but my heart was bleeding.

CHAPTER FORTY-SEVEN

~

FREE

Haven't you had enough fighting, Ha-Le?' I chided myself. 'Why do you keep causing problems when you should be making things right with Hong-An and Travis? Why do you keep doing this over and over again?' I felt so defeated by my actions. It was time for me to put my armour and shield away. I had fought all of my life. The time for fighting was over. Now was the time for me to celebrate my many victories. I'd survived a terrifying journey across the seas, detainment in Hong Kong, and I'd overcome cancer twice. Yes, I'd done enough fighting. It was time for me to put my hands up and surrender.

I walked outside and stood under a big Liquidambar tree in my front yard. I let the breeze blow through my hair and closed my eyes, letting the sun seep into my skin. I could feel the force of surrender begin to rise inside of me. 'Let it go and lose yourself, Ha-le!' I said to myself, trying to will some sort of release to happen magically inside of me.

I looked up at the leaves on the tree outlined against the clear blue sky. I could see old leaves growing and new leaves sprouting right alongside them. They were all different shapes and sizes. I contemplated the rough long older leaves that had lived through sun, rain, and wind, but we're still hanging on to the branch, their rough texture folding imperfectly with age. Yet, they were so beautiful, blowing in the wind. No one could argue that they were perfect. They had been worn by time and exposure, perfectly imperfect. Perfection was a challenge I was batting inside of me, and I could feel that it was holding me back. I looked back up at the leaves, 'Let it go and lose yourself Ha-Le!' I said once again to myself.

It was no wonder that this was hard for me, I had a lifetime of fighting against abuse, a broken family, war and hardship. All of these things made me want to spare Hong-An from this suffering and somehow this has turned into wanting perfection for her. It was this battle for perfection that forced my behaviour. I began to come to the slow realisation that I had to accept that life was in fact not perfect at all. Nothing was, not even the leaves on the trees. I had to allow my daughter to live her own life in all of its messy, imperfect glory.

'You can both do whatever you like,' I murmured, speaking as if Hong-An and Travis were both in front of me. 'I can't stop you from making your own life choices. Your choices are yours to make. The consequences of your choices are your own responsibility and a part of your unique life journey. It was not right for me to judge you.'

I walked back inside and found Minh inside reading his book in the lounge room. I went to him with my thoughts.

'Minh, we can't cancel the wedding, as I threatened Travis. They are adults. They can run a wedding by themselves. The more we try to help, the more we end up hurting. We hurt them, and we hurt ourselves. We hurt our family. We have to leave it alone, or the fighting will never stop.'

With this new realisation, my anger and pain began to slowly melt away. I was finally thinking clearly.

'I take full responsibility for my actions,' I continued. 'Hong-An was right to be angry with me, but the way she expressed that anger was not right. That is on her to take responsibility for her actions. We've all been wrong here, but we will all learn and grow through this. We will all overcome this and become better people. From now on, I will do my best to allow the unknown to unfold as it will and not worry. I've made mistakes in the past, but I'll do better moving forward.' I had to remind myself, as I often did, that we can only control the present.

Minh stared at me, with a furrowed brow.

'What are you saying, Ha-Le?' he asked. 'Does this mean that we will accept Travis?'

'Yes! That's right, Minh,' I said. 'We kept trying to change them, and when we did this, we went beyond our boundaries as parents. It's time to change ourselves and our perspectives. Let's make the right decision. Let's make this right today.'

I choked on my words then, feeling suddenly stuck. My mind was flooded with memories of twenty-three years ago when the three of us were held as prisoners. But then, the miracle had happened. Remembering this gave me hope. If we could get past that, then, surely, we could get past this.

💙 💙 💙 💙

The days that I spent at Whitehead Camp were gruelling and long. I lay there, in the blistering heat of the metal building, starving and broken and fully accepting that death would be better than this.

The new camp may have been just built, but it was starkly inhospitable. There were no trees, and the buildings were left to bake exposed in the sun. Everyone rushed in madly to claim their spots, but our family walked around aimlessly. We had given up. I had been using every ounce of my energy to look after Hong-An. Minh had invested all of his strength and motivation into the screening process. It was like the authorities were toying with us before they would inevitably send us back to Vietnam.

Though I longed to be settled in another country, the thought of returning to Da Nang, despite the danger and uncertainty, felt like a welcome option. We were just so exhausted and fed up. We couldn't find ourselves a bed; they were all taken. Defeated, I collapsed in the sun, like a broken doll, unable to go on.

Minh negotiated a small bed for us to share as a family, but it was no relief. For a week, I could barely eat and sleep. I existed in a no man's land of consciousness, devoting myself to feeding my constantly hungry daughter, but I was never able to produce enough milk for her.

'I don't think I can continue, Minh,' I said, in between the spoonful of rice he was forcing me to eat.

'Just one more spoon, please.'

'No, not the rice. I mean this,' I said, spreading my hands. 'Everything. Life. I honestly think I am not going to make it.'

Minh persevered doggedly, refusing to hear me, but I truly felt at the edge of death. If the heavenly light had shone down and invited me in, I would have gratefully accepted, had it not been for the insistence of the little girl in my arms. She cried and cried, bullying me back to life.

On the final afternoon, when Hong-An was sleeping, I closed my eyes too and was instantly transported to the edge of the river in Da Nang. I kicked a stone back and forth, waiting for my mother to arrive on the ferry. It was never going to come. I picked up a stone and threw it as far as I could towards the other side. It landed just a few meters into the river and disappeared immediately into the water. I watched the ripples spread across the water until they faded and eventually disappeared entirely.

'Ha-Le! Ha-Le! Wake up.'

Opening my eyes felt like being dragged out of the river.

'Ha-Le!' Minh said. 'They just called our names. We need to go to the office.' He helped me to a sitting position and cradled both of my cheeks in his hands. 'I think this is it. This could be our answer.'

The thought brought me to full consciousness and gave me enough energy to walk across the grounds, with Minh supporting me.

The official greeted Minh in English and then turned to the interpreter. 'Go on, tell them. You know the details.'

The interpreter looked at us blankly, then the edge of a grin appeared and spread across her face. 'You are the first three people to be accepted as refugees. Tomorrow morning you will be transferred to an open camp. Congratulations. You are free!'

Minh dropped to his knees and thanked God.

I burst into tears, and for the first time in a long time, they were tears of joy. Hong-An looked up at us with earnest eyes. Prison life was the only life she knew.

'We are free!' I said. 'My darling girl, we are free!'

Not everyone understands what freedom really feels like. For a person who has always been free, they don't feel it. They take it for granted. They don't even notice the tremendous beauty of their lives. On the day that we were accepted as refugees, I knew that I would never take my freedom for granted again. I felt like Jean Valjean in the last scene of Les Misérables. It was one of my favourite movies, and it was in my mind that day. I remembered the way Jean had walked away from Javert. Freedom manifested itself in his walk like he wanted to dance. His eyes lid up with joy when he looked up to the sky with a smile and new a hope for his life.

I had been a prisoner in Hong Kong for an entire year. It had been difficult from the very start, but once Hong-An was with me, the imprisonment became unbearable. I longed for my child's freedom far more than I longed for my own.

We left the office feeling as if we were walking on clouds. The coin had flipped, and we went from near exhaustion to having boundless energy. The news was like an antidote to the poison that had been in me since we'd left Vietnam. It was like finding a stream in the desert. We were free! Word quickly got around that we had been granted refugee status, and we hadn't even made it back to our bed before the crowds packed around us, congratulating and admiring our situation.

No one had been accepted yet. It was Minh's genius had made it all happen. There was no doubt that there was a sting of jealousy amongst the crowd, but they fought through it and partied until midnight, long after we had slipped away and fallen asleep. The three of us slept well for the first time in months.

The day finally arrived when we would be transferred to the open camp, which was just one small piece of administration away from being resettled in another country. When this day finally broke, we woke up charged with energy and excitement.

The whole camp spilled around the gate as we left. We felt like heroes as they sang and cheered and wished us luck. Until the officers insisted it was time to leave, Minh was huddled around a group of men and women, giving them advice on planning for their screening. He promised he would do his best to continue to provide them with guidance from outside. People believed they had a chance now. We had given them a taste of that rare delicacy: hope. Minh had not beaten the system. He had used his intelligence to make the system understand our situation and given us what was required under their laws.

For many, it was too late. They had already received their rejection and were waiting to be sent home. Then others were stuck in limbo, waiting and hoping that their eventual answer would be good news. Whatever their situation, they wore big smiles for us, and we waved and cried back at them from the bus bars.

As we drove away and the camp disappeared under the green ridge of the hill, I was flooded with a strange feeling that I had not had for so long. It was so unfamiliar that I could not instantly place it. Was it inspiration? Motivation? It felt like, all of a sudden, my appetite for life had returned. A better future suddenly seemed probable, possibly even. Hong-An bounced up and down with joy, absorbing our energy, swimming in her parents' happiness for the first time since her birth.

Since I had first stepped onto the boat with all my reluctance and fear, everything that I'd endured suddenly came flooding back to me. It was like a movie playing in my mind. I smiled with every fibre of my being, and it was a smile of victory for Hong-An, Minh, and me. Life was so delicious. I was deliciously free, and so were the two people that I loved the most. Tears fell from my eyes.

The past year had transformed me into a tough woman.

It wasn't just because of my spirit that I'd come through this experience stronger and better. Having my baby daughter by my side had helped me through. She was my rock, and I was hers. We had clung to each other, with a great need on both sides, through all of the cold, hunger, and emotional turmoil that living as detainees had brought down on us. Hong-An, my angel, had been with me all along the way, fighting my battles with me. She was my tiny co-warrior. We had won the fight together.

♥ ♥ ♥ ♥

Our freedom was slow to materialise.

Upon our arrival at Tuen Mun open camp, we were taken on a building tour and shown our beds. It was not that much different from Hei Ling Chau, except the people walking around looked different. They were dressed much more formally, and they looked healthier, happier, and more relaxed. I told Minh that I wanted to taste the free life outside, so we took Hong-An out for her first walk.

Together, we walked Hong-An through the gates for our first freedom steps since we set our foot on Hong Kong's land. No one stopped us or even looked at us. We just walked through the gates and out onto the road. We walked across a bridge and towards a market. I couldn't believe it. It felt like I was dreaming. I pinned on my thighs a couple of times to make sure what I experienced was true.

The scenes and smells of things there took us by surprise and excitement, and Hong-An started crying due to over-stimulation. Not even our daughter's tears could break our satisfaction at finally being able to walk around in the open air. I bought some vegetables at a stall, and the thrill of the act made me shiver with excitement.

I cooked vegetable soup for the family and us next to the bed where we lived. Freedom soup, I called it, and we ate every drop.

Getting out of the camp would take a month or two, Minh had assured us. Soon, officials from one of the countries accepting refugees would come and interview us, and then we would be granted asylum. I found so much hope in his words.

I fell asleep holding Hong-An and dreaming about her bright future.

There would come a time when I would stand gazing through the airport glass at the tail of a huge Qantas plane for the very first time. The red triangle with the leaping white kangaroo somehow promised the secrets of our new home. The logo was replicated on stickers, which all of the refugees wore with pride, marking us out as a group and branding us as newcomers to the Promise Land. With my heart full of dreams, I watched Australian commercials on television.

'The country of honey and milk,' Minh said with sparkling eyes. I could not wait to see Hong-An chase a kangaroo, jump around in the warm, sandy outdoors, and run across endless green fields. I wanted all of this for my daughter more than my heart could bear, but I would have to wait for these moments. I would have to wait, with bated breath, for the day that my child would indeed be free.

That day would come, but it would be two long, arduous years of waiting. Freedom does not come for free. It is bought with the hard-earned sweat of tenacity and perseverance.

My heart was set on Australia. I knew nothing about Australia before leaving Vietnam, but now it occupied my every waking thought. My first impression of Australia was seeing kangaroos jumping around a vast field, with indigenous Australians playing the didgeridoos. I felt a calling for Australia. My heart reached for that place. It somehow just felt right.

'I only want to have a peaceful life,' I said to Minh, over and over again. 'We can have a peaceful and happy life in Australia.'

After a few months, we learned that Australia had changed their policy on refugees, and we had no idea when they would interview us again. I felt weighed down. When I'd first received news of my refugee status, it had been uplifting. It had given me renewed strength. Receiving official refugee status was like a shiny veneer laid out over my vision, colouring my perspective of everything I thought and saw. It had temporarily energised me and given me great happiness. But now, all of those blissful feelings were wearing off as I struggled under the burden of the new challenges we faced. The exhaustion and sleeplessness tortured me. I wanted to be settled in Australia now. I was so ready to start my new life.

Of course, Minh and I could have tried to move somewhere else, but none of the other options sounded right for us. I was devastated as I heard terrible stories of refugees seeking to settle in America. They were not supported properly and had to work day and night in order to earn enough to survive and send money back to their relatives. Under this societal pressure, a lot of them were stealing and gambling and getting into all sorts of trouble.

We did find a way to guarantee ourselves asylum in America, but there was a condition attached that had a cost that was too severe to stomach. We would have to spend the next six months in the Philippines 'getting used to the culture.' My old school friend, Ngoc, had completed the process. She told us life in the Philippines' camp was even harder than that in Hong Kong. Her mother had died there of a heart attack.

It didn't feel right, so we waited, and hoped and waited some more. We only wanted Australia and hoped that it would open its doors to us.

CHAPTER FORTY-EIGHT

~

REBUILD

We had assumed that Hong-An would come home for New Year. We were wrong.

She had a return flight scheduled to bring her home in time. Spending Christmas apart was devastating enough but bringing in the New Year together was even more sacred to our family. I knew I had made a mess of the situation, but I really felt confident that I would do what was needed to change my own behaviour going forward. Despite this vow to work harder, I was still left with a stale taste in my mouth from the choices I had already made. I could not take back my words. They still lingered sharply in the air like breath on a cold day. They just wouldn't disappear. They were stuck on a loop in my mind. Was the damage already done?

I kept thinking of the few cold text messages I had sent after I had the big fight with Travis, and Hong-An had left for the Goal Coast by herself. I had sent these texts, fuelled by more than half a bottle of wine, and I regretted them so deeply. One even ended with the mortifying words: 'You are dead to me.'

These words were harsh, and I couldn't get this mistake out of my mind even if I had committed to myself and to Minh to do better. I had turned a leaf, but my phone still remained silent. There was not even a text reply from Hong-An.

In that horrible, stinging silence, my blindness was exposed. I hung my head and accepted that my fear, selfishness, ego, jealousy, misery, and even my desire for wanting good, had blocked the person I wanted to be.

Realising this made me feel so ashamed and gave me the courage to try to unpeel the layers of my emotions to reveal my better self. 'Come out and take control.' I insisted. She stirred a little, day by day, until the anger, worry and remorse eased. I found a space in me to forgive and move on, but without being able to see Hong-An, it had nowhere to live but in my imagination. It felt vitally important that she would return for New Year so that I could present to her my rediscovered self. I would prove to her that I was healed and capable of moving onward to the wedding and beyond in a spirit of love and compassion.

I had tried to protect Hong-An, and that had torn us apart. Nevertheless, I'd tried my best as a mother, and I learned many lessons from what I had done.

Hong-An will survive with the man she loved. If she struggles with her new life, that will be a good lesson for learning and growing! My new thinking had set me free as I could see clearly that I couldn't control the future! There was no such thing as perfect. The future has to become what it wants, my feeling aside.

I found the courage to text Hong-An once again.

'What time do you land in Sydney?' I asked, 'Let me know, and we will pick you up.'

'I will stay back here in the Gold Coast for the New Year,' she replied without a flourish.

I was numb and sat down on the couch after reading Hong-An's words.

I missed Hong-An so much, but I tried to remember how much we had been through. If we can survive all of that together, we can certainly get through this.

I moved around the lounge room for the entire day, looking through the big window, down to the end of our cul-de-sac, in the hopes of seeing my daughter appear from afar, with her warm and familiar smile. She would hug me at the door and said, 'we are good now, Mẹ' as usual after our fights. I kept waiting and prayed that we would spend the New Year together. When darkness fell, I couldn't see the cul-de-sac anymore, putting all my hopes on hearing her footsteps.

But she never came. Even at 11 PM, an hour before the New Year when Minh was asleep in the bedroom, I entertained the thought that she would knock on our door. Instead, I watched the fireworks on television, each burst pummelling the landscape of my already-wounded soul.

It was only last year that Hong-An had been waiting, with tears streaming down her face, as I recovered from my surgery. I was still coming out from under the effects of the anaesthesia, but I could still recall the way Hong-An had rushed up to me as I was wheeled out from the operation theatre, crying out, 'Mẹ! Mẹ! I love you!' She had held my hands tightly, showing me just how much she loved me.

I had faded in and out of consciousness as all of this happened, but Minh filled in the blanks for me.

'Hong-An was so worried about you!' he told me. 'Our daughter loves you so much, Ha-Le. She cried all the way home!'

We had been through so much worry and pain during this time. We carried around daily the worry that we would be torn apart by cancer and death itself. How ironic that it was not cancer but our own actions that had caused this divide. But really, wasn't this a much easier problem than cancer to solve?

There were only twenty-three days until Hong-An's wedding. We would make this right; I knew we would.

I have survived so many things in my life, even that long, lonely night waiting for the new year to begin alone which seemed impossible to recover from at the time, even that moment had new dawn. I simply slept, and the sun rose again, and I did survive.

I always survive.

❤❤❤❤

After Hong-An didn't come home for the New Year, I expected she would come home by the second or third of the month, but that didn't happen, and her next text message left me in shock.

It read, Hi Ba! Mẹ! I've decided to stay with my friends until the wedding. I don't want any more trouble in our family affecting the wedding.

When Minh read that message, he shook his head.

'We caved in and gave in to everything that she wanted!' he vented. 'But it wasn't enough! Nothing is enough to mend these wounds!'

I sat down in front of my computer, trying to find the courage to write another plea to Hong-An. I had to insist that she come home for the wedding. An email was the only way that I could connect with my daughter, I didn't know where she was staying.

I sniffled and fought back the tears while I typed the words out on the keyboard. I wrote to her in Vietnamese, starting with the words: 'To my dearest, only daughter, and my son-in-law.'

I poured out all of the words that I had in my heart. I opened up to Hong-An and Travis about my lack of control over my moods lately. I told them how I missed them and regretted my actions and told them how I prayed to God that we would all reconcile. I told them I wanted to forget the past. Clinging to the past was unhelpful, and all that I really wanted was a new beginning for all of us.

I ended up with an email expressing to Hong-An how much I loved her. I told her of the huge, vast love that I had in my heart for her.

Ba, Mẹ miss you so much, my dear! I wrote. Come back home and let us take care of you one last time before you start your new life with Travis. Please let Mẹ cook for you a few more times before moving away, starting your own life, and cooking for your own family. Your wedding will be in three weeks. You need to be comfortable and healthy in the weeks leading up to it. Ba and Mẹ love you always, no matter what else had happened!

Hong-An's response came not long after, and her words brought a new wave of tears to my swollen eyes.

I have missed you so much, Ba and Mẹ. I cried a lot with Travis over Christmas and New Year. I've been so sad about everything that has happened in our family.

But then, as I continued to read, my heart sank.

I still want to stay with friends until the wedding. I don't want to have any other negative effects on my wedding.

She still seemed upset with me.

Then I read Travis's reply, and my heart sank even further.

I forgive you, Ha-Le,' he said. 'But please don't cause any more trouble to Hong-An. I don't want you to be a liar!

Minh fumed when I showed him the email. 'How rude!' he said. 'What an insulting email!'

I could see that he was very upset.

But I responded differently. My perspective had shifted, and I wasn't angry anymore.

Actually, in contrast to Minh's feelings, I found myself chuckling at Travis's response. His words showed me that he cared a lot about my daughter. It also showed me that he feared me, and I need to be well behaved if I wanted to see better outcomes.

I tried to explain my new way of thinking to Minh.

'This is a good thing,' I said to him. 'This is opening up the lines of communication between us. This will make the relationship between the four of us better for the future. I don't want to fight or make any more problems. We need to let this go.'

Minh nodded in sympathy, and I was glad to see that he was on my side.

I made one last attempt to convince Hong-An to come home. I told her about my new commitment to accept Travis and my intention to support their relationship. I also mentioned that our family would be arriving soon. This persuaded her to come.

'Dear Mẹ! You are right! I will be home before Uncle Five's family, and grandma arrive.'

I had the peace that I wanted at last. My soul was flooded with relief.

Hong-An did indeed return to stay at our house for two weeks before the wedding.

A week before she came, I had managed to convince Travis to accept a lunch invitation to speak with me. When he arrived, I hugged him warmly, but he remained suspicious. I had prepared a special Vietnamese meal for him, hoping to win his heart through his appetite. We spoke about the plans for the wedding, and I remained calm and supportive, even though the news of each decision without my input made me feel increasingly side-lined.

'Can you do me a favour?' I asked him tentatively. He put down his spoon and looked at me sceptically.

I spoke gently. 'You may not think this, considering the recent events, but Hong-An needs to be close to her family. I wonder if, after the wedding, you both would move into the other half of the house. You would have your private lives with a separate entrance. Hong-An is very spoiled, and it would be great if we could support your wife which would allow her to have less stress. If we are neighbours, then we can support each other and rebuild our family together.'

His answer was immediate and clear.

'No!'

He seemed to be gaining confidence in delivering their decisions to me.

'We are already happy in our own lives; we are making our own decisions. Thank you.'

I smiled, betraying the choking feeling inside me. 'I respect your decision, Travis. And thank you for having lunch with me. You are always welcome in this house.'

Travis's firm rejection of my heartfelt offer left me feeling deflated and embarrassed, but I held strong.

My own life of hardships had taught me a lot. I had learned many lessons that I wanted to share with my daughter. I wanted to use my mistakes to help my daughter manage her own life, but she wanted to make her own mistakes. In a way, I understood this. Yet, it was still so hard to train myself to pull back and keep my thoughts to myself. It is hard to let a child start making their own choices, especially when you can see, as a parent, that their choices may hurt them. I never wanted my Hong-An to have pain, worry, or stress but perhaps that was an unrealistic wish.

So, when Hong-An arrived home, looking slightly embarrassed and awkward, I decided to be on my best behaviour. I observed her progress in the final organisation of the wedding, offering to help when I saw her struggling. She always refused, and I always retreated. I felt like I was abusing her by not helping. Every cell in my body wanted to lift her out of the stress and take control of the situation. I had given up trying to reclaim the wedding to match my expectations. I honestly just wanted to see my daughter happy and relaxed for her special day. The internal struggle was a mighty battle of willpower.

I focussed my energy on preparing a surprise for the wedding ceremony. I had written a song for her and with the help of a friend, recorded it. The plan was to sync it to a slide show of photos of Hong-An's life. I spent my evenings barricaded in the study, sifting through and arranging photos in order by date. It was an epic procedure as we had taken thousands of pictures—so many good memories of our pride and joy over the twenty-three years of her life. I brought out all the photo albums. I wanted to arrange a beautiful slide show for Hong-An's wedding.

A cyclone of emotions swirled about in my heart as I viewed all of the pictures that we'd accumulated over the years. Time had passed so quickly. It seemed like mere days ago that I'd held Hong-An in my arms back at the Hei Ling Chau detention camp. When she was only seven days old, and she fought with me for survival. She had been a warrior since the womb. Tears pricked at my eyes once more as I prayed that my brave daughter would continue to fight. I hoped she would be strong and bravely face up to all of the challenges that would come down on her as a married woman. She would have to be brave and strong and independent as she set out into the world, now with her own new family to take care of.

I didn't know what the future would bring for my daughter, but I did know that it was my role, as her mother, to support her in this transition. I wanted to create something that would echo all of the love that I held for her in my heart. I truly hoped that she would appreciate my efforts. She was trying to do so much on her own. She didn't want any help from me, but that was all that I wanted to do. Watching her wrapping heart-shaped chocolates for her guests stung me. A bride shouldn't have to do such things for her own wedding.

I was in contact with Travis's parents, who emailed me their photographic contributions of Travis's life. Seeing him as a baby, a toddler, a child, and a teenager opened my heart to him more and more. I saw the world through his eyes. I climbed trees with him, shook hands with Prime Minister John Howard, celebrated his football wins, studied and travelled the world with him. Seeing the photos of him as he got older, I cried, witnessing depression and tiredness gradually take hold of his features. But his big, honest smile linked the whole collection together, and I welcomed him into my life, all of him.

I felt moved, not only seeing Hong-An's beautiful face as she grew older through the series of photographs but also seeing my own journey. I had fought so many battles of survival, and I'd thought that my battles were over. But now, I was learning that life was a series of challenges. That is what it was to exist as a human being. Life was a series of moving from one challenge to the next, overcoming one only to move on to another.

But I knew now that I would always have the strength in me to face whatever came. I was just like that fiery red flower that would grow and rise up again, even stronger than before, even after being burnt to the ground. I was a Waratah. I would always overcome, and my daughter would too. She was made of exactly the same stuff as me.

CHAPTER FORTY-NINE

~

A PILE OF CINDERS

On the day before the ceremony, the wedding party we attended a rehearsal at the church. Hong-An had allowed me to decorate it with ribbons and purple roses. I had taken to it with a heap of energy, and Erin had been kind enough to help me. I found myself feeling so grateful to her, watching her jumping around and climbing up and down the ladder. She was there for more than four hours decorating with me. The church looked elegant and beautiful by the time we'd finished, and I was happy to finally be able to contribute to the event in a meaningful way. I stood off to the side and watched my daughter practising walking down the aisle, laughing with her bridesmaids.

'Slower, slower,' they yelled. 'What's the rush?'

Travis, although not yet in his suit, looked dashing and confident. It was great to see him interacting with his own friends and witness their support for him. I took a long breath. 'Maybe everything is going to be OK,' I thought. It was incredible to me that he was about to become a part of my family. I don't think I'd truly grasped this until that moment. My family was about to grow. Everything had happened so quickly. I was feeling an overwhelming sense of awe and appreciation for the forward march of life. Change, change, change, that was all that we could ever really count on in life.

I had not planned to reveal my slide-show surprise to them yet, but the pastor insisted on testing the equipment. As they fiddled with the cables, images began to appear on the screen. There were two portions of the slide show. The first part was paired with the song I'd written and recorded and was mostly pictures of Hong-An and Travis, while they were engaged, but there were also some pictures of Hong-An with Minh and me, as a child and as an adult.

The first portion started with pictures of Travis and Hong-An together, smiling, kissing, and holding hands. I heard the opening bars of my song that I'd recorded to go with the slides, and I rushed to turn the computer off.

'No, Mẹ, let's keep watching, please!' Hong-An pleaded.

'OK, darling,' I said. I was utterly moved. I let the slide show continue to play, but I muted the song. I wanted to save that for the day of the ceremony.

'Beautiful lyrics!' Travis's friends commented, watching the translation that Minh had done for my song, scrolling down to the screen's bottom.

The second portion of the slide show was pictures of Hong-An and Travis as babies, small children, and then teenagers.

Hong-An's bridesmaids erupted into shouts of wonderment. They cooed over a picture of Hong-An as a newborn, lying on our makeshift bed in the camp. Beside her were five oranges, an apple and a can of milk powder, her first possessions, laid out almost as proudly as our child. That was our definition of abundance at the time. I was sitting by her side, in front of the cloth and newspaper that made up the makeshift wall of our home. You could see that I was weakly smiling. Opposite that picture, I had placed a photo of Travis in his mother's arms on a hospital bed, with a squiggly red line connecting the two babies together.

There was Travis, posing with a soccer ball under his foot, grinning proudly at the camera. There was Hong-An, grinning in a sparkly red sequined dress. There Travis, posing in front of a wall of children's artworks, and then Hong-An wearing a vibrant patterned dress with a matching umbrella over her shoulder. Each of these photos were portrayed in a line, alternating with photos of Hong-An and Travis, as if symbolising that their fates were always intertwined, even years before they'd ever met.

The whole group watched as the pictures automatically flipped over, telling the story of their lives; Travis on a tricycle, grinning in the back-seat of a car, standing with an Easter egg balancing on his head; Hong-An on our camp bed again, this time in a donated red dress, more apples in the background. Hong-An wearing Minh's glasses in our apartment in Hong Kong. Hong-An teetering on her newly-found legs in Sydney harbour. Hong-An posing proudly in front of a glass cabinet in Minh's parents' house. Then the two of them on separate toy telephones at three years old, positioned together as if they were calling each other, across the lines of time and fate.

I looked at my daughter. She had relaxed a bit now and was enjoying the show. I wondered how much her friends knew about our story. To me, it was still truly remarkable to see my child, barely walking, with the Sydney Opera House in the background. Back in the camp, we had seen postcards of Sydney Harbour and constantly imagined ourselves, free, walking as a family along the shore. Just a couple of photos, a few months apart, held an impossible journey across continents and a transformation in the direction of our lives.

The slide show continued, now at a faster pace, through their early years of school, successes in sports and academia, holidays, questionable fashion choices, posing with friends in high school, graduations and university days. Then there were more pictures of the two of them as an engaged couple. Their individual lives came together then in a series of shots and selfies as a couple: Jumping high in the air at the beach, arm in arm near a waterfall, kayaking in Ha Long Bay, paddle boarding on the Gold Coast. They looked happy and alive. I had made sure to choose images that captured them at their best, carefully arranging them on the screen in a dedication of love and support.

Then there were a series of shots of them with their families. Travis with his huge tribe of relatives from the Gold Coast, and Hong-An with our extended family in Da Nang. I had cried putting them together, wishing deeply that Hong-An had her relatives around when she was growing up. Vietnamese culture is almost unimaginable without swarms of relatives being constantly involved. Our choices had led to our trio braving it, almost alone, in Australia.

The slide show ended with a beautiful selfie of the two of them, with the Sydney Harbour Bridge in the background. I had added some decorative hearts around their smiling faces, and the words, 'We are Merried!!!' scrolled above their heads. Everyone laughed when they realised my unintentional spelling mistake. On any other day, I would have been deeply mortified with humiliation, but this time, I laughed along happily just to be part of the joyful spirit.

I felt uplifted, coming back from the church. The delegation of my family had arrived from Vietnam already and was preparing for the big day. Everything was going as smoothly as could be expected, and finally, I felt like I was part of the event.

But my good mood was dampened when I arrived home to a quiet house. We should have had colourful lanterns and decorations over the front door just like we would've had in Vietnam. Their absence sparked a flood of frustrations in me, shattering the short-lived happiness I had found at the church. Inside, Uncle Five and his family and my mother were waiting for us to arrive home. They waited in a house that was glaringly bare. There was not even a hint of the traditional Vietnamese celebration that should have surrounded us. We should be enjoying a huge party with my mother, Uncle Five's family, and some of the great friends who had known Hong-An since she was in my tummy and as a baby. We should be cheering and laughing together, joyously acknowledging this important milestone in Hong-An's life. I felt empty and embarrassed, and I could feel threads of loneliness creeping up on me, burrowing into my soul.

I was trying hard at this moment to fight off old feelings and old patterns. I had worked so hard to come this far, and I didn't want to start to slip back into unwanted thinking again, but everything just felt so bitterly unresolved.

I tried to remind myself that there are always hurdles to climb over mental setbacks on a path to change. I knew that somehow, I just needed to push past this part in my mind. But even as I had this thought, I could feel the familiar feelings of disappointment creeping back. It was like a fog settling slowly and silently into the tender valleys of my mind.

'This was not how a Vietnamese mother should be spending the night before her daughter's wedding,' I thought. I had always loved Australia, but in my heart, in my soul, I was Vietnamese first and foremost. It was an integral part of my identity. That night, I felt more Australian than Vietnamese. This wedding was one suited to an Aussie family but completely lacking in aspects of Vietnamese culture. I felt deflated, disappointed. I felt so lonely in Australia; I was so far away from my homeland, culture, and family. I once again rallied commanded the bitterness to go away. I beckoned and pleaded with it to leave me in peace, but I finally succumbed to a compromise of the mind and allowed myself to indulge in the nostalgic indulgence of thinking of what I felt was missing.

If we were in Vietnam, we would be entertaining a whole house full of relatives. All of Hong-An's uncles, aunties, and cousins would be hugging her and expressing their abundant happiness for her. This was what was missing. It was this absence that watered the seeds of disappointment deep in my mind.

I went to my bedroom and buried my face in the pillow. I was overwhelmed by my fatigue and sadness. I wanted to regain my emotional footing. I had come so far and made so much progress, but I felt myself sinking once again to the depths of my darker emotions. I was not ready to give my daughter away. This was not what I wanted after raising her and caring for her for so many years. I was her mother, and I knew her better than anyone. She needed more time to mature and grow. She wasn't ready to start a family of her own.

I could feel the world I had created collapsing like a pack of cards right before my eyes. It was a world made of paper. The paper was on fire, and I was trying to put out the fire with more paper. There was nothing left to burn. My soul was a pile of cinders. How could I possibly recreate the illusion of a happy mother for tomorrow's ceremony? Why should I have to keep struggling after all that I had endured? I needed to find my inner strength once again. Why was it trying so hard to hide itself from me?

~

CHAPTER FIFTY

SHE LED ME THROUGH

I remembered bringing Hong-An to San-Yick Camp's nursery centre when she was only just ten months old. I took her there, and she played with the toys and the equipment and laughed a lot. I had thought she liked it, but she became distressed when I was gone to do volunteer work at Tuen Mun camp for a few hours. Hong-An clung to me, full of tears in her eyes when I came back to pick her up.

After only half a day of having my first job in Hong Kong, I stopped going back there. I decided to find another way to let Hong-An enjoy other children but I would still be by her side.

One day, I put on my high-heeled shoes and best clothes and took my daughter to the open camp. I had remembered that they offered a free childcare service for the children of Vietnamese asylum-seekers. I marched straight in and asked them if they had any work available. After a brief interview, they not only offered me a job, but they told me I could bring Hong-An along as well. I was so ecstatic and thrilled. I took the offer without a second thought.

Hong-An had taught me to love children. She showed me how adorable and sweet they were. It is because of her that I am so passionate about them.

Obviously, those little people needed the love and attention of their parents, and in their absence, I found I was able to give it to them. In their innocent, earnest eyes, I witnessed the sensitive soul that I, too, had as a child. I remembered the constant longing for my mother and father's presence. It was now my turn to give my love back.

Just as our lives were settling into a strong rhythm, we saw our numbers appear on the camp notice board one Sunday afternoon after church. 'We are going to Australia on the 26th of June.' Minh cried out with joy as he hugged Hong-An and me and covered us with his kisses.

We had been granted asylum in Australia after waiting for two years to get to this country!

I literally danced with Hong-An along the street the next morning, all the way to the childcare centre. My boss, Ronnie, had to calm me down in order to get a word out of me.

'Hey, hey, what's going on? You are going to scare the kids,' she laughed.

'We go Australia!' I said in broken English. 'Our name on board. Happy, wow. We go, we go!'

She hugged me. 'Oh, that is amazing, Ha-Le! I'm so happy for you guys.' She looked me in the eyes then, and her expression was sad. 'But we will miss you here.'

'I will miss you too, Ronnie,' I said and hugged her again.

'What will you do in Australia?' she asked.

No one had ever asked me what I would do when I got to Australia. Everybody's field of vision ended at the moment we were accepted as refugees. I looked around the room and saw the little faces of the kids looking back at me as if they were waiting for my answer too.

'Childcare,' I said. 'I will build a little heaven for kids. I will make my own childcare centre.' This answer also brought me back to the time that I made a deal with God, on the very last night I was in Vietnam. 'God,' I said, 'If you bless me to get through this trip and out of Vietnam this time, I will submit my life to serve children.' And so, I did.

We flew to Australia on a massive, red plane. Emblazoned on the side was a big red kangaroo. Hong-An recognised the animal.

'Kangaroo!' she cried out with delight.

This was the first time in my life that I'd been on a plane. I was getting to enjoy this new experience, right alongside my daughter. We boarded that plane, and I felt as though I were walking into a dream. We had fought so hard for this opportunity, and as I saw this dream finally coming true, my heart was light, dancing and jubilant inside of me.

Once we arrived, I felt nearly numb with joy. We walked through the airport, marvelling at the space and staring at all the blonde-haired people. Outside, it did not look like the postcards we had seen. It was pouring rain, grey, and dull. We didn't see the sparkling harbour, the Opera House, or even any promised kangaroos and boundless fields. We just drove through the rain to the outer suburb of Canley Heights to stay with Minh's brother while we found our feet. I was suddenly flooded with the feeling of the loss of Hong Kong. I missed the smell of it.

I missed the delicious smells of fried tofu, rice congee, dumpling noodles, BBQ pork, and five spices that found the way to reach every city's corners. I missed the city sounds as well. In Hong Kong, there were so many different sounds that filled the air. It was the sound of the music of the city. I missed Hong Kong's businesses and shops, buses, trams, scooters, and hurried pedestrians. I missed the bubbling murmurs of the Cantonese language, interspersed here and there with the languages of refugees and immigrants from various cultures.

We set to work building our new lives. I still wanted to start a childcare business more than anything, but it was another long hard fight to make this dream come true. Dreams are usually like this. They don't come easily. The first step towards achieving that dream was to learn English. We moved into a tiny one-bedroom apartment in Cabramatta, furnishing it modestly with our Centrelink incomes.

Cabramatta is the heart of the Vietnamese diaspora in Sydney. I began to feel more supported. I began to feel a part of the community. I did not know it at the time, but this was one of the very best times in my life. This was the most beautiful time for the Three Musketeers. We didn't have anything in our first new home yet. We owned nothing in the world! Yet, we were filled with hope. We had hope for the future and love for each other. This was all that we really needed. I felt like I could do anything.

I enrolled in a three-month-long English course offered to us for free as migrants. Even though it broke Hong-An's heart to see me go off to class, I loved it. I had the most limited knowledge of the English language in the class, and there were endless embarrassing moments when I stumbled and jumbled my words in front of my fellow students.

One day, Mary, my first and most favourite English teacher in Australia, greeted me cheerfully at Fairfield AMES. 'How are you going, Ha-Le?'

I answered confidently and without hesitation, 'By train Mary.'

'Oh! By train,' Mary repeated back to me with an indulgent smile. Reading her face, I knew that something was wrong with my English.

I bent over with a deep belly laugh when Minh explained to me what the question Mary had asked actually meant. 'She was just casually asking how you were doing.' Minh explained.

Another day, I went to the office wanting to change one class for another.

'Hang on, Ha-Le!' Mary said to me, as she was with another student. I looked around and tried to find some rope to hold on to while I waited for my teacher. Minh and I laughed even louder when I later told him this story.

I felt ashamed of my English, but this only made me want to try even harder. I studied with every spare moment that I had and added new words to my vocabulary all the time. My dictionary was filled with red marks on almost every page!

When Minh applied for a postgraduate degree in Applied Linguistics, I understood that I had to pause my dream in order to look after Hong-An at home. Even though my duty as a mother was stronger than my career plans, Minh's absence as he went to the library almost every day left me with my solitude and my loneliness only began to grow. With our limited income, it was difficult to do much more than stay at home or go window shopping at the local shopping centre.

One day, while taking a different route through the park, I heard children playing. Hong-An had wandered over towards the sound, and I joined her at the gate of a childcare centre. We stood there for a few moments watching the kids play and run around. I was transported back to my job in Hong Kong and felt instantly reconnected to the joy of serving the needs of children. After six months of being in Australia, my dream of opening my own centre had been relegated to the realms of fantasy.

One of the educators came over, bent down and said to Hong-An, 'Hello sweetie. Do you want to come over and play?'

Hong-An looked up at me. 'Mẹ, she is speaking English.'

'Yes dear,' I said. 'She is asking if you want to play with the other kids. But I'm sorry, we can't, we just don't have the money.'

'Come inside just for a little bit, OK?' she said. Hong-An looked at me again for approval, and I, of course, had to accept.

'Thank you,' I said to the woman.

'I'm Jan, and Ellie is our Coordinator,' she said, pointing to the other lady. 'Are you new to Australia?'

Jan was very friendly, and I told her a little of our story, mentioning that I had worked in a childcare centre in Hong Kong.

After our conversation began to grow, Jan came to understand better our challenges, and her kindness took hold. She could see I was skilled with children, and eventually, she made me an offer to volunteer working at the centre in exchange for Hong-An's childcare's fee. I was thrilled. It was the perfect opportunity to get experience working in Australia and also practice my English. This was the first of so many small steps I took on my way to achieving my dream. I so wanted to own my own childcare centre; I could nearly taste it.

I was motivated by the idea that I could still be with Hong-An while I worked by opening my own centre.

I kept my dream and my vow to Hong-An alive by searching the papers for childcare centres for sale. There were plenty of centres, but they were all way above what we could afford. Finally, I discovered one in the suburb of Birrong, which was much cheaper and available for sale as freehold. I didn't understand what that meant at first, but I convinced Minh to go and look at it with me.

The centre was located in a beautiful leafy cul-de-sac, and I fell in love with it immediately. This place had everything that we needed. There were three bedrooms for our family, and then the preschool was in the back, with a separate entrance. I couldn't have found a more perfect location, and I knew that I had to find a way to make it work. Selling our current house would only cover half of the price of the freehold. The other half would need to be covered by an additional loan, which the bank, unfortunately, had already rejected. Determined to find a way, I went to a Vietnamese broker and managed to find an option where we could just barely scrape through. Minh was apprehensive.

'Why do you insist on pursuing this? What we have already achieved as a family is the dream of millions of people coming here,' he said.

He was right, but what he didn't understand was this was not something of my own. It was our family's success, not my dream.

Even though he didn't fully understand, and the risk made him nervous, Minh did support me in the end. After discussing it at length, he agreed to buy the centre.

I dove into the deep water and finally opened the centre. The seeds of which had been planted all that time ago in Hong Kong. My dream had finally come true. But the struggle had really only just begun.

There were so many challenges. I hired the wrong staff and was disappointed by their attitudes and behaviours. Also, the parents were not so welcoming. They had enrolled their children there under the management of someone else, and now they were somehow meant to put their trust in a Vietnamese woman with a heavy foreign accent. This was no small matter, and to my dismay, the parents started pulling their kids out of the centre one by one. The stress of the management, staffing problems, and lack of kids pushed me to my breaking point. I came to the difficult decision to close the doors after only three months.

It was not a complete financial disaster. The building was still our house, and Minh's job could cover the mortgage repayments if we lived a simple life. I was very thankful to Minh during this time. He ended up taking on a second job to cover the cost of the large mortgage. I knew that he was working twice as hard as he should have, and he was doing it all to finance my dream. He didn't always agree with me, but he was always on my team. He was my constant partner, supporting my vision even when he didn't share it.

The setback was a massive blow to my confidence and willpower. I focused on getting my health back, and when I was well enough, I took a job at another childcare centre. After a week there, observing the dissatisfaction of the staff and the sad faces of the children, I became motivated to reopen my centre. A few parents had started to stop me in the street and at the local shopping centre to ask if I would be opening again. They had moved their kids to other centres but quickly recognised that mine was preferable.

I reopened my preschool with new energy, and the rooms filled rapidly with great support and encouragement from parents such as Sue McDermott, and Sue Pearson. For the next ten years, I lived the peaks and valleys of my dream while also studying to gain a Bachelor of Education.

After nearly eight years of pursuing what I really passionate to learn, I received my degree, finalised the deal to build a brand-new centre close by, allowing us for the first time to separate our home and my workplace. All the pieces of the puzzle we had been arranging our whole lives were now in place. We were a successful, well-respected family in the community. Hong-An was a model student and a model daughter and was about to embark on her own dreams. My life had been a struggle for survival but now, looking ahead, I felt like I could finally relax and enjoy what we had worked so hard to build.

Now thinking back on those days, so much has changed. Each struggle has led us to where we were now. Things were different, and it was now Hong-An building her own life. The challenges that I faced were different. I knew that I had to stop worrying so much about what the future might bring. I knew I had to focus on the moment. I had to help make sure tomorrow, Hong-An's wedding day would be both memorable and special. Once again, I repeated the mantra to myself that I had carried with me throughout life.

'Let it go; you can only worry about the present,' I quietly whispered to myself as I finally began to win the battle for sleep.

CHAPTER FIFTY-ONE

OUR CULTURE

'C an you please stop crying, so I can put on your eyelashes?' Tanya, the make-up artist, said to me.

It was impossible. My face looked like a swollen piece of fruit. I could hardly open my eyes to look in the mirror.

It was like trying to put a bandage on to stop the wound from spreading any further.

So much emotion had led up to this moment. I'd started to feel slightly better yesterday. After hours of worrying and stress, I had finally found peace. But that peace was gone once more, and it had somehow slipped through my fingers like sand. No matter how hard I tried to grab hold of it. It was not healthy for me to keep going through the cycle of negative thinking and blame. I knew this in theory, but somehow, I still struggled immensely to put this thought into practice.

The main thing that kept nagging at me was the thought that I was the one who had exposed Hong-An to a different culture in the first place. I couldn't rest that this act was the ultimate trigger that caused her to drift away from her Vietnamese self.

When we fled Vietnam, looking for a new place to call home, Australia had opened its arms to us. I wouldn't have ever wanted to shield Hong-An from her new home's cultural and social norms. But I had also assumed that we could somehow be both Vietnamese and Australian at the same time. Vietnam was where we had come from. It was important to retain ties to those roots, but we couldn't simply close ourselves off to the culture of Australia.

There were so many 'what if' scenarios playing out in my mind. One that persistently plagued me was the thought that if Minh and I had a better relationship, maybe Hong-An would have more respect for her parents and culture.

Ultimately, I had to face the reality that Hong-An would not do everything the way that we, as her parents, wished. I had to accept somehow and let go. She had gotten to the point in her life where she was making her own choices. I knew this was something that every mother had to deal with as her children grew up and left the nest.

I wondered how I would ever make it through the ceremony. I was sure that I would somehow break down in tears and grief against my will.

I sat in the chair, waiting for my hair and make-up to be finished, and still kept lecturing myself. I had gotten more robust, and I was clear what I needed to do to take control of my own thoughts, but this was a journey, and I was still a human battling for control of my mind.

'Try to control yourself, Ha-Le,' I whispered gently to help calm my thoughts and get me back on track. Inside me was a small flame of clarity and hope that I was trying desperately to grow bigger with only my own breath.

'The wedding is happening soon. Accept the present exactly as it is, see it, love it and make peace with it. Move forward into the next moment, breathe deeply and fill your lungs full of happiness. You can do this.'

It was indeed time to let go, time to get over it, time to grow and change.

I grit my teeth together, clenched my jaw hard and then noticed the tension and took one big deep breath releasing it all. I was learning, and I was growing. The process of change is not perfect. I didn't know exactly how I would get there, but I knew I didn't want any more sorrow or pain in my heart. I didn't want to waste another minute on something that I didn't like in my life. I needed to stop focusing on the things that were out of my control. I had to give my attention to the things that were within my power to change.

I closed my eyes, willing myself to relax as I was fighting back the tears. I didn't want to keep ruining my make-up even before it finished.

When my face was dry, Tanya finished putting on my make-up, and I looked in the mirror. What I saw caused me to laugh out loud in surprise.

I couldn't stop laughing, it was just too absurd, and the laughter had somehow replaced the tears. My skin was a dark brown. She had given me a tan look, a very tan look, rather than using a foundation that matched my actual skin tone.

'Tanya!' I cried through the laughter that now I just couldn't contain. 'This is not the colour of my skin. You made me tan so that I'd look hot and sexy, didn't you?' I said, nearly falling out of my chair.

'No!' Tanya insisted. 'Your face was swollen and bumpy, so I used this powder to cover up the uneven skin tone. Also, it makes your face look slimmer!'

I didn't think I'd be able to show my now-far-too-brown face at my daughter's wedding, but it was funny, and there was little to do at this point but laugh at the ridiculousness of it all.

Tanya agreed to try and fix it and to attempt to disguise the monstrosity of my face. She kept applying and reapplying different substances in varying amounts. Tanya was right, and my face was swollen and bumpy. My sadness could not be hidden, no matter how much cosmetics were applied.

By the time I left the salon, I was wearing a thick and heavy mask.

When I arrived home, Minh was waiting anxiously for me.

When I walked in, he took one look at me, and his expression changed from frustration at my lateness to pure and utter confusion. He stared in amazement and cocked his head to one side as if he had accidentally addressed a total stranger as his wife. 'What the… What happened to you Ha-Le?' was all he managed to get out.

Seeing his face with such a twisted state of confusion written all over it somehow only made me laugh like a mad person. 'This is the face you married, Minh. This is the real monster. Get used to it!' I said between fits of laughter.

'You look ridiculous. You look like a total stranger. You don't look like your pretty self. Go and look in the mirror. Do you even know what you look like? You will regret it if you don't fix it,' Minh replied, now starting to hold back laughter of his own, mixed with his confusion.

He was right; I did look like a different person. I wore an impenetrable mask. It was ironic really, given everything, there was nothing to do but laugh. I wiped a few layers of the make-up off, exposing my puffy eyes, and smudging my painted eyebrows in the process. But really, I was kind of past the point of caring.

I only had a few more hours of battling my own mind to push through. I had to keep my mask in place. Somehow, it was funny but I kind of needed the disguise in the end to hide my emotions. But I'd already wiped away several layers of make-up, so I was left with nothing to hide behind but my own strength now.

Hong-An came into the living room then. She was wearing her wedding dress, beaming and turning about so that we could see her dress from all angles. It was a beautiful dress, and Hong-An looked stunning in it, but it was missing something vital.

'Where is the veil?' I asked. I couldn't stand to see her bareheaded in her wedding dress!

'I can't remember where I put it,' Hong-An said, with a flippant wave of her hand. 'But I'm not worried about it.'

I kept my lips pinned together. I didn't say anything. But I was terribly disappointed. Hong-An had asked me to order the veil from Vietnam, as she couldn't find it in her size in Australia. I didn't know if Hong-An had misplaced the veil out of stress or distraction or if she really didn't care about all the trouble I'd taken to find it for her. But I once again turned to my inner voice to quiet my emotions and win the battle to keep my words to myself.

'You look beautiful, darling,' I murmured.

'Cam on, Mẹ,' Hong-An said in Vietnamese, excitedly. 'Let's get some family photos!'

The photos too, were rushed and a source of disappointment, but even if I had taken my heavy mask of make-up off, I still kept on a mask of civility. Once we were at the church, I let my frustrations and anxieties rise and fall amidst the chaos of the crowd. I greeted Travis's parents warmly and accepted everybody's compliments about the beauty of the venue. The pastor came and reminded me to wait for the wedding March to play before walking my daughter into the church from the entrance door.

'There is no going back now, Ha-Le,' I told myself. 'Hong-An will be married in only a few minutes.'

It was true. The arrow had been shot. All that we could do now was breathe, surrender to the moment and let go.

CHAPTER FIFTY-TWO

THE CEREMONY

I wrung my hands together, standing in the foyer of the church, with Minh and Hong-An at my side. This was it. The ceremony was about to start, and Minh and I were giving Hong-An away. She was leaving us and going to Travis, and from the look of it, it seemed like it was a change that she couldn't wait to make. Hong-An was smiling, as I'd never seen her smile before. Her eyes danced with jubilation. She was chattering excitedly to Minh, but I could hardly hear what she was saying. I was overwhelmed by this day. I felt ready to collapse. I wish I could have just stayed home and waited for it all to be over, but I was doing my best to find my inner strength and hold onto it.

I watched Hong-An, twirling her bouquet of flowers in one hand and smoothing the fabric of her bridal gown with the other. She was radiant. She looked like an angel in her white dress. Her hair was down and had been styled into long, loose curls that cascaded over her thin shoulders. This was the hair that had received millions of kisses from me over the years. Was this really my daughter? Was this the infant I had clung to in the Hong-Kong refugee camp? The little life I had fought for on the boat escaping Vietnam? Yes, it was, and yet, I couldn't believe it. I couldn't totally accept it. Where had the years gone? My tiny baby was a grown woman now. She had been with me for my journey, and now she was going to start her own. My daughter was a beautiful and happy grown woman. She didn't need me anymore.

The pain welled up in my heart. Tears stabbed at my eyes, like tiny pinpricks. My throat felt thick and tight like something hard and unmanageable was forming in its centre. My breath shortened. Each inhale was a struggle.

Hong-An turned to me, smiling with her eyes alight, and said something. My thoughts were too fuzzy and distracted to really listen. All that I could think about was how I'd held her to me as a baby, how I'd taken her in my arms for the first time and been overcome with a love that I didn't know was possible. My love for my baby consumed me. Even though now she was older and independent, that love had not lessened. I was still as fiercely devoted to her as ever, but she no longer required that level of devotion from me. What was I supposed to devote myself to now?

I forced a smile onto my face.

'I'm sorry, darling,' I said. 'I didn't hear you. Say it again.'

'I asked if you're ready?' she repeated. 'The ceremony is going to start soon. Are you ready to walk me down the aisle?'

More tears welled up in my already wet eyes. I blinked rapidly, trying to fight them off, but it was no use; several tears escaped, travelling down my cheeks in heavy streams.

Hong-An frowned, a furrow formed in her eyebrows.

She watched me crying but didn't say anything. She was an intuitive girl. I know that she could sense all of the feelings I was carrying around inside of me.

The music began just as my storm of tears worsened.

Directly next to us stood the youngest members of the wedding party. Uncle Five held his one-year-old with two big red love hearts in his tiny little hands. There were the flower girls and ring bearer, small children with bright smiles that reminded me Hong-An would never be my child in the same way again. My sobs deepened. Minh looked over at me but didn't say anything. I believe he tolerated my display of emotions because he felt his own but just not letting them out.

I watched as the fabric of the bridesmaids' dresses swished against their legs as they began to walk down the aisle. I felt a sense of pride well up in me. Hong-An had allowed me to be a part of her wedding, even if, ultimately, I hadn't been as involved as I would've liked to have been.

I had chosen the material for the bridesmaid's dresses and designed them myself. Hong-An's closest friends were dressed in floor-length gowns of light purple. The skirts were soft and flowing, while the bodice of the gowns was more fitted and covered with a delicate lacy material that swirled about.

The dresses matched the gorgeous purple bouquets that the girls carried. My own dress was made in a similar style but was slightly different so that I matched the rest of the wedding party and was also set apart as the bride's mother. My dress was also a soft purple, but instead of being sleeveless as the bridesmaids' dresses were, mine had full-length sleeves, and the whole dress was entirely covered by floral lace, intertwined with sequins and beading that flashed as the sunlight struck them.

I nodded and smiled through my tears. We made quite the picture. I felt proud of my contribution to my daughter's wedding. All of the dresses were so beautiful, and they had been coordinated with the decorations in the church. At the end of each wooden pew, there were great swaths of white taffeta looped over, with purple and pink flowers cascading down from the centre of the loop and down over the material, nearly brushing the floor. Despite my fear and sorrow, I couldn't help but stand in awe. This was my daughter's wedding, and it was a breath-taking scene.

The wedding planner saw my tears of emotion hurried over to me with a tissue, which I used to blot frantically at my eyes, but I knew it was no use. My make-up was ruined, and I was an emotional disaster. This wasn't a mess that tissues could clean up.

I grit my teeth together and braced myself for the dreaded moment, when Hong-An would let go of my hand, let go of Minh's hand, and take both of Traviss. That moment was speeding towards me, and I'd never felt more unprepared for anything in my life.

The music shifted, intensifying, and Hong-An clutched my hand without looking at me. She was staring straight ahead, poised on the balls of her feet, as if ready to spring forward. My Hong-An couldn't wait to start her new life. But this new beginning for her was an ending for me, an ending that I wasn't ready for.

My heart hammered and then slowed, feeling as though it'd skipped a beat, and then it sped back up again, this time pounding in my ears. I had to steady myself by placing the palm of my hand against the wall.

'It's time,' the wedding planner told us. 'Everyone ready?'

I nodded numbly. I felt so much, and at the same time, didn't feel anything at all. I was lost in an ocean of emotions that would be impossible to describe. It was as though I had so many feelings, careening around inside of me, that they'd all blended together and now I could hardly feel anything at all. But this numbness did not really hide the churning sentiments trapped inside me, they were still there, causing sweat to bead up along my hairline and my fingers to tremble.

Hong-An took hold of my arm on one side, and Minh's on the other. We stepped through the doors, the three of us all in a row. The Three Musketeers stood together for what felt like the very last time. As we stepped out into the aisle of the church, all heads turned our way. I heard a chorus of murmuring as everyone saw how beautiful and elegant Hong-An was in her wedding gown.

My lower lip trembled. I fought to keep it together. All eyes were on us. I couldn't ruin this moment for my daughter!

But as we took our first steps through the church, the floodgates opened. I cried openly in front of all of our family and friends. My eyes were turned downward, but still, in the periphery of my vision, I could see the flash of many cameras, documenting every moment of my incredible sadness. I heard murmurs from the crowd, many exclamations of 'aww' and more than one guest joined me in shedding tears. This was how this moment would be forever remembered! Here I was, sobbing all through my daughter's walk down the aisle. I wanted to stop, but I felt as though I couldn't control myself. My tears poured out of me as though they came from an external source. I cried a river at that moment, just like the river that had separated me from my mother all those years ago in Vietnam, just like the river that Hong-An and I had walked along during our last visit to our home country. But I was crying a new river now. Each tear that fell was for the widening separation between my daughter and myself. I feared I might drown in the sadness that engulfed me.

I continued to shake and sob all the way up the aisle. My footsteps felt heavy and leaden, as though I was walking to my own execution. My body gave no indication that this was the happiest day of my daughter's life. The stage came closer and closer. Travis stood there beaming. His eyes were alight, and he didn't even seem to notice that Hong-An's mother clung to her sobbing like a crazy woman. His eyes were only on Hong-An. His smile was bright and exuberant. I had never seen him look so happy. He looked like he couldn't wait to take Hong-An as his wife like this was the moment he had been waiting for his whole life.

A new emotion swept through me then, intermingling with my heavy sadness and stabbing fear. I was struck, at that moment, by how much Travis truly loved my daughter. I'd never seen a groom look so blissfully at peace while also so excited and eager. His face was an exquisite depiction of the tender love that Travis carried for Hong-An.

And then I was struck just as suddenly by the realisation that Hong-An returned that love to him in equal measure. She had been bouncing up and down all morning, eagerly preparing for this very moment. She had chatted animatedly with her bridesmaids, expressing that this was the happiest day of her life and that she couldn't wait to start the rest of her life with Travis.

As we took our last few steps before Hong-An would be given away, snippets of their relationship, the moments that I had witnessed, flashed in my memory.

I recalled the way they laughed and talked together as if nothing could make either of them happier than simply to converse and interact with one another. I recalled the way Travis looked at Hong-An when she wasn't paying attention. I recalled the way they'd sequestered themselves away on our family vacation, always preferring to be alone together.

I took a deep, shuddering breath, bracing myself as if for impact. I felt like life was coming at me full force.

I had been wrong. I had been wrong about it all!

Travis was the right man for my Hong-An, because he was the man who loved and treasured her. He saw Hong-An as the special and amazing person that I knew she was.

I had been so worried that Travis would not be able to properly care for Hong-An, but I hadn't stopped to think that he had been doing exactly that for as long as I'd known him. He treasured Hong-An, and Hong-An treasured him back.

I don't know why it took me so long to get to this moment or why it was the walk down the aisle that finally brought it to the forefront of my consciousness, but the timing was perfect. This realisation was exactly what I needed at that moment. I considered the possibility that maybe a force greater than myself, maybe God, had helped to further my perspective and had laid the groundwork for me to come to this new understanding.

I let go of Hong-An's hand and placed it into Travis' outstretched palm. As I gave my daughter away, I felt peace finally settle into my heart. It was true that our relationship would never be the same, but I was finally ready to accept that this was a good thing. Life is ever-changing. To be a living creature is to be in a constant state of change. We grow, we mature, we age.

This is what my Hong-An had done. Was it normal that I was so resistant to let her go? Was it normal that I'd fought against this marriage from the very start? Maybe. Maybe not. But even if my actions were not the norm, I knew that my emotions were. When a mother's young leaves the nest, it is a painful and emotionally draining process. I knew this now first-hand.

My tiny family had been through so much more than many others. The Australian families that I knew had never lived through war, death, and finally, relocating to a completely new country, one fundamentally different in every single aspect. I could see it now. I could see the reasons for my own behaviour. I had lost so much throughout my life. I had fought tooth and nail to give my daughter a better life. Now, it was time for her to go off on her own and enjoy that better life that I'd made possible. Now was the time for me to let go and know that I'd given my baby everything that I could.

I had tried to live for Hong-An. Now I knew, the best way for me to live for Hong-An was to give her space and focus on becoming the best me that I could be. I wanted to make Hong-An proud of me. I would show her my new independence. I would prove that I could live life on my own, without constantly worrying about her. I felt jubilant when my mind hit this point. I was braving great changes, even stepping outside the norms of Vietnamese culture.

I felt like dancing, like when I was a little girl having competitions with my younger brother, Hien. If only little Ha-Le could see me now.

As Hong-An took Travis's hands and stepped up to the altar, facing the pastor and preparing to speak her vows, my heart was still and peaceful for the first time all day.

Hong-An was such a special and one-of-a-kind girl. She had so many unique attributes that she should be proud of. Minh and I were both certainly very proud of her. We could not be happier with the amazing daughter that we had been blessed with. All of the Three Musketeers should be proud of who they were, who they'd become, and who they would go on to become. We are all continually growing and changing. My family was the way it was because of our experiences, both shared and individual. We should embrace our imperfections. It was our imperfections that actually made us perfect. We should take pride in all that we'd done and proclaim it for the entire world to hear! We had a right to acknowledge our strength and all the struggles that we had overcome. At that moment, I knew I had enough. I had my family. I didn't need anything else.

I took my seat next to Minh, and the tears continued to flow, only they were different tears now. There was less urgency and desperation in my crying because now I could see that our lives were playing out exactly the way they were supposed to. Hong-An would be ok. My fears as a mother had blinded me to who she really was. She was not a weak and spoiled child, as I'd convinced myself. I had told myself that she needed me, only because I needed her. She was not any of the things that I'd thought she was. She was a warrior. Like me. Like her grandmother. Like her great-grandmother. She had strength and wisdom inside of her. She had a sharp intelligence and a heart full of love. My daughter was going to be fine. And so was I.

As a grown Hong-An said, 'I do.' I could hear a much younger Hong-An in my mind, a soft voice from the past reaching out to grab hold of me.

'Happy or sad tears, Mẹ?' I heard her ask. I smiled softly.

Sometimes, they are the same thing.

CHAPTER FIFTY-THREE

~

A NEW BEGINNING

'Wow! What a ceremony! Your family is like an icon for us to look up to,' Jan laughed as she hugged me in congratulations.

I smiled but knew that Jan didn't know the full story. People always saw my family as so perfect, but we were just as flawed and damaged as any other family. Yet, for the first time, I was starting to realise that this was alright. Perfection wasn't attainable. We all have our struggles, and part of being living creatures was to simply learn to accept this. I'd had a revelation, but I knew that truly coming to its acceptance would take work. I would continue to stumble and fall and mess up, but I knew that I was on the right path. Great change takes excellent work, but it all starts with a shift in mindset. The hardest part was over.

My mood continued to lift as more and more people came up to me to offer their congratulations. I was hugged and kissed and had an abundance of kind words and well wishes heaped upon me. I knew that I was very blessed. My heart was warm and light. I felt as though I'd lived a lifetime since that morning, even if only in my soul. We are never done growing. We are never done learning and becoming better versions of ourselves. That is why it is so important to overcome the past. The past is over and done with, and the present is all that we can control. It is all that we have any power over.

'Life didn't go as we planned! But we kept on moving on our new path and made the best of it!' I felt happy with this thought. My heart was no longer heavy.

We had so much to be grateful for. We had a beautiful home. We had a community of friends and family to love and support us. We had it all, and for far too long, I'd let myself fall into a mindset of negativity. When we allow negative thoughts to consume us, when we take on a mindset of lack, this makes it difficult for us to see the positive aspects of our lives. When we are only focused on what we do not have, it makes it nearly impossible for us to be grateful for what we do have.

'Enough is enough, Ha-Le! It's time to focus on your joys and hopes now!'

I said this to myself as the lyrics of one of my favourite hymns, Amazing Grace, began to play in my mind. I found myself humming along, feeling moved beyond belief.

'Amazing Grace, how sweet the sound
That saved a wretch like me
I once was lost, but now I am found
T'was blind, and now I see!'

These poetic lyrics described me perfectly. I had been lost, and now I felt like I was found. A divine force had caused me to confront the error of my ways with such suddenness and accuracy. Now, I could see. My love for my daughter was powerful, so powerful and wholly encompassing that it had blinded me. But that blindness had been lifted from me. I was shaking with the power of my emotions.

I watched Hong-An and Travis walk out of the church, hand in hand, moving forward to start their family. My heart was pumping with emotion. They had become husband and wife in front of God and all of the people who loved them most. Travis was now officially my son-in-law. I took everything in with a great amount of overwhelming feelings. I felt as if I was swimming through a great ocean of emotions. Each wave was connected and equally powerful. As soon as one emotion came crashing down, lessening in force and lapping against the shore, another would build and strengthen and then come roaring at me full force. But this time, I wasn't fighting against my feelings. I was tranquil and accepting, taking each wave in stride, floating along, with a heart at rest. My soul was at rest. I had been fighting and worrying for far too long. I made a promise to myself. 'From now on, I won't let what is in my mind destroy the best part of each moment. I vow to keep this promise today, tomorrow, and forever!'

The four of us were starting a brand-new chapter in our lives. I opened my heart to it all, letting it swing wide open and readying myself for the endless possibilities before me. I welcomed all of the potential surprises and unknown adventures that life might bring.

When the car turned to our cul-de-sac, I could see our beloved house where the three musketeers had lived happily together for the longest time. It felt different now, and my eyes once again fought back emotion.

'Oh, my baby, we are going to miss you a lot!'

♥ ♥ ♥ ♥

After getting into the house, I decided I needed a quick nap if I really wanted to make a beautiful mother of the bride. I laid down in my bed to rest. I felt an exquisite sense of comfort all over me. Harmony reverberated throughout my whole being.

When I woke up, I found Minh, beaming as he looked at me.

'Wow!' he said, 'You seem one-hundred times better now!'

'Don't flirt with me!' I teased. 'I know that you didn't like my monster face, but that was the true me!'

'You look beautiful with your natural face, Ha-Le.'

Minh's sweet words brought me back to the time when we were dating. I smiled with tears. That had been so long ago. Another lifetime ago.

My mother came into the room then, smoothing her hair, as she readied herself to leave for the reception.

'Where did you get that maroon dress Ha-Le?' she asked. 'It fits you perfectly!'

'Here in Australia, Ma!' I answered. 'It's crazy that I found a nice dress actually to fit my tiny body.'

I was pleased with everything, my make-up, my dress, and I could even feel my heart singing. I was ready to celebrate! Of course, we were celebrating my beloved daughter's wedding, but somehow, I also wanted to celebrate a new me as well!

I really was like a brand-new person. When we arrived at the reception, I waved and smiled, greeting all of the friends and family surrounding us. It was such a contrast from the flood of emotions that had run through me like a river that morning. It felt like I was completely cleansed of anything negative. I felt as light as air.

I looked around at the decorations and elegant setting, feeling truly happy. The restaurant looked wonderful. They had listened to and implemented all of our requests.

The candles that I'd bought for each table complimented a small vase of flowers, made the room warm and charming. There were also lanterns, Chinese firecrackers, and Asian pictures and artwork. These decorative elements blended so well with the Western chairs, tables and walls. It was a harmonious and gorgeous pairing of cultures. It was so perfectly symbolic of the wedding that had just taken place, only hours ago.

The music from the band made me happy. They played some Christian songs that I often sang at church. They reminded me of God's love and gave me comfort.

'The only thing left to do now is to be happy,' I told myself. 'My only job now is to enjoy the party to the fullest. No matter what happens!'

Tennille announced the bride and groom, and to my surprise, Hong-An arrived without wearing the dress that I'd bought for her in Vietnam. At first, I felt a bit hurt. But then I remembered my new resolve, and I realised that I was focusing on what I did not have instead of remembering the blessings that I did have. Once I revised my thinking, I was truly able to see how breath-taking my daughter was. She looked truly beautiful, in a gentle dress that she had chosen for herself.

'She did that without counting me in?' I thought to myself. 'You know what? That is just fine. She doesn't need to include me in every decision she makes. It's time for her to do whatever is right for herself.' I processed these thoughts with feelings of acceptance.

There was a collective 'wow' from the guests, as an entire line of waitresses brought out the meal.

Soon, it was time for the speeches.

Tom and Travis gave their speeches first. Tom gave such a long speech and sounded so passionate. He talked about how his ancestors had come from England to Australia. He described how they had managed to keep their traditional culture. He then went on to say they were now accepting a new culture into their family, as they warmly welcomed a Vietnamese daughter-in-law.

'We will live in harmony with each other, and I am so proud of Australia, where we embrace such a diversity of so many enriching cultures.'

Travis's speech was equally wonderful and heartfelt.

'We are all becoming a family, and we will enjoy the competition of yummy foods from chefs Tom and Ha-Le!'

There were whistles and cheers from the guests. They all smiled, happy to see the way love could bring together two very different cultures.

The Vietnamese side of the hall became very excited and noisy when Minh and I came to the stage. Minh spoke English, and I translated his words into Vietnamese.

'Today, we felt so moved to give away our beloved only daughter!' The room was quiet as Minh spoke with emotion. 'But in return, we gain a handsome, hot, and beautiful son-in-law!' He danced with his words, and you could see his happiness as he spoke.

As I translated what Minh was saying, my heart was also dancing with a happy tune, 'He will be our only son, and we love him so much!' I added.

I took my seat, with my heart glowing. I was filled with joy and anticipation. The slideshow that I had so lovingly created and paired with my heartfelt song that I'd written with care and sung with deep emotion was about to be presented. It was my gift to her, my way of showing her my heart, and all the love that I held inside of it, for her, my only child.

The first image came onto the screen. It was a picture of Travis and Hong-An. Hong-An was smiling as Travis kissed her hand, bowing slightly as if he were a chivalrous knight, and she the lady who had stolen his heart.

The music began to play, and more images came onto the screen. They were all of Hong-An and Travis as a happy, engaged couple. I felt a swell of pride as my voice was heard, singing in Vietnamese, with the English translation of the lyrics scrolling across the bottom of the screen, beneath the pictures.

"Today, my beloved daughter is getting married.

You have grown up and met the person whom you love with all your heart.

When Ba and Mẹ looked at you in the wedding gown, tears were welling up in our eyes.

Oh! Time has passed by so quickly with numerous sweet loving memories.

It was not long ago when I held you lovingly in my arms

It was not long ago with you still little and naive

and we cheerfully dancing and merrily singing

with every happy tune to our family life.'

Pictures of Hong-An as a small child came then. There was one of her at her first birthday party. Then another of her as a small child, standing back-to-back with me and looking at the camera with a playful attitude, arms crossed. Then there were pictures of Hong-An with both me and Minh. I heard many murmurs and sounds of 'wow!' and 'aww!'' through the crowd. I could see the eyes of the guests lighting up.

As I looked out into the audience, I could see so many of our Vietnamese relatives' eyes well up with emotion upon hearing Minh's words.

The final image came onto the screen; a beautiful selfie of the two of them, taken at their engagement party, with the Sydney Harbour Bridge in the background.

The room exploded in applause. Many people stood up to clap.

After this, it was time for Hong-An and Travis to deliver their speeches.

I watched my daughter deliver her speech. There was joy dancing in her eyes. In a way, I was saying goodbye to my daughter. She would not need me so much anymore. She would be independent and able to make her own choices. I probably would not see her as often. But I felt ready, finally, to embrace this chance.

'Goodbye, my Hong-An,' I whispered. 'Mẹ loves you so much!'

CHAPTER FIFTY-FOUR

ONE LAST PUSH

I was beautifully happy.

I was as happy as I'd ever been. There had been so many changes in my life, in the months and years after the wedding, it wasn't all good news. That is life. Life is never all good or all bad. It is always a mixture of both. As my relationship with Hong-An and Travis was gradually repaired and strengthened, I also began to face many personal struggles. Even as I found myself growing and thriving in ways I'd never before imagined, I unfortunately still struggled. I was finally moving to a place of acceptance and true peace. I did my best to move forward one small step at a time and to try to understand Hong-An and Travis a bit more. It wasn't easy to get back to a place of normalcy after all of the turbulence our family had suffered, but little by little, we began to make it happen. I remained patient and started to see positive changes begin to materialise. My heart became still and welcoming. After the emotional epiphanies that had occurred for me at Hong-An's wedding, I now realised that the best was still yet to come.

But I was also faced with a new challenge, lumps started to form on my face and groin, and very quickly, they increased in size combined with a terrible cough. It was nerve-wracking. I had already been through two cancers, and so any time my body was doing anything out of the ordinary, I became very concerned.

I went to see my doctor and the news I received confirmed my worst fears.

My GP, Wendy, looked at me with very serious eyes.

'These are abnormal tumour growths,' she said. 'To be on the safe side, we need to book you a biopsy. I'll schedule you an appointment at Westmead Hospital.'

Oh, another biopsy! I hated it. It was a painful and terrible procedure.

When my blood test results came back, I was referred for an MRI, and then a second appointment was made.

'Perhaps you should bring your husband in for this appointment,' Wendy said when I spoke to her on the phone. 'Or someone else in your family.'

Minh would be working, and I decided not to bother Hong-An. I went in alone, with my heart racing. Wendy asked me to sit down.

'Ha-Le, I can see in your file that you've had cancer twice. We've cross-checked the results of all your tests, and unfortunately, I have to inform you that you have Non-Hodgkin Lymphoma.'

'Not again! Not again!' I was so shocked by the news of another deadly disease. My soul left my body. It was exactly like the moment when I'd found out I was pregnant with Hong-An.

'Why me again?!'

Tears came flooding down my cheeks.

Wendy started talking about chemotherapy.

'We'll schedule an appointment with the oncologist so that you can start to talk about your treatment plan,' Wendy paused, looking at me with very sad eyes. 'I'm so sorry to see you like this, Ha-Le,' she said softly.

I nodded without saying anything. I felt numb. I didn't know what to say or do.

'I'll give you a consent form so that I can book you to see the specialist and start chemotherapy soon,' Wendy continued.

She concluded our meeting by handing me a pile of documents and pamphlets full of advice on caring for oneself during cancer treatment.

My head buzzed with the events of the past hour as I walked, slowly and sadly, out of the doctor's office, and down to where I'd parked my car. The drive home was only five minutes, but it felt like ages. All of my emotions tumbled together, but still, I felt surprisingly clear-headed.

When I arrived home, I went straight up to my bedroom and threw open the bedroom window. I let the cool air sweep through my hair. I felt the chill flush my cheeks.

Our bodies are made mostly of water. We have oceans inside us. I closed my eyes and listened to the wind. My cancerous cells were at work inside me, attacking like warring fleets on the sea. I knew what to do. This time, I would not accept chemotherapy. To truly heal my cancer, I had to heal the root cause of my sickness. There must be something inside my body as a sign of another cancer. I needed to do something for it to rescues myself.

'What are you going to do, Ha-Le?' Travis asked when he and Hong-An came to visit that night.

'I will heal myself,' I said. 'I will use my knowledge to heal myself.'

'Please don't put yourself at risk, Mẹ,' Hong-An said.

'All the specialists will do is put me down for chemotherapy,' I argued back to Hong-An. 'That's all that they can do for cancer patients. It's the only option they have. I have to find another way. I know what is wrong with me, and I will fix it! Knowledge will replace my fear!'

The irony was not lost on me that now it was my daughter that disapproved of my choices. It was like the tables had turned, and now our roles had been reversed.

Hong-An's wedding really had proven to be a huge turning point in my life. All of the pain and hopelessness in my heart had pushed me to find a way out.

Right after Hong-An's wedding, I became dead set on changing my inner world's landscape. I wanted to find more moments of happiness in each day. Like searching for seashells on a beach full of sand, I found that the more I hunted the more beauty I discovered. I wanted to take away all the fixations I'd had before. I tried to free my own mind. I knew I needed more resources, but I couldn't have told you at the time what they were. But, little by little, I started to dig, hunting for clues along the way.

In the beginning, I did what most people do. I turned to Google in pursuit of answers. Of course, what I found was merely an endless sea of words in front of me. But like most things in life, serendipity took hold and just by chance, I picked up the first clue of many along my path. It was nothing grand. I selected an eBook, '101 things successful people do differently.' I was about to discard it unceremoniously as it appeared to have little to offer in the way of wisdom, but then a name stuck out at me.

Brian Tracey. I visited his website and right away bought his course 'Success Made Simple.'

When you look back at all the dots of your life connected in reverse, its easy to see how they make sense. The resources I sought out to help and inspire me were all just small steps along a bigger journey, but I couldn't see it at the time. I could only inch forward like a slow caterpillar in hopes of finding the right branch on which to blossom into a butterfly. These were the first small, simple steps that I needed to loosen the hard surface I had built up over a lifetime. It was just the right little push to crack me open and peel back the layers of myself. This was where my inner journey began.

But just like a rock picking up speed as it is pushed down a hill, I could feel myself changing faster and faster as I learned more and more. I found myself having so many 'aha' moments I could no longer count them.

Brian led me to a deep understanding of the power of the subconscious mind. I started exploring my emotions in greater detail. These were already things I had begun on my own before even picking up a book. During my breakthrough at Hong-An's wedding I was already beginning to be more conscious of my inner world and the great power I had over it if only I tried. Now I was examining more deeply how my life view impacted my behaviour. I was still trying desperately to escape being trapped in a cycle of pain and problems.

And then, one day, I had a breakthrough. I began to find more and more well-known doctors, masters and healers and resources that supported me to reach a greater level of understanding. Layer by layer, my barriers began to fall away, and my mind began to open up. I started to understand myself on different levels than I had ever before.

My body came alive with electricity as I began to slowly release so much that I had held on to. I explored all the trapped emotions that had kept hidden inside me for a lifetime. The more I explored, the more I came to understand that I was not just a human of flesh and bone, but in fact a product of every moment of my entire life. Every single event I had endured over the years had shaped me. Every experience had become a part of me.

As I considered this thought, hundreds of moments that made up my life flashed before me like a movie theatre without popcorn. The American planes, little me being held over the well, the times I disappointed by my father, or was upset with my mother. I could clearly see all the violence I had witnessed between my parents. I could see the places of trauma that were still embedded deep in my bones. The Death House, the tunnels, running from the Viet Cong, escaping on the ship, dead bodies on the side of the road. I could even feel Chi Thoi's curse as if it was still in me ... My life seemed overpopulated with traumatic emotionally charged events. But these events were mine, they were what built me, and they were resting just under my skin. Moments that were now embedded forever in my cells. I could not remember a time in my life when I was not led forward by the blind emotion of the past. These feelings were always there.

'Bye Travis, bye Hong-An,' I gave them each a goodbye hug and kiss with sadness in me. I just wished they could stay a bit longer and asked me how I felt inside my heart with the news of having a Non-Hodgkin Lymphoma. They did not know how much I needed them to support me to go through the new challenges!

I walked to the backyard and sat under the verandah looking at the wind blow through the gumtrees and the clouds began to form above in the sky. It was 8 pm, but the daylight was still there as it was summer.

'How could these things not have shaped you Ha-Le?' I said out loud to no one in particular. I started to understand so clearly how these experiences impacted me now. The past was still alive and present in me every day. I came to understand that we could not run away from the past but we need to make peace with it at present.

I looked down at my feet, I touched my legs and examined my hands a bit closer, feeling each wrinkle on every finger. I started to imagine all the tiny cells inside. Millions of tiny cells were each nothing by themselves, but together they make up all of me. No wonder I had gotten cancer twice. If all these negative emotions I had experienced were simply trapped, there must be a raging war going on inside of my body.

My first cancer was thyroid. By the time the doctor had diagnosed it, it had spread throughout my neck and was very serious. Hong-An had started her second year of high school at Meriden at the time, and my main thought was for her well-being. What if I died? She did not have a big family to look out for her. It would be just her and Minh. I would not get to see her grow up, finish year twelve, graduate from university, or get married. I would not see my beloved daughter in a beautiful wedding gown.

I received five horrible radiotherapy treatments in ten years. I will never forget the lonely times in the hospital, with no one around for days, because of the radiation leaking from my body.

Thinking back on this, I was angry at myself for agreeing to this treatment. 'I was so stupid to add more toxins and destruction to my body!' I cried out with regret.

Ovarian cancer was next, leading to a full hysterectomy. I begged everyone to leave me alone. I needed to focus on my own self-healing. My gut told me that was what I needed most. If I'd had good knowledge of self-healing, as I do now, I would never have let anyone rough up my body with their sharp knives from the start.

I looked again at my hands. I watched the blood pumping through the veins on my wrist. My body still looked young on the outside, but on the inside, it must be a wasteland after the amount of toxic chemicals that had entered my body to treat both cancers. But even the poisonous chemicals had not killed the negative emotions trapped inside my cells.

I now found renewed hope and vigour inside of myself. I was learning so much and gaining so many new tools. I spent all of my energy learning about self-healing.

I signed up for a pivotal course with the renowned Dr. Bradly Nelson, and without realising it, began the next incredible phase of my journey. It was like I was following breadcrumbs; I didn't know exactly where this was leading to, but I could feel it when I found something good. I could use a tool to more deeply understand myself and slowly release all the pain hiding deep in my cells. I knew that I was the only one that had the power to do this. Finding the right teachers was just what I needed to uncover this power.

I learned that I was not only a victim; I was a victim of victims. I was a victim of my parents, Chi Thoi, and the Vietnam War. And of course, they were all victims too, which is why this cycle of abuse had continued. I started to understand that I was trapped in a bubble of problems. It was like I was bouncing around without gravity at the whim of my own weightlessness. I was stuck airborne inside this bubble, a mere victim of the experiences that floated by. It was, in fact, these little micro experiences, these tiny moments, like a slap of Chi Thoi's hand that had left an imprint on me. These imprints had created a map of emotions inside me. I had used this map as a guide in my life, without ever even being aware of it. I had lived in this world for such a long time, feeling as though there was really no way out. I'd thought that my life was the way that it had to be. I didn't believe I had any power in its creation. I'd thought that I needed to accept my fate as it was laid out before me.

Now, I recognised this negativity, as one tiny moment was only a small part of me. There were all the other moments, too—the sweet breath of my baby on my cheek. The crisp smell of the ocean breeze as it hit my skin. My husband's kind gaze from across the room. These were there too. The negative ones were only a fraction of who I was, and there were so many good parts of me too. I only had to let them out, to let them shine. I started to immerse myself in all the joys of my life, in all the joys of being me, and I took it all in with open arms, ready to accept the abundance the universe offered me.

I can't say I could have done this alone. I needed these teachers and these guides to find this new lens to see myself from the inside out. There were so many exciting teachers to choose from once I began to discover this path. I was like a kid in a candy store. I started to explore so many topics, like the study of Psychosomatics with Herman Muller. I found out more about the profound inner strength of a human being and the connection of mind and the body through his teachings.

But despite these teachers, the true knowledge and wisdom came from within me. It was resting quietly there all along and only needed to be uncovered, like lifting a mossy stone in the forest. I could find it when I tapped into my true self.

It was through this process of discovery that I also began to love myself. This may sound both overly simple and a bit cliché, but it is in fact, the truth. All my life, I had been waiting for others to give me what I could best give myself. That little child waiting for her mother so far across the river to only love her. I now knew I could give that love to myself. And with this love came greater objectivity.

My perspective slowly widened. I started to understand why other people treated me the way that they did. I knew that I had to forgive them all. I had to forgive each and every person in my past, and even more importantly, I had to forgive myself.

Even though I began to live with this new perspective daily, it was not enough to clean away the past from every cell in my body. Don't mistake me for saying that personal growth is either easy or quick. There were still more layers that needed to be shed off. I was like a moulting reptile; every time I grew just a bit, I could shed one more layer of skin.

Now, faced with a third bout of cancer, my newfound understanding guided me forward. I knew that there must be something hidden inside of me. I had to figure out the root cause of the problem.

I was on a mission, a mission to be the best possible Ha-Le! The more that I learned, the more my resolve strengthened. I knew more and more clearly than ever that I would not have chemotherapy. It was hard to be a lonesome warrior when people around me were against my choice. It was hard to take such a scary risk when everyone kept trying to convince me that it was a bad idea. I knew that others said this only because they cared about me and wanted me to get better, but I truly felt in my heart that the path I'd chosen was the right one. I could heal myself with wisdom and strength.

I needed to fight my cancer by looking deep into my own heart and purging all of the shadows from within it. I promised myself that I would fight with all my strength for my survival, and I made this vow with tears glistening in my eyes.

I had a growing thirst for knowledge, and I yearned to know more about how I could heal myself. I set my course, preparing to fight an enemy that I could not see, but I trusted in my path so far. The universe delivered support that I hadn't been expecting. I found a mentor.

I wandered through the Mind and Body Festival at Home Bush when a voice hit my ears.

'Do you want to sign up for an NLP Breakthrough?'

I turned in the direction of the voice, finding a smiling man as its source. I had never heard this word before, but he had a warm face and an inviting smile, so I felt drawn to know more.

'Hi!' he said, with a friendly wave. 'I'm Arthur, and I'm from Mind and Body College.'

'What is NLP?' I asked.

'NLP stands for Neuro-Linguistic Programming. It is a powerful way of improving our health, relationship and business and so on.' Arthur answered enthusiastically. He seemed to read what I needed.

I spoke with him for a few minutes, feeling hypnotised by his words. I found myself signing up for three trainings with him.

My hard exterior, built up through so many years of hardship and pain, cracked just a bit more with each step forward. I knew I couldn't walk this path alone and began to understand that so many before me had already taken this journey, and I was simply building on their knowledge and making it my own.

I trained in various practices of the mind and body. Therapies that guided me to release the past from my cells. Like popping little infected pimples and releasing what was inside so they could heal, with each new training, I gained something new. The name of these disciplines was not initially familiar to me, but like any good education, they became part of the vocabulary of my healing. I learned the value of NLP, Timeline Therapy, Hypnosis, EFT, and Positive Psychology, and studied to a master level in many disciplines. I felt even more at home in my own skin with each new revelation. I was rebuilding myself, and I needed the knowledge and tools to do it right.

The more of my true self was uncovered the more negativity and false beliefs could be shed. I could let it slip away like dead leaves blowing in the wind from a healthy tree.

It was not an easy process; every cell of my body was tired, each part of my body ached, and my mind didn't have any more room for stretching, but I kept going. I put my head down, studying day and night, fighting urgently to rescue myself from more chemotherapy. And I did.

My parents, my country, my marriage, my daughter, my life experiences, all of these had built layer upon layer of hard scabs that buried my true beauty. They also buried my true authentic self. I was finally about to claim what I deserved as my birthright.

'Ha-Le,' I whispered to that little girl on the river's edge. 'Don't wait there any longer; go run and play.'

I knew that playful little girl who had been so eager to know more about the world was still buried deep inside of me just waiting to be uncovered. I would be with her on my new journey, and we would dance and sing together.

I studied hard and worked through so many layers of myself as I did. Sure, I received Diplomas from a well-known NLP and Hypnosis school, Tad James, and accolades for my effort, but it was not what I sought. In these moments of hard work and perseverance, I found true wisdom. Truth revealed itself to me. I clearly understood that I needed to accept my life circumstances as they were.

Whatever was happening to me at any given moment, I needed to face it with full acceptance. By living a life without acceptance, I'd learned to be negative, and the negativity of my experiences had built up in my body. All of my life experiences were stored up in my body's cells. My own trauma, alongside the trauma of my parents and grandparents, had all settled deep inside me. Hurt and pain snowballed through the ages, building upon itself, one layer after another. Generations of pain were hidden within the cells of my body. These memories would decide my fate. The only way to survive was to fight to rid myself of this pain. I had to fight to regain my true self! This was the only way to keep myself alive.

I knew now that a person's internal self-talk has a very real effect on the outside world. Our perspective shapes our reality.

I had changed my heart. I had changed my mind. I'd dared to look at the hardships of my life. Sharpening my eyes had given me greater clarity. I was now able to see all of the details that I'd never noticed before. My struggles had all served a purpose. They have helped me to become more attune to life both outside and inside of me. I watched my internal world and my external world begin to weave more closely together. They had always been intertwined, but I'd never been able to see it somehow.

So much had changed since the tearful day of Hong-An's wedding, the day when I'd had the first glimmer of my 'aha!' moment, a moment that had since fully actualised. I was better now, and my relationships were better now too. Now, I understood why I'd caused so much trouble for Hong-An, why I'd been so resistant to her marrying Travis, and why I'd been so afraid of Travis's well-being. I was finally ready to take responsibility for my actions and admit that many of the problems in my life had been the result of my own doing. I made peace with myself, and I made peace with all of the people in my life that I'd harboured negativity towards for far too long.

♥ ♥ ♥ ♥

I sat quietly at my favourite spot in the house, a long, soft green sofa. My thoughts mingled with the giant gumtrees I could see in the backyard through the big wooden framed window. I had spent a lot of contemplative moments here, rearranging things in my mind. Today was different; today, things started to fall into place in a way they hadn't before.

I came to understand that over the years, I'd pointed the finger of blame at everyone around me, my parents, Minh, Travis, and Hong-An. I had blamed the Vietnam War. I had blamed Chi Thoi. I had blamed everyone and everything else. I had told myself that they were the problem and that I was only a helpless victim. But that just wasn't true. I knew now that I was not a victim. Far from it, I had great strength and fortitude in me. It was only now, with this new set of skills, that I was equipped with a true lens to see the world, and the world started to present itself to me as it really was. At that moment, looking out at the gum trees bending ever so gently with the wind, it all came into focus, like a camera lens that was suddenly turned to just the right spot. I realised that I could not change the past, but I could change the way I viewed it. I could change the way that I continued to allow it to hold power over my life. I didn't need to give it power anymore, and enough was enough.

Feeling enlightened, I closed my eyes and began the healing journey of making peace with my loved ones. Making peace with the past and making peace with my choices.

I started to slowly forgive myself and those around me, to let it all go. I could hear Minh in the other room reading and gently turning the pages. His presence suddenly filled me.

At that moment, I chose to forgive myself for the unfair feelings I had suffered towards Minh. I had chosen him to be my husband. I had chosen him, and it wasn't fair of me to expect him to be someone that he wasn't, when I had chosen him knowing who he was. I needed to take responsibility for this choice. I had to be fair to Minh. I also had to be fair to myself. It was unfair to both of us that I relied on him for my happiness. But now I understood that I could only rely on myself for happiness.

Minh had been my partner through the darkest and most terrifying moments in my life. We disagreed and clashed, but he had tried his best to be a good husband and father, just as I'd tried my best to be a good wife and mother. Any mistakes he had made were forgiven, just as I wanted my own mistakes to be forgiven.

I remembered that Minh told me why he did not attend my 21st birthday. He confessed that he didn't dare to face the reality that I would not choose him out of all the other men who wanted me. It touched my heart to hear him speak of this vulnerability and fear of rejection.

I am so thankful for Minh now, despite all the struggles we had together. Everything we'd been through had brought me to where I am today. Minh had been an important element in my personal growth. He had helped to make me into the woman that I am now.

Minh cared so deeply for me. 'I love you so much Ha-Le' he would say to me almost every day. This thought filled my eyes with tears even as I sat there alone on the sofa, I could feel his love for me.

'Sorry for being nasty with you sometimes, Minh!' I whispered sincerely from my heart. I had not been the only one to sometimes suffer in our marriage. He had also suffered. I could not deny this. It was time for him to choose the best path for his life, with his true ability as a man.

I came up to my husband sitting on a chair in the other room. I buried my face in Minh's chest and said, 'I love you for who you are Minh and want to grow old with you!' Minh wiped his tears as he replied.

'I always want you in my heart. God has joined us together in this world. He has given me no other greater blessings than you in this life.'

Forgiveness, I breathed it in and let go.

♥ ♥ ♥ ♥

I felt so moved by what had shifted in me.

I placed my two hands above my chest to feel my heart beating. I hugged myself tightly and took a moment to bless my body for all it has given me. I began to look at my past as a gift, and suddenly it transformed from treachery into my pearls of wisdom. I honoured all the hardships and sorrows in my life as steps on the path to greatness. I began to understand there were deep meanings behind all the experiences that I went through. I gave thanks to my soul for having woken me from my slumber on life's journey.

I also needed to forgive myself for the mistakes that I made when Hong-An decided to take Travis as her husband; these mistakes were due, in large part, to the pain and negativity I carried with me in my subconscious.

I lay back down on the sofa and took a deep breath gripping hard to the pillow next to me as I did. I knew I needed to let go of this pain once and for all. I knew that forgiveness was the only way forward. I forgave myself, knowing that I'd done my best at the time with what I had. The past had been deeply rooted in me, I was only trying my best to protect her, I just didn't know that what I was doing was wrong.

I forgave myself for being so foolish. I'd been foolish to forget that Hong-An had naturally gained a lot of wisdom and survival skills from her parents. Now the relationship between Hong-An and I was being mended, slowly but surely. Forgiving myself was all that was left to keep us moving forward. I considered my actions and realised so much of what went wrong was only the result of me holding on to the past—clinging onto it like a life vest out at sea, trying to stay afloat.

My thoughts moved to an earlier time, a time when Hong-An had been small and dependent, back when she had been my entire world, and I had been hers.

'We will be together, as the smallest tribe,' I remembered whispering to an infant Hong-An. I wanted us to stick together, giving one another a safe refuge from all the bitterness and sorrow of the world. The thing I did not consider at that moment is that Hong-An would grow up as she now has. I sensed it was again this clinging to the past that was impacting my behaviour in the present.

I now took out this new lens I was using to see my world and focused it in a new way. I wasn't losing a daughter; I would always be a mother. I had raised an amazing daughter, and now I could watch the beauty I had created walking free in the world from a distance.

Again, I understood it was Hong-An who had been a gift for me. She had given me a reason to keep living when times were hard. She had given me the opportunity to be her mother and had always made me feel like the very best mother in the world. I now understood that I had projected many of the problems from my own childhood onto Hong-An. What I lacked as a little girl, as a daughter, I wanted to make up for in my relationship with Hong-An. But that was an unfair burden on her, and in doing this, I had hurt our relationship.

I walked over to our memory cabinet, where we kept some mementos and photographs of the main events of the adventures of the Three Musketeers. I glanced down at a picture of a one-month-old Hong-An, and my vision blurred with tears. This time they were happy tears. This picture had been taken at Hei Ling Chau Camp. That had been such a challenging time.

I thought back to all of the pain that I'd lived through during our twenty-five-day trip on the big vast sea, with my daughter still inside of my belly. I recalled the loneliness of my days in Victoria Prison and then San Yuk Hospital. I recalled being slapped by the Indian officer. I recalled my terror and homesickness. All of this came back to me in full force, careening about like a cyclone in my mind.

I lifted the picture frame and lovingly rubbed the image of Hong-An's young face. She laid on a blue mat that I'd sewn for her. She looked strong, like a baby warrior. We had all fought like warriors, and we had won. Our prize had been our new lives in Australia, and since moving here, we had won many more battles, side by side, as a family. I let myself drift back into the past, riding on the soft waves of memories. The pain had left my heart, leaving room for it to fill with joy.

I realised that there was now a new chapter. We were no longer the Three Musketeers, but we could become the Fantastic Four. My gaze turned to newer pictures. My walls were now covered with images of us all together. I smiled happily, looking at a picture of me, Minh, Hong-An, and Travis. As always, Travis was smiling at Hong-An, looking at her like she was the most precious gift he could ever receive. He really loved her, and I knew that he had grown to love Minh and me as well.

I placed my fingertip on a picture of the four of us, hung close to the dining room table.

'Aww, Travis!' I murmured. 'Mẹ loves you, my son.' Travis never calls me 'Mẹ' as I wished, but I could apply it by myself. I felt grateful to have Travis in my life. He has a beautiful and honest soul. He played a big part in my journey of finding myself. I believed that we had come into each other's lives for a purpose. The universe had a sense of order to it. There was a divine plan, and each one of us living creatures was only a small piece of the cosmic puzzle.

It has been five years since I gave my daughter away; time had passed so easily despite a lot that had shifted inside of me.

'What time do you want to go to the restaurant, Travis?' Minh asked over the phone. It was Travis's 29th birthday, and we had made plans to celebrate together.

I had written a poem for the occasion, pouring out all of my feelings onto paper.

Dear Travis,
You have been a blessing from the beginning.
I love you, my son-in-law, with all my heart.
I adore your humour.
I appreciate your hugs.
I admire your heart,
and most of all,
I thank God for having brought you to me
as a beautiful and precious present.
Love you always,
Ha-Le

'Wow!' Travis had exclaimed when I gave him the poem that I had nicely framed.

'It's beautiful!' he said as he smiled and happily kissed my face.

I smiled back and thrilled that I'd been able to write a poem that properly expressed all of my love for my son-in-law.

'I love you so much, Travis,' I told him.

I could not count the number of times that I'd said this to him. I'd started out feeling sceptical of him, not believing that he would make a positive addition to our family, but I had been so very wrong about that. I was grateful to have Travis in my life now. Travis had a beautiful and honest soul.

I recalled how upset I had been by the cost of the engagement ring he'd given to Hong-An. I could see now how silly I'd been to care about the price of the ring. It didn't matter if the ring was two dollars or twenty-thousand dollars. Either way, he was a remarkable and caring husband for my Hong-An. That was all that mattered. Hong-An's words had been true. The ring was only a symbol. It was a symbol of their love, and the love between them was solid and pure.

Travis had strengthened and enhanced my daughter's life. As a mother, there was nothing more that I could ask for in a son-in-law. I'd gotten so caught up worrying about Travis's mental health problems. I'd blinded myself to everything wonderful that he added to Hong-An's life, and eventually once I'd let my guard down, to my life too.

In the midst of our worst moments of fighting, Hong-An had said something to me.

'You want Travis to be the perfect man for me,' she'd said. 'But what if in two or three years, he got cancer or some other serious illness? Would you accept him then?'

Hong-An's words had stayed with me, and I knew now that it was because her words echoed with the truth. Travis's mental illness was not the end of the world, and once I'd realised this, my family had been able to come together once more through love and understanding. Travis was a blessing to Hong-An's life. My past had created many fears in me and robbed me of my confidence in Hong-An's abilities to live a good life with Travis.

'Please forgive me!' I whispered. 'Forgive me for once making your heart hurt! Please forgive me for all of the fears that I had inside of me! I was blinded. I couldn't see how beautiful and pure you were! Thank you for being a good husband to my daughter. You are more than I ever could have hoped for, as my daughter's husband. You are a blessing to her and me!'

I sent my message and prayers to God and hoped that Travis would somehow connect to the good energy I'd sent his way.

♥ ♥ ♥ ♥

'Ah, my dear daughter, Ha-Le,' my mother would cry out in excitement whenever she saw my face through our video call.

How are you today, Ma?' I asked her, and tears welling up in the corner of my eyes as I had to admit that I too was so happy to see her face after my breakthrough.

'I am good, and why are you crying, darling?' my mother asked, looking worried.

'No reason, don't worry Ma! I just feel so blessed that I still have you in my life. I love you so much, Ma' I said, but my words got choked up once again with tears.

'I understand; I feel blessed as well and love you a lot too!' my mother looked a bit emotional with her words as she spoke.

'I love your top, Ma; it looks so beautiful on you!' I said as I tried to shift the energy to stop Ma from getting overly emotional.

Before I said goodbye to my mother over the phone, she and I talked a lot about my father. We spoke of him as if he was still alive.

'He loved you so much, Ha-Le!' my mother kept repeating over and over again, as if the more she said it, the more it would ring true.

I just wanted to imagine that both of them were in front of me. I wanted to be able to hug them and bury my face between them just as I would have as a little girl.

I retrieved an old photograph of the two of them. It was one of my favourites, taken the very first time that I went back to Vietnam to visit, in 1992. I held the picture in my hands. My parents both looked so beautiful and happy. I knew that their smiles covered years of pain and heartbreak. Both of my parents had their own scars, hates, vulnerabilities, and fears. And still, they had enriched my life. They had let me be who I was. They had protected me and taught me.

I could see now that all of the pain with my daughter had started with the relationship I had with my own parents. Growing up was confusing for me. I wanted to stay a little girl for longer so that I could get more of the happiness I deserved. I didn't know how to be a grown-up, even as the people around me said that I was a very mature and smart girl. I wore a mask that fit other people's thinking in my life and covered my true self. I knew how to appear just as they thought I should be. But inside my heart, I struggled to stand on my own two feet. It was because I'd always felt distant from my parents. I was always reaching out for their love, grasping at fragments. Their love was a phantom, always just out of reach of my stretching fingertips. At least, that was how it felt to young Ha-Le.

I could see now that I had been too stuck in my own perspective, never considering that my parents were living their own life experiences, and trying their best through their own challenges and hurt. My parents had never meant for me to feel distant from them. They never meant to do that to me. They just weren't properly equipped for parenthood, and they were trying to raise children during one of the most tumultuous times in Vietnam's modern history. They raised kids through the Vietnam War and the rise of communism. This was no easy feat. I could see now that I should applaud them for all of their efforts.

'Ma and Ba, I love you both very much!' I whispered, with tears in my eyes. 'Thank you for bringing me into this world, even with your broken souls and broken relationships! Thank you! Thank you!'

Indeed, I could never thank them enough for being their daughter. They'd always tried to give me everything. But most of all, they allowed me to have the freedom to explore the world to its fullest. Not many parents could do that for their children.

It was easier to forgive my parents with this broad perspective. But as I thought of them, Chi Thoi's face suddenly appeared in my mind. It was much harder to forgive her, but I did. I took a deep breath, and I let go. I allowed myself to forgive the person who had infected some of the deepest of my wounds. She had been the worst antagonist of my childhood, but I knew now that she also carried the worst pain in her own heart. I had to forgive her if I was really going to release myself from the pain of the past. I had to unshackle myself from the resentment and anger that held me back. The image of Chi Thoi appeared in my mind. I could see her pretty face, fair skin, and dry red hair so close to me.

'I forgive you, Chi Thoi,' I said. 'You beat me and verbally abused me. All of that pain has followed me into the present. But now, I set myself free from all of it. I forgive you for all that you did to me.'

I sent this message out to the wind, with tears drying on my cheeks. My heart swelled with love and understanding for the teenage girl who had hurt me. I felt sorry for that teenager now. Her life was full of distortions and misfortune. She hadn't known what to do with her pain and hurt, so she had hurt me. It wasn't her fault. I stood there in my mind on the river banks which had now become such a symbol in my life. I imagined her standing in front of me there with the wind blowing away our collective grief. I gave Chi Thoi a hug, wrapping my arms firmly around her and truly loving her with everything I had. I kissed and blessed her and then released her pain and mine together to the wind.

♥ ♥ ♥ ♥

In March of 2018, I was given the great news that my Lymphoma was in remission. I cried with joy as I left the cancer centre in Bankstown Hospital. I knew that I'd made the right choice in going without chemotherapy. All I needed was to uncover the abundant strength and power already inside of me. Everything I needed was there all along.

The Lymphoma had been the very last push that I needed. It made me fight twice as hard to release all of the darkness in my heart. The pain that had been fermenting in my soul was gone now. I felt like a butterfly who had just popped out of a cocoon and was now unfolding my wings. The door had been opened, and now an endless world of possibilities was in front of me. A bright future was on the horizon. Now, I understood that change mind would lead to a change of life. Then I turned to embrace and focus on my future instead of my past.

Silent tears ran down my face as I drew the final pieces of the puzzle together. It was time to lift the curse. I had let go and forgiven those around me. But now, it was time to set us all free. The breeze sighed softly in answer. It was time.

CHAPTER FIFTY-FIVE

~

OH, DAUGHTER

I looked out across Bach Dang River. On the other side, I thought I could just make out the form of Hong-An. I waved to her and called her name, but the river was too wide. I looked for the bridges, but there were none. Next to the water was a small fishing boat. A man was nervously trying to start the motor. I could only see his back. When I got closer, I asked him if he could take me across.

'My daughter is there. I think she needs me.' When he turned around, it was my father, as a young man.

'I can't start the motor, princess. You can go, but you have to row yourself,' he gave me the oars.

'Come with me, Ba, I want you to meet Hong-An.'

He wiped his hands on his pants, full of oil and sweat. 'No, Ha-Le. I can't. This is my home, I'm happy here.'

The river seemed wider than before, but my body swelled with courage. My daughter needed me.

I rowed with a strength that I did not know I had. I thought I saw, once, a face in the water, swollen and decaying. But maybe it was just a fish, or a plastic bag. I dared not look at it.

When I got closer to the shore, my daughter stood up. From a distance, I could now see she was only a toddler. Only about three or four and all alone.

'I'm coming, my darling,' I called. She came down to the water's edge and dipped her feet in. I could see something, red and shimmering in her hand as she slowly, carefully, came towards me.

'Stay back,' I shouted. But the wind was blowing, and she could not hear me.

'Mẹ?' she called.

'Yes, darling, wait, I'm nearly there.'

'Me, is that you?' she asked, not hearing me.

I reached her just as her head dipped below the water. I jumped out of the boat and whisked her to safety. 'It's ok, sweetheart. I'm here now.' I placed her gently down on the bank, and she hugged her knees, her wet hair covering her face. I bent down to meet her gaze as I would with any child under my care.

It was only then that I could see what she held in her hand. A flower, cup-shaped, bright red, and startling in its intensity. I knew it immediately.

The wind that had whipped up seemed to be the start of a storm, and I took off my scarf and wrapped it around her shoulders. She was shivering. 'I just want my mother,' she cried.

I patted her head soothingly. 'Shhh. I'm here. I'll always be here for you, Hong-An.'

The little girl stopped shivering abruptly and looked up. Through strands of wet hair, her eyes shone with bright electricity that leapt into my body. 'I'm not Hong-An,' she said. It was the voice of a child but had the gravity of many generations of wisdom. With a shock, I recognised her face. Inside me, every cell danced.

It was me.

'I'm not your daughter,' she repeated.

'But Hong-An needs me,' I said, but it felt like a script as if I was reading someone else's lines.

'Hong-An is over there,' she said, pointing back across the river to where I came from. The shoreline had completely changed. It was now crammed with tall buildings, a bridge and a big beautiful blue sky arching high above. It looked exactly like Sydney Harbour. She was right. My daughter was over there, but it was impossible to see her amongst the crowds of tourists, cars, and chaos of the city.

When I turned back to the little girl, she was shivering again, and I hugged her. Her little arms wrapped around my waist, and for a moment, we felt like the same person. I carried her up and over the grass, across the dirt road and towards my old house.

As we walked through the streets of my childhood, the little girl lost all the intensity I had felt by the water. She was just like any other three-year-old but especially vulnerable, a little open heart, so exposed and so pure. I thought of all of the little children who had been in my life. A thousand precious souls, all were needing love and attention—all vulnerable. Hong-An was one of them, but she was no longer a little girl, and neither was I. I had given birth to her, but she was not mine to keep.

The girl in my arms, sensing my attention wandering, snuggled closer. She was dirty and worn, and even at her young age, I could tell she was feeling rejected and afraid. I knew exactly what she needed. She needed the comfort only I could give.

'It is not your fault when your baby brother goes hungry and thirsty, little one,' I told her, stroking her hair and loving her the way she longed to be loved. She leaned her head on my shoulder. I wasn't sure if she understood my words, but I hoped that she would remember this moment one day and that it would give her the courage to keep going.

'You have always tried your best,' I encouraged her as I would any child. 'It's not your fault your parents fight; they fight because of their own problems. It's not because of you,' I kept speaking now as I could see my words were clearly soothing her like salve on an open wound. As I spoke, I could see her relaxing deeper into my arms. She looked at me with her sweet black eyes. 'It's not your fault that your father hit your pregnant mother with the broom,' I continued.

As I spoke, I took my hands and stroked her as if I was soothing every cell in her body. In my mind's eye as we walked back by the lake, I took all of her sadness and guilt and wiped it away with my hands, releasing the pain to blow freely across the water. She would carry it no longer.

I no longer had to worry about this small, vulnerable child, for I now knew that she had a constant companion, even in the darkest moments. She had a warrior within; her pain was no longer her friend.

EPILOGUE

'O h! Yummy! BBQ pork belly and rice noodle!' Hong-An cried out with delight. I could see my baby, forever as she always was, when I cooked for her.

'We are spoiled again, Ha-Le,' Travis said as he hugged me sweetly, with a wide, beautiful smile. 'We just finished all the yummy food you packed for us last time,' he added.

I loved them both so much, and I have had so many beautiful moments, just like this one, in the last two years. My heart danced with gratitude for what I had. I finally felt I was enough. I felt complete. The sensational feeling of joy for being a mother rushed from my toes to my head, even though we still had not had the chance to sit alone together or to even share the coffee I had longed for. But I was happy to see her even just once a week and have a meal with her and Travis.

'We may put the house up for rent and move to Maroubra,' Travis suddenly announced.

Hong-An looked a bit nervous and didn't look at us.

'Just thinking about it, we haven't made the decision yet,' Hong-An responded when she saw the worried look on her father's face.

'Do whatever you both feel is right, dear. If the change helps Travis with his well-being, and it is good for your work, go for it. Your father and I support you both. Don't we, Minh?'

'We love the comfortable house you built for us and all you have done to support us,' Travis started, trying to comfort us. 'We love the area, love to be around you guys, but I think Maroubra is better for my health.'

'Go for what you really want. Think about yourselves first,' I reassured them one more time.

They both looked surprised but smiled at me with their beautiful smiles.

'I really am proud of you both,' I added. 'I admire you two for all the hard work you have done and how you run your lives so well, so independently! Well done, Kings!'

They chuckled as I jokingly referred to them by Travis's surname. I liked to use it when I was half-serious and half-joking.

They both looked back at me with love, and I returned it in full measure. My heart was bursting with joy and abundant love for both of them.

I had found true peace. 'Good job, Ha-Le,' I thought. I patted myself on my back with a smile.

I was ready for my baby to go wherever she wanted. My heart would be forever with my beloved daughter.

In such a short time, my life had changed so much. My daughter had gotten married and moved away. I had temporarily lost her, and now I had her back, but in a new way. Our relationship had matured. It had grown, and so had I.

I felt strong. I felt happy. I felt connected to the love and energy of the universe in a brand-new way. I felt so moved by what had shifted in me. I gave thanks to my new life, which began a new unfolded journey.

The pain that encompassed me had blinded me from everything wonderful that I had. My negativity had consumed me until all that I could see was the darkness when there was so very much light. I was finally ready to be my best self. I was finally ready to take responsibility for the ways that my own mindset affected my life in very real, tangible ways. With this responsibility, I was blessed. I loved myself enough now to hold myself accountable, and this would enable me to live my best life. My heart was open to all possibilities. My soul was free, and I started falling in love with life and its un-limitedness. My taste of the future was so delicious!

Life is a constant state of flux. Life is gaining and losing at the same time. I understood this now, and I knew that I could overcome anything that came my way with time and hard work. I was resilient. I would always bounce forward with zest and life. I could flourish even under the most tenuous circumstances. I am a Waratah, and nothing would ever quell my spirit.

HA-LE THAI

Author, Early Childhood Educator, Assessor & Trainer, Parenting and Life Coach, Speaker, Facilitator, Energy Medicine Healer.

Ha-Le is a survivor of a dysfunctional family, child abuse, the Vietnam War, a 'boat people' and a refugee in Australia. She is a three times survivor from three different cancers. Ha-Le also taught herself English and obtained a Bachelor of Teaching, Diploma in Child Studies, Positive Psychology, Diploma in NLP and Hypnosis and has a host of other qualifications in her toolkit.

Ha-Le was a founder, former Director and Authorised Supervisor of Birrong Preschool in Sydney. She was very successful in her educational business. She taught and cared for the young children with her great passion.

Ha-Le had written five books:
- WARATAH *(Memoir)*
- HABITS TO BENEFITS - *Volume 1 (Parenting Book)*
- AWAKENING THE INBORN WARRIOR WITHIN *(Ebook)*
- KAYLA KOALA AND HER MAMA *(Children Picture Book)*
- DAZZA SAVES THE KOALA *(Children Picture Book)*

Ha-Le now is on a mission to help everyone unleash their inborn warrior, and she is especially passionate about helping children to thrive in this world now and become a happy and prosperous adult later no matter what challenges life may present. Ha-Le also is on a mission of part-time writing, and She is very fascinated by this work. Her focus is on Personal Growth Parenting, and children's educational picture Books.

Her upcoming books are:

- 'G' DAY, CANCERS!' How To Live With Cancers Every Day.

- EYES AND LIPS - Let Your Soul Shines Through.

- HABITS TO BENEFITS - Volume 2 *(Parenting Book)*.

Using her W.A.R.A.T.A.H formula which is an acronym for WARRRIOR, ADAPTABILITY, RESILIENT, ACCEPTANCE, TRANFORMATION, AUTHENTICITY & HOPE. Ha-Le has helped many people find their strength, overcome challenges and difficulties and get their lives to shine again.

A favourite saying of Ha-Le is, 'Life is so abundant. Enjoy it to the fullest!!!'